Cooperative Agreements Between Public Authorities

Kris Wauters

Cooperative Agreements Between Public Authorities

The influence of CJEU case law on national legal systems

intersentia

METRO

Ius Commune Europaeum

Kris Wauters

Cooperative Agreements Between Public Authorities. The influence of CJEU case law on national legal systems

Intersentia Publishing Ltd
Sheraton House | Castle Park
Cambridge | CB3 0AX | United Kingdom
Tel.: +44 1223 370 170 | Email: mail@intersentia.co.uk

ISBN 978-1-78068-312-6
D/2015/7849/57
NUR 823

Cover photograph © iStock-Thinkstock.com

British Library Cataloguing in Publication Data. A catalogue record for this book is available from the British Library.

CONTENTS

ACKNOWLEDGEMENTS

I would like to thank everyone who has contributed to the conduct of my research. My special thanks goes to my supervisors, Professors Rosa Greaves and Noreen Burrows. Throughout these six years, they each contributed to the realisation of this work. Several times we met in Glasgow to comment on the different chapters. Especially, Rosa Greaves has helped me significantly in different kinds of ways during the final few months, which were really hard. Her help was a substantial element in the realisation of the PhD. I thank also Yseult Marique, who read the whole text and made some fundamental comments, which improved the text. A special thanks goes to the examiners of my Viva Professors Tom Mullen and Martin Trybus, who added some precious remarks which improved the content of the PhD.

Some people also granted material help. I thank them also: Johan Herbots and the law office Monard-D'Hulst. Major material support I got from my parents, who were my first source of inspiration to work hard. They also gave me opportunities in my youth and encouraged me to start university studies. Jan Ghysels granted me the freedom to finish this PhD. Last but not least, I also thank my secretary at the Université de Louvain, Marie-Elise Bouchonville, and Ann-Sophie Vanwinsen, who structured the text, verified the footnotes and the bibliography.

Finally, I thank those who have demonstrated a lot of patience during the last years of this PhD. Mainly, weekends and holidays were spent on this text. Every time the family left on holiday, place was made for a pile of books and photocopies. A special thanks to my son, Chiron, and my wife, Goddy Haerden. My wife has motivated me to accomplish this work, although she suffered the most. I hope she can forgive me. I dedicate this book to her.

Chapter 1

INTRODUCTION

This book regards how and to what extent EU law can influence national administrative law. The possible influence on one aspect of national administrative law is examined. The study looks to what extent EU law has an impact on how national public authorities take decisions as to how to organise the manner in which they discharge some of their public tasks. The research was then narrowed to cooperation between public authorities as a means to organise or discharge public service tasks. The objectives of this work are to detect such an influence, to explain the influence, to examine the extent of influence.

1. Contextual background

1.1. Phenomenon of cooperation

The role of the State was greatly expanded in the 20th century. It was at this time that the '*État gendarme*' became an '*État providence*'; social protection and the economic prosperity of the citizen became important objectives (tasks of general interest) for the State. The practice of intervention by public authorities[1] in every day life was profoundly changed.[2]

The intervention of public authorities in the social and economic life of citizens was particularly necessary in the second half of the 20th century. This was because, namely, Europe had two major World Wars and a great depression. Europe had to be rebuilt after 1945 and State intervention was felt to be necessary.[3] This emergency was especially prominent in the European countries that were hit the hardest by the wars. It was believed

1 The concept 'public authority' refers in the first instance to the concept of 'contracting authority' as used in public procurement Directives: for this concept Cf. S. Arrowsmith, *EU Public Procurement Law an introduction*, www.nottingham.ac.uk.pprg and see also chapter 3. The Court of Justice of the Europan Union has defined the term 'public authority' for service concessions in Case C-91/08, *Wall AG v. La ville de Francfort-sur-le-Main and Frankfurter Entsorgungs- und Service (FES) GmbH* [2010] *ECR* I-2815, at [49] (see also chapter 3). In the present book the concept 'public authority' normally refers to both concepts unless expressly mentioned otherwise.

2 H.W.R. Wade and C.F. Forsyth, *Administrative law* (Oxford: OUP, 2009), p. 3.

3 E. Szyszczak, *The regulation of the State in competitive markets in the EU* (Oregon: Hart Publishing, 2007), p. 1.

that public authorities were necessary to provide protection and further prosperity to their citizens. The public interest required the presence of an overarching public authority that would accomplish tasks and deliver services to its citizens: a public service or a task of general public interest. In France, for example, the deliverance of public services justifies the existence of public authorities and was and is still fundamental to their existence (see chapter 6).

This book is not concerned with the activities of public authorities themselves but the way that public authorities accomplish their public service tasks and the instruments these public authorities need to accomplish those tasks. The public authorities' main function is to meet the needs of the general public, and to do this they organise themselves in a number of different ways. There are three main ways to provide service delivery: the State can i) make use of its own resources (in house), ii) create (unilaterally) separate entities or iii) make agreements (cooperation) with other entities for this purpose (outsourcing). For a long time public authorities did not need the help of third parties as their intervention in public life was limited. The rise of social democracy and welfare states, the sophistication of modern society increased public interventionism and in many areas public authorities no longer had the capacity of doing everything themselves.[4] This is where third parties came in.

A public authority may either cooperate with the private sector or it may cooperate with other public authorities. It is the latter that is the central object of the study undertaken in this book. A distinction must be made between vertical (agreement with a self-established legal person or with a subsidiary of which the public authority is a member) and horizontal (agreement with a non-related public authority) cooperation. Cooperation between public authorities has increased in several Member States[5] as a means to improve the organisation and management of public services. Today many public services are ensured through the cooperation between public authorities.[6] For example, as will be explained in Chapter 6, in England and Scotland public authorities share more and more (public) services.

1.2. Ways and areas of cooperation

As Arrowsmith confirmed recently 'collaborative agreements between public bodies in procurement and in the delivery of public services – sometimes referred to in some forms as "shared services" arrangements or (under EU law) "public-public partnerships" – have been given increased emphasis in recent years'.[7] Cooperation is sometimes useful for

4 T. Kaarreselo, 'Procuring in-house: the impact of EC procurement regime' (*PPLR*, 2008), p. 242.

5 The European Union is an international organisation created by different countries and composed of different countries in Europe. These countries are called 'Member States'.

6 J. Wiggen, 'Public procurement rules and cooperation between public sector entities: the limits of the in-house doctrine under EU procurement law' (*PPLR*, 2011), p. 157.

7 S. Arrowsmith, *The law of public and utilities procurement*, Vol. I (London: Sweet & Maxwell, 2014), p. 97.

delivering a service at a lower cost and to have a more efficient service delivery.[8] This kind of cooperation between public authorities has to realise efficiencies through collaboration in purchasing, provision of accommodation, and support services. In France, cooperation between public authorities is used in almost every administrative policy and action.[9] Chapter 6 also emphasizes the increasing use of shared services in England and Scotland. In most Member States public authorities use different means of cooperation, in order to organise their public services. These different ways of cooperation are used in different areas of public service delivery.

1.2.1. Ways of cooperation

Throughout the European Union public authorities cooperate. This cooperation takes different forms. The present section will distinguish different criteria to categorise the ways of cooperation.

A first distinction could be made between informal and formal cooperation.[10] The criterion used to distinguish between these two forms of cooperation, is the fact that there is a written document confirming the formal cooperation. Even when the cooperation is in a written form, a distinction can be made between agreements and 'real' contracts.[11] The main difference between these two categories is the legal enforceability of 'real' contracts. The research considers only 'real' contracts. All other types of cooperation and categorization are outside the scope of the study (see also Chapter 3).

Forms of cooperation can also be divided according to the type of contracting party. Public authorities cooperate with the private sector or with the public sector. It is this last kind of cooperation, cooperation with the public sector, which is the object of the study. Some 'public' cooperation takes place between public authorities on an equal legal footing, or between public authorities of different kinds or between public authorities and public companies or independent regulatory agencies.[12] For example agreements are signed in England between local authorities and central government where councils

8 One can find on the internet economic studies to explain the advantages of cooperation in some situations: E. di Porto, 'Cooperation among local governments to deliver public services: Evidence from France', www.ieb.ub.edu/files/Di%20Porto.pdf; G. Bel and M.E. Warner, 'Factors Explaining Inter-municipal Cooperation in Service Delivery: A Meta-Regression Analysis', www.union.wisc.edu/pmra2013/Paper%20Submissions/Renamed/Factors%20Explaining%20Intermunicipal%20Contracting%20A%20Meta%20Analysis.pdf.

9 J.-D. Dreyfus, *Contribution à une théorie générale des contrats entre personnes publiques* (Paris: L'Harmattan, 1997), p. 178.

10 Professor Arrowsmith uses in her latest handbook on public procurement the distinction between informal (loan of staff) and formal collaboration (joint committees): see S. Arrowsmith, *The law of public and utilities procurement*, Vol. I (London: Sweet & Maxwell, 2014), p. 97.

11 See for this distinction P. Vincent-Jones, *The New Public Contracting* (Oxford: OUP, 2006), p. 16.

12 See J.-B. Auby, 'Comparative approaches to the Rise of Contract in the Public Sphere' (*PL*, 2007), p. 42.

commit themselves to improve their services in exchange for more funds.[13] In Europe, one of the best known forms of cooperation between public authorities on the same level is inter-municipal cooperation.[14, 15]

A distinction can also be made according to the object of the cooperation. Cooperation can serve several aims: to set mutual management objectives, to exchange staffing, to coordinate policies, mutual consultation, etc. The object of this book is limited to cooperation as a means of organising public services. In chapter 5 a distinction is made between horizontal or contractual cooperation on one hand and vertical or institutional cooperation on the other. Cooperation can also be achieved either by a simple agreement concluded between independent public authorities or by a merger or amalgation taking place between public authorities. The next section below examines in which areas public authorities cooperate as to the organisation and management of public services.

1.2.2. Areas of cooperation

Public authorities cooperate in different areas of policy to deliver public services. It is outside the scope of the research to provide an exhaustive overview of all the areas where public authorities cooperate in the various Member States. This is not the object of the study. However, it is relevant to give a few examples to underscore the social and economic importance of this topic.

In general, a distinction can be made between operational tasks and coordination tasks managed through cooperation: Operational tasks have been defined as 'the joint production of public services: municipalities strive to overcome the limitations or inefficiencies of small-scale local government. ... Coordination tasks refer to the regulation of externalities of local policies and to an allocation of resources and costs that is rational from a *supra*-local perspective'.[16]

In England, the Local Government Association has launched a national shared services compendium and map which shows the councils engaged in shared service arrangements.[17] A selection is also made according to the type of shared service arrangement.[18]

13 Local Public Service Agreements (LPSAs): K. Young, 'Local public service agreements and performance incentives for local government' (*Local Government Studies*, 2005, 1), pp. 3–20. See also Article 1 of the French law of 7 January 1983 on urban planning: "les collectivités locales concourent avec l'Etat à l'administration et à l'aménagement du territoire, au développement économique, social, sanitaire, culturel et scientifique, ainsi qu'à la protection de l'environnement et à l'amélioration du cadre de vie".

14 Municipalities establish a corporation and transfer specific tasks and sometimes authority to such corporation.

15 R. Hulst and A. van Montfort (eds.), *Inter-Municipal cooperation in Europe* (Dordrecht: Springer, 2007), 238 p.

16 R. Hulst and A. Van Montfort, 'Inter-municipal cooperation: a widespread phenomenon', in R. Hulst and A. van Montfort (eds.), *Inter-Municipal cooperation in Europe* (Dordrecht: Springer, 2007), p. 11.

17 Www.local.gov.uk/shared-services-map.

18 Https://www.google.com/fusiontables/DataSource?docid=1AFBbo_u05-L8VStILuB2beiDxdK6-3-CbbY7reFB#rows:id=1.

Arrangements are made for the purpose of sharing knowledge, resources and services to provide technology solutions, support the professional development needs of young people advisers, the provision of ICT, legal and HR, sustainable management of waste. In Germany, the means of cooperation are chosen to maximise resources and enhance service delivery in expensive areas: water/energy supply, waste/sewage disposal, public transport, IT-infrastructure and maintenance.[19] In France, public authorities cooperate in the areas of water, energy, waste, soil pollution, security, maintenance, infrastructure, IT.[20] The same kind of cooperation can be found in Belgium. Arrowsmith also enlisted areas where collaboration between public authorities is used: payroll, human resources, leisure facilities, health services, refuse collection.[21]

Inter-municipal cooperation takes place throughout Europe in a wide range of tasks: the coordination of local spatial plans for new housing or business parks, the mutual adjustment of local policies concerning investments in recreational and cultural facilities, infrastructure or economic development to increase the competitiveness of the region in the national or European market, social services, refuse collection or music education, and coordination of local employment or housing policies, the joint operation of a music school, a fire service department, waste processing units or public transport.[22]

The case law discussed in Chapters 5 and 6 below also demonstrates in which areas public authorities cooperate or are willing to cooperate. The CJEU case law gives several examples of specific tasks performed through cooperation. Several decisions or rulings of the CJEU concern operation, construction or maintenance tasks.[23] Sometimes public authorities transfer the management of a service or several public service(s) to another public authority.[24] Inter-municipal cooperation is normally created to deliver public tasks for municipalities.[25] The municipalities then finance collectively this provision. Sometimes public authorities cooperate to share the performance of a public task.[26]

19 M. Burgi, '"In-House" Providing in Germany', in Comba, M. and Treumer, S. (eds.), *The In-House Providing in European Law* (Copenhagen: Djøf Publishing, 2010), p. 73.

20 Ph. Neveu, 'Contractualisation et mutualisation, outils de l'intercommunalité', in (*La Semaine juridique Administrations et Collectivités territoriales*, 2010, n° 30), p. 2242 et s. See also chapter 6.

21 S. Arrowsmith, *The law of public and utilities procurement*, Vol. I (London: Sweet & Maxwell, 2014), p. 97.

22 R. Hulst and A. Van Montfort, 'Inter-municipal cooperation: a widespread phenomenon', in R. Hulst and A. van Montfort (eds.), *Inter-Municipal cooperation in Europe* (Dordrecht: Springer, 2007), p. 11.

23 C-107/98, *Teckal Srl v. Comune di Viano* [1999] *ECR* I-8121; C-231/03, *Consorzio Aziende Metano (Coname) v. Comune di Cingia de' Botti* [2005] *ECR* I-7287; C-573/07, *Sea Srl v. Comune de Ponte Nossa* [2010] *ECR* I-08127; Case C-458/03, *Parking Brixen GmbH v. Gemeinde Brixen and Stadtwerke Brixen AG* [2005] *ECR* I-08585.

24 Case C-295/05, *Asociación Nacional de Empresas Forestales (Asemfo) v. Transformación Agraria SA (Tragsa)* [2007] *ECR* I-02999; C-324/07, *Coditel Brabant SA v. Commune d'Uccle and Région de Bruxelles-Capitale* [2008] *ECR* I-8457; C-183/11, *Econord SpA v. Comuni di Cagno, Comune di Varese, Comune di Solbiate* [2012] *ECR* I-00000.

25 G. Bel, W. Fageda and M. Mur, 'Why do municipalities cooperate to provide local public services? An empirical analysis' (*Local Government Studies*, 2013), http://dx.doi.org/10.1080/03003930.2013.781024.

26 C-480/06, *Commission of the European Communities v. Federal Republic of Germany* [2009] *ECR* I-04747.

1.3. *Applicable law*

Cooperation between public authorities was for a long time governed in the different Member States by national administrative law. It was considered to be an aspect of the freedom of a public authority to organise its own services. This possibility or principle of self-government has also been recognised at the European level in the European Charter on Local Self-Government (15 October 1985).[27, 28] In the last couple of decades the national administrative law of the Member States has been influenced by case law from the Court of Justice of the European Union (CJEU).[29] One of the main objectives of this research is to examine this influence and more specifically the influence of EU law on cooperation between public authorities. The study is only interested in this kind of cooperation that can be qualified as a public contract or service concession.

The EU owes its existence to the fear of further wars in some 'Western' European countries after 1945. Cooperation among the different countries was seen as a hopeful and effective way to avoid such wars as well as a means to enable Europe to establish a place for itself in the new world order.

In the aftermath of World War II the European nations were not ready to relinquish their sovereignty to an international organisation. The sentiment was that such a step would be easier to take within a framework of economic objectives.[30, 31] Six countries founded the European Coal and Steel Community in 1951. On 25 March 1957, these same six countries signed two further treaties: the Euratom Treaty in matters of nuclear energy and the Treaty establishing the European Economic Community. The latter later became the cornerstone of an intensive and wide-ranging cooperation that ultimately led to the creation of the European Union (EU) (which as of 2014 has 28 Member States).

With the establishment of the European Economic Community (EEC)[32] in 1957, the Member States implicitly opted for a closer union through economic objectives. The EU

27 Article 6(1) of the Charter provides: 'without prejudice to more general statutory provisions, local authorities must be able to determine their own internal administrative structures in order to adopt them to local needs and ensure effective management'.

28 The European Charter on Local Self-Government, 15 October 1985. See on this Charter: J. Andrews, 'European Charter on Local Self-Government' (ELRev 1986), pp.180–181; J. Smith, 'The European Charter on Local Self-Government: does the UK Government comply' (*Journal of Local Government Law*, 2002), pp. 90–96.

29 Lord Denning spoke in general of an incoming tide that cannot be held back: *HP Bulmer Ltd v. J. Bollinger SA* [1974] 2:401,418–19. See also H.W.R. Wade and C.F. Forsyth, *Administrative law* (Oxford: OUP, 2009), p. 176.

30 See on the economic objectives of the EU in general N. Reich, *Understanding EU law: Objectives, Principles and Methods of Community Law* (Antwerp – Oxford: Intersentia, 2005), p. 400; K. Lenaerts and P. Van Nuffel, *European Union Law* (London: Sweet & Maxwell, 2011), pp. 106–111.

31 One of the exceptions to this was NATO.

32 Hereafter we will use the concept 'European Union'. This concept was introduced with the Treaty on the European Union signed at Maastricht on February 7, OJ [1992] C 224. The European Union was the overarching structure for the European Communities and intergovernmental pillars. The Treaty of

is an example par eminence of how the Member States endeavoured to achieve peace and stability through economic integration. The idea of economic unity came after the realisation that a common market with free movement of goods, persons, capital and services and free competition could provide a stable and prosperous economy. This liberal conception precludes excessive State intervention. When the EEC was established, the Member States transferred some of their sovereignty to the new international organisation. This transfer would have an impact on the competences of the Member States.

The importance of a 'free market' has grown steadily in the EU, whereas at the national level the need for State intervention remains the prevailing theme. The growing influence of EU law has impacted on national policy regarding the tasks of a public authority (State intervention) and the way that public authority organises itself to accomplish the public service tasks.

The founding treaties of the EU[33] had very few provisions directly aimed at relieving this tension. In Articles 31 and 90 EEC (now Articles 37 and 106 TFEU[34] respectively) the founding Member States of the Treaty tried to balance between the free market and, the potential for State intervention. These provisions regulate situations only when public undertakings may be subject to European competition law. Yet there was no other provision that tried to seek such a balance.

Due to a lack of provisions in the founding treaties and the lack of action of the European Commission the CJEU was, for a long period, the motor that drove the development of EU law.[35] In CJEU case law there is a tendency that makes many States' measures or decisions fall within the scope of EU law. As a result of a functional interpretation of EU law the CJEU found itself competent to rule on certain cases that, arguably, may fall under the competency of the Member States. State action and intervention thus risk falling completely under the scope of EU law, which jeopardizes the competence of Member States in traditional national branches of law. In several areas the CJEU seems to struggle with this tension between State action or intervention (competence Member States) and the internal market (competence European Union).[36] Accordingly, the CJEU

Lisbon (OJ [2007] C306) removed the pillar structure and adopted the single title of European Union with full legal personality.

33 The Treaty of Paris establishing the European Coal and Steel Community, the Treaty of Rome establishing the European Economic Community, the Treaty of Rome establishing a European Atomic Energy Community.

34 Treaty on the Functioning of the European Union OJ 2010 C 84 (erratum: OJ [2010] C 181/1).

35 T. Trimidas, 'The Court of Justice and judicial activism' (*ELRev*, 1996), p. 199; B. Bertrand, *Le juge de l'Union européenne, juge administratif* (Brussels: Bruylant, 2012), pp. 22–23. K. Lenaerts, *Le juge et la Constitution aux Etats Unis d'Amérique et dans l'ordre juridique européen* (Brussels: Bruylant,1988).

36 See the case law on golden shares: C. Gerner-Beuerle, *Shareholders between the market and the state; The VW law and other interventions in the market*, CMLRev. 2012:97–144; Case C-367/98, *Commission v. Portugal* [2002] *ECR* I-4731; Case C-483/99, *Commission v. France* [2002] *ECR* I-4781; Case C-503/99, *Commission v. Belgium* (2002) *ECR* I-4809; Case C-98/01, *Commission v. United Kingdom* [2003] *ECR* I-4641; Joined Cases C-282 & 283/04, *Commission v. Netherlands* [2006] *ECR* I-9141; Case C-112/05, *Commission v. Germany* [2007] *ECR* I-8995; Joined Cases C-463 & 464/04, *Federconsumatori and*

has through its case law determined the competence of the EU or its Member States to adjudicate on a particular matter.

Through its interpretation of the public procurement Directives,[37] the CJEU has made it clear that agreements (public contracts) concluded between public authorities could also fall within the scope of EU law. Thereafter, the CJEU case law extended the scope to include service concessions concluded between public authorities.[38] That is why the study uses the concept of 'cooperative agreements'. The definitions of 'public contract' and 'service concession' contained in the public procurement Directives[39] each refer to the element 'contract' to determine the meaning of these concepts. Through the element 'contract' the CJEU confirmed agreements (or cooperation) between public authorities fall under the scope of the Directives[40] and of the principles of equality. In several Member States the decision to conclude such an agreement did not need the organization of a tendering procedure. A public authority did not have to guarantee an equal treatment. The choice to cooperate with another public authority was considered to belong to the liberty of public authorities to organize and discharge their public service tasks. The CJEU case law restrains the liberty of public authorities to organize and discharge public service tasks. It is this influence that is central.

In this way EU law intervenes in an area (organization of public services) where normally the competences still belong to the Member States.[41] The CJEU case law on cooperative agreements also determines the division of powers between the EU and its Member States in EU law. The criteria created by the CJEU in its case law determine the application of EU law on cooperative agreements between public authorities and, thus, influences the delimitation of powers between the EU and its Member States.

Case law concerning cooperative agreements between public authorities has continued to evolve. One of the aims of the study is to determine how the CJEU intentionally or unintentionally seeks, through its case law on cooperative agreements, to find a balance between States' actions, that which falls outside the scope of EU law, and an internal market situation subject to EU law.

Others and Associazione Azionariato Diffuso dell'AEM SpA and Others v. Comune di Milano [2007] *ECR* I-10419; Case C-171/08, *Commission v. Portugal* [2010] *ECR* I-06817; Case C-543/08, *Commission v. Portugal* [2010] *ECR* I-11241.

37 Directive 2004/17/EC of the European Parliament and Council Directive OJ [2004] L134/1 coordinating the procurement procedures of entities operating in the water, energy, transport and postal services sectors and Directive 2004/18/EC of the European Parliament and Council Directive OJ [2004] L134/114 on the coordination of procedures for the award of public works contracts, public supply contracts and public service contracts.

38 Case C-458/03, *Parking Brixen v. Gemeinde Brixen* [2005] *ECR* I-8585.

39 Articles 1(2)(a) and 1(4) Directive 2004/18/CE.

40 See Case C-107/98, *Teckal Srl v. Comune di Viano* [1999] *ECR* I-8121.

41 See also D. Casalini, 'Beyond EU Law: the New "Public House"', in G. Olykke, C. Hansen and C. Tvarno (dir.), *EU Public Procurement – Modernisation, Growth and Innovation* (Copenhagen: Djøf Publishing, 2012), pp. 151–153.

2. EU law impact on national administrative law

The influence of EU law on national administrative law had long been an unknown factor because until 25 years ago EU law was not a compulsory subject in several universities. Legal experts did not always have sufficient knowledge of this EU law so its possible influence was unclear. In 1992 Jurgen Schwarze wrote: 'there is less awareness of the influence of European Community law in the other direction on the general administrative law of the Member States'.[42] Even afterwards, EU law and national administrative law were seen as two different legal domains that were studied separately.

The effect of EU law on national administrative law is becoming ever more palpable. National administrations or public authorities need to take into account EU law more, when they make a decision.[43] Recent years have seen a quantitative increase in scholarly research on the influence of EU law on national administrative law[44] although academic literature has in general remained limited. Some scholars named this research field 'European administrative law'.[45]

The book aspires to be a constructive addition to this research. As mentioned earlier, cooperative agreements between public authorities is the central focus of this research. This specific form of cooperation is traditionally handled under national administrative law. The study will now focus on the influence of EU law on this specific national body of law that in principle defines the ways in which a public authority can collaborate with another public authority. Thus, the study demonstrates the possible influence of EU law on national administrative law.

National administrative law is a legal domain that basically remains under the competence of the Member States. One of the principles of national administrative law is unilateral actions by the public authority, based on the general public interest. To the extent that the general interest can justify intercession by a public authority, the latter has discretion as to how to proceed. However, in EU law this unilateral action is subject to the internal market rules and EU competition law.

42 J. Schwarze, *European administrative law* (London: Sweet and Maxwell, 1992), p. 1453.

43 See Discussion paper 3; EU administrative law and national administrations: http://ec.europa.eu/justice/events/assises-justice-2013/files/administrative_law_en.pdf.

44 J.H. Jans, R. Delange, S. Prechal and R.J.G.M. Widdershoven (dir.), *Europeanisation of Public law* (Groningen: Europa Law Publishing, 2007); G. Eckert, Y. Gautier, R. Kovar and D. Ritleng (dir.), *Incidences du droit communautaire sur le droit public français* (Strasbourg: Presses Universitaires de Strasbourg, 2007); J.-B. Auby and J. Dutheil de la Rochère (dir.), *Droit administratif européen* (Bruxelles: Bruylant, 2007), p. 1122); J.-B. Auby (dir.), *L'influence du droit européen sur les catégories du droit public* (Paris: Dalloz, 2010); J.-B. Auby and J. Dutheil de la Rochère (dir.), *Traité de droit administratif européen* (Bruxelles: Bruylant, 2014). In regard to this book that examines the influence of EU law on French and English administrative law, see also J.-F. Flauss, 'Rapport français', in J. Schwarze (ed.), *Das Verwaltungsrecht unter europaïschem Einfluß* (Baden-Baden: Nomos, 1996), pp. 31 and 273.

45 J.-B. Auby and J. Dutheil de la Rochère, 'Introduction générale', in J.-B. Auby and J. Dutheil de la Rochère (dir.), *Droit administratif européen* (Bruxelles: Bruylant, 2007), pp. 3–4.

The increasing influence of EU law on national administrative law is based on well-established general principles of EU law, namely, the principles of i) direct effect,[46] ii) primacy[47] and iii) loyalty.

The doctrine of direct effect is well established and means that EU law can be invoked directly by EU citizens before national courts if clear, unambiguous and unconditional. This is important because the legislative acts adopted in the public procurement field in the EU are directives. Secondly, a fundamental principle of EU law is the principle of supremacy; this means that EU law prevails over national law. Thus if there are national rules in the field of public procurement that contradict EU law, the latter will prevail. Both principles explain why EU law can have an influence on national law and to what extent.

Article 4(3), first subpara. TEU confirms the principle of sincere cooperation or Union loyalty[48] and expresses the principle of good trust set down in Article 2(2) of the UN Treaty.[49] Case law regards this principle as being of a constitutional nature or as integral to the very core of EU constitutional law.[50] It flows from the very nature of the EU, which can be described as cooperation between the Member States with transfer of sovereign rights in specific and limited fields. From this transfer was born a new legal order with its own legal rules and principles. The Member States must take all requisite measures to ensure the effective application of EU law, even if it concerns measures related to the organisation of public service tasks. This obligation of the Member States has been recently confirmed in CJEU case law on cooperative agreements between public authorities.[51]

Given the trend of the Europeanisation of national administrative law, noted by some legal scholars, specialised in administrative law, the effect of EU law in national

46 See on this principle K. Lenaerts and P. Van Nuffel, *European Union Law* (London: Sweet & Maxwell, 2011), pp. 753–816; P. Craig and G. De Burca, *EU Law* (Oxford: OUP, 2011), pp. 256–301; A. Dashwood, M. Dougan, B. Rodger, E. Spaventa and D. Wyatt, *Wyatt and Dashwood's European Union Law* (London: Hart Publishing, 2011), pp. 235–286.

47 See on this principle K. Lenaerts and P. Van Nuffel, *European Union Law* (London: Sweet & Maxwell, 2011), pp. 753–816; P. Craig and G. De Burca, *EU Law* (Oxford: OUP, 2011), pp. 180–217; A. Dashwood, M. Dougan, B. Rodger, E. Spaventa and D. Wyatt, *Wyatt and Dashwood's European Union Law* (London: Hart Publishing, 2011), pp. 235–286.

48 J.H. Jans, R. De Lange, S. Prechal en R.J.G.M. Widdershoven, *Inleiding tot het Europees bestuursrecht* (Nijmegem, Ars Acqui Libri, 2002), p. 69.

49 B. De Witte, 'Interpreting the EC Treaty like a constitution: the role of the European Court of Justice in comparative perspective', in R. Bakker, A.W. Heringa en F. Stroink (eds.), *Judicial Control* (Antwerpen: Maklu, 1995), footnote 33.

50 See K. Lenaerts and P. Van Nuffel, *Constitutional law of the European Union* (Oxford: OUP, 2005), pp. 115–123; R. Widdershoven, 'The principle of loyal cooperation. Lawmaking by the European Court of Justice and the Dutch Courts', in F. Stroink and E. van der Linden, *Judicial Law-making and Administrative Law* (Antwerpen: Intersentia, 2005), p. 6; J.T. Lang, 'Article 10 EC – The most important 'General Principle' of Community Law', in U. Bernitz, J. Nergelius en C. Cardner (eds.), *General Principles of EC Law in a Process of Development* (Alphen aan den Rijn: Kluwer Law International, 2007), pp. 76–78.

51 Case C-15/13, *Technische Universität Hamburg-Harburg, Hochschul-Informations-System GmbH v. Datenlotsen Informationssysteme GmbH* [2014] *ECR* I-00000, at [22].

administrative law can no longer be ignored.[52] For example, in Paul Craig's book on English administrative law a whole chapter is devoted to EU law.[53]

3. Research questions

The main objective is to examine if EU law has had some impact and influence on how national public authorities take decisions as to how to organise the manner in which they discharge some of their public tasks. In order to test this, this study

(i) narrows the research to cooperative agreements between national public authorities within the EU law on public contracts and service concessions
(ii) limits the EU Member States to France and the UK.

The two key and main research questions to comply with this objective are the following:

A) Do agreements between national public authorities whereby they cooperate in discharging their public tasks come within EU law and, in particular, within the scope of the EU public procurement Directives?

In order to answer this question the following sub-research questions have been identified:

(a) What kinds of situations regarding the organisation of public tasks are influenced by EU (public procurement) law? (chapter 3)
(b) How can these situations have been influenced by EU law? (chapter 4)
(c) Which elements of EU internal market law are relevant to the understanding of the CJEU case law? (chapter 4)
(d) To what extent these situations are influenced by EU (public procurement) law? (chapter 5)

B) Has there been influence of EU (public procurement) law in shaping or changing national administrative law of France and the UK?

In order to answer this question the study has identified the following sub-research questions

(a) How do public authorities in France discharge their public service tasks? Do they cooperate with each other? (chapter 6)
(b) How do public authorities in the UK discharge their public service tasks? Do they cooperate with each other? (chapter 6)
(c) What, if any, has been the influence of EU law (both legislative and case law) on how France and the UK organise the manner in which their national public authorities discharge their tasks? (chapter 6)

52 H.W.R. Wade and C.F. Forsyth, *Administrative law* (Oxford: OUP, 2009), p.176.
53 P. Craig, *Administrative law* (London: Sweet and Maxwell, 2012), pp. 275–297.

4. The importance of the research

It is submitted that in 2008 at the beginning of this study there was a gap in the literature that this book seeks to fill. The gap, namely how EU public procurement rules (and generally EU law) are applied to cooperative agreements between public authorities, was identified as a direct consequence of practising as a lawyer in this field. In advising national public authorities and private companies in regard to the application of the public procurement Directives it became clear that there was such a gap.[54] In practising law and in researching for this manuscript, questions arose often from public authorities that wished to establish a cooperative association (horizontal or vertical) or to become a member of an existing cooperative association.

Law practitioners specialised in national administrative law have the tendency to fall back on national laws and principles regulating analogous situations. However, practical experience in dealing with the public procurement Directives and the CJEU case law indicated that the interaction between CJEU case law and the research questions identified is where the answers were likely to be found. Thus, practice awakened the curiosity and produced the idea to undertake a more fundamental investigation of this matter.

CJEU case law on cooperative agreements between public authorities has induced public authorities to rethink how they organise the service delivery to the public: 'As recent legal analysis and the transaction cost economics pointed out long since, market solutions may be well-suited for some public purposes but not for others'.[55]

Each time a public authority wants to cooperate with another public authority, which happens regularly in certain Member States (see chapter 6 on the French and English system), the public authority has to review EU law, i.e. the public procurement Directives and the principle of equality.

The influence of CJEU case law on cooperative agreements between public authorities through the interpretation and application of the public procurement Directives has been underscored in different Member States[56]:

54 The author approached the University of Glasgow in 2007 to write the present work.

55 D. Casalini, 'Beyond EU Law: the New "Public House"', in G. Olykke, C. Hansen and C. Tvarno (eds.), *EU Public Procurement – Modernisation, Growth and Innovation* (Copenhagen: Publishing, 2012), p. 153.

56 Extended studies on in-house situations were accomplished in Spain: J.J. Pernas Garcia, *Los operaciones in house y el Derecho comunitario de contratos publicos* (Madrid: Iustel, 2008); in Italy: D. Casalini, *L'organismo di diritto pubblico e l'organizzazione in house* (Napoli: Jovene Editori, 2003); in Belgium: F. Gosselin, C. Molitor, P. Nihoul and Ph. Quertainemont (eds.), *Les modes de cooperation des services publics locaux au regard du droit européen* (Waterloo: Kluwer, 2008); In Germany: K. Hardraht, *In-House-Geschäfte und Europäisches Vergaberecht* (Berlin: Dunckler & Humblot, 2006).

- United Kingdom / England[57]:

'Shared service models have been successfully used by public authorities for many years and their use is anticipated to increase following the United Kingdom's coalition government's Comprehensive Spending Review and the need for public bodies to achieve efficiency savings. Procuring a service provider can sometimes be a lengthy, uncertain and expensive process, so understandably, contracting authorities are keen to take advantage of what is now commonly known as the "*Teckal*" or "in-house" exemption.

Whether public authorities can contract with one another and the extent to which they can involve the private sector without the need to conduct a formal EU procurement process has been considered on a number of occasions by the ECJ and domestic courts and the resulting decisions are complex and sometimes contradictory'.[58]

- France:

Chapter 6 demonstrates the impact of the CJEU case law on cooperative agreements between public authorities in France. It influences one of the constitutional cornerstones of French society: the 'service public' and the liberty for public authorities to organize how they deliver their public service tasks.

- In Germany:

'Die Rechtsprechung des Europäischen Gerichtshof zu den In-House-Geschäften hat die Beurteilung von In-House Vergaben im deutschen Recht wesentlich geprägt'.[59]

- General view:

'Today, many tasks within the public sector are carried out through cooperation between different public sector entities, often through the use of contracts or contract-like mechanisms. The question as to whether Directive 2004/18 (the Directive) applies to such cooperation has long been the subject of debate, as the application of the Directive to such cooperation may be seen as interfering in the Member States' freedom to organise their public sector as they see best fit. The so-called in-house doctrine developed by the Court of Justice of the European Union (CJEU) has long been the centre of attention in this debate'.[60]

57 See also in Scotland: 'Shared services in the Scottish public service: impact of the EU public procurement rules', www.scotland.gov.uk/Resource/Doc/1265/0051647.pdf.

58 Procurement Lawyers' Association Sharing Services Working Group [2011:3] help.procureweb.ac.uk/2508.file.dld.

59 K. Lott, *Die Rechtsprechung des EuGH und die In-House-Vergabe in Deutschland* (Saarbrücken: VDM Verlag Dr. Muller, 2008), p. 58.

60 J. Wiggen, 'Public procurement rules and cooperation between public sector entities: the limits of the in-house doctrine under EU procurement law' (*PPLR*, 2011), p. 158).

The possible influence of EU law on cooperative agreements can also be illustrated with an example from Belgian law.[61] In Belgium, under Article of 162 para. 4 of the Constitution; municipalities may either work together on the basis of an agreement (horizontal), or they may jointly create a new legal person (vertical). According to Belgian law, municipalities can freely enter into such cooperative associations, even if private companies are involved. Creating such cooperative associations is considered to be an element of the free choice to discharge public service tasks. Clearly, vertical cooperative associations (inter-municipal cooperation) between municipalities are frequently made in Belgium, particularly, in the sectors of electricity, gas, water supply, transport, and waste collection (major economic sectors).

According to CJEU case law municipalities must ascertain whether they are subject to EU law every time they wish to set up such a cooperative association. The cooperation can be classified as a public contract or service concession contract. Therefore, EU law restricts the freedom of choice of the Belgian municipalities. They must investigate whether the manner in which this cooperative association is constituted meets the criteria set out in the CJEU case law to determine whether such association falls outside the scope of EU law. The same questions arise when a municipality wishes to become a member of such a cooperative association. Thus the municipality, taking into account the CJEU case law, can make an informed decision how to organise its administration and how it discharges its public service tasks.

The application of EU law implies the holding of a competitive tendering procedure. This takes time, and also gives rise to subsidiary expenses that could run very high if the agreement is classed as a public procurement. In that case the public authority would have to engage in a complex tender procedure.

Public authorities and private enterprises should be made aware as far as possible of the potential impact of EU law on certain types of cooperative agreements. This knowledge will prevent situations where the public authorities are post facto confronted with lawsuits that might force them to withdraw completely from cooperative associations that are already underway. It also enables private enterprises to be aware that in this context they may benefit from an open market.

The research considers briefly the new legislative initiatives at EU level, that now contain specific provisions on cooperative agreements between public authorities.[62]

61 It is also the case in other Member States: Cf. M. Comba and S. Treumer (eds.), *The In-house Providing in European Law* (Copenhagen: Djøf Publishing, 2010). During a work experience sojourn in a Scottish attorneys' office it became clear that in Scotland as well the issue of the influence of EU law comes up whenever public authorities apply the system of sharing services.

62 Proposal for a Directive on procurement by entities in the water, energy, transport and postal services sectors COM(2011)895final; Proposal of the European Commission for a directive of the European Parliament and the Council on public procurement, COM(2011)896 final; Proposal of the European Commission for a directive of the European Parliament and the Council on the award of concession contracts, COM(2011)897final. See chapter 5.

5. Methodology and structure

As stated previously, this book is concerned with the identification of specific EU law that has an impact on a specific area of national administrative law, namely the organisation of public services through cooperation between public authorities. This impact is found in the EU law applicable to public procurement and to service concession contracts, primarily due to the interpretation the CJEU has given to EU law.

The book draws on legal mechanisms adopted by the EU and selected Member States. At the EU level, the study focuses on certain provisions of the TFEU and on the public procurement Directives. Any investigation on the application of EU law on cooperative agreements between public authorities must start with an analysis of the legal texts. Accordingly, each national legal system has its own rules, regulations and principles that could apply when public authorities cooperate.

However, the importance of the relevant case law is not to be underestimated. It is the rulings and judgments of the CJEU on cooperative agreements between public authorities that has developed a large portion from existing public procurement rules and regulations. In the light of research done, the CJEU's case law illustrates the manner in which the CJEU generally exercises its competence in interpreting EU law; that is, in a manner that influences national administrative law. This book then explores how this influence on national administrative law manifests itself. In England and France – the two legal systems selected to illustrate this influence – it is especially evident in their case law. Accordingly, an analysis of national case law is also relevant in this domain.

This investigation proceeds from the assumption that the CJEU has developed specific case law that can potentially influence how national administrative law does *de facto* determine the ways in which public authorities cooperate. Accordingly, the first part of the research was an analysis of this case law. Such an analysis brought clarity to the TFEU provisions, to the general principles of EU law, and to the elements of CJEU case law that can conceivably be said to underlie the evolution of this specific case law.

After considering the relevant CJEU case law on cooperative agreements, certain elements from EU primary law upon which the CJEU case law is putatively based have been selected. First, several standard literature works[63] were reviewed to select the relevant EU primary law. Next, the relevant EU primary law (provisions and principles) were subject to a more detailed analysis. It is important to note that except for the study of the concept 'services of general (economic) interest', European competition law was not deemed

63 P.J.G. Kapteyn, A.M. McDonnell, K.J.M. Mortelmans and C.W.A. Timmermans, *The Law of the European Union and the European Communities* (Alphen aan den Rijn: Kluwer Law International, 2008); D. Chalmers, G. Davies and G. Monti, *European Union Law* (Cambridge: Cambridge University Press, 2010); K. Lenaerts and P. Van Nuffel, *European Union Law* (London: Sweet & Maxwell, 2011); P. Craig and G. De Burca, *EU Law* (Oxford: OUP, 2011); A. Dashwood, M. Dougan, B. Rodger, E. Spaventa and D. Wyatt, *Wyatt and Dashwood's European Union Law* (London: Hart Publishing, 2011).

relevant. This does not mean that European competition law was not considered, but only that no clear link with the enforcement of EU competition law was identified.

After an examination of the case law on cooperative agreements the thesis explores what influence it has had on the national administrative law of the selected Member States. Throughout the book remember that the EU consists of 28 Member States; hence, material and linguistic limitations make it impossible to study the influence of EU law in all Member States. Difficulty of language justifies the choice of legal systems.[64] Thus, given the language limitations of the author, the Member States that could be studied were the United Kingdom, Ireland, Belgium, the Netherlands, France and Luxemburg. However, there are no rules or regulations and little case law that are concerned with this issue in The Netherlands. As for Luxemburg, its market is too small to provide significant data for this study and it is substantially influenced by the French system. Belgium and Ireland borrow liberally from the French and English legal system, respectively. The selection has been narrowed to France and England (and Scotland in some instances): 'English and French administrative law are bound to be taken as examples given their representative status for different legal traditions'.[65, 66]

These two Member States are also representative of the two major forms of legal systems in Europe: civil law and common law.[67] Each in its own way influences how the position of a public authority is conceived within the respective legal systems and the principles that govern their competences. It is reasonably presumed that one legal system is more sensitive than the other to the influence of EU law. This choice of two diverse legal systems should make differences more readily apparent, and also provide the opportunity to contrast the two legal systems to show how differently they might conceptualise the same situation, i.e. cooperation between public authorities. In both countries EU law has had an influence on national administrative law.

It is acknowledged that the Member States that have been selected are not necessarily those that are most often brought before the CJEU. The biggest 'client' of the CJEU as far as this topic is concerned is Italy. In 50% of the cases it is an Italian case that sets the agenda. The first case adjudicated on this matter was an Italian case.[68] Second in importance quantitatively are cases of German origin. Nevertheless the choice of France and England is justified as explained above.

The thesis is divided into seven chapters. The *first chapter* sets out the objectives, research questions and the manner in which the thesis is structured.

64 See M. Rüffert, 'The Transformation of Administrative Law as a Transnational Methodological System', in M. Rüffert (ed.), The Transformation of Administrative Law (Sellier, European Law Publishers, 2007), p. 9.

65 M. Rüffert, *o.c.*, p. 9.

66 See also chapter 6 for other justification regarding the choice of France and England.

67 The author is aware of the fact that this distinction is simplistic and does noet cover all EU countries: see J. Ziller, 'Les droits administratifs nationaux: caractéristiques générales', in J.-B. Auby and J. Dutheil de la Rochère (dir.), *Traité de droit administratif européen* (Bruxelles: Bruylant, 2014), p. 744.

68 Case C-107/98, *Teckal Srl v. Comune di Viano* [1999] *ECR* I-8121.

The *second chapter* provides a contextual background to the public procurement Directives. This chapter examines the historical evolution of this body of legislative measures and regulations and outlines the basic objectives they seek to achieve. It helps the reader to understand the historical basis and purposes that partially underlie CJEU law on cooperative agreements between public authorities. This case law has its origins in how the CJEU has interpreted certain provisions of the public procurement Directives. That is why these Directives are considered in the present thesis as the original framework. Afterwards the CJEU expanded its case law to service concessions, reason why the present thesis also regards the influence of EU primary law. Taking into account the research questions of the thesis it would not be logic to have a section on primary EU law in this chapter. Chapter 3 and chapter 4 examine to what extent primary EU law could be important for the subject of the book.

The *third chapter* examines what kind of situations regarding the organisation of public tasks could be influenced by EU law. The result of this chapter is a description of the scope of the study. The chapter analyses the concepts of 'public authority', 'cooperation' and 'public service tasks'. More specifically, relevant CJEU case law is examined together with the public procurement Directives, as to the meaning of the first two concepts. The *ratione personae* and *ratione materiae* scope of the thesis will be defined by these terms to avoid any confusion over terminology, since in fact each national legal system has its own terms for 'public authority' and 'cooperation'. The concept *'public service tasks'* is important because cooperative agreements between public authorities are a means to organize these tasks. Only these tasks qualified as *"public service tasks"* are relevant to this study. This concept is very similar to the concept 'services of general (economic) interest'.[69]

The *fourth chapter* examines certain provisions and principles of EU primary law in order to help clarify CJEU case law on cooperative agreements. The chapter explains how EU law could have an influence on these kinds of agreements. Different elements of the scope of applicability of the internal market rules could explain this influence. These aspects are analysed. The chapter looks for the element that appears to explain why under certain circumstances cooperative agreements between public authorities are excluded from the scope of EU law.

The *fifth chapter* focuses on CJEU case law on cooperative agreements between public authorities. The chapter discusses in depth the relevant case law: its origins, the evolution of the case law and the lessons that can be derived. The case law was considered on the basis of the following division: vertical or institutional and horizontal or contractual cooperation. As the CJEU[70] stated recently these two kinds of cooperative agreements are governed by another type of criteria to determine if they fall out of the scope of EU law.

69 N. Fiedziuk, 'Putting services of general economic interest up for tender: reflections on applicable EU rules' (*CMLR*, 2013), pp. 87–88.

70 Case C-159/11, *Azienda Sanitaria Locale di Lecce, Università del Salento v. Ordine degli Ingegneri della Provincia di Lecce and Others* [2012] *ECR* I-00000, at [31] to [34].

This book proposes a general explanation for the CJEU case law on cooperative agreements between public authorities. Finally, the study examines in this chapter the new Directives that were adopted in 2014 and which contain specific provisions on cooperation between public authorities.

In the *sixth chapter* two selected national legal systems will be analysed. First the French legal system is presented by analysing the concept of '*public service(s)*' and second by focussing on the phenomenon of cooperative agreements between public authorities. The chapter demonstrates the influence of EU law on one area of national administrative law i.e. how public authorities are constraint in discharging their public tasks if they choose to engage in cooperative agreements with other public authorities. Finally, the book will similarly discuss the English legal system, examining the same kind of questions as for the French system.

The last chapter sets out the general conclusions.

Chapter 2

THE ORIGINAL FRAMEWORK: THE PUBLIC PROCUREMENT DIRECTIVES

This study endeavours to show that European Union (EU) law has impacted on cooperative agreements between national public authorities. It is not intended to investigate the impact of each and every aspect of EU law. This book examines only the consequences of particular case law of the Court of Justice of the European Union (CJEU) on the aforementioned cooperative agreements. This case law has been developed from the preliminary references submitted to the CJEU by national courts concerning the interpretation of public procurement Directives.[71] These Directives constitute the original framework of the CJEU case law on cooperative agreements.

In this context it is relevant to explore the genesis and evolution of these Directives. This book makes clear to what extent these Directives contain provisions concerning cooperative agreements between public authorities and how these Directives may have an impact even in situations that are not a focal point of the Directives. On the basis of these Directives and the fact that they are a mere expression of the fundamental freedoms found in the Treaty on the Functioning of the European Union (TFEU) the CJEU expanded its case law on cooperative agreements to service concessions. Chapter 4 examines how EU law could have had a bearing on cooperative agreements between public authorities. That is why primary EU law, as a framework of the research and of the public procurement Directives, is not examined in this chapter but in chapter 4.

The chapter (i) sketches the historical background of the public procurement Directives, (ii) gives a general view of present (iii) and recently adopted Directives, and (iv) explains the objectives of this specific body of EU law.

[71] Case C-107/98, *Teckal v. Comune di Viano* [1999] *ECR* I-8121 on vertical cooperative agreements. Case C-480/06, *Commission of the European Communities v. Federal Republic of Germany* [2009] *ECR* I-4747 on horizontal cooperative agreements.

1. Historical background of the public procurement Directives[72]

The first and most important pillar of the EU concerns above all the establishment of an internal market, resting on four fundamental freedoms: free movement of goods, persons, capital, and services. The EU has the competence to achieve these objectives.[73] Each Member State must guarantee that the citizens of any other Member State has equal access to its territory to the end of providing services to economic operators and private persons, establishing residence, and engaging in gainful activities. Member States cannot take measures that hinder free movement.

Public authorities in the different Member States need goods, services and people to manage tasks of general interest and for which they conclude contracts with third parties. The decision to conclude such a contract might also be considered a measure that could hinder the realisation of the internal market.[74] Thus in taking these kinds of decisions Member States have to ensure they abide by EU law.

The CJEU has by its case law created the means of exercising a degree of control on what a public authority may or may not do when looking for a contract partner. The driver is not principles of private contract law, but the strictly economic objective that defines the EU, namely the greatest possible competition between economic actors. To ensure free competition between the different undertakings interested in concluding such a contract, a public authority has to treat equally these undertakings and to ensure transparency.

The Treaty on the European Union (TEU) and the TFEU contain a number of negative obligations imposed on the Member States, all to the end of achieving the internal market. Member States quite quickly discovered that these obligations were not in themselves sufficient to banish each and every form of discrimination or every difference. Thus, a difference in legislation could put economic actors from some Member States in an unequal position. Therefore, to maintain effective competition harmonisation of the different national legislation was necessary in certain areas. So, the Member States were encouraged to take positive action. Harmonisation of national rules with the aim of eliminating distortions of competition is conducive to the attainment of the internal market.[75]

72 S. Arrowsmith, *The law of public and utilities procurement* (Londen: Sweet & Maxwell, 2005), pp. 140 et seq.; Ch. Bovis, *EC Public Procurement: case law and regulation* (Oxford: OUP, 2006), pp. 95 et seq.; J.M. Fernandez Martin, *The EC Public procurement rules: a critical analysis* (Oxford: Clarendon Press, 1996), pp. 4 et seq.; P. Trepte, *Public procurement in the EU* (Oxford: OUP, 2007), pp. 27 et seq.; F. Weiss, *Public procurement in European Community Law* (Londen: Athlone, 1993), pp. 40 et seq.

73 The European Union is an overarching name, comprising the EC and EAEC (formerly Euratom).

74 See further Chapter 4.

75 Case C-300/89, *Commission of the European Communities v. Council of the European Communities* [1991] *ECR* I-2901, at [23].

The EU Council and the European Commission have two main instruments at their disposal to harmonise legislation: the regulation and the directive.[76] They have made abundant use of these instruments. The directive as a legal instrument is used when it is necessary to implement a goal in different ways in the various Member States. How a matter is handled may involve social and economic choices or a variety of administrative procedures, depending on the individual Member State. Every Member State has the possibility to adjust the content of the directive to its own legal and judicial system. The law applicable to public contracts was in a lot of continental EU member states administrative law. This branch of law is rather different from Member State to Member State. This explains why the tendering of public contracts was best regulated through directives.

Harmonisation has also led to the EU assuming a regulatory role in matters that *prima facie* did not come under the provisions of the treaties. A typical example, as adduced by legal scholars, is the adoption of Directives on public procurement, in which the EU – via these measures – encourages the Member States to harmonise with one another.[77] It was deemed more necessary to harmonise in this area, because national public authorities seemed to have a very strong protectionist tendency when tendering and awarding public contracts.[78] Purchasing activities by Member States were identified as considerable non-tariff barriers.[79] The TEU and TFEU, like the prior EU Treaties, contain no specific provisions on public procurement.[80]

The economic importance of public contract markets in the EU needs no further emphasis.[81] In light of the realisation of the internal market, it should be stated that public authorities are normally not bound by market principles when taking decisions. Their decisions are based on the pursuit of the general public interest and public authorities therefore, need not worry about competitiveness and financial attractiveness. It would regularly come about that public authorities gave the advantage to their own national undertakings. Such decisions could distort the market.[82] These two

76 On directives see S. Prechal, *Directives in EC law* (Oxford: OUP, 2004).

77 K. Lenaerts and P. Vanuffel, *Constitutional law of the European Union* (London: Sweet & Maxwell, 2005), pp. 268–269.

78 M. Trybus and R. Caranta, 'European Union Law of Public Contracts: Public Procurement and Beyond', in M. Trybus, R. Caranta and G. Edelstam (eds.), *European Union Law of Public Contracts* (Brussel: Bruylant, 2013), p. 3.

79 Ch. Bovis, 'Public procurement in the EU: jurisprudence and conceptual directions' (*PPLR*, 2012), p. 247.

80 See for the reasons M. Trybus, 'Public contracts in European Union Internal Market Law: Foundations and Requirements', in R. Noguellou and U. Stelkens (eds.), *Comparative law on Public Contracts* (Brussel, Bruylant, 2010), pp. 83–84. On the absence of public procurement dispositions in the original Treaty of Rome see M.A. Flamme, 'La liberation de la concurrence dans les marchés publics au sein de la C.E.E.' (*RMC*, 1965), p. 277, footnote 2: according to the author the national parliaments would not have accepted such provisions in the Treaty because of the protectionist traditions of certain Member States.

81 M. Monti, 'A New Strategy for the Single Market: At the Service of Europe's Economy and Society' (May 9, 2010), http://ec.europa.eu/bepa/pdf/monti_report_final_10_05_2010_en.pdf.

82 S. Arrowsmith, 'The past and future evolution of EC procurement law: from framework to common code?' (PCLJ, 2006), p. 339.

circumstances were major factors making the introduction of public procurement Directives necessary. The provisions of the EU treaties were not sufficiently specific to prevent public authorities from taking discriminatory decisions fostering unequal treatment.

The first sign of positive action in the field of public procurement appeared in two general programmes, adopted by the EU Council in 1962, which effectively removed all obstacles on freedom of cross-border services and establishment.[83] These two general programmes contained several dispositions on public procurement. The need was recognised for the adoption of European legislation (via directives) on the specific subject. Public procurement was (and is) considered a very important aspect of the common / internal market.[84, 85] The acquisition of work, goods and services of public authorities represents a major activity in the EU economy. Barriers to these kinds of trade would jeopardize – to a great extent – the realization of the internal market. Two directives concerning public procurement were then issued on the basis of these two programmes.

The first legislative initiatives were Directive 70/32/EEC[86] and Directive 71/304/EEC.[87] Directive 70/32/EEC forbade measures hindering free movement of goods. Directive 71/304/EEC, which had been exclusively applied to the completion of public work contracts, obliged Member States to i) lift restrictions affecting the right to enter into or award public works contracts, ii) perform or participate in the performance of such public works, on behalf of the State, regional or local authorities, or legal persons governed by public law. However, these Directives did not yet compel Member States to bring their national laws on public contracts into harmony with one another.

More important, however, was the adoption of Directive 71/305/EEC.[88] This Directive sought not simply to facilitate freedom of establishment and the free provision of cross-border services in the area of public procurement, but also to provide a competitive market for potential candidates. In the event, the drafters of the Directive attached special significance to the provision of adequate information for potential bidders. Thus the very first Directive on public procurement contained an indication of the principle of

83 The General Programme for the abolition of restrictions on freedom to provide services OJ 2/32 English Special Edition Series II Volume IX pp. 3–6 and the General Programme *for the abolition of restrictions on freedom of* establishment OJ 2/36 English Special Edition Series II Volume IX pp. 7 – 15.

84 See S. Arrowsmith, *The law of public and utilities procurement*, Vol. I (London, Sweet & Maxwell, 2014), p. 1: 19% of GDP of the 27 EU Member States and 21,6% of the GDP in the UK.

85 M.A. Flamme, 'La libération de la concurrence dans les marchés publics au sein de la C.E.E.' (*RMC*, 1965), p. 277.

86 Commission Directive 70/32/EEC of 17 December 1969 on provision of goods to the State, to local authorities and other official bodies, OJ [1970] L 13.

87 Council Directive 71/304/EEC of 26 July 1971 concerning the abolition of restrictions on freedom to provide services in respect of public works contracts and on the award of public works contracts to contractors acting through agencies or branches, OJ [1971] L 185/1.

88 Council Directive 71/305/EEC of 26 July 1971 on the coordination of procedures for placement of public contracts for the completion of public works, OJ [1971] L. 185/5.

transparency.[89] The second co-ordination directive was Directive 77/62/EEC.[90] The two Directives are comparable in structure and content. However, both Directives allowed autonomy to Member States in the implementation of the Directives into national legislation. In particular, these Directives set out no specific awarding procedures that contracting authorities should follow. They merely laid down several conditions for whenever a contracting authority uses its own procedures.

The two Directives were not successful since the Member States were not inclined to follow them. Moreover, public authorities awarded less public (work) contracts in that period. Finally, a number of activities of general interest did not fall under these Directives (utility sectors). Hence, it was recognised that new initiatives would need to be implemented. It was clear that the Directives contained no provisions that could be applied to cooperation between public authorities. Taking into account the insignificant influence of the Directives on national administrative law, this first period is not important to the research being undertaken.

However, in 1985, with the adoption of the White Paper on the Internal Market,[91] the position changed radically. The Internal Market programme required the harmonisation of Member States laws in many sectors that had a direct impact on achieving the EU Internal market by 1992. The adoption of the Single European Act in 1989 ensured that unanimity was no longer required for the adoption of harmonising directives that were necessary to achieve the Internal Market. This radical approach manifested itself particularly in the legislation adopted in the field of public procurement. There is no doubt that the internal market project largely influenced the evolution of the second generation of public procurement Directives.

In the 1980s there was an attempt made to improve the Directives. Thus, respectively Directive 88/295/EEC[92] and Directive 89/440/EEC[93] were adopted amending the previous Directives. In themselves these Directives brought few changes to the existing Directives, but they did add a plethora of new provisions that concerned, in particular, the introduction of a negotiating procedure, the application of EU standards, rules of notification. As there was no coordination between the new and the old Directives the sense of the regulatory measures was quite difficult to interpret.

89 This is discussed in greater depth in chapter 4.

90 Council Directive 77/62/EEC of 21 December 1976 coordinating procedures for the award of public supply contracts, OJ [1977] L 13/1.

91 European Commission White Paper for the Completion of the Internal Market (COM) 85 310 final.

92 Council Directive 88/295/EEC amending Directive 77/62/EEC coordinating procedures for the award of public supply contracts as well as for the repeal of some provisions of Directive 80/767/EEC, OJ [1988] L127.

93 Council Directive 89/440/EEC amending Directive 71/304/EEC concerning the abolition of restrictions on freedom to provide services in respect of public works contracts and on the award of public works contracts to contractors acting through agencies or branches, OJ [1989] L210.

Ultimately this led to new coordinating Directives, namely, Directive 93/36/EEC[94] and Directive 93/37/EEC,[95] closely followed, by yet other set of Directives: Directive 89/665/EEC,[96] Directive 93/38/EEC,[97] Directive 92/13/EEC[98] and Directive 92/50/EEC.[99]

In Council Decision 94/800/EC,[100] the Council of the EU made its approval contingent on the Government Procurement Agreement (GPA), the objective of which is to establish a multilateral framework of equal rights and obligations in the area of public contracts with a view to further liberalisation and expansion of world trade. The GPA is to date the only legally binding agreement in the World Trade Organisation (WTO) focusing on the subject of government procurement. It is a plurilateral treaty administered by a Committee on Government Procurement, which includes the WTO Members who have signed the GPA, and thus have rights and obligations under the Agreement. This resulted in two new Directives that applied the obligations flowing from the GPA to the previous Directives: Directive 97/52/EC[101] and Directive 98/4/EC.[102]

An examination of the Directives mentioned in this section shows that they did not provide much information as to their application to cooperative agreements between public authorities.

94 Council Directive 93/36/EEC of 14 June 1993 coordinating procedures for the award of public supply contracts, OJ 1993, L199/1.

95 Council Directive 93/37/EEC of 14 June 1993 concerning the coordination of procedures for the award of public works contracts, OJ [1993] L199/54.

96 Council Directive 89/665/EEC of 21 December 1989 on the coordination of the laws, regulations and administrative provisions relating to the application of review procedures to the award of public supply and public works contracts, OJ [1989] L395/33.

97 Council Directive 93/38/EEC of 14 June 1993 coordinating the procurement procedures of entities operating in the water, energy, transport and telecommunications sectors, OJ [1993] pp. 84–138.

98 Council Directive 92/13/EEC of 25 February 1992 coordinating the laws, regulations and administrative provisions relating to the application of Community rules on the procurement procedures of entities operating in the water, energy, transport and telecommunications sectors, OJ [1992] L 76/14.

99 Council Directive 92/50/EEC of 18 June 1992 to the coordination of procedures for the award of public service contracts, OJ [1992] L209.

100 Council d ecision 94/800/EC of 22 December 1994 concerning the conclusion on behalf of the European Community, as regards matters within its competence, of the agreements reached in the Uruguay Round multilateral negotiations (1986–1994), OJ [1994] L336/1.

101 Directive of the European Parliament and the Council Directive of 13 October 1997 amending Directives 92/50/EEC, 93/36/EEC and 93/37/EEC concerning the coordination of procedures for the award of public service contracts, public supply contracts and public works contracts respectively, OJ [1997] L328/1.

102 Directive of the European Parliament and the Council Directive of 13 October 1997 coordinating the procurement procedures of entities operating in the water, energy, transport and telecommunications sectors, OJ [1998] L101/1.

2. The public procurement Directives of 2004[103]

Until recently there were mainly two Directives regarding public procurement in the EU.[104] They are Directive 2004/17/EC coordinating the procurement procedures of entities operating in the water, energy, transport and postal services sectors[105] (telecommunications thus is no longer one of the utility sectors) and Directive 2004/18/EC on the coordination of procedures for the award of public works contracts, public supply contracts and public service contracts.[106]

However, the genesis of these Directives was a long ordeal. In 1996 the European Commission drafted a Green Paper entitled 'Public procurement in the European Union: exploring the way forward'.[107] The purpose of this Green Paper was to provide a context for a wide-ranging debate on public contracts within the EU. The most important targets were: an effective implementation of the existing case law; better accessibility to contracts; access to the markets of non-EU Member States; and coordination of policy on public contracts as well as other areas of policy. There was no doubt that Member States were not adequately implementing the Directives. The complex regulations and the rigid system for complex contracts were also touched upon in this Green Paper.

However, the Green Paper elicited over 300 responses, from which it became clear that some fundamental changes were needed to the existing Directives. The reactions ultimately led to a Commission Communication of 11 March 1998 entitled *'Public procurement in the European Union'*.[108] Its objective was to achieve a more efficient system that would result in a better public service, economic growth, greater competition, job creation, an assault on corruption, and lastly, clearer and more flexible rules and procedures. The catchwords for the impending regulation were: flexibility, modernisation and simplification. The interaction between the Commission and the various stakeholders and policy-makers eventually produced, in 2000, two proposals for directives, one for

103 S. Arrowsmith, 'An Assessment of the New Legislative Package on Public Procurement' (*CMLR* 41, 2004), pp. 1–49; V. Bertrand, 'La réforme européenne des marchés publics dans les secteurs classiques' (*JTE*, 2005), pp. 1–11; R. Beuter, 'European public procurement reform: main innovations in the Public Sector Directive – a preliminary assessment' (*Eipascope* 3, 2005), pp. 5–11; D. D'Hooghe, I. Vos and Ph. De Keyser, 'Recente evoluties in het aanbestedingsrecht', in K. De Ketelaere and A. Verbeke (eds.), *Jaarboek Bouwrecht 2004–2005* (Brugge, Die Keure, 2005), pp. 4–20; A. Mattera, 'Vers un Code européen des marchés publics. Simplification, modernisation et clarification de la reglementation existante' (*RDUE*, 2000), pp. 528–570; I. Ramsey, 'The New Public Procurement Directives: a partial solution to the problems of procurement compliance' (*EPL*, 2006), pp. 275–294; R. Williams, 'The New Procurment Directives of the European Union' (*PPLR*, 2004), pp. 153–159; X., 'Les Nouvelles directives européennes' (*ACCP* 33, 2004), pp. 45–68.

104 See also Directive 2009/81/EC of the European Parliament and of the Council of 13 July 2009 on the coordination of procedures for the award of certain works contracts, supply contracts and service contracts by contracting authorities or entities in the fields of defence and security, and amending Directives 2004/17/EC and 2004/18/EC, OJ [2009] L 216.

105 OJ [2004] L. 134/1.

106 OJ [2004] L. 134/114.

107 COM(96)583.

108 COM(1998)143.

the public sector[109] and one for the utility sectors.[110] However, the proposals generated abundant discussion among the Commission, Council and Parliament,[111] and it was only in 2004 that the new Directives were finally approved.

Simplification and clarification found expression first and foremost in the fact that the four different Directives were replaced by only two Directives (2004/17/EC and 2004/18/EC). The Directives in the classical sectors (works, supplies and services) have been consolidated into one Directive, which in itself entailed a significant trimming of the aggregate set of provisions (48 Articles). Further, discrepancies among the various Directives have been eliminated by incorporating the same provisions into each type of public contract. Second, the provisions are listed in the chronological order of the award procedure. Third, the number of pecuniary thresholds was reduced and they are now expressed in Euros. Fourth, concepts are explicitly defined in the Directives and specific interpretations from the case law of the Court of Justice, have now been inserted in the Directives. Finally there are provisions relating to the general principles of equal treatment, non-discrimination, and transparency.

For flexibility a new type of award procedure, namely, competitive dialogue[112] was adopted. Any economic operator may request to participate and the contracting authority conducts a dialogue with the candidate admitted to the procedure for the purpose of working out one or more suitable alternatives capable of meeting the requirements. On that basis the selected candidates are invited to tender (Article 1, no. 11, (c) Directive 2004/18/EC). This procedure is intended for public contracts of a particularly complex nature, where the contracting authorities are unable to determine what means would best meet the requirements of the contracting authority or evaluate what technical, financial and legal alternatives the market has to offer. Innovative projects also benefited from such a procedure.

Second, provisions on the use of framework agreements are explicitly employed. A framework agreement[113] is defined as an agreement between one or more economic operators for the purpose of fixing, for a specified period, the conditions for awarding

109 Proposal for a Directive of the European Parliament and the Council coordinating the procurement procedures of procedures for the award of public supply contracts, public service contracts and public works contracts, COM(2000)275.

110 Proposal for a Directive of the European Parliament and the Council coordinating the procurement procedures of entities operating in the water, energy and transport sectors, COM(2000)276.

111 A more detailed overview is found in S. Van Garsse, *Nieuwe richtlijn overheidsopdrachten. Codificatie van het Europees aanbestedingsrecht in de klassieke sectoren* (*NjW*, 2004), pp. 945–946.

112 See F. Lichère, 'New Award Procedures', in M. Trybus, R. Caranta and G. Edelstam (eds.), *European Union Law of Public Contracts* (Brussel: Bruylant, 2013), pp. 83–95; A. Rubach-Larsen, 'Competitive Dialogue', in R. Nielsen and S. Treumer (eds.), *The New EU Public Procurement Directives* (Copenhagen: Djøf Publishing, 2005), pp. 71–80.

113 See F. Lichère, 'New Award Procedures', in M. Trybus, R. Caranta and G. Edelstam (eds.), *European Union Law of Public Contracts* (Brussel: Bruylant, 2013), pp. 95–99; R. Nielsen, 'Framework Agreements', in R. Nielsen and S. Treumer (eds), *The new EU Public Procurement Directives* (Copenhagen: Djøf Publishing, 2005), pp. 81–96.

contracts, namely, the price, and the projected quantity (Article 1.5 Directive 2004/18/EC).

Third, it is now permitted to operate through central purchasing bodies. A central purchasing body is a contracting service that acquires specific deliveries and/or services for other contracting services or grants public contracts and concludes framework agreements in respect of specific works, deliveries or services for contracting authorities (Article 1.10 Directive 2004/18/EC).

In the spirit of modernisation, the Directives encourage the use of electronic media in communication and information exchange. The use of electronic media shortens the award procedure. The Directives also introduce a number of innovative, electronic award techniques that concern electronic security. Public authorities can make use of dynamic purchasing systems. A dynamic purchasing system is an electronic process for purchases of common use and with general features available on the market that meet the requirements of the contracting authority. They are time limited and are permanently open to every economic operator that meets the criteria of selection.

Finally, the Directives also introduce a number of innovations in regard to selection and award criteria and the integration of social and environmental objectives in the award of public contracts as well as in respect of technical specifications. The Directive for the utility sectors now includes a general mechanism for exclusion. In those cases where an activity carried out in a Member State is directly open to competition in market areas to which access is not restricted, the Directive is not applicable (Article 30 Directive 2004/17/EC).

Chapter 5 demonstrates that some of the provisions of the 2004 Directives were already much clearer on the application of the Directives to cooperative agreements between public authorities. But until 2004 none of the Directives provided specific provisions that made clear to what extent cooperative agreements between public authorities fall out or within the scope of EU law. This explains why this situation has been dealt with by the CJEU, which has elaborated criteria to exclude, under certain circumstances, such cooperation from the scope of EU law (see chapter 5). The CJEU based its case law on certain concepts (contract, operator) already used in the Directives, but interpreted these concepts in a functional and autonomous way. This interpretation not only broadened the possible scope of EU law, but also created jurisprudential rules as to the extent to what cooperative agreements fall under the scope of EU law.

The public procurement Directives adopted in 2004 contain no specific provisions concerning cooperative agreements between public authorities (see chapter 5), from which it may be inferred that the powers of the Member States are still quite ample. However, the CJEU has via its case law had an impact on these powers (see chapter 5). In doing so the CJEU has made use of a broad interpretation of the Directives and thus, as a consequence of the direct effect of some of the provisions of Directives. The CJEU based its case law on the objectives of the public procurement Directives and the internal market rules to elaborate an innovative application of EU law on cooperative agreements between public authorities. The Member States and their public authorities are bound by the CJEU interpretation. By such a device EU law has had an influence on some aspects of national administrative law; namely, the organisation of public service tasks.

In *Stadt Halle* the CJEU explained that vertical cooperative agreements between public authorities, where one of them is a semi-public company, would clash with the objective of free and undistorted competition and the principle of equal treatment.[114] The CJEU stated in *Carbotermo*[115] that the *Teckal* criteria[116] 'are aimed at preventing distortions of competition'. The CJEU, thus, asserts that cooperative agreements between public authorities could potentially clash with certain of the EU objectives. According to the CJEU, this observation also corroborates the application of EU law (i.e. public procurement Directives and principle of equal treatment), when these objectives are jeopardised as a consequence of a State measure. The objectives are imperilled whenever a cooperative agreement fails to meet the criteria the CJEU has developed in its *Teckal* case.

According to *Commission v. Germany* horizontal cooperative agreements between public authorities do not undermine the principle objective of the EU rules on public procurement, that is, the free movement of services and the opening of undistorted competition 'where implementation of that cooperation is governed solely by considerations and requirements relating to the pursuit of objectives in the public interest and the principle of equal treatment of the persons concerned, referred to in Directive 92/50, is respected, so that no private undertaking is placed in a position of advantage vis-à-vis competitors'.[117] Thus a potential clash with the objectives of the EU raises the issue of the applicability of EU law. In *Ordine degli Architteti*[118] the CJEU developed criteria that concretise these objectives. If a horizontal cooperative agreement fails to meet these criteria, EU law is applicable.

Directives 2004/17/EC and 2004/18/EC are the framework of the present book. If a Member State has failed to implement the Directives or has implemented them incorrectly, nationals can invoke most provisions of the Directives in a direct way before national

114 Case C-26/03, *Stadt Halle and RPL Recyclingpark Lochau GmbH. v. Arbeitsgemeinschaft Thermische Restabfall- und Energieverwertungsanlage TREA Leuna* [2005] *ECR* I-00001, at [51].

115 Case C-340/04, *Carbotermo SpA and Consorzio Alisei v. Comune di Busto Arsizio and AGESP SpA* [2006] *ECR* I-04137, at [59].

116 Case C-107/98, *Teckal v. Comune di Viano* [1999] *ECR* I-8121. The public procurement Directives are not applicable to cooperation between public authorities if the public authority exercises a control on the second on which is similar to that which it exercises over its own departments and, secondly, the second public authority carries out the essential activities with the controlling authority or authorities. See chapter 5.

117 Case C-480/06, *Commission of the European Communities v. Federal Republic of Germany* [2009] *ECR* I-04747, at [47].

118 Case C-159/11, *Azienda Sanitaria Locale di Lecce, Università del Salento v. Ordine degli Ingegneri della Provincia di Lecce and Others* [2012] *ECR* I-00000.

courts: 'that the substantive rules of the procurement directives, such as the obligations on advertising, conducting the competition, evidence and criteria for selection and award criteria, in general have direct effect'.[119] THE CJEU recently ruled as follows in this regards in a matter concerning the public procurement Directives: 'that ... whenever the provisions of a directive appear, so far as their subject-matter is concerned, to be unconditional and sufficiently precise, they may be relied on before the national courts by individuals against the State where the latter has failed to implement the directive in domestic law by the end of the period prescribed or where it has failed to implement the directive correctly'.[120] If the national court is not sure about the application or meaning of the provision of EU law, it can start a preliminary procedure before the CJEU. A lot of case law on cooperative agreements finds its origin in this kind of procedures.

3. New developments

In December 2011, as announced in the Single Market Act,[121] the Commission adopted its new proposals on public procurement. These proposals are part of an overall program aimed at a thorough modernization of public procurement in the EU. This program includes the revision of Directives 2004/17/EC (procurement in water, energy, transport and postal services sectors) and 2004/18/EC (public works, supply and service contracts), as well as the adoption of a directive on concessions, which were until now not regulated at the EU level.

These proposals originated in the European Commission communication on smart, sustainable and inclusive growth.[122] Public procurement is one of the market-based instruments for achieving the objectives set out in the 2020 strategy. Europe 2020 wants to develop an economy based on knowledge and innovation, the promotion of a low carbon, resource efficient and competitive economy, the fostering of a high-employment economy delivering social and territorial cohesion. The European Commission issued a Green Paper on the modernisation of EU public procurement policy[123] to initiate a consultation on new proposals. One of the issues elaborated in the Green Paper is on cooperative agreements between public authorities.

On 20 December 2011 the Commission published its proposals for two new procedural directives on public procurement, one[124] to replace Public Sector Directive 2004/18/EC

119 S. Arrowsmith, *The law of Public and Utilities Procurement* (London: Sweet and Maxwell, 2005), p. 1393 referring to case law in footnote 40.

120 Case C-425/12, *Portgás – Sociedade de Produção e Distribuição de Gás SA v. Ministério da Agricultura, do Mar, do Ambiente e do Ordenamento do Territó* [2013] *ECR* I-00000, at [18].

121 Communication from the Commission to the European Parliament, the Council, the Economic and Social Committee and the Committee of the Regions: *Towards a Single Market Act – For a highly competitive social market economy*, COM (2010) 608.

122 Communication from the Commission of 3 March 2010 – *Europe 2020 A strategy for smart, sustainable and inclusive growth*, COM(2010) 2020 final.

123 Green Paper on the modernisation of EU public procurement policy, COM (2011) 15 final.

124 Proposal for a directive on public procurement, COM (2011) 896 final.

and the second[125] to replace Utilities Directive 2004/17/EC, with the stated aims of; simplification' and 'flexibilisation' of the rules to improve value for money.[126] The proposals aim also to enable public contracts to be better used to support other EU policies. The Commission also proposed a new directive to regulate the award of concessions.[127] It based this new proposal on work done in 2004.[128]

These proposals sparked many discussions within the European Parliament and led to numerous amendments. Compromise texts were the result.[129] These compromise texts were submitted to the vote in January 2014 in the plenary session of the European Parliament. They were published in the Official Journal of the European Union (OJ) on 28 March 2014.[130]

The different proposals of the EU Commission contained dispositions on the cooperative agreements between public authorities. A comparison between the texts originally accepted by the EU Commission and the published texts makes clear that major amendments had been inserted. The new provisions led to many discussions, which demonstrate the sensitive nature of the matter. Many Member States feared a too great interference of EU law on their national competences. The compromise texts seek a new balance in the distribution of powers between the EU and the Member States, inter alia regarding cooperative agreements between public authorities. These dispositions are not studied in-depth here.[131] The new dispositions on cooperative agreements between public authorities are not the main focus of the present work.

125 Proposal for a directive on procurement by entities in the water, energy, transport and postal services sectors, COM (2011) 895 final.

126 See e.g. the Explanatory Memorandum to the proposal for a directive on public procurement, p.2.

127 Proposal for a directive on the award of concession contracts, COM (2011) 897 final.

128 See, in particular, European Commission, *Green Paper on public-private partnerships and Community law on public contracts and concessions* COM(2004) 327 final and *Communication from the Commission to the European Parliament, the Council, the European Economic and Social Committee and the Committee of the Regions on Public-Private Partnerships and Community Law on Public Procurement and Concessions*, COM (2005) 569 final.

129 Proposal for a directive of the European Parliament and of the Council on public procurement (Classical Directive) (First reading) – Approval of the final compromise text – 2011/0438 (COD).
Proposal for a Directive of the European Parliament and of the Council on the award of concession contracts (First reading) – Approval of the final compromise text – 2011/0437 (COD).
Proposal for a directive of the European Parliament and of the Council on procurement by entities operating in the water, energy, transport and postal services sectors (First reading) – Approval of the final compromise text – 2011/0439 (COD).

130 Directive 2014/25/EU of the European Parliament and of the Council of 26 February 2014 on procurement by entities operating in the water, energy, transport and postal services sectors and repealing Directive 2004/17/EC; Directive 2014/24/EU of the European Parliament and of the Council of 26 February 2014 on public procurement and repealing Directive 2004/18/EC; Directive 2014/23/EU of the European Parliament and of the Council of 26 February 2014 on the award of concession contracts JO 2014 L94.

131 See chapter 5.

4. Objectives of the public procurement Directives[132]

A number of general objectives on which the public procurement Directives are based are described. These objectives guide the CJEU in its task of interpreting the various provisions of the Directives. These objectives help to explain in what measure public procurement Directives and the principles of equal treatment and transparency are applicable to cooperative agreements between public authorities.[133]

The public procurement Directives were, and remain, one of the major legislative acts furthering the achievement of an internal market; their legal basis is found in the TFEU provisions on free movement. Both Directives and the TFEU provisions on free movement seek EU integration.[134] The Directives should be considered a further concretization to the TFEU provisions. In that sense it is comprehensible that the CJEU applies the same principles on cooperative agreements of public authorities without making a distinction regarding the kind of contract that governs the cooperation. The EU public procurement system is the outcome of a progressive development over a period of several decades with the ultimate goal of opening up public markets to competition as an ideal means of promoting economic efficiency.[135] Early CJEU case law on public procurement is regularly based on Treaty provisions concerning free movement.[136]

In Directive 71/305/EEC freedom of establishment and the free performance of services were the primary objectives of the opening of public markets. However, the authors of this Directive added the following aim as well: *"To ensure development of effective competition in the field of public contracts"*.

In its first judgment in this area the CJEU laid especial stress on the freedom of establishment and free movement of services as objectives to the achievement of the

132 On this subject see S.E. Hjelmborg, P.S. Jacobsen and S.T. Poulsen, *Public procurement* law (Copenhagen: Djøf Publishing, 2006), pp. 19–33; A.S. Graells, *Public procurement and the EU Competition Rules* (Oxford: Hart Publishing, 2011), pp. 189–220; C.R. Hansen, *Contracts not covered or not fully covered by the Public Sector Directive* (Copenhagen: Djøf Publishing, 2012), pp. 51–56; S. Arrowsmith, 'The purpose of the EU Procurement Directives: ends, means and the implications for national regulatory space for commercial and horizontal procurement policies' (*CYELS*, 2011–2012), pp. 1–47.

133 See Chapter 5.

134 G.S. Olykke, 'How does the Court of Justice of the European Union pursue competition concerns in a public procurement context?' (*PPLR*, 2011), p. 181.

135 P. Wang, R. Cavallo Perin and D. Casalini, 'Addressing purchasing agreements between public sector entities: what can the WTO learn from the EU's experience?', in S. Arrowsmith and R.D. Anderson (Eds.), *The WTO regime on government procurement: challenge and reform* (Cambridge: Cambridge University Press, 2011), p. 255.

136 See P. Trepte, *Regulating procurement. Understanding the ends and means of public procurement regulation* (Oxford: OUP, 2004), pp. 350–351. Case 45/87, *Commission v. Ireland ("Dundalk")* [1988] *ECR* 4929; Case C-3/88, *Commission v. Italy ("Re Data Processing")* [1989] *ECR* 4035; Case C-243/89, *Commission v. Danmark ("Storebaelt")* [1993] *ECR* I-03353; Case C-359/93, *Commission v. Netherlands ("UNIX")* [1995] *ECR* I-00157.

internal market.[137] In later case law the CJEU tends to see the achievement of a free market as a goal for facilitating attainment of the internal market and for making it easier for undertakings to pursue their business interests.[138] In any event, the realisation of the internal market and the attainment of the conditions for a dynamic and effective competition[139] now stand side by side as parallel objectives in the context of public procurement Directives.[140] According to the CJEU the widest possible opening-up to competition is contemplated not only from the point of view of the EU's objective of achieving the free movement of goods and services but also from the interest of the contracting authority, which will thus have greater choice as to the most advantageous tender which is most suitable for the needs of the public authority in question.[141]

The Court of Justice has described the purpose of the public procurement Directives as follows: 'the Directive ... is aimed at eliminating restrictions on the freedom of establishment and the free movement of goods and services in the area of public procurements for the purpose of opening tenders to real and effective competition'.[142] The CJEU sees this objective in broad terms as: 'attaining the widest possible opening-up of public contracts to competition'.[143] The Directives' purpose is to put an end to 'practices that seek to limit competition in general, and the participation of subjects of other Member States in tender calls, in particular, by facilitating access to procurement procedures for service providers [in other Member States]'.[144] In other words, the intention is to protect market participants established in another Member State,[145] i.e. to avoid favouritism.[146]

137 Case C-31/87, *Gebroeders Beentjes BV v. the State of the Netherlands* [1988] *ECR* 4635, at [9].

138 Case C-532/06, *Emm. G. Lianakis AE, Sima Anonymi Techniki Etaireia Meleton kai Epivlepseon and Nikolaos Vlachopoulos v. Dimos Alexandroupolis and Others* [2008] *ECR* I-251, at [39]; Case C-454/06, *Pressetext Nachrichtenagentur GmbH v. Austria, APA-OTS Originaltext-Service GmbH and APA Austria Press Agentur registrierte Genossenschaft mit beschränkter Haftung* [2008] *ECR* I-4401, at [31].

139 Case C-95/10, *Strong Segurança SA v. Município de Sintra and Securitas-Serviços e Tecnologia de Segurança* [2011] *ECR* I-01865, at [37]. For a more extended study regarding the influence of the 'competition objective' in the public procurement Directives see A.S. Graells, *Public procurement and the EU competition rules* (Oregon: Oxford and Portland, 2011), pp. 190 et seq. See also C. Estevan de Quesada, 'Competition and transparency in public procurement markets' (*PPLR*, 2014), pp. 229–244.

140 Case C-454/06, *Pressetext Nachrichtenagentur GmbH v. Republik Österreich (Bund), APA-OTS Originaltext-Service GmbH and APA Austria Presse Agentur registrierte Genossenschaft mit beschränkter Haftung* [2008] *ECR* I-04401, at [31]; see also Case C-480/06, *Commission v. Germany* [2009] *ECR* I-04747, at [47].

141 Case C-305/08, *Consorzio Nazionale Interuniversitario per le Scienze del Mare (CoNISMa) v. Regione Marche* [2009] ECR I-12129 at [37].

142 Case C-399/98, *Ordine degli Architetti delle province di Milano e Lodi, Piero De Amicis, Consiglio Nazionale degli Architetti and Leopoldo Freyrie v. Comune di Milano, and Pirelli SpA, Milano Centrale Servizi SpA and Fondazione Teatro alla Scala* [2001] *ECR* I-05409, at [52].

143 Case C-94/12, *Swm Costruzioni 2 SpA, Mannocchi Luigino DI v. Provincia di Fermo* [2013] *ECR* I-00000, at [34].

144 Case C-92/00, *Hospital Ingenieure Krankenhaustechnik Planungs-Gesellschaft mbH v. Stadt Wien* [2002] *ECR* I-5553, at [44].

145 Case C-226/09, *European Commission v. Ireland* [2010] *ECR* I-11807.

146 Joint cases C-285/99 and C-286/99, *Impresa Lombardini SpA – Impresa Generale di Costruzioni v. ANAS – Ente nazionale per le strade and Società Italiana per Condotte d'Acqua SpA and Impresa Ing. Mantovani SpA v. ANAS – Ente nazionale per le strade and Ditta Paolo Bregoli* [2001] *ECR* I-09233, at [35].

The intent of the Directives is to constrain public authorities and to get them to allow their works to be done in a similar manner as the private sector; i.e. permitting them to seek the best and cheapest solution. In this sense they may not favour certain situations without good reason and all similar situations must be treated in a like manner.

On the basis of these objectives one can argue that if a State measure (the decision to cooperate) does not put the aims of the Directives at risk, application of EU law is not relevant.[147] The present book argues that CJEU case law on cooperative agreements is based on this presupposition.

The objectives of the EU public procurement Directives differ radically from the objectives the Member States sought to achieve via the national regulations on tendering of public contracts. Several Member States desire, first and foremost, best value for money or aim at a revitalisation of the national economy by granting public contracts to their domestic firms. The Directives, together with the interpretation given to some of the Directives' provisions by the CJEU, entailed a complete rethinking of how a public contract has to be tendered. This gave rise to tensions in the past between EU and national objectives. This tension is one of the important objects of study of the present book.

5. Conclusions

The public procurement Directives are among the most important directives focussed on the realization of the internal market. These Directives are subject to a rapid evolution. Both the reality and the functional interpretation of the Directives by the CJEU made several amendments throughout the last 4 decades necessary.

However, the amendments have had as a result that the mission of Member States to implement these Directives is more and more difficult and the task of public authorities to apply the provisions of the Directives is rather hazardous. This now raises the question of whether the endeavour of the EU to achieve the economic objectives might impair the workings of national public authorities and thus the general public interest that they serve. Indeed, regular changes in the Directives for economic reasons, means that the Member States must adopt new national implementing measures that people must be retrained and that undertakings must adapt anew. This also takes energy, time and money. It would be better to introduce such innovations every two or three decades but not every ten years. Ten years is not enough time for the Directives to prove themselves.

147 The 2004 public procurement Directives also took into account secondary or horizontal policies or objectives (see S. Arrowmith and P. Kunzlik (eds.), *Social and environmental policies in EC procurement law* (Cambridge, Cambridge University Press, 2009), 509 pp. However, the present book demonstrates that the CJEU case law on cooperation between public authorities can be explained on the basis of the economic objectives of the Directives.

Despite the numerous changes in the Directives, the main objectives of the public procurement Directives remain almost the same: the realization of the internal market and effective competition. Preamble (1) of Directive 2014/24/EU states: 'The award of public contracts by or on behalf of Member States' authorities has to comply with the principles of the Treaty on the Functioning of the European Union (TFEU), and in particular the free movement of goods, freedom of establishment and the freedom to provide services, as well as the principles deriving therefrom, such as equal treatment, non-discrimination, mutual recognition, proportionality and transparency. However, for public contracts above a certain value, provisions should be drawn up coordinating national procurement procedures so as to ensure that those principles are given practical effect and public procurement is opened up to competition'.[148]

This also means that the provisions of the Directives must still be implemented and interpreted taking into account the more general European objectives. Another consequence of this will be that cooperative agreements between public authorities must be construed in terms of this perspective. Thus, the national objectives on the best organization of public service tasks[149] are triggered by the economic objectives of the EU.

148 See also Preamble (2) Directive 2014/25/EU.

149 Cooperative agreements between public authorities are considered in the present work to be a means of organising public service tasks.

Chapter 3

CONCEPTS

The starting point of this research is that public authorities or contracting authorities work together in order to organize or to discharge their publics' or general tasks interest. They cooperate and they contract with each other. This type of cooperation is influenced by EU law. The aim of the study is to examine this influence.

In order to mark out the research field of the study and to make clear where EU law has a bearing on national administrative law the relevant concepts must be defined. The field of study is principally concerned with EU law. So the definitions of these concepts are found in this law. The central actor of the study is the (i) *public or contracting authority*. It determines the *ratione personae* scope of the study. The situation that was studied is the cooperation between public authorities, i.e. cooperative agreements. The concept of (ii) *'cooperative agreement'* determines the *ratione materiae* scope of this book. The influence is felt regarding the organization and management of (iii) *public tasks or tasks of general interest*. As such the presence of these concepts in a particular situation does not exclude the application of EU law, but under certain circumstances cooperative agreements between public authorities ensuring the implementation of public service task fall outside the scope of EU law.

The CJEU normally uses a teleological interpretation to give a meaning to the concepts used in EU law.[150] In a teleological interpretation the judge endeavours to discover the purpose or object of a particular term and will interpret the term such that an *effet utile* is the outcome: 'in interpreting a provision of Community law it is necessary to consider its wording, context and aims'.[151] Thus, a text must be so construed that its potential consequence in practice would be in consonance with the perceived purpose (doctrine of effectiveness). Such a method of interpretation is similarly discernible in Article 31.1 of

[150] For an extensive explanation on the CJEU's approach to legal interpretation and the reasons for the teleological interpretation see N. Fennelly, 'Legal Interpretation at the European Court of Justice' (*Fordham International Law Journal*, 1996), pp. 656–679.

[151] Case C-84/95, *Bosphorus Hava Yollari Turizm ve Ticaret AS v. Minister for Transport, Energy and Communications and others* [1996] *ECR* I-03953, at [11]; Case 337/82, *St. Nikolaus Brennerei v. Hauptzollamt Krefeld* [1984] *ECR* 1051, at [10]; Case C-83/94, *Leifer and Others* [1995] *ECR* I-3231, at [22].

the Vienna Convention on the Law of Treaties.[152] 'A treaty shall be interpreted in good faith in accordance with the ordinary meaning to be given to the terms of the treaty in their context and in the light of its object and purpose'. In *casu* the interpretation must promote the further development of the EU.[153]

This method of interpretation was applied by the CJEU as early as in the ruling in *Van Gend & Loos*.[154] The CJEU interprets EU law in the light of the political, economic and social objectives that constitute the foundations of EU law. Clearly, these objectives evolve continuously over the course of time; therefore, such a method of interpretation is likewise evolutionary by nature and hence EU law is not a given. This is also the principal criticism levied at the CJEU; namely, that by giving preference to this method of interpretation the CJEU appears to have assumed a legislative role.[155] This interpretation method has to guarantee the widest possible application as to ensure the realization of the internal market.

The CJEU has realised two fundamental ideas through its use of the teleological method of interpretation: i) a greater unity of EU law and the creation by the Court of its own legal system, i.e. the unity and autonomy of EU law.[156] And ii) fundamental principles such as direct effect and primacy of EU law, the liability of Member States for failure to acknowledge EU law are all products of the aforementioned teleological interpretation.

In public procurement cases the CJEU refers regularly to the preambles of the Directives setting out their context and objectives (see Chapter 2). The concepts 'public or contracting authority' and 'cooperation or contract' are interpreted on the basis of the teleological method, i.e. the objectives of the public procurement Directives and internal market law. When defining them, one must take into account both the context of the provision as well as the objectives of the public procurement Directives.[157] The CJEU gives two reasons for the need for an autonomous interpretation. First, the provisions in the Directives do not refer to national law for determining the meaning and scope of its provisions. Therefore it is logical in this context that it be defined at the supranational level. Secondly, an autonomous interpretation ensures a uniform application of European Union law that benefits the equal treatment of EU nationals.

152 Opened for signature May 23,1969,1155 U.N.T.S. 331, 8 I.L.M.679.

153 On the objectives of EU internal market law, see chapter 4.

154 Case C-26/62, *NV Algemene Transport- en Expeditie Onderneming van Gend & Loos v. Netherlands Inland Revenue Administration* [1963] *ECR* 00001.

155 H. Rasmussen, *On Law and Policy in the European CJEU. A Comparative Study in Judicial Policy-Making* (Dordrecht: Martinus Nijhoff Publishers, 1986); P. Neill, *The European CJEU: A Case Study in Judicial Activism* (London: European Policy Forum, 1995); T.C. Hartley, 'The European Court, Judicial Objectivity and the Constitution of the European Union' (*The Law Quarterly Review*, 1996), pp. 95–109.

156 P. Pescatore, 'Le recours, dans la jurisprudence de la Cour de Justice des Communautés Européennes, à des normes déduites de la comparaison des droits des Etats membres' (*RIDC*, 1980), p. 337.

157 Case C-373/00, *Adolf Truley GmbH v. Bestattung Wien GmbH* [2003] *ECR* I-1931, at [40].

The consequence of the principle of autonomous interpretation is that only the CJEU will be able to determine authoritatively what these concepts means. Trepte notes that this signifies that the CJEU case law will be difficult to predict, given its tendency to interpret broadly its scope.[158]

1. The meaning of 'public authority' or 'contracting authority'

Only decisions of a particular kind of legal person form the subject of the study. The book qualifies these legal persons in general as 'public authorities'. The meaning of 'public authority' cannot be found in any treaty concluded between the EU Member States.[159] Two kind of cooperative agreements (public contract and service concession) are object of this study. For each of these agreements a different concept determines the scope of application ratione personae of the research. The public procurement Directives that form the basis for the research, use the concept of 'contracting authority'. These Directives define it in a precise way. Regarding service concessions the Court of Justice uses the concept 'public authority'. Hereafter, which authorities are a 'contracting authority' and which are a 'public authority' is defined in detail.

1.1. Contracting authority[160]

1.1.1. Preliminary remarks

Both the Public Sector Directive (2004/18/CE) as well as the Utilities Directive (2004/17/CE) use the same definition of 'contracting authority': '"Contracting authorities" are States, regional or local authorities, bodies governed by public law, associations formed by one or several of such authorities or one or several of such bodies governed by public law'.[161] First the definition lists a number of traditional authorities, then includes 'bodies governed by public law' and finally mentions the concept of 'association'. These three categories are discussed further hereafter. The Directives do not contain a definition for each of the categories and thus the intervention of the CJEU has been necessary. Member States do not have the competence to exclude entities from these categories. They are bound by the definition of the Directives, as interpreted by the CJEU in its case law.

Regarding the concept of 'contracting authority', the public procurement Directives did not limit the term to traditional authorities, but have also extended the term to include other legal entities which are under the control of traditional public authorities. The public procurement Directives employ their own definition of 'contracting authority'

158 P. Trepte, *Public procurement in the EU* (Oxford University Press, Oxford, 2007), p. 104.

159 Chapter 4 establishes the concept 'Member State', used in the EU treaties, covers to a great extend the concept 'public authority'.

160 *The present study will only take into account the concept 'contracting authorities' and not the other entities falling under the scope of Directive 2004/17/EC or 2014/25/EU. These entities are less important for the present study.*

161 Article 2.1 (a) Directive 2004/17/EC; Article 1.9 Directive 2004/18/EC.

since the different legal cultures of the Member States had to be taken into account. Thus, the term is not limited to an entity regulated by public law.[162]

The CJEU defines 'contracting authority' in such a broad manner that it embraces a large number of legal situations falling inside the scope of the public procurement Directives, considering that any evasion of the rules is a disadvantage for the realization of a unified internal market. Legal entities that do not come within the scope of the term 'contracting authorities', are, therefore, not bound by the strict rules of the Directives.

Once a body is recognized as a contracting authority, the public procurement Directives will apply to all contracts offered by the contracting authority, both those that are part of its activities in the general public interest as well as those with a purely commercial character.[163] This was confirmed by the CJEU in its judgments in *Mannesmann*[164] and *Commission v. Germany*.[165] Making a distinction based on the tasks of a contracting authority would not serve the 'effet utile' of the public procurement Directives nor would it promote legal certainty.

A body that performs only commercial tasks will not be part of the 'State'. The sole commercial character of a body rules out the specific connection with a public authority that is necessary in order to be considered a 'contracting authority' according to the functional interpretation given by the CJEU to the term.[166] It was not necessary to include such commercial bodies within the scope of the public procurement Directives, since competition is not in jeopardy given the lack of government interference. The decisions of commercial bodies are normally market based and do not imperil free trade and free competition.[167] Only in the presence of governmental interference decisions can be taken which can favour an economic operator.

The 2014 public procurement Directives do not substantially alter the personal scope. The definition of contracting authority remains in essence the same.

1.1.2. Traditional authorities

Among the traditional authorities a distinction must be made between the State, regional and local authorities. The Directives do not always define these terms in detail, so the CJEU case law has done so.

162 Case C-214/00, *Commission v. Spain* [2003] *ECR* I-4667.

163 S. Arrowsmith, *The law of public and utilities procurement* (London: Sweet & Maxwell, 2005), p. 253: "*This reflects the directives, which apply to the State and regional and local authorities regardless of the nature of their activities.*"; P. Trepte, *Public procurement in the EU* (Oxford: OUP, 2007), p. 99.

164 Case C-44/96, *Mannesmann Anlagenbau Austria AG and Others v. Strohal Rotationsdruck GesmbH* [1998] *ECR* I-73.

165 Case C-126/03, *Commission v. Germany* [2004] *ECR* I-11197.

166 Opinion Advocate General Alber Case C-306/97, *Connemara Machine Turf Co. Ltd v. Coillte Teoranta* [1998] *ECR* I-8761, at [27–29].

167 See, however, Articles 101–107 TFEU.

The 'State' is the main contracting authority and is usually the principal user of public contracts. Although the meaning of the State seems obvious, the CJEU had to address some specific situations in order to define with more clarity the concept of a State.

First, the CJEU considered bodies having an organic relationship with the public authority. Bodies that have an organic relationship with the State should in any case be regarded as a 'State'. In *Vlaamse Raad*, the CJEU clarified what is the 'core' of the concept 'State'.[168] The CJEU stressed that the concept 'State' necessarily encompasses all bodies with legislative, executive or judicial powers. This also applies to the bodies that exercise those powers at a regional level.[169] Consequently, the CJEU concluded that the *Vlaamse Raad*[170] is a part of the concept 'State'. The CJEU did not have to use the term 'State' in order to classify the *Vlaamse Raad* as a contracting authority since the *Vlaamse Raad* is an integral part of the Flemish Community of the Flemish Region, and could therefore be considered to be a 'regional or local authority'.[171] The current Directives in particular refer to the regional or local authorities as contracting authorities. The concept of a 'State' is an autonomous concept that does not depend on a national interpretation.[172]

Secondly, the CJEU has also accepted as part of the State bodies with no organic relationship to the State. Thus even those bodies without an organic relationship with the State can be considered an integral part of the State. In *Beentjes*[173] the CJEU applied a functional interpretation of the term 'State'. This case was also the first one where the CJEU applied this interpretation method to enlarge the scope of the Directives.

In *Beentjes* the CJEU was faced with a local land consolidation committee, a body that had no legal personality and therefore could not be considered as a 'body governed by public law'. Nor was there an organic relationship with a contracting authority, so that the committee was not considered to be an integral part of the State in accordance with the early case-law of the CJEU.[174] Therefore, the public procurement Directives would normally not be applied to the local land consolidation committee. The CJEU could only resolve this void in the Directives through a broader interpretation of the term 'State'.

The CJEU considered that the local land consolidation committee was a part of the State although it was not formally an integral part of it. In these situations, the CJEU deems the fact that the composition and functions of the committee are governed by national legislation important. Also that the committee depends on a local contracting authority

168 S. Arrowsmith, *The law of public and utilities procurement* (London: Sweet & Maxwell, 2005), p. 255: "core" entities.

169 Case C-323/96, *Commission v. Belgium* [1998] *ECR* I-5063, at [27].

170 Flemish Parliament. Flanders is one of the Regions in Belgium.

171 E.H. Pynacker Hordijk, G.W. Van Der Bend and J.F. Van Nouhuys, *Aanbestedingsrecht* (Den Haag: SDU, 2004), p. 38.

172 Case C-323/96, *Commission v. Belgium* [1998] *ECR* I-5063, at [42].

173 Case 31/87, *Gebroeders Beentjes BV v. State of the Netherlands* [1988] *ECR* 4635.

174 The organic and formal interpretation: Case 36/74, *B.N.O. Walrave and L.J.N. Koch v. Association Union cycliste internationale* [1974] *ECR* 1405; Case 249/81, *Commission v. Ireland* [1982] *ECR* 4005.

(province) as far as the appointment of its members are concerned; that it is bound to apply rules laid down by a central committee established by royal decree whose members are appointed by the Crown; and that the State ensures observance of the obligations arising out of measures of the committee and finances the public works contracts awarded.[175]

In other words, the CJEU considers also factors and indications such as the intention and the purpose of establishment of an entity, in order to determine whether it is part of the State.[176]

The CJEU based its reasoning on the objectives of the public procurement Directives and the fundamental principles enshrined in the TFEU. These principles are compromised when the public procurement Directives are deemed not applicable, simply because the contract is awarded by a body which, although created to perform tasks of general public interest, is not formally a part of the government's administration.

The CJEU case law has been consistent in its application of a functional interpretation to the term 'State'.[177] The CJEU has adapted the concept of 'State' into a sort of safety net for bodies that are likely to fall outside of the scope of the public procurement Directives. These bodies, despite their close ties with the traditional public authorities have no formal links with them nor can they be considered as 'bodies governed by public law' due to their lack of legal personality. This is in line with CJEU case law, which has always attempted to widen the scope of the public procurement Directives as much as possible in order to guarantee both a maximum protection of equality between the contractors as well as an optimal competitive environment.

Arrowsmith suggests that only bodies without legal personality can be considered as a 'State'. Therefore, if they have legal personality, there is a high probability that they are 'bodies governed by public law' and there will be no need for a safety net.[178]

In *Scala*[179] the CJEU stated that a municipality is a regional or local authority within the meaning of Article 1, para b of Directive 93/37 on public works[180] and therefore falls

175 Case 31/87, *Gebroeders Beentjes BV v. State of the Netherlands* [1988] *ECR* 4635, at [8].

176 C. Bovis, *EC Public Procurement: case law and regulation* (Oxford: OUP, 2006), p. 365.

177 Case C-353/96, *Commission* v. *Ireland* [1998] *ECR* I-8565; Case C-306/97, *Connemara Machine Turf Co. Ltd v. Coillte Teoranta* [1998] *ECR* I-8761.

178 S. Arrowsmith, *The law of public and utilities procurement* (London: Sweet & Maxwell, 2005), p. 255.

179 Case C-399/98, *Ordine degli Architetti delle province di Milano e Lodi, Piero De Amicis, Consiglio Nazionale degli Architetti and Leopoldo Freyrie v. Comune di Milano, and Pirelli SpA, Milano Centrale Servizi SpA and Fondazione Teatro alla Scala* [2001] *ECR* I-5409, at [57]. In case of public work contracts: Case C-220/05, *Jean Auroux and Others v. Commune de Roanne* [2007] *ECR* I-385, at [43].

180 Directive 93/37/EEC concerning the coordination of procedures for the award of public works contracts [1993] *OJ* L199/54.

within that provision given the definition of the concept 'contracting authority'. Regional or local authorities are, by definition, contracting authorities.[181]

1.1.3. Associations formed by one or several authorities

The term 'associations formed by one or several authorities' seems to refer to an inter-municipal and an inter-provincial body.[182] The CJEU has stated that this category of contracting authorities is a residual category. This is also illustrated by the position of this phrase in the Directive's text.[183]

Therefore, one must first determine whether a body is not a 'State, Community, Region, province or municipality', or a 'body governed by public law', before it can be captured under this heading. This obviously depends on whether the association has legal personality. This category is only relevant for situations where public authorities cooperate contractually. Once they have created another legal person, it cannot be considered anymore as an association. In that situation the concept 'body governed by public law' will be relevant.

1.1.4. Body governed by public law

Article 1.9 Directive 2004/18 states that

> *'A "body governed by public law" means any body:*
>
> *(a) established for the specific purpose of meeting needs in the general interest, not having an industrial or commercial character;*
> *(b) having legal personality; and*
> *(c) financed, for the most part, by the State, regional or local authorities, or other bodies governed by public law; or subject to management supervision by those bodies; or having an administrative, managerial or supervisory board, more than half of whose members are appointed by the State, regional or local authorities, or by other bodies governed by public law.'*

Article 1.9 of Directive 2004/18/EC adds: 'Non-exhaustive lists of bodies and categories of bodies governed by public law which fulfil the criteria referred to in (a), (b) and (c) of the second subparagraph are set out in Annex III'. This annex then groups together per Member State a number of bodies that are considered to be 'bodies governed by public law' under the public procurement Directives. The CJEU has repeatedly confirmed that

181 Case C-126/03, *Commission* v. *Germany* [2004] *ECR* I-11197, at [18]. See also joined Cases C-182/11 and C-183/11, *Econord v. Comune di Cagno, Comune di Varese, Comune di Solbiate* [2012] *ECR* I-00000, at [25].
182 C. De Koninck and P. Flamey, *Overheidsopdrachten* (Antwerpen: Maklu, 2006), p. 29.
183 Case C-360/96, *Gemeente Arnhem and Gemeente Rheden v. BFI Holding BV* [1998] *ECR* I-6821, at [27].

this list is not exhaustive.[184] On the other hand, the inclusion of a body in this list by a Member State does not create an irrefutable presumption that it is a 'body governed by public law'. Even if this is the case, an examination of the nature and characteristics of the body is required.[185] A Member State does not have the possibility to extend the meaning of the term. It cannot include bodies, which do not comply with the definition of 'body governed by public law'.

Following the wide interpretation of the term 'contracting authority' in *Beentjes*, the CJEU has also interpreted the concept 'bodies governed by public law' in a functional and autonomous way. Thus, the CJEU stated in *Commission v. France* that 'it is in the light of those objectives that 'contracting authority', including a body governed by public law, must be interpreted in functional terms'.[186] The CJEU has repeated this several times[187] and added that the concept should be given a broad interpretation.[188]

The idea behind the broad interpretation is to include as many bodies as possible in the definition of 'contracting authority.[189] Every entity that has the possibility to take decisions without bothering if it will have an effect on its economic functioning or financial standing could be defined as a 'contracting authority'. The aim of the concept 'body governed by public law' is to include entities that are closely linked to traditional public authorities. From this rationale the terms 'bodies governed by public law' and 'contracting authorities' will have their own meaning under EU Law. Each element of the definition to determine the presence of such an entity will be interpreted in a same manner.

An entity is a 'body governed by public law' when it meets three conditions: (i) established for the specific purpose of meeting needs in the general public interest not having an industrial or commercial character; (ii) having legal personality; and (iii) demonstrating a certain degree of dependence on a contracting authority.

The three conditions are cumulative[190] and will be discussed individually below. Although the term at first glance might suggest something else, a 'body governed by

184 See f.e. Case C-373/00, *Adolf Truley GmbH v. Bestattung Wien GmbH* [2003] *ECR* I-1931, at [39]; Case C-283/00, *Commission* v. *Spain* [2003] *ECR* I-11697, at [77].

185 Case C-300/07, *Hans & Christophorus Oymanns GbR, Orthopädie Schuhtechnik v. AOK Rheinland/Hamburg* [2009] *ECR* I-04779, at [42–43].

186 Case C-237/99, *Commission v. France* [2001] *ECR* I-939, at [43]. For the autonomous interpretation, see Case C-84/03, *Commission* v. *Spain* [2005] *ECR* I-139, at [27]; Case C-373/00, *Adolf Truley GmbH v. Bestattung Wien GmbH* [2003] *ECR* I-1931, at [36].

187 Case C-470/99, *Universale-Bau AG, Bietergemeinschaft: 1) Hinteregger & Söhne Bauges.m.b.H. Salzburg, 2) ÖSTÜ-STETTIN Hoch- und Tiefbau GmbH v. Entsorgungsbetriebe Simmering GmbH* [2002] *ECR* I-11617, at [53]; Case C-84/03, *Commission v. Spain* [2005] *ECR* I-139, at [27]; Case C-283/00, *Commission* v. *Spain* [2003] *ECR* I-11697, at [73]; Case C-214/00, *Commission* v. *Spain* [2003] *ECR* I-4667, at [53].

188 Case C-373/00, *Adolf Truley GmbH v. Bestattung Wien GmbH* [2003] *ECR* I-1931, at [43].

189 At [43].

190 Case C-18/01, *Arkkitehtuuritoimisto Riitta Korhonen Oy and* Others *v. Varkauden Taitotalo Oy* [2003] *ECR* I-5321; Case C-373/00, *Adolf Truley GmbH v. Bestattung Wien GmbH* [2003] *ECR* I-1931; Case

public law' does include private bodies that meet the mentioned conditions. In this manner, the CJEU avoids the danger that the application of the Directives would be nullified when entities regulated by public law permit autonomous bodies, ruled by private law, to award contracts on their behalf.

Under the first condition, the body must be established for the particular purpose of meeting needs in the general public interest, not having an industrial or commercial character. Some legal scholars pretend that this criterion derives from French administrative law.[191]

The CJEU has made clear that both the aspect of 'general interest' and 'not having an industrial or commercial character' have to be examined separately.[192] Both have to be present in order to have a body governed by public law. Indeed, there are needs that, although they have an industrial or commercial character, are to be considered as needs in the general public interest.[193]

The words 'established for the specific purpose' suggest that the objective of the general public interest must be explicitly apparent in the articles of Association.[194] However, the CJEU has ruled otherwise. It is necessary to consider the activities that the body actually carries out.[195] The legal form is irrelevant.

The term 'general interest' is vague and hard to define. Its definition depends on time and social context, and thus fluctuates. It is not a surprise that in practice the interpretation of this concept presents most of the problems.[196] The CJEU has always maintained that the 'general interest' is an autonomous concept of EU law. The judgment in *Agora* and *Korhonen* makes clear that the body cannot solely act in an individual interest.[197] Where the activities of the body meet the needs of an indefinite number of people, the general public interest seems to be apparent.

C-237/99, *Commission v. France* [2001] *ECR* I-939; Case C-283/00, *Commission* v. *Spain* [2003] *ECR* I-11697; Case C-214/00, *Commission v. Spain* [2003] *ECR* I-4667.

191 M.P. Chiti, 'The EC concept of Public administration: the case of the bodies governed by public law' (*EPL*, 2002), p. 489.

192 Joined Cases C-223/99 and C-260/99, *Agorà Srl and Excelsior Snc di Pedrotti Bruna & C. v. Ente Autonomo Fiera Internazionale di Milano and Ciftat Soc. coop. arl.* [2001] *ECR* I-3605, at [32] et seq.; B. Schutyser, 'Het toepassingsgebied van de wetgeving overheidsopdrachten: een aantal evoluties in de rechtspraak van het Hof van Justitie (1998–2003)' (*TBP*, 2004), p. 261.

193 Case C-360/96, *Gemeente Arnhem and Gemeente Rheden v. BFI Holding BV* [1998] *ECR* I-6821.

194 E.H. Pynacker Hordijk, G.W. Van Der Bend and J.F. Van Nouhuys, *Aanbestedingsrecht* (Den Haag: SDU, 2004), p. 47.

195 Case C-470/99, *Universale-Bau AG, Bietergemeinschaft: 1) Hinteregger & Söhne Bauges.m.b.H. Salzburg, 2) ÖSTÜ-STETTIN Hoch- und Tiefbau GmbH v. Entsorgungsbetriebe Simmering GmbH* [2002] *ECR* I-11617, at [56].

196 E.H. Pynacker Hordijk, G.W. Van Der Bend and J.F. Van Nouhuys, *Aanbestedingsrecht* (Den Haag: SDU, 2004), p. 40.

197 Joined Cases C-223/99 and C-260/99, *Agorà Srl and Excelsior Snc di Pedrotti Bruna & C. v. Ente Autonomo Fiera Internazionale di Milano and Ciftat Soc. coop. arl.* [2001] *ECR* I-3605, at [34]; Case C-18/01, *Korhonen and Others* [2003] *ECR* I-5321, at [44].

It is immaterial that such needs are also met or can be met by private undertakings. More important is the decision of a State or a local or regional authority to meet the needs, or to retain a decisive influence over the body in question.[198] This decision will be made when it is clear that the private sector cannot partially or fully meet such a need. The desire to retain a decisive influence over the body indicates precisely that it discharges tasks of general interest.[199] On that matter there seems to be a parallel with the *quasi in house* case law of the CJEU.[200] Where contracting or public authorities conclude contracts with each other, which may fall within the scope of the public procurement Directives or of the EU Treaty rules, it seems that the object of that contract (public service tasks, required in the general public interest) will also determine whether one contracting authority exercises a control over the other contracting authority as it would have over its own departments.

The CJEU has come to the following general definition in its case law: needs are in the general interest when they are not met otherwise by the availability of goods or services in the market place and, for reasons associated with the general interest, the State chooses to provide, or over which the State wishes to retain a decisive influence.[201] Trepte considers that the CJEU has looked towards state requirements with a specific task that must be achieved.[202]

The needs of general public interest that a body meets cannot be of commercial or industrial nature. This latter characteristic is significant for the application of the public procurement Directives and does specify the nature. The CJEU, therefore, takes into account all relevant factual and legal elements such as the circumstances prevailing when the body concerned was established and the conditions under which it exercises its activity.[203]

To determine these elements the CJEU uses a number of 'negatively' and 'positively' expressed considerations. In order to meet this criterion, a judge examines whether the body carries on its activities in a competitive environment.[204] The existence of significant competition does not in itself justify the classification of 'commercial or industrial in nature', nor does the activity of the body solely for the benefit of commercial undertakings.[205]

198 Case C-393/06, *Ing. Aigner, Wasser-Wärme-Umwelt, GmbH v. Fernwärme Wien GmbH* [2008] *ECR* I-2339, at [40]. See also a comparable definition for the concept 'service of general interest' in the present Chapter section 3.

199 Compare Case C-373/00, *Adolf Truley GmbH v. Bestattung Wien GmbH* [2003] *ECR* I-1931, at [51] and [52].

200 This case law will be discussed in Chapter 5.

201 See Case C-360/96, *Gemeente Arnhem and Gemeente Rheden v. BFI Holding BV* [1998] *ECR* I-6821, at [50] en [51] and Joined Cases C-223/99 and C-260/99, *Agorà Srl and Excelsior Snc di Pedrotti Bruna & C. v. Ente Autonomo Fiera Internazionale di Milano and Ciftat Soc. coop. arl.* [2001] *ECR* I-3605, at [37].

202 P. Trepte, *Public procurement in the EU* (Oxford: OUP, 2007), p. 104.

203 At [41].

204 Case C-393/06, *Ing. Aigner, Wasser-Wärme-Umwelt, GmbH v. Fernwärme Wien GmbH* [2008] *ECR* I-2339, at [41].

205 Case C-18/01, *Arkkitehtuuritoimisto Riitta* Korhonen *Oy and* Others *v. Varkauden Taitotalo Oy* [2003] *ECR* I-5321, at [50].

In addition, a judge must also examine whether the body operates in normal market conditions, whether it does not primarily aim to make a profit, whether it does not bear the losses associated with the exercise of its activity, and whether the activity has public financing.[206] All the criteria expressed, to a greater or lesser extent, the idea that the body concerned can take into account factors other than the economic considerations when closing a contract. A private undertaking will, on the other hand, always be driven by economic motives when choosing a contractual partner.

Why should the needs in the general interest be other than of commercial or industrial nature? The answer is obvious: 'the need to compete may force the entity to purchase in a commercial matter'.[207]

The second condition to be categorised as a 'body governed by public law', is to have legal personality. This condition is clear and does not instigate much discussion. Stated once more: The public or private nature of the entity is not decisive.

This criterion though, is vital for determining whether a judge considers a body to be a contracting authority that falls within the category of traditional public authorities or whether it falls within the category of bodies governed by public law. An association of contracting public authorities belongs to the traditional authorities if they have no legal personality. When the body has legal personality, it is not part of the traditional authorities, unless of course it is itself a traditional contracting authority. In the case of the presence of a legal personality, the body can only be a body governed by public law if it satisfies all other conditions.[208]

The third condition requires a close dependence on another contracting public authority. There are three criteria provided in order to establish this dependence: funding, supervision, and composition of the body. The objective of the third condition is to make the public procurement rules applicable to legal entities over which a contracting authority has a lasting influence. It is possible that the contracting authority, directly or indirectly, influences this entity to act in a non-market conform way in the awarding of contracts by that entity.[209]

These three criteria are alternative, not cumulative.[210] The three criteria in the third condition each reflect the close dependence of a body on the State, or on local or regional authorities or on other bodies governed by public law.[211] Thus, it is sufficient that only

206 Case C-283/00, *Commission* v. *Spain* [2003] *ECR* I-11697, at [81].

207 S. Arrowsmith, *The law of public and utilities procurement* (London: Sweet & Maxwell, 2005), p. 269.

208 See Case C-353/96, *Commission* v. *Ireland* [1998] *ECR* I-8565, at [32]; Case C-306/97, *Connemara Machine Turf Co. Ltd v. Coillte Teoranta* [1998] *ECR* I-8761, at [27].

209 J. De Staercke, 'De toepassing van de algemene reglementering overheidsopdrachten op privaatrechtelijke (onderwijs)instellingen na het Cambridge-arrest van het Hof van Justitie' (*RW*, 2002–2003), p. 162.

210 Ch. Bovis, *EU public procurement law* (Cheltenham: Edgar European Law, 2012), p. 290.

211 Case C-380/98, *The Queen v. H.M. Treasury, ex parte The University of Cambridge* [2000] *ECR* I-8035, at [20]; Case C-526/11, *IVD GmbH & Co. KG v. Ärztekammer Westfalen-Lippe* [2013] *ECR* I-00000, at [20].

one of these conditions is met for sufficient dependency. If one of the criteria is fulfilled the contracting authority is able to influence the decisions of the other body.[212] Hence, this body cannot behave as a private company and accordingly violate the rules of the market.

The first alternative criterion for the dependence condition to be met is that the activities are financed for the most part by the traditional contracting authorities or bodies governed by public law. Based on the decisions concerning this criterion, a judge seems to be obliged to examine three elements: i) what is the amount of financing, ii) where does the financing come from and iii) is there anything in return for the finance awarded?

First, Article 1(9) of Directive 2004/18 requires that the financing of the activities comes from the contracting authorities. The phrase 'for the most part' must be interpreted in its ordinary meaning, i.e. 'more than half'.[213] To determine correctly the percentage of public financing of a particular body account must be taken of all of its income, including that which results from a commercial activity.[214]

According to the CJEU the way in which a particular body is financed is not an 'absolute criterion'.[215] The CJEU pointed out that not all payments made by a contracting authority have the effect of creating a specific relationship of subordination, as set out by the third criterion. In other words, not all funds that flow from a contracting authority to a public body are eligible to be qualified as 'financing' within the meaning of the public procurement Directives. The CJEU clarifies that 'only payments which go to finance or support the activities of the body concerned without any specific consideration therefor may be described as 'public financing'.[216] Advocate General Alber opined that financing can only consist of supporting the general activity of the body.[217]

On the contrary, an indemnity for an activity, based on a reciprocal contract freely negotiated between the contracting parties, does not fall within the concept of 'public financing'. The CJEU admits that such funds flows could create a relationship of subordination, but the nature of the relationship is not the same as the specific relationship as set out by the third criterion: 'rather, it is analogous to the dependency that exists in normal commercial relationships'.[218]

212 Case C-526/11, *IVD GmbH & Co. KG v. Ärztekammer Westfalen-Lippe* [2013] *ECR* I-00000, at [20].

213 Case C-380/98, *The Queen v. H.M. Treasury, ex parte The University of Cambridge* [2000] *ECR* I-8035, at [30]; Case C-337/06, *Bayerischer Rundfunk a.o. v. GEWA* [2007] *ECR* I-11173, at [33].

214 Case C-380/98, *The Queen v. H.M. Treasury, ex parte The University of Cambridge* [2000] *ECR* I-8035, at [36].

215 At [21].

216 At [21].

217 Opinion Advocate General Alber, C-380/98, *The Queen v. H.M. Treasury, ex parte The University of Cambridge* [2000] *ECR* I-8035, at [40].

218 Case C-380/98, *The Queen v. H.M. Treasury, ex parte The University of Cambridge* [2000] *ECR* I-8035, at [25].

The term 'normal commercial relationships' seems not the exclude that some activities, based on contractual provisions, could be deemed to be 'financed by a contracting authority'. Some forms of payments, following a commercial agreement, can indeed be addressed, where such an agreement does not exist in a pure commercial context. Advocate General Alber explicitly states that an indemnity for a contractual activity could nevertheless create a relationship of dependence as set out in the third criterion, in particular when a contractual activity of the body simultaneously constitutes an activity that is of general interest or that serves academic purposes.[219]

To determine what can be considered as being a purely commercial agreement, Arrowsmith suggests applying the same principles that are found in state aid regulations.[220] Advocate General Alber pointed out what he seems to consider as being 'normal commercial relationships': 'As a rule such dependency does not arise precisely where an establishment receives payment as consideration for an activity which it offers in the same way as an undertaking operating on the market independently in competition with private undertakings and on the basis of a specific contract for the supply of services'.[221]

From all these principles, the CJEU concludes that grants for the support of research work may be regarded as financed by a contracting authority. This is financing that goes to the institution as a whole in the context of its research work.[222] Similarly, scholarships may be classified as 'public financing', since there is no contractual consideration.[223] However, payments for finance activities of executing a specific research or the organisation of seminars cannot be regarded as public financing. The contracting authority has in fact an economic interest in providing this service.[224]

Where direct financing by the contracting authority is concerned, there is no problem in concluding that the first alternative criterion is fulfilled. The CJEU has considered the question whether the same applies in the case of indirect financing. Bodies benefiting from indirect financing are, according to the CJEU, eligible to be regarded as 'contracting authorities'.[225] Article 1.9 of Directive 2004/18/EC does not clarify the way in which the financing should be done. *Bayerischer Rundfunk* concerned a German public television

219 Opinion Advocate General Alber, C-380/98, *The Queen v. H.M. Treasury, ex parte The University of Cambridge* [2000] *ECR* I-8035, at [44].

220 S. Arrowsmith, *The law of public and utilities procurement* (London: Sweet & Maxwell, 2005), pp. 258–259.

221 Opinion Advocate General Alber, C-380/98, *The Queen v. H.M. Treasury, ex parte The University of Cambridge* [2000] *ECR* I-8035, at [45].

222 Case C-380/98, *The Queen v. H.M. Treasury, ex parte The University of Cambridge* [2000] *ECR* I-8035, at [22].

223 At [23].

224 At [24].

225 Case C-337/06, *Bayerischer Rundfunk e.a. v. GEWA* [2007] *ECR* I-11173, at [60]; Case C-526/11, *IVD GmbH & Co. KG v. Ärztekammer Westfalen-Lippe* [2013] *ECR* I-00000, at [23].

station of which more than half of its income was generated by contributions paid by citizens. The contributions were collected by a central agency in Germany.

The CJEU took the following facts in account in order to conclude that the said case concerned 'public financing':

- The contribution by which the activities of the body concerned were financed is based on a Staatsvertrag, which constitutes a government act. In other words, the contribution does not follow from an agreement between this body and the users, and definitely not from an agreement between the body and the central agency. The mere possession of a television set is sufficient to be liable for payment of the contribution.
- The amount of the contribution is set by the Parliaments and governments of the Länder.
- When collecting the contribution, the central agency disposes of powers of a public authority.

In that regard it is of no relevance whether the government collects the contribution and subsequently makes it available to the broadcasting organisations or whether the government attributes the right to collect the contribution directly to these organisations. As a consequence, indirect public financing is also regarded to be public financing in the light of the financing criterion. In other words, the CJEU applies an extensive definition of the concept 'financed for the most by bodies of public law'.[226]

This decision seems logical, as a contribution that is independent from the actual use of the television set constitutes a form of public funding. This is not the case with subscription payment or pay-per-view for commercial networks, where the payment follows an agreement between the networks and the receivers.[227]

The CJEU decided similarly in a case where a legal health insurance fund made an announcement for the request of offers for manufacturing and delivering shoes.[228] As the contributions payable by the insured to the legal health insurance funds are imposed, calculated and collected in accordance with rules of public law, such funds can be regarded as being bodies of public law and should therefore apply the public procurement Directives.[229]

The dependence of a contracting authority can also result from the degree of supervision such authority has over the management of the concerned body. Contrary to the criteria

226 R.S., 'Un organisme public de radiodufffusion percevant une redevanve est-il un pouvoir adjudicateur?', under Case C-337/06, *Bayerischer Rundfunk a.o. v. GEWA* (*BJCP* 4, 2008), p. 98.

227 A. Brown, 'Whether German public broadcasters are financed for the most part by the state so as to fall within the EU procurement directives: Bayerischers Rundfunk (C-337/06)' (*PPLR*, 2008), NA126.

228 Case C-300/07, *Hans & Christophorus Oymanns GbR, Orthopädie Schuhtechnik v. AOK Rheinland/Hamburg* [2009] *ECR* I-04779.

229 At [59].

of financing and composition of the decision-making body, which are quantitative criteria, the criterion of management supervision is of a qualitative nature.[230] This results in the inevitable consequence that the supervision criterion will require interpretation.

The CJEU has underlined that the management supervision must give rise to dependence on the contracting authorities equivalent to that which exists where one of the other alternative criteria is fulfilled (financing and composition of decision making body).[231] The supervision should nonetheless lead to the possibility for the public authority to influence the decisions of the body in relation to public contracts.[232] Supervision in relation to public contracts can emerge from a strong general dependence (possible also influencing other fields) not only through a supervision specifically directed to the award processes.[233] An indirect supervision is sufficient.[234] The possibility of supervision must also exist prior to the making of the decisions. A possible control a posteriori is not sufficient.[235]

The question arises as to which criteria should determine whether the degree of supervision by the government over an entity leads to a strong dependence. Following Advocate General Mischo's view, the legal and regulatory framework surrounding the concerned entity is the determining criterion.[236] From such framework several possible powers of control emerge, which can lead to the conclusion that sufficient dependence exists. Such exercise was made by the CJEU in the cases *Commission v. France*[237] and *Adolf Truly*.[238]

In *Commission v. France*, the CJEU seemed to distinguish between two hypotheses either the rules of management are not detailed or very detailed by law. In the latter case, the regulator has already limited the operating radius of the entity. In such situation, regular supervision suffices, so it seems, to consider it as strong influence. Under 'regular supervision' it is understood that the public authority does not have the power to interfere directly with decisions of the management of the entity (in casu a social housing company). A regular supervision is therefore not sufficient to establish dependence within the meaning of Article 1(9) of Directive 2004/18/EC where the rules of management are not in detail governed by law.

230 C. Bovis, *EC Public Procurement: case law and regulation* (Oxford: OUP, 2006), p. 366.
231 Case C-237/99, *Commission v. France* [2001] *ECR* I-939, at [49].
232 Case C-237/99, *Commission v. France* [2001] *ECR* I-939, at [59]; Case C-373/00, *Adolf Truley GmbH v. Bestattung Wien GmbH* [2003] *ECR* I-1931, at [69]; Case C-306/97, *Connemara Machine Turf Co. Ltd v. Coillte Teoranta* [1998] *ECR* I-8761, at [34]; Case C-353/96, *Commission v. Ireland* [1998] *ECR* I-8565, at [39].
233 S. Arrowsmith, *The law of public and utilities procurement* (London: Sweet & Maxwell, 2005), p. 260.
234 Case C-306/97, *Connemara Machine Turf Co. Ltd v. Coillte Teoranta* [1998] *ECR* I-8761, at [34]; Case C-353/96, *Commission v. Ireland* [1998] *ECR* I-8565, at [39].
235 Case C-373/00, *Adolf Truley GmbH v. Bestattung Wien GmbH* [2003] *ECR* I-1931, at [70]; Case C-526/11, *IVD GmbH & Co. KG v. Ärztekammer Westfalen-Lippe* [2013] *ECR* I-00000, at [29].
236 Opinion Advocate General Alber, C-380/98 *ECR* I-8035, at [51].
237 Case C-237/99, *Commission v. France* [2001] *ECR* I-939.
238 Case C-373/00, *Adolf Truley GmbH v. Bestattung Wien GmbH* [2003] *ECR* I-1931.

In particular these 'strict rules' consist of the fact that; i) the law determined the activities of the social housing company; ii) the articles of association contained provisions included in an annexe to the law providing standard provisions; iii) that the technical characteristics; and iv) the cost price of the activities of the entity were fixed by an administrative act.

The CJEU subsequently deducted the existence of sufficient supervision from several specific elements. The public authority had the power to dissolve the entity and to appoint a liquidator. In addition the public authority could suspend the governance bodies and appoint an administrator. This last power did not fall within the scope of the regular supervision, but implies a true interference by the government. Although in this case the government could only execute these powers on an exceptional basis (in particular in case of serious irregularities on behalf of the management), a situation of permanent supervision was nevertheless present. In addition, the public authority could impose a certain management profile on the entity. There also existed, by decree, an inter-ministerial service of supervision over the entity, controlling in particular any persons, to whom a measure is imposed by the minister, would also actually execute such measure.

In the *Adolf Truley* case, the CJEU took into account the following elements. The public authorities verified not only the annual accounts of the entity (by definition *a posterior* control, thus not sufficient to create supervision), but also its conduct from the point of view of proper accounting, regularity, economy, efficiency and expediency. The public authorities were in addition authorised to inspect the business premises and facilities of the entity and to report the results of those inspections to the regional authority, which held all the shares in the entity in question.[239]

The CJEU does not clarify how important it considers each of these criteria to be, and whether any specific criterion is considered to be decisive, nor whether the criteria are cumulative. The CJEU simply states that, if the criteria are fulfilled, a situation of 'supervision' is present. In any case, there exists a different interpretation than the description of the term 'control', as it results from the 'quasi in house' case law. In particular when a public authority exercises a control over another legal person in a similar way as it does over its own service, such cooperation is not subject to the regulation with regard to public contracts.[240]

In accordance with the third alternative dependence criterion, this dependence is established when the majority of the members of the governance, managing, or the supervising body have been appointed by other contracting entities.

Despite the fact that the legal provision explicitly mentions 'more than half', Pynacker Hordijck et al. are of the opinion that such provision must also be interpreted in a

239 Case C-373/00, *Adolf Truley GmbH v. Bestattung Wien GmbH* [2003] *ECR* I-1931, at [74].
240 Case C-107/98, *Teckal Srl v. Comune di Viano* [1999] *ECR* I-8121.

functional way.[241] This would mean in the first place that dependence would also be established in case the public authority, instead of appointing the nominal majority of the members of the decision making body within the entity, has appointed a number of members who together hold a decisive majority.

The CJEU has not yet rendered a decision by which it expresses the meaning of the third dependence condition. In *Connemara*[242] the CJEU considered the concerned entity to be an entity of public law and stated that the State had the power to appoint the principal officers of the entity. In addition, the CJEU mentioned that the State had been given the possibility to 'control' the entity, so that it is not clear which element has lead to the establishment of dependence.

At what point in time should one determine whether the three conditions have been fulfilled? The CJEU explicitly stated that the determination must be made on an annual basis and that the budgetary year during which a procurement procedure is commenced must be regarded as the most appropriate period for calculating the method of financing of that body. An entity, which is considered to be a contracting authority at the commencement of the procurement procedure, will maintain such qualification until this procedure has been completed.[243]

As the Directives do not provide any indication as to how to identify the moment at which the evaluation should be done, the CJEU has based its decision on the provisions regarding indicative notices. According to these provisions contracting authorities should make public the indicative notices as soon as possible after the beginning of the budgetary year, where the total amount of the procurement that they envisage awarding during the subsequent twelve months, amounts above the thresholds. According to the CJEU, the provisions imply that the contracting authority retains that status for twelve months from the beginning of each budgetary year.[244]

Advocate General Alber had suggested in his Opinion preceding the *University of Cambridge* judgment a possibility to reassess the entity's status during the procedure in case of significant changes in funding.[245] Such changes could indeed have as a consequence that the entity does no longer comply with the three conditions, in a way that, while the procedure is pending, no mention can be made of a 'contracting authority'. However, the CJEU has not taken into account such consideration in the judgment in *University of Cambridge* case. The CJEU attached great importance to the principle of legal certainty, requiring that the rules are clear and their application foreseeable for all those

241 E.H. Pynacker Hordijk, G.W. Van Der Bend and J.F. Van Nouhuys, *Aanbestedingsrecht* (Den Haag: SDU, 2004), p. 52.

242 Case C-306/97, *Connemara Machine Turf Co. Ltd v. Coillte Teoranta* [1998] *ECR* I-8761, at [32–35].

243 Case C-380/98, *The Queen v. H.M. Treasury, ex parte The University of Cambridge* [2000] *ECR* I-8035, at [40] and [43].

244 At [39].

245 Opinion Advocate General Alber, C-380/98, *The Queen v. H.M. Treasury, ex parte The University of Cambridge* [2000] *ECR* I-8035, at [74].

concerned.[246] In other words, third parties and, of course, the contracting authority itself should know from the commencement of the budgetary year whether the contracts they envisage for the subsequent year fall within the scope of the public procurement Directives.

1.2. Public authority

The CJEU case law on cooperative agreements between public authorities does not only apply to contracts normally falling within the scope of the public procurement Directives. The CJEU has extended its case law also to service concessions. This type of agreement, however, falls outside the scope of the public procurement Directives.[247]

This means that for these contracts, in principle, the concepts as set out in the aforementioned Directives are not relevant. The scope of the Directives is based on, amongst others, the concept 'contracting authority'. Contracting authorities are subject to the public procurement Directives. The question arises whether this concept can be transposed to service concessions in order to understand the *ratione personae* scope of this category of contracts.

As until recently no specific directives with regard to service concessions existed, the provisions of the TFEU applied.[248] It is obvious that a parallel exists concerning the *ratione personae* scope of the TFEU and of the public procurement Directives. It is also on these Treaty provisions that the CJEU has based its case law that public authorities, which conclude service concession contracts, must comply with the principle of equal treatment and the duty of transparency.[249] The provisions on free movement (Articles 34, 49 and 56 TFEU) determine their *ratione personae* scope. According to these provisions, the scope is determined based on the concept of 'Member State'.[250]

The Treaty, however, does not provide a definition of 'Member State'. According to the CJEU, there are the traditional public authorities, as listed by Directive 2004/18/EC: the State and the territorial bodies.[251] It further deals with professional organisations or

246 Case C-380/98, *The Queen v. H.M. Treasury, ex parte The University of Cambridge* [2000] *ECR* I-8035, at [40] and [43], with reference to Case C-44/96, *Mannesmann Anlagenbau Austria AG and Others* [1998] *ECR* I-73.

247 Article 17 Directive 2004/18/EC.

248 In Chapter 4, it will be submitted that the public procurement Directives fall within the scope of the TFEU provisions that regard free movement.

249 Case C-324/98, *Telaustria Verlags GmbH and Telefonadress GmbH v. Telekom Austria AG, joined party: Herold Business Data AG* [2000] *ECR* I-10745, at [60–62]; Case C-206/08, *Wasser- und Abwasserzweckverband Gotha und Landkreisgemeinden (WAZV Gotha) v. Eurawasser Aufbereitungs- und Entsorgungsgesellschaft mbH* [2009] *ECR* I-0000, at [44].

250 M. Szydlo, 'Contracts beyond the scope of the EC procurement directives – who is bound by the requirement for transparency?' (*ELR*, 2009), pp. 724–730; See B. Nabli, 'L'autorité publique et la puissance publique', in J.-B. Auby (dir.), *L'influence du droit européen sur les categories du droit* public (Paris: Dalloz, 2010), pp. 334–343.

251 Joined cases C-46/93 and C-48/93, *Brasserie du Pêcheur v. Bundesrepublik Deutschland and The Queen v. Secretary of State for Transport, ex parte: Factortame Ltd and others* [1993] *ECR* I-1839; Case C-1/90,

other institutions of public law, such as universities.[252] Also all institutions under the strict control or supervision of a member state fall within the scope of the concept 'Member State' within the meaning of the provisions on free movement.[253] The free movement principles apply to private bodies supported by the state through finance.[254] The element of dependence can also be found in the public procurement Directives when they provide a definition of a 'body governed by public law'.

In *Coditel Brabant*,[255] a case which concerned a service concession, the CJEU referred to *a public authority which is a contracting authority,*[256] thus suggesting that it considers the terms 'public authority' and 'contracting authority' to be synonyms. Legal scholars already built upon the concept of 'contracting authority' to characterize the concept 'public authority' in the context of awarding government contracts[257] other than public contracts.[258] This is how the CJEU ruled in its decision *Wall AG.*[259]

In *Wall AG*, the CJEU had its first opportunity to examine the public entities to which the principles applicable to service concessions (equal treatment and duty of transparency) apply. The case concerned a matter in which the city of Frankfurt signed a concession agreement with the Frankfurter Entsorgungs- und Service GmbH (FES), a legal person governed by private law. The execution of a part thereof was subcontracted by FES to Wall AG, in particular the performance of the advertising services. At a certain moment, FES changed its subcontractor and the question arose as to the nature of FES. Is it a 'public authority' bound by the provisions on free movement, the principle of equal treatment and the duty of transparency?

Aragonesa de Publicidad v. Departmento de Sanidad [1991] *ECR* I-4151; Case C-103/88, *Fratelli Costanzo* SpA v. Comune di Milano [1989] *ECR* 1839.

252 Case 71/76, *Jean Thieffry v. Conseil de l'ordre des avocats à la Cour de Paris* [1977] *ECR* 765; Case C-419/92, *Ingetraut Scholz v. Opera Universitaria di Cagliari and Cinzia Porcedda* [1994] *ECR* I-505.

253 M. Szydlo, 'Contracts beyond the scope of the EC procurement directives – who is bound by the requirement for transparency?' (*ELR*, 2009), p. 725.

254 C. Barnard, *The substantive law of the EU* (Oxford: OUP, 2013), p. 35.

255 Case C-324/07, Coditel Brabant *SA. v. Commune d'Uccle and Région de Bruxelles-Capitale* [2008] *ECR* I-8457.

256 At [34].

257 The concept 'government contract' is used in the present book to characterize all contracts concluded by public authorities.

258 R.G.T. Bleeker and E.R. Manunza, 'De invloed van het Europees recht op het Nederlandse aanbestedingsrecht' in A.S. Hartkamp, C.H. Sieburgh and L.A.D. Keus (eds.), *De invloed van het Europese recht op het Nederlandse privaatrecht* (Deventer: Kluwer, 2007), part 42–2, pp. 566 et seq.; D. Ruiz-Jarabo Colomer, 'L'engagement contractuel dans la jurisprudence de la Cour de justice des Communautés européennes', in *Conseil d'Etat. Rapport public 2008. Le contrat, mode d'action publique et de production de normes* (Paris: La documentation française, 2008), pp. 371 et seq.; S.E. Zijlstra, 'De grenzen van de overheid', in X., *Privaat bestuur?* (Den Haag: Boom Juridische Uitgevers, 2008), pp. 34–42; K. Wauters, *Rechtsbescherming en overheidsovereenkomsten* (Antwerpen: Intersentia, 2009), p. 23, nr. 24.

259 Case C-91/08, *Wall AG v. La ville de Francfort-sur-le-Main and Frankfurter Entsorgungs- und Service (FES) GmbH* [2010] *ECR* I-02815.

The CJEU followed the reasoning that the definition of the term 'contracting authority' in the public procurement Directives can inspire to find a definition of 'public authority': 'To establish whether an entity with characteristics such as those of FES may be equated to a public authority bound by the obligation of transparency, some aspects of the definition of 'contracting authority' in Article 1(b) of Directive 92/50 on public service contracts should be taken as guidance, to the extent that they correspond to the requirements produced by the application to service concessions of the obligation of transparency flowing from Articles 43 EC and 49 EC'.[260] The idea behind this consideration seems to be that only those entities, which are not inspired by economical needs and thus can choose a contracting partner, should be subject to the principle of equal treatment and the duty of transparency.

According to the CJEU, an entity must comply with two conditions to be considered a 'public authority': first, the undertaking in question is effectively controlled by the State or another public authority, and, secondly, it does not compete on the market. The first condition corresponds to the dependency criterion, by which the Directive 2004/18/EC provides, amongst others, a definition of a 'body governed by public law'. The second condition seems to be similar to the element of 'general interest, not having an industrial or commercial character' as set out in the definition of the concept 'body governed by public law'.

The CJEU did not further explain the two conditions in this case. However, the CJEU did check whether the factual elements of the case complied with the conditions, in order to decide whether FES constituted a 'public authority'. As regards the first condition, the CJEU concluded that although 51% of the share capital of FES is owned by the city of Frankfurt, a majority of three quarters of the votes is needed for the decision of a general meeting of shareholders. In addition, on the supervisory board of FES, the city of Frankfurt has only a quarter of the votes. As far as the second condition is concerned, the CJEU concluded that FES operates in the market and that it obtains more than half its turnover from bilateral contracts.

The same objectives as those guiding the public procurement Directives serve as a base to describe the concept 'public authority'. The CJEU refers in *Wall AG* to the following objectives: the free movement of services and the opening up of the market to undistorted competition in the Member States.[261] These objectives necessitate a broad interpretation of the concept of a 'public authority'. *Wall AG* contains criteria that could determine whether an entity is a public authority for any contract that does not fall within the scope of the public procurement Directives.[262]

260 At [47].

261 Case C-91/08, *Wall AG v. La ville de Francfort-sur-le-Main and Frankfurter Entsorgungs- und Service (FES) GmbH* [2010] *ECR* I-02815, at [48].

262 A. Brown, 'Changing a sub-contractor under a public services concession: Wall AG v. Stadt Frankfut am Main C-91/98' (*PPLR*, 2010), pp. 160–166.

The recently published Directive on service concessions (Directive 2014/23/EU) now uses the concept of 'contracting authority' and defines it in Article 6. It received the same definition as the concept used in the public procurement Directives. It can be presumed that the CJEU interprets the concepts in the same way taking into account the objectives of the internal market rules and the provisions on the fundamental freedoms.

2. Cooperative agreements

Considering the focus of the research, not every form of cooperation between public authorities will be addressed. This book is limited to the forms of cooperation between public authorities that have all the characteristics of a public contract or a service concession. To determine the object of the study, it is important to determine the meaning of 'public contract' and 'service concession'.

In this context it is not the intention to analyse the two terms in all its components. In the case of public contracts only the element 'contract' will be addressed. As will become apparent, this element forms the starting point for the CJEU case law on cooperative agreements that will be examined in Chapter 5 (2.1.). The concept 'service concession', which is also a contract, will be compared in particular with the concept 'public contract' (2.2.).

2.1. Public contract

The subject of this book falls into the scope of Directive 2004/17/EC and Directive 2004/18/EC. Article 1 of Directive 2004/18/EC determines for the public sector the scope of the public procurement regime: "Public contracts' are contracts for pecuniary interest concluded in writing between one or more economic operators and one or more contracting authorities and having as their object the execution of works, the supply of products or the provision of services within the meaning of this Directives'. Directive 2004/17/EC contains a comparable definition. (Article 1.2.(a)) The distinguishing characteristics for the ratione materiae scope are: (i) a contract, (ii) for pecuniary interest, (iii) concluded in writing, and (iv) the execution of works, supply of products or provision of services.

Not all the elements are decisive to define the concept 'public contract'. The element (iii) is not relevant. This element does not determine the presence of a public contract. The elements (ii) and (iv) are not important to explain the CJEU case law on cooperative agreements. They will not be analysed in detail. For the purpose of this research, it is submitted that the relevant element or starting point for the CJEU case law on cooperative agreements between public authorities was the existence of a contract.[263, 264]

The application of Directives 2004/17/CE and 2004/18/EC requires the presence of a 'contract'. In general the CJEU emphasizes the importance of the element 'contract' to determine whether there is a public contract.[265]

First, within the public procurement Directives, the concept 'contract' has an autonomous meaning. As with defining other concepts in the public procurement Directives, the CJEU uses a functional interpretation[266] of the term 'contract'. Consequently, CJEU case law seems to distinguish several elements that have to be established in order to be in the presence of a 'contract'.

An analysis of the relevant CJEU case law demonstrates that it is not possible to have a consistent definition of the concept 'contract'. The definition of many of the concepts used in the public procurement Directives has evolved over a number of CJEU judgments[267] and is not yet definitive. The principles developed in the context of EU internal market law influence and impact on the meaning of 'contract'. The CJEU distinguishes two elements in its case law to define the concept of 'contract' within the meaning of the public procurement Directives: two different wills and the freedom to negotiate.

A first attempt at defining the term 'contract' can be found in the Opinion of Advocate General Cosmas in *Teckal*.[268] He emphasizes that a contract is synallagmatic. There is a meeting of wills between two different persons, the contracting authority and the supplier. In other words, there are mutual acts of performance, the creation of rights and obligations for the parties to the contract and interdependence of their respective acts of performance. According to the Advocate General, for public procurement Directives to apply it is essential that the party entering into the contract with the public authority, namely the supplier, has a real third-party status *vis-à-vis* that public authority; that is to

263 E. Fatome and L. Richer, 'Procédures de passation des contrats et pouvoir d'organisation du service public' (*ACCP* 12, 2002), p. 61; K. Weltzien, 'Avoiding the procurement rules by awarding contracts to an in-house entity – scope of the the procurement directives in the classical sector' (*PPLR*, 2005), pp. 239–240; T. Kaarreselo, 'Procuring in-house: the impact of the EC procurement regime' (*PPLR*, 2008), p. 244; A.L. Durviaux in its Phd-thesis categorizes the in house case law under the personal characteristics of the concept 'public contract': A.L. Durviaux, *Logique de marché et marché public en droit communautaire* (Bruxelles: Larcier, 2006), pp. 176–189.

264 See chapter 5.

265 Case C-451/08, *Helmut Müller GmbH v. Bundesanstalt für Immobilienaufgaben* [2010] *ECR* I–02673, at [46].

266 Case 130/87, *Gebroeders* Beentjes *BV v. State of the Netherlands* [1988] *ECR* I-4635.

267 A.L. Durviaux characterizes the concept 'public contract' as 'une concept en "devenir"': A.L. Durviaux, 'La 'logique de marché' dans les relations contractuelles entre le secteur public et le secteur privé: développements récents', in N. Thirion (ed.), *Le marché et l'Etat à l'heure de la mondialisation* (Bruxelles: Larcier, 2007), p. 42.

268 Opinion of G.Cosmas, case C-107/98, *Teckal Srl v. Comune di Viano* [1999] *ECR* I-8121, at [52].

say, the supplier must be a separate person from the public authority.[269] This could be inspired from the traditional French definition of an administrative contract ('contrat administratif').[270]

In its ruling in this case the CJEU did not give any complete definition. It limited itself to characterizing a contract as an agreement between two separate persons.[271] It seemed that the CJEU would follow a more traditional definition of the concept: there is a consensus between both parties either as to the choice over whether to enter into a relationship. Also the choice over whether to accept particular terms or the possibility for one of the parties or a third party to override and/or alter the agreed terms.[272] The presence of two independent legal bodies is in all events the first element to determine whether there is a contract.

Nevertheless, the unilateral nature of certain decisions in the context of the award of a public contract does not rule out the term 'contract' as shown by the CJEU in the *Scala*-case.[273] *Scala* involved the restoration and renovation of the historic building of the Scala Theatre, the renovation of the municipal buildings of the Ansaldo complex and the construction of a new theatre in the quarter Bicocca. The City of Milan decided to integrate the works into a major renovation of an entire site (unilateral decision) where the owner of that site, according to Italian law as the holder of a subdivision permit, should be responsible for the carrying out of the works. It was also agreed that the owner would be responsible for the infrastructure works. The parties to these transactions were of the opinion that there was no contract.

In this case the CJEU noted that the City of Milan did have a choice under the relevant building and planning regulations as to how to arrange for the construction of the development project. The City may deviate from the rule of immediate construction of the project by the contractor and opt for the later construction of the project by another contractor under an award procedure. This option would give the contracting entity an opportunity to award the works contract to another contractor and would therefore justify the application of the Directive. The CJEU concluded that a contract did exist.

269 At [53 et seq.].

270 For a definition of the concept 'contrat administratif' see A. de Laubadère, F. Moderne and P. Delvolvé, *Traité des contrats administratifs*, T. 1 (Paris: LGDJ, 1981), pp. 29 et seq.; see also D. Truchet, "Le contrat administratif, qualification juridique d'un accord de volontés", in L. Cadier (ed.), *Le droit contemporain des contrats. Bilan et perspectives* (Paris: Economica, 1987), p. 186; F. Lichère, *Droit des contrats* publics (Paris: Dalloz, 2005), p. 10; X., "Contrat, loi et décision administrative unilatérale: des imbrications croissants", in *Rapport public 2008. Le contrat, mode d'action publique et de production de normes* (Paris: La documentation Française, 2008), pp. 92–93.

271 Case C-107/98, *Teckal Srl v. Comune di Viano* [1999] *ECR* I-8121, at [49].

272 S. Arrowsmith, *The law of public and utilities procurement* (London: Sweet & Maxwell, 2005), p. 284, 6.2.

273 Case C-399/98, *Ordine degli Architetti delle Province di Milano e Lodi, Piero De Amicis, Consiglio Nazionale degli Architetti and Leopoldo Freyrie v. Comune di Milano, and Pirelli SpA, Milano Centrale Servizi SpA and Fondazione Teatro alla Scala* [2001] *ECR* I-05409.

More important than the presence of two legal bodies to determine the concept of 'contract', is the manner in which these two legal bodies relate to each other. In principle, it is essential that the two agree. It is only by the convergence of the wills of both parties that legal effects can arise. This expresses the idea of freedom of contract. Contracting parties choose freely with whom they want to contract, how they want to contract, and what they want to contract. Yet, the CJEU ruled that if a contracting authority cannot choose its contracting party, the categorisation of a 'contract' under the public procurement legislation is not excluded (*Scala*).[274] Under EU law freedom of choice is not relevant for a contract to exist.

On the other hand one can also find herein the principle of consensualism. To determine whether a contract exists under the public procurement Directives, one must, according to the CJEU in *Scala*, investigate whether there is a possibility of negotiation on the actual content of the performances.[275] Some specific legal effects must be realized due to the consensus of the parties. In *Scala* the parties decided which infrastructure works the promotor was to construct and what the relevant conditions were. The contracting authority receives, as a result of the consensus, also a legal title to the facilities.[276] There can be no question of a contract when the contracting authority unilaterally imposes obligations on the entrepreneur that differ from the contractual terms that the entrepreneur normally applies.[277]

To date, the CJEU has not made any definitive statements concerning the degree of negotiation that is sufficient to decide whether a contract exists. Perhaps, as a starting point, a different judgment of the CJEU[278] can be considered where the CJEU had to rule on a modification to a contract and to what extent this change constitutes a new contract. The CJEU refers in this case to considerations from earlier case law involving a modification when the parties renegotiate the essential terms. Thus, one could argue that a contract exists when parties negotiate and reach an agreement on the essential terms of a contract.

Another judgment of the CJEU that is relevant to this issue is a case that concerns an ambulance providing service. The ambulance service had signed a contract with a contracting authority where the funding conditions were regulated with respect to the operation of the service. Based on the actual facts, however, the CJEU could not exclude that the ambulance service did not derive the power for the execution of this contract

274 At [52].

275 See also J. Wiggen, 'Public procurement rules and cooperation between public sector entities: the limits of the in-house doctrine under EU procurement law' (*PPLR*, 2011), p. 170.

276 At [71].

277 Case C-220/06, *Asociación Profesional de Empresas de Reparto y Manipulado de Correspondencia v. Administration General del Estado* [2007] *ECR* I-12175, at [54]; see also Opinion Advocate General Mazak joined cases C-197/11 and C-203/11, *Libert and Others ECR* I-00000 [88].

278 Case C-454/06, *Pressetext Nachrichtenagentur GmbH v. Republik Österreich (Bund), APA-OTS Originaltext-Service GmbH and APA Austria Presse Agentur registrierte Genossenschaft mit beschränkter Haftung* [2008] *ECR* I-04401, at [34].

directly from the law. When a person provides services under its own powers derived directly from the law, it does not constitute a contract within the meaning of the directives on public procurement.[279] In such a situation there is not really a third person on whose demand the contract is executed, so there is no question of consensualism. The contractor, who executes an agreement under a regulatory or statutory provision, is not in a contractual relationship.[280]

Conclusion

Based on the relevant case law, it is clear that the CJEU is not bound by the categorisation of a cooperation or agreement when establishing the existence of a contract. The CJEU analyses the facts of a case and then assesses to which degree negotiation between the present parties is possible, making abstraction of the unilateral or reciprocal nature of a decision.

This case law has the great disadvantage of being very unpredictable since the CJEU, in its quest, will again and again be guided by the goals of the public procurement Directives that were set out in Chapter 2. Furthermore, an evolving definition has the advantage of being able to adapt to the subtleties of public authorities in order to avoid the application of the public procurement Directives. Finally, the analysis of the case law does not support a contention that the CJEU is far removed from national traditions when defining the term 'contract'.

2.2. *Service concession*

Service concession is the second form of contract concluded by a public authority that has been subjected by the CJEU to the application of EU law and more specifically to the principle of equality. First, it will be analysed how this concept was introduced in EU law. Thereafter this concept will be defined taking into account the public procurement Directives and the CJEU case law. Finally this section deals with the main difference between a service concession and a public contract: the transfer of risk.

2.2.1. Foundations in EU law

The Treaty of Rome[281] did not contain any specific provision on 'service concessions', nor can this concept be found in the amending treaties. The concept 'concession' appeared for the first time in EU law in 1962. The General Programme for the abolition of restrictions on freedom to provide services[282] and the General Programme for the abolition of restrictions on freedom of establishment[283] contain each a reference to this

279 Case C-532/03, *Commission v. Ireland* [2007] *ECR* I-11353, at [37].

280 See Preamble of Directive 92/50/EEC of 18 June 1992 relating to coordination of procedures for the award of public service contracts.

281 Treaty of 27 March 1957 establishing the European Economic Community.

282 Series II Volume IX pp. 3–6.

283 Series II Volume IX pp. 7–15.

concept. Both programmes provide obligations for the Member States to abolish restrictive provisions and set out actions in regard to citizens of other Member States. These obligations concerned also obtaining concessions or licences delivered by the State or another public body.

A description of the concept 'concession' can be found for the first time in Article 3.1. of Council Directive 71/305/EEC.[284] This provision directly makes a link with the concept 'public work contract' (article 1(A)) and indicates the distinctive element between both contracts: 'a contract of the same type as that indicated in article 1 (A) except for the fact that the consideration for the works to be carried out consists either solely in the right to exploit the construction or in this right together with payment'. The right to exploit was already a major element of the concept 'concession'.

This Directive did not contain any definition of the term 'service concession'. The first generation of Directives on public procurement did not concern 'public service contracts'. Thus, it was logical that the first Directives did not contain any definition of the concept 'service concession'. For the first time Directive 92/50/CEE[285] provided specific dispositions related to the tendering of public service contracts. In the proposal for the Directive a definition of the concept 'service concession' was included: 'a 'public service concession' is a contract other than a public works concession within the meaning of Article 1(d) of Directive 71/305/EEC, concluded between an authority and another entity of its choice whereby the former transfers the execution of a service to the public lying within its responsibility to the latter and the latter accepts to execute the activity in return for the right to exploit the service or this right together with payment' (Article 1, h).

Although the Commission itself was in favour of including a regulation on service concessions in the Directive, there was a difference of opinion between the Member States within the Council.[286] France and the other Latin countries felt especially that such *intuitu personae* agreements could not be competitively awarded. These countries also feared an increased competition for their business interests in such enterprises, which regularly exercise such activity in a monopoly.[287] As a result, the final text of the Directive did not contain any reference to the term 'concession'.

Directive 2004/18/CE for the first time contained a definition of the concept 'service concession'. Article 1, paragraph 4 of Directive 2004/18/CE defines the concept 'service concession' as 'a contract of the same type as a public service contract except for the fact

284 Series I Volume 1971(II), pp. 682–692.

285 Council Directive 92/50/EEC of 18 June 1992 relating to the coordination of procedures for the award of public service contracts, OJ [1992] L 209 pp.1–24.

286 Case C-324/98, *Telaustria Verlags GmbH and Telefonadress GmbH v. Telekom Austria AG, joined party: Herold Business Data AG* [2000] *ECR* I-10745, at [48].

287 M.A. Flamme, Ph. Matheï, Ph. Flamme, A. Delvaux and Cl. Dardenne, *Praktische commentaar bij de reglementering van de overheidsopdrachten*, 1A (Brussel: NCB, 1996–1997), p. 134. See also Ch. Bovis, *EU public procurement law* (Cheltenham: Edgar European Law, 2012), p. 337.

that the consideration for the provision of services consists either solely in the right to exploit the service or in this right together with payment'. This contract is still excluded from the scope of the public procurement Directives.

As already mentioned above the EU institutions have for the first time approved in 2014 a whole new Directive on concessions.[288] The main characteristics of the concept 'concession' are maintained.[289] This Directive provides a detailed regulatory regime for the tendering of work and service concessions.

2.2.2. Basic elements[290]

On the basis of Article 1, paragraph 4 Directive 2004/18/CE the CJEU has developed the meaning of 'service concession'. The CJEU interprets the concept autonomously: 'The question whether the agreements at issue should or should not be classed as service concessions must therefore be considered exclusively in the light of Community law'.[291]

The concept 'service concession' was mentioned for the first time in the *BFI* judgment.[292] Unlike the CJEU, Advocate General La Pergola advanced in this case a number of criteria to qualify a service concession: the beneficiary of a concession is the user and not the awarding public authority, the payment of a sum of money by third parties to the contract holder, the concession operator operates a service of general interest and the concession operator bears the economic risk of the operation of the service.[293]

In his Opinion in *Telaustria Verlag*[294] Advocate General Fennelly relies on the definition of the concept of 'public service contract' to define the concept of service concession. He considered the lack of consideration on the part of the contracting authority as a basic characteristic of a service concession. According to Fennelly the concessionaire had itself the largest or at least the substantial economic risk associated with the exploitation of the service concession.

288 Directive 2014/23/EU.

289 H. Hoepffner, 'La nouvelle directive Concessions' (*Europe*, 2014, June), p. 10.

290 See on the early case law: U. Neergaard, 'Public service concessions and related concepts – the increased pressure from Community law on Member States' use of concessions' (*PPLR*, 2007), pp. 387–409. See also more recently: C.R. Hansen, 'Defining a Service Concession Contract will the proposed new definition of service concession contracts increase legal legality in the field of concessions', in G.S. Olykke, C.R. Hansen and C.D. Tvarno (eds.), *EU Public procrurement – Modernisation, Growth and Innovation* (Copenhagen: Djøf publishing, 2012), pp. 239–250.

291 Case C-382/05, *Commission of the European Communities v. Italian Republic* [2007] *ECR* I-6657; Case C-348/10, *Norma-A SIA and Dehon-ASIA v. Latgales planasanas regions* [2011] *ECR* I-0000, at [40].

292 Case C-360/96, *Gemeente Arnhem and Gemeente Rheden v. BFI Holding BV* [1998] *ECR* I-6821.

293 Opinion Advocate General La Pergola Case C-360/96, *Gemeente Arnhem and Gemeente Rheden v. BFI Holding BV* [1998] *ECR* I-6821, at [26]; see also Ch. Bovis, *EC Public Procurement: Case law and Regulation* (Oxford: OUP, 2006), pp. 334–335. Opinion Advocat General Alber Case C-108/98, *RI.SAN srl and Comune d'Ischia, Italia Lavoro SpA and Ischia Ambiente SpA* [1999] *ECR* I-05219, at [50].

294 Opinion Advocate General Case C-324/98, *Telaustria Verlags GmbH and Telefonadress GmbH v. Telekom Austria AG, joined party: Herold Business Data AG* [2000] *ECR* I-10745, at [30].

In defining the concept the CJEU was inspired, prior to a definition in the public procurement Directives, by the term 'public works concessions'.[295] Article 1, paragraph 4 of Directive 93/38/EEC referred only to contracts for pecuniary interest concluded in writing and, without making express reference to public service concessions. It provided only indications about the contracting parties and about the object of the contract, defining them in particular in the light of the method of remunerating the service provider and without drawing any distinction between contracts in which the consideration is fixed and those in which the consideration consists in a right of exploitation.[296]

There is only a question of a service concession when there is a contract.[297] This could be inferred from the case *Sporting Exchange*.[298] In this case the CJEU literally considers: 'the issue of a single licence is not the same as a service concession'.[299] On the one hand, the CJEU states that a licence, a unilateral legal act, is not a service concession. On the other hand, the CJEU always adds the term 'contract' when it talks about a service concession.

What does not appear necessary is that a service concession concerns a public service. If the public nature should have been a condition, the Directive would also have mentioned it. Usually it will of course involve a public service, precisely because it is a task that a public authority transfers to a third party.

The CJEU for the first time defined implicitly the concept 'service concession' in *Telaustria*[300] as a contract in which the consideration consists in a right of exploitation. This is also the first distinctive criterion approved by the CJEU regarding a service concession, more specifically the transfer of the right to operate the service. The service provider is not reimbursed by the public authority concerned but by third parties who use the service.[301] A service concession is not a contract for pecuniary interest like a public contract falling under the scope of the public procurement Directives.

The provider takes the risk for operating the services in question. The public body hands over the risk of exploitation, which the CJEU considers to be the second important criterion of the concept 'service concession'. This element cannot be found in the Directive's definition. Thus, the CJEU once again took a 'legislative' role. This element

295 L. Richer, *L'Europe des marchés publics* (Paris: LGDJ, 2009), p. 205.

296 Case C-324/98, *Telaustria Verlags GmbH and Telefonadress GmbH v. Telekom Austria AG, joined party: Herold Business Data AG* [2000] *ECR* I-10745, at [43].

297 See also E.H. Pynacker Hordijk, G.W. Van Der Bend and J.F. Van Nouhuys, *Aanbestedingsrecht* (Den Haag: Sdu Uitgevers, 2009), p. 100.

298 Case C-203/08, *Sporting Exchange Ltd v. Minister van Justitie* [2010] *ECR* I-04695.

299 At [46].

300 Case C-324/98, *Telaustria Verlags GmbH and Telefonadress GmbH v. Telekom Austria AG, joined party: Herold Business Data AG* [2000] *ECR* I-10745, at [43].

301 Case C-458/03, *Parking Brixen GmbH. v. Gemeinde Brixen and Stadtwerke Brixen AG* [2005] *ECR* I-08585, at [40].

will now be examined in detail, because it was the source of most of the case law on the meaning of 'service concession'. It is the most distinctive element.[302]

2.2.3. Transfer of risk

In different cases the CJEU had the opportunity to clarify the second important criterion to qualify a service concession: to what extent the public authority has to transfer the risk?

In *Eurawasser*,[303] although rendered in the framework of Directive 2004/17/EC, the CJEU specified that it is irrelevant whether the fee paid by third parties or consumers is governed by private or public law. In the same ruling, the CJEU held that the actual risk assumed by the provider does not have to be significant.[304] It is only required that the public authority hands over all or a substantial part of the risk. The general risks resulting from possible amendments to the contract, made in the course of performance of the contract, cannot be taken into account.

The right to exploit the service, either alone, or together with payment, entails that the provider of the service takes the risk of operating the service. That risk may, at the outset, be very limited. It is necessary for classification as a service concession that the contracting authority transfers to the concession holder a significant share of the risk which it faces.

In that regard, it must be stated that the risk of the economic operation of the service must be understood as the risk of exposure to the vagaries of the market,[305] that may consist of the risk of i) competition from other operators, ii) that supply of the services will not match demand, iii) those liable will be unable to pay for the services provided, iv) the risk that the costs of operating the services will not fully be met by revenue, or v) liability for harm or damage resulting from an inadequacy of the service.[306] By contrast, risks such as those linked to bad management or errors of judgment by the economic operator are not decisive for the purposes of classification as a public service contract or

302 C.R. Hansen, 'Defining a Service Concession Contract will the proposed new definition of service concession contracts increase legal legality in the field of concessions', in G.S. Olykke, C.R. Hansen and C.D. Tvarno (eds.), *EU Public procrurement – Modernisation, Growth and Innovation* (Copenhagen: Djøf publishing, 2012), p. 240.

303 Case C-206/08, *Wasser- und Abwasserzweckverband Gotha und Landkreisgemeinden (WAZV Gotha) v. Eurawasser Aufbereitungs- und Entsorgungsgesellschaft mbH* [2009] *ECR* I-8377, at [55].

304 At [71].

305 See also Case C-206/08, *Wasser- und Abwasserzweckverband Gotha und Landkreisgemeinden (WAZV Gotha) v. Eurawasser Aufbereitungs- und Entsorgungsgesellschaft mbH* [2009] *ECR* I-8377, at [66] and [67].

306 Case C-274/09, *Privater Rettungsdienst und Krankentransport Stadler v. Zweckverband für Rettungsdienst und Feuerwehralarmierung Passau* [2011] *ECR* I-1335, at [37]; Case C-348/10, *Norma-A SIA and Dehon-ASIA v. Latgales planasanas regions* [2011] *ECR* I-0000, at [48].

a service concession, since those risks are inherent in every contract, whether it be a public service contract or a service concession.[307]

In *Privater Rettungsdienst* the CJEU confirmed that the fees allotted to the provider by another public body did not suffice to cover all operating expenses.[308] The providers faced a deficit and they were exposed to this risk. Finally, it was proved that there was competition on the market for this activity. Under those circumstances the CJEU concluded that the contract must be defined as a 'service concession'.

As regards the exposure to the vagaries of the market the CJEU examined in the case of *Norma-A* the applicable legislation and the terms of the contract.[309] Having regard to the terms of the contract and to the national law provisions, the CJEU concluded that the provider did not bear a significant share of the operating risk. The public authority would reimburse the service provider for any operating losses.

The CJEU has in its case law further described the term 'operating risk' or 'risk of the economic exploitation', which is the risk of being exposed to the fluctuations of the market. According to the CJEU, this could be manifested in different, non cumulative, ways: the risk of competition from other market participants; the risk of mismatch between the supply and the demand of services; the risk of insolvency of those that must pay for the services that are supplied; the risk that the costs are not fully covered by the income; or the risk of liability for damages due to defective services.[310]

3. Public tasks

The concept 'public service' or 'public task' is unknown in EU law and has also not been defined by the CJEU in its case law. However, for a better grasp of the case law on cooperative agreements between public authorities it is necessary to make clear what is meant by 'public service', 'public interest tasks' and 'public tasks'.[311]

In this book it is argued that these terms must be given a comparable meaning to the meaning given to 'service of general interest' (SGI) (see 3.2.). The definition of SGI should be used as a reference to the understanding of the term 'public task'. First, the historical evolution of the place of 'public tasks' and 'services of general interests' in EU law is briefly set out, followed by a more detailed analysis of this concept.

307 Case C-274/09, *Privater Rettungsdienst und Krankentransport Stadler v. Zweckverband für Rettungsdienst und Feuerwehralarmierung Passau* [2011] *ECR* I-1335, at [38].

308 At [40].

309 Case C-348/10, *Norma-A SIA and Dehon-ASIA v. Latgales planasanas regions* [2011] *ECR* I-0000, at [51] to [54].

310 At [48].

311 In the latest case law the CJEU uses the concept 'public task' in English and the concept 'service public' in French: Case C-159/11, *Azienda Sanitaria Locale di Lecce, Università del Salento v. Ordine degli Ingegneri della Provincia di Lecce and Others* [2012] *ECR* I-00000.

3.1. *Historic development*

The organisation of a public authority or the management of its 'public (service) tasks' falls outside the scope of the EU Treaty provisions. That is why in the original provisions of the EEC Treaty there is no mention of public tasks. Only Article 77 EEC (now Article 93 TFEU) contained a reference to the term 'public service' in the context of transport policy and Article 90 EEC (now Article 106 TFEU) addressed 'services of general economic interest'.

As public authorities in social welfare states took upon themselves more tasks that touched upon the economic sector, the need arose to define the public service tasks that come within the scope of the EU Treaty and, therefore, governed by EU law.[312] Member States such as France wished to maintain an extensive autonomy in respect of the organization and the management of public service tasks or services of general interest. As a result a tension occurred between the pursuit of the internal market objective and the conservation of Member States competences.

Public (service) tasks and SGI, however, have their place in the EU. Only the approach between the national philosophy and the goals of the EU are different. The term 'public service' is perceived in legal systems that are inspired by French law from the idea of a public authority as an entity with special prerogatives, while the institutions of the EU act within the objective to achieve an internal market. In this latter context, however, the SGIs do matter. In certain circumstances they can be considered to be an economic activity and, thus, EU law will have its impact. (see also Chapter 4) An approximation of both approaches should be possible since the perceptions should cross at some point.

With the Treaty of the EU,[313] signed in Maastricht on 7 February 1992, several non-economic policy issues were introduced at the European level such as the creation of a European citizenship conferred on all nationals of the EU Member States. Thus EU nationals secured rights not only in their roles as economic actors in the EU market but also in their own rights as EU citizens. Thus certain safeguards have been granted to EU citizens to access the services of general interest. Access to SGI is perceived as a fundamental right. However, wherever access is mentioned, the right to an optimal service of general interest is also necessarily implied. Thus when a public authority appeals to a third party to carry out a service of general interest, EU citizens will be well served if these third parties are selected through a competitive procedure.

312 For an overview of the conflicting opinions on the place of the CJEU's concept of 'public service task' or 'service of general interest' see H. Schweitzer, 'Services of general interest: European Law's Impact on the Role of Markets and of Member States', in M. Cremona (ed.), *Market Integration and Public Services in the European Union* (Oxford: Oxford University Press, 2011), pp. 11–62; M. Nettesheim, *Les services d'intérêt general en droit communautaire entre libre concurrence et état social* (*RIDC*, 2008), pp. 608–615.

313 OJ 1992 L 191.

The European Commission was the first to give the SGI a place within the EU law by publishing a Communication[314] to this effect. In this Communication the Commission placed services of general interest at the heart of the EU's society. The services of general interest, according to another Commission's Communication,[315] are a key aspect in the EU model of society. In 1999, the Member States inserted, through the signing of the Treaty of Amsterdam on 2 October 1999, Article 16 in the EC Treaty (now Article 14 TFEU). By introducing this EU Treaty provision it seems that the carrying out of services of general economic interest is perceived as an obligation imposed on the EU and on the Member States[316] and that the access to services of general economic interest is a fundamental right of European citizens.

The European Commission issued two documents on services of general interest: the Green Paper on services of general interest[317] and the White Paper on services of general interest.[318] In both documents, the Commission tries to distinguish between non-economic services of general interest falling outside the scope of the EU Treaty, and the services of general economic interest, which fall within it.

Social objectives have acquired more importance in the current version of the EU Treaty (or EU priorities). Some important Treaty articles have been altered or new articles added by the Treaty of Lisbon. The Treaty of Lisbon altered Article 16 EC (now Article 14 TFEU) as follows:

'Without prejudice to Article 4 of the Treaty on European Union or to Articles 93, 106 and 107 of this Treaty, and given the place occupied by services of general economic interest in the shared values of the Union as well as their role in promoting social and territorial cohesion, the Union and the Member States, each within their respective powers and within the scope of application of the Treaties, shall take care that such services operate on the basis of principles and conditions, particularly economic and financial conditions, which enable them to fulfil their missions. The European Parliament and the Council, acting by means of regulations in accordance with the ordinary legislative procedure, shall establish these principles and set these conditions without prejudice to the competence of Member States, in compliance with the Treaties, to provide, to commission and to fund such services'.

Finally, the 26th Protocol to the Treaty of Lisbon emphasizes the importance of the SGEIs. This Protocol gives Member States the competence to provide, to commission and

314 Communication on services of general interest in Europe of the Commission d.d. 11 September 1996, COM(96)443final; D. Simon en F. Lagondet, *La communication de la Commission sur les services d'intérêt général en Europe continuité ou rupture?* (*Europe* 1, 1997), pp. 4–6.

315 Memorandum of the Commission on services of general interest in Europe OJ 2001 C 17/4.

316 K. Lenaerts, 'Les services d'intérêt général et le droit communautaire' in *Rapport public du Conseil d'Etat* (2002), p. 427. Article 36 of the Charter of fundamental rights of the European Union OJ [2012] C 326, pp. 391–407.

317 COM/2003/0270.

318 COM/2004/0374.

to organize non-economic services of general interest (Article 2 of the Protocol). The Charter of Fundamental Rights of the EU of 7 December 2000 recognizes the right of every European citizen to access the services of general economic interest (Article 36).

These documents emphasize a trend that gives the concept 'service of general interest' economic or non-economic, a EU meaning. These services play an important role in achieving a social, economic, and territorial EU cohesion.[319] In all the sectors the EU institutions are competent; this EU concept will gradually define to what extent that competence can be used. According to some, the services of general (economic) interest (SG(E)I) have acquired a constitutional dimension as a consequence of this increased attention.[320]

3.2. *The concept 'services of general interest'*

According to the CJEU, a public authority has the ability to perform its public tasks with its own administrative, technical and other resources without having to use a tendering procedure.[321] The CJEU further adds that public authorities may exercise the possibility to use their own resources to perform the public interest tasks conferred on them in cooperation with other public authorities.[322] Finally, it has been accepted that EU law does not require public authorities to use any particular form in order to carry out jointly their public service tasks.[323]

The concept 'public (service) task' or 'public service obligation' determines whether a particular agreement or cooperation between public authorities falls within or outside the scope of EU legislation. EU law does, however, use the concept of service of general (economic) interest (SGEI) (see Article 106 TFEU). It is generally agreed that the terms 'public service' and 'services of general interest' are closely interrelated.[324] The General Court of the EU itself admitted as follows: 'that the concept of public service obligation … corresponds to that of the services of general economic interest as designated by the

319 F. Malvasio, 'Les catégories du droit administratif économique et du service public', in J.-B. Auby (dir.), *L'influence du droit européen sur les catégories du droit public* (Paris: Dalloz, 2010), p. 763.

320 U. Neergaard, 'Services of general economic interest under EU law constraints', in D. Schiek, U. Liebert and H. Schneider (eds.), *European Economic and Social Constitutionalism after the Treaty of Lisbon* (Cambridge: Cambridge University Press, 2011), p. 181.

321 Case C-26/03, *Stadt Halle and RPL Recyclingpark Lochau GmbH v. Arbeitsgemeinschaft Thermische Restabfall- und Energieverwertungsanlage TREA Leuna* [2005] *ECR* I-00001, at [48].

322 Case C-324/07, *Coditel Brabant SA v. Commune d'Uccle and Région de Bruxelles-Capitale* [2008] *ECR* I-8457, at [49].

323 Case C-480/06, *Commission v. Germany* [2009] *ECR* I-04747, at [47].

324 N. Fiedziuk, 'Putting services of general economic interest up for tender: reflections on applicable EU rules' (*CMLR*, 2013), pp. 87–88; J. Sirinelli, *Les transformations du droit administratif par le droit de l'Union européenne* (Paris: LGDJ, 2011), p. 269; F. Malvasio, 'Les catégories du droit administratif économique et du service public', in J.-B. Auby (dir.), *L'influence du droit européen sur les catégories du droit public* (Paris: Dalloz, 2010), p. 763; L. Dubouis, 'Service public et droit de l'Union européenne un perpétuel débat', in *Juger l'administration, administrer la justice: Mélanges en l'honneur du Daniel LABETOULLE* (Paris: Dalloz, 2007), p. 295.

contested decision and that it does not differ from that referred to in Article 86(2) EC'.[325] Therefore, the concept of 'public service task' can be explained by the concept of 'services of general interest'.[326] If the CJEU case law on cooperative agreements needs to have the same consequences in all Member States, this concept also has to receive the same interpretation.

The question remains what is meant by services of general interest? Generally no treaty or other secondary legal text in EU law contains a definition of this concept. In principle it is national law that determines the meaning of 'services of general interest', its nature and its extent.[327] The influence of EU law on the meaning of the term is perceptible when the CJEU investigates whether a State has classified an activity as a SG(E)I in order to avoid applying EU law (Article 106 TFEU). Member States enjoy a wide discretion, subject only to control for manifest error.[328] However, 'A Member State's power ... to define services of general economic interest is not unlimited and cannot be exercised arbitrarily for the sole purpose of exempting a particular sector ... from the application of competition rules'.[329]

EU competition law will serve as a basis to define the concept 'service of general interest'. This definition should ascertain the meaning of the term within the context of the rules governing the fundamental freedoms. The fact that little attention has been given to the above term in the context of the fundamental freedoms can be explained by the fact that the concept SG(E)I is not decisive to determine if a situation falls under the scope of the internal market rules. However, the definition takes on a significant role when the application of the free movement rules to cooperative agreements between public authorities is at issue.

The European Commission proposed in 2003 a definition for the concept SGI: 'The term 'services of general interest' cannot be found in the Treaty itself. It is derived in EU practice from the term 'services of general economic interest' and covers both market and non-market services delivered by public authorities as being of general interest and subject to specific public service obligations'.[330] Two elements are important to analyse the concept 'SGI': i) it is either economic or non-economic; ii) it must be of a general interest. Both aspects are examined.

Services of general interest are either economic or non-economic in nature. How is this distinction established? The distinction is not obvious. Indeed, like other concepts in

[325] Case T-289/03, *British United Provident Association Ltd (BUPA), BUPA Insurance Ltd and BUPA Ireland Ltd v. Commission of the European Communities* [2008] *ECR* II-81, at [162].

[326] See in this regard Case T-289/03, *British United Provident Association Ltd (BUPA), BUPA Insurance Ltd and BUPA Ireland Ltd v. Commission of the European Communities* [2008] *ECR* II-00081, at 165: Here the CJEU makes use of the term 'service of general interest' when it is a matter of applying Article 106.2 TFEU and Article 107 TFEU.

[327] Case T-289/03, *British United Provident Association Ltd (BUPA) v. Commission* [2008], at [167].

[328] At [166]; Case T-17/02, *Fred Olsen v. Commission* [2005] *ECR* II-2031, at [216].

[329] Case T-289/03, *British United Provident Association Ltd (BUPA) v. Commission* [2008] *ECR* II-81, at [168].

[330] Green paper on services of general interest COM(2003) 270 final, at [16].

European law, this will be interpreted functionally and evolutionary.[331] At times there is a reference to the concept of 'economic activity' as used in competition law and the rules relating to fundamental freedoms.[332]

An economic activity within the meaning of competition law is 'any activity consisting in offering goods and services on a given market'.[333] It concerns 'market services'.[334] The case law on market services[335] is too numerous to be considered here. Moreover, the distinction between economically or not economically as used in competition law is irrelevant to this study, which is concerned only with the free movement rules. Indeed, in both cases, the presence can lead to the inapplicability of EU law, specifically with regards to the principle of equality and public procurement Directives.

In the context of the rules on free movement, the carrying out of a non-economic general interest service could be an economic activity when it is carried out for remuneration from a public authority.[336] Thus, the concept of economic activity has a different meaning in competition law than it has in internal market law.

Some authors advocate and recognize a common meaning for the term 'economic activity'. The only valid criterion to be applied in order to determine whether an activity falls within the scope of the EU Treaty's provisions on free movement of goods or services[337] is whether the service is marketable.[338] Thus two questions need to be answered: (a) is there a market and (b) does the entity that provides the service of general interest, provides a good or service? From the CJEU case law it can be seen that a public

331 W. Sauter, 'Services of General Economic Interest and Universal Service in EU Law' (*ELR*, 2008), p. 175.

332 U. Neergaard, 'Services of General Economic Interest', in M. Krajewski, U. Neergaard and J. Van Den Gronden (eds), *The Changing Legal Rramework for Services of General Interest in Europe* (TMC Asser Press, 2009), p. 23; M.T. Karayagit, 'The Concept of Services of General Economic Interest Revisited' (*EPL*, 2009), p. 586.

333 Joined Cases C-180/98 to C-184/98, *Pavel Pavlov and Othus v. Stichting Pensioenfonds Medische specialisten* [2006] *ECR* I-6451, at [75].

334 N. Fiedziuk, *Services of General Economic Interest and the Treaty of Lisbon: Opening Doors to a whole new approach or, maintaing the 'status quo'* (*ELR*, 2011), p. 233.

335 Case C-205/03P *Federación Española de Empresas de Tecnología Sanitaria (FENIN) v. Commission of the European Communities* [2006] *ECR* I-6295, at [25]; Case C-309/99, *J.C.J. Wouters, J.W. Savelbergh and Price Waterhouse Belastingadviseurs BV v. Algemene Raad van de Nederlandse Orde van Advocaten* [2002] *ECR* I-1577, at [48–49]; Case C-244/94, *Fédération Française des Sociétés d'Assurance, Société Paternelle-Vie, Union des Assurances de Paris-Vie and Caisse d'Assurance et de Prévoyance Mutuelle des Agriculteurs v. Ministère de l'Agriculture et de la Pêche* [1995] *ECR* I-4013, at [21]; Case C-41/90, *Klaus Höfner and Fritz Elser v. Macrotron GmbH* [1991] *ECR* I-1979, at [22].

336 For several examples, see B. Bossard, 'Le traitement communautaire des services d'intérêt général non economiques' (*RDP*, 2006), p. 1315; L. Driguez and S. Rodrigues, 'Services sociaux d'intérêt social et droit communautaire' (*AJDA*, 2008), p. 193.

337 G. Eckert, 'La distinction entre les services d'intérêt économique général et les services d'intérêt général non-économiques', in L. Potvin-Solis (dir.), *Huitièmes Journées d'Etudes du Pôle Européen Jean Monnet, la libération des services d'intérêt economique général en réseau en Europe* (Bruxelles: Bruylant, 2010), p. 10.

338 M.T. Karayagit, 'The concept of services of general economic interest' (*EPL*, 2009), p. 583.

authority decides whether a market exists and when the service should be placed on the market. There is a need for public service when the market actors have no sufficient incentives to do so and market forces may not result in a satisfactory provision.[339] The choice of a public authority to organize its services in a particular way does not suffice to rule out an economic relationship.[340]

The services must be of general interest. Indeed the CJEU case law on cooperative agreements does not make any difference between economic public tasks or non-economic public tasks. When are services of general or of particular interest? Public authorities consider SGI being of particular importance to citizens so that if there was no public intervention the services would either not be supplied satisfactorily or would be supplied under different conditions.[341]

Society has also an interest in the public service being completed. Service is of public interest and not only for an individual or a group of individuals,[342] but for everyone, it is universal. The service or task has an essential character, which promotes social cohesion.[343]

In the *BUPA* case, the CJEU attempted to convey some minimum criteria to characterize a task or service of general economic interest: 'These are, notably, the presence of an act of the public authority entrusting the operation in question with an SGEI mission and the universal and compulsory nature of that mission'.[344] On this basis the following criteria can be added to the concept 'service of general interest': a person must be entrusted with the exercise of the activity through an act of public authority.[345]

Some legal scholars defend the proposition that there is throughout the European Union a 'common denominator' underlying public services: 'the fact that they are regarded as being in the public interest, and as such are performed by public law or private law organizations under state control or subject to specific state intervention'.[346] According to other legal scholars the term 'public task,' as used in the CJEU case law on cooperative agreements between public authorities (see Chapter 5), can be defined as a task carried

339 Communication from the commission, services of general interest, including social services of general interest: A new European commitment, COM(2007), 725 final.

340 Case T-155/04, *SELEX Sistemi Integrati SpA v. Commission* [2006] *ECR* II-4797, at [87] and [89].

341 M.T. Karayagit, 'The concept of services of general economic interest' (*EPL*, 2009), p. 576.

342 U. Neergaard, 'Services of General Economic Interest', in M. Krajewski, U. Neergaard and J. Van Den Gronden (eds), *The Changing Legal Rramework for Services of General Interest in Europe* (TMC Asser Press, 2009), pp. 21–22.

343 See S. Rodrigues, *Les qualifications concurrentes des activités d'intérêt général en droit communautaire* (*AJDA*, 2006), p. 86.

344 Case T-289/03, *British United Provident Association Ltd (BUPA) v. Commission* [2008] *ECR* II-81, at [172].

345 See also Case C-49/07, *Motosykletistiki Omospondia Ellados NPID (MOTOE) v. Elliniko Dimosio ECR* [2008] I-4863, at [45].

346 E. Malaret Garcia, 'Public service, Public services, Public functions, and Guarantees of the Rights of Citizens: Unchanging needs in a changed context', in M. Freeland and S. Sciarra (eds.), *Public services and citizenship in European law* (Oxford: Clarendon Press, 1998), p. 57.

out according to an obligation under public law.[347] These definitions emphasize the convergence between the concepts 'public services' / 'public tasks' and 'services of general interest'.

4. Public / private divide

The way the CJEU has defined the examined concepts influences the public / private divide in the legal systems of the Member States. The public / private divide is a well-known distinction in legal theory. In most EU Member States this classic distinction exists in one way or another. It is one of the most important distinctions in legal theory.[348] However, the meaning of this distinction, what is understood under public and private law, differs from one Member State to another. Member States use different criteria to make the distinction.[349] Several reference points can be used to categorise a situation or act as public or private.[350] Thus it is difficult to make general statements about the distinction and about the meaning of the concepts of 'private law' and 'public law'.

This explains why EU law does not take into account national distinctions. EU law adopted a functional approach: 'Primary and secondary law was, and largely still is, organised along the lines of the overall objective of (economic) integration as reflected in different subject matters'.[351] Every action or decision (public or private) which endangers the realisation of the internal market comes within the scope of EU law. Notwithstanding this indifference, the public / private divide co-exist within the domain of EU law[352] as it will be illustrated briefly below. This will then be followed by an examination of the divide in two Member States: France and the UK (especially England) which are the selected two EU Member States. Next, the book will examine the relationship between the CJEU case law on the cooperation between public authorities and the divide in the EU and the Member States.

In 2010 Odudu distinguished three phases in the evolution of the public and private distinction in the EU.[353] In a first phase the distinction corresponded, according to Odudu to the divide between the internal market rules applicable to the State and the competition rules applicable to undertakings/private partners. In a second phase the

347 F.L. Hausmann and G. Queisner, 'In-House Contracts and Inter-Municipal Cooperation – Exceptions from the European Union Procurement Law should be applied with caution' (*EPPPL*, 2013), p. 236.

348 C.M. Donelly, *The delegation of Governmental Power to Private parties: A comparative perspective* (Oxford: OUP, 2007), p. 6: 'one of the grand dichotomies of Western thought'.

349 J.-B. Auby, 'La distinction du droit public et du droit privé', in J.-B. Auby (dir.), *L'influence du droit européen sur les catégories du droit public* (Paris: Dalloz, 2010), p. 295.

350 C. Semmelmann, 'Theoretical reflections on the public-private distinction and their traces in European Union law' (*Social legal series*, 2), http://opo.iisj.net/index.php/osls/article/viewFile/102/71, pp. 29–30.

351 C. Semmelmann, 'The Public-Private Divide in European Union Law or an Overkill of Functionalism', http://papers.ssrn.com/sol3/papers.cfm?abstract_id=2056311, p. 13.

352 I. Pelikánová, 'The Role of Competition Law in the Evolution of Community Law', in H. Kanninen et al. (eds.), *EU Competition Law in Context: Essays in Honour of Virpi Tiili* (Oxford: Hart Publishing, 2009), p. 27.

353 O. Odudu, 'The public/private distinction in EU Internal Market Law' (*RTDE*, 2010), 826 et seq.

nature of the activity and the identity of the entity that undertakes the activity, become important to determine if competition (market activity) or internal market (regulatory activity) rules are applicable. Finally, in the third phase the CJEU seems to reject the public private divide. The distinction has therefore become more and more blurred.[354]

4.1. France

France is one of the Member States in which the public-private divide is acknowledged by the judicial system. The organisation, management and actions of French government are regulated by a separate branch of the legal system, namely administrative law. Chapter 6 explains the rules to determine in what situations administrative law will be applicable. The nature of the legal entity involved in the legal relationship, as well as the nature of the activity to which this legal relationship relates are essential. Administrative and constitutional law (i.e. public law) are in France separate branches of the legal system from private law.

Three debates are ongoing in France in relation to the public-private divide: 1) Private law scholars and public law scholars are both under the impression that respectively private law or public law are becoming more important; 2) The divide between private law and public law is not impermeable; 3) The divide between private law and public law is merely ideological.[355] These evolutions in the divide will be reviewed briefly.

Firstly, the premise that is gaining widespread acceptance is that in situations in which citizens are involved, the law applicable to the factual situation cannot change depending on whether one of the parties involved is a public entity. In tort law, for instance, "public law" and "private law" are moving closer.[356] On the other hand, the role of public authority in society, as well as the way in which it serves the public interest, is changing. In the framework of this book, it is important to note that even in France, public authorities are cooperating more and more with the private sector to manage the delivery of services of general interest or to organize their public service sector.[357, 358] More frequently, public authorities are applying instruments of private law to fulfil their public service obligations, or they simply delegate certain competences or tasks to the private

354 M. Poiares Maduro, 'The Chameleon State: EU Law and the Blurring of the Private/Public Distinction in the Market', in R. Nickel (ed.), *Conflict of Laws and Laws of Conflict in Europe and Beyond – Patterns of Supranational and Transnational Juridification* (Antwerp – Oxford – Portland: Intersentia, 2010). See also W. Sauter & H. Schepel, State and Market in European Union Law: The Public and Private Spheres of the Internal
Market before the EU Courts (Cambridge: Cambridge University Press, 2009).

355 C. Beaud, 'La distinction entre droit public et droit privé: un dualisme qui résiste aux critiques', in J.-B. Auby and M. Freedland (eds.), *The Public/Private Divide: une entente assez cordiale*? (Paris: Editions Panthéon-Arras, 2004), pp. 31–38.

356 E. Picard, 'The Public-Private Divide in French law through the History and Destiny of French Administrative Law', in M. Rüffert (ed.), *The Public-Private Law Divide: Potential for transformation* (London: British Institute of International and Comparative Law, 2009), p.77.

357 An explanation of this concept can be found in Chapter 6.

358 E. Picard, *o.c.*, p. 78.

sector. The public service sector is itself becoming more compelled to behave as an economic operator.

New tendencies in the way in which public authorities manage public service, imply a shift in the public-private divide. The divide itself, however, continues to retain its place in France.[359]

4.2. *England*

For a long time, a separate branch of administrative or public law did not exist in England. (see further Chapter 6) For this reason, the concept of a "divide" did not even apply. This finding results from the fact that in England separate courts, competent to review decisions of public authorities, never existed.

The divide was introduced for the first time in the 1970s and 1980s by judges to secure a stronger and more extensive system of judicial review.[360] Public lawyers have propagated the existence of an independent public law, on the basis of the observation that public authorities have special prerogatives and that therefore private law simply does not apply. The most important objective of administrative law is to keep the powers of public authorities under control.[361] This is the role of judicial review (see Chapter 6). According to some, public law concerns the exercise of power by public bodies and the control mechanisms.[362] Public authorities also accomplish specific tasks, causing these services to be considered public.[363] They serve the public interest, an interest not of an economical nature. Public law rules should facilitate the accomplishment of these tasks. Moreover, public authorities act on behalf of citizens, to whom they are accountable. Specific rules govern accountability, rules that are also to be considered public.[364]

Law scholars have considered liberalization, privatization and management a threat to the existence of a separate public law classification.[365] According to some of them, a separate public law remains necessary, even when using instruments of private law: it makes the government accountable to citizens, it facilitates contracting activities and it protects the contractor.[366]

359 L.-A. Barrière, 'Une approche historique de la summa divisio droit public-droit privé', in B. Bonnet et P. Deumier, De *l'interet de la summa divisio droit public-droit prive? (*Paris: Dalloz, 2010), pp. 28–30.

360 C. Harlow and R. Rawlings, *Law and administration* (Cambridge: Cambridge University Press, 2009), p.19.

361 W. Wade and C. Forsyth, *Administrative law*, 11th edition (Oxford: OUP, 2014), p. 4.

362 N. Bamforth and P. Leyland (eds.), *Public law in a Multi-Layered constitution (*Oxford: Hart Publishing, 2003), p. 1.

363 A. Davies, *The public law of government contracts (*Oxford: OUP, 2008), p. 64.

364 A. Davies, *Accountability: a Public Law Analysis of Government by Contract* (Oxford: OUP, 2001), chapter 2.

365 M. Freedland, 'From the Contract of Employment to the Personal Work Nexus' (*Industrial Law Journal*, 2006), nr. 35, p. 107.

366 A. Davies, *The public law of government contracts (*Oxford: OUP, 2008), p. 83.

More and more often, certain social, economic and regulatory matters are being managed by institutions, which are not public bodies. This does not simplify the task of understanding the divided between public and private law.[367] The lack of clarity of the divide remains even today.[368] Some might even call it a paradox: on the one hand the divide still exists; on the other hand it appears outmoded.[369] Private law is determined in referral to phenomena such as privatization, contracting out, public-private partnerships, internal markets, etc. Authority is shared between public authorities and private parties. Therefore, the distinction is heavily criticized. Some authors even advocate a uniform judicial system without such a division.[370]

In general, this book maintains that a public law and private law divide exists, but that it is subject to evolution. Whereas citizens used to be fully subject to public authorities, they are nowadays becoming more and more equal parties. However, even in the latest state of the relationship, there are interests that require rules of public law.

4.3. EU

EU law applicable to service concessions and public contracts results in free competition, which is a primary aim of the EU, influencing the public authorities' decisions. The paramount aims are not the interests of the public authorities, but the interests of the market. (see chapter 2). This already demonstrates a shift in the public/private divide at a national level. The most important aim of public procurement rules at a national level was the maximisation of the profit for public authorities (public purpose). The public procurement Directives aim to eliminate restrictions on the freedom of establishment and the free movement of goods and services in the area of public procurements for the purpose of opening tenders to real and effective competition (private purpose) (see Chapter 2).

Moreover, the personal scope of this specific area of EU law results in a categorization of private entities (e.g. hospitals) as public authorities, and in a submission of these private entities to rules of law which are of a rather public law-nature[371] (see further Chapter 3). The criteria determining the presence of a contracting or public authority demonstrate that the activity of the entity determines the application of the 'public' procurement rules and thus influences the public / private divide. One might say that in doing so, EU law takes into account the shifts within the public/private divide at a national level.

The legal acts, carried out by private legal entities undertaking these tasks, are 'public contracts' because the legal entities, which are largely subject to private law, when

367 S. Arrowsmith, *Civil liability and public authorities* (Winteringham: Earlsgate Press, 1992), p. 3.

368 A. Davies, *The public law of government contracts* (Oxford: OUP, 2008), pp. 73–76.

369 P. Cane, 'Accountability and the public-private Distinction', in N. Bamforth and P. Leyland (eds.), *Public law in a Multi-Layered constitution* (Oxford: Hart Publishing, 2003), pp. 247–276.

370 C. Harlow, '"Public" and "Private" Law: Definition without Distinction' (*CMLR*, 1980), p. 241; D. Oliver, *Common values and the Public-Private Divide* (London: Buttersworth, 1999).

371 See also S. Arrowsmith, *Civil liability and public authority* (Winteringham: Earlsgate Press, 1992), p. 95 et seq.

entering an agreement categorizes as a service concession or as a public contract, have to behave as if they are public legal entities. In this situation, the impact of EU law has the surprising effect, namely that the use of an instrument of private law results in the application of public law 'tinted' legislation. In our opinion, this unintentional influence defeats the privatisation of law applicable to public authorities and to acts of public authorities. A question therefore arises as to whether EU law should take into consideration certain tendencies emerging in the Member States, or to shape them by exercising its influence.

The cooperation between public authorities is a characteristic of the contractualisation of the government, and of the use of instruments of private law by public authorities. Chapter 6 demonstrates that in France this category of agreements was entered into freely without application of certain principles of public law. When discussing the English system, it will become clear that, in principle, all contracts made by a public authority are regulated by common law (see, however, chapter 6 regarding the principles of judicial review). Through the law of public contracts, rules of administrative law have penetrated this field. Moreover, the CJEU reduces the free disposition of a public authority to cooperate with whom it pleases. Chapter 5 will point out that if a public authority chooses a contract with another public authority, of which a private entity is a shareholder, public procurement law normally will apply.

As a result, the Court ignores tendencies that are evolving in most Member States. Thus a situation or cooperation, which in many EU Member States is considered to be governed by private law, is influenced by administrative law due to the impact of CJEU case law on cooperation. As a result, a backwards evolution takes place, causing the "public" element in the divide to become more relevant again. In France, for instance, all agreements closed by a government are now being categorised as a "contrat public" (see chapter 6), whereas classically a distinction was made between "contrats administratifs" and "contrats de droit privé".[372]

5. Concluding observations

The subject of this work is cooperative agreements between public authorities. Chapter 3 has explained the concepts of 'cooperative agreement' and 'public authority'. The following chapters consider only this kind of cooperation. The research tries to prove that the CJEU case law on this type of cooperation has an impact on the way public authorities in the Member States organize or manage their public tasks. To understand this influence a definition of the concept 'public task' was necessary. The book proposes an EU definition inspired by the concept 'service of general interest'.

[372] See D. Ritling, 'L'incidence du droit de l'Union Européenne sur les catégories organiques du droit administratifs', in J.-B. Auby and J. Duteuil de la Rochère (eds.), *Traité de droit administratif européen* (Bruxelles: Bruylant, 2014), pp. 1072–1073.

Each term has been given an autonomous EU definition. As a result situations, which are normally covered by national administrative law, do come within the scope of EU law. The chapter demonstrates that the functional interpretation of the CJEU brings more and more situations under the scope of EU law. This evolution in CJEU case law also explains in part why cooperative agreements between public authorities are influenced by EU law. However, the concept of general interest raises the question if these agreements do not take a special place in EU law, even if they regulate an economic activity. It is one of the questions this book examines.

The examined concepts also prove that EU law does not only have an influence on national concepts, but that the definitions of certain EU concepts are also influenced by national law.

Chapter 4

INFLUENCE OF EU LAW ON PUBLIC AUTHORITY DECISIONS

In chapter 6, it is shown that the public authorities in France and the United Kingdom cooperate with one another in the organisation or management of their public service tasks. The way a public authority organises its public service tasks does not normally fall within the scope of EU law. EU law is first and foremost oriented toward economic objectives and in principle is predominantly concerned with setting rules in the economic sector. It concerns public authority decisions that have an influence on free trade or free competition. One of the distinguishing features of a public authority is precisely that in principle it has no economic objectives,[373] which is why the organisation of its departments and the management of its public service tasks falls *a priori* outside the regulatory activities of the EU. The objectives of a public authority are first and foremost 'social'[374] in nature, and the European Economic Communities (EEC) did not pursue such objectives in 1957.[375]

However, as this book will strive to make clear, EU law does have bearing on how a public authority organises and discharges its public service tasks. The starting point is the case law of the Court of Justice of the European Union (CJEU) based on public procurement Directives and the applicability of the Directives to cooperative agreements between public authorities, as examined in detail below in chapter 5. Taking the principle of equality as a general principle of EU law, the Court has expanded the case law to include service concessions concluded between public authorities.[376] As developed in chapter 3 the notion 'cooperative agreement' is only of relevance to the thesis if it has the characteristics of a public contract or a service concession.

One of the research goals of is to discover how it is possible the EU law could have an influence on cooperative agreements concluded between public authorities. The inquiry of

373 Chapter 3 of the present book explained the notion 'public authority'. One of the featuring elements to define this notion is the activity of this kind of entity. A public authority needs to have activities of general interest, which are not industrial or commercial in nature.

374 The notion 'social' is used here to explain that a public authority serves the interests of the public.

375 In regard to the place of social objectives in EU law see P. Craig, *The Lisbon Treaty* (Oxford/ OUP, 2010), pp. 286–330. These objectives have been occupying more and more space since the Lisbon Treaty. Article 3(3) TEU refers explicitly to a social market economy, social progress, social exclusion, social justice and solidarity.

376 This specific CJEU case law is comprehensively explored in Chapter 5 of this book.

this case law has brought to light a number of possible elements of influence and by the same token has dismissed a number of others as not being germane to the issue. This chapter takes up the conclusions of the research and situates the relevant case law within the larger body of EU law. The CJEU already confirmed that secondary legislation and its interpretation must always be understood within the scope of the relevant Treaty provisions.[377]

The first issue to be determined is the basis of public procurement Directives in EU law and the legal principles implicit in the conclusion of government contracts,[378] or to put it more precisely: is the basis the internal market rules or the EU competition law. The objectives and provisions of one of these areas of EU law help to explain the genesis and content of public procurement Directives. CJEU case law on cooperative agreements could also be explained and understood in this broader framework. But taking this further, it will be even more important to explore how it is possible that such cooperative agreements may be influenced by EU law.

The investigation should demonstrate that the internal market rules lie at the basis of the public procurement Directives and of the principles applicable to certain categories of government contracts. The scope of applicability of these rules and principles should thus also help to explain why certain types of cooperative agreements between public authorities do not come under EU law. This chapter will also seek to identify which aspects of EU law are germane to the specific CJEU case law on cooperative agreements. Which aspect of the scope of applicability could explain this case law whereby these agreements are, under certain conditions, excluded from the scope of EU law? The following aspects are analysed: 1) state measure, 2) interstate interest, 3) restriction and 4) justification.

1. Internal market law or competition law?

In chapter 3, the book concluded that public procurement Directives, the interpretation of which is at the very source of CJEU case law on cooperative agreements, are aimed ultimately at the realisation of the internal market and are oriented toward free competition. This raises the question of which area of EU law public procurement Directives are more properly situated: the internal market rules or competition law? (1.1.) After answering this question, the study then goes on to examine briefly the more specific framework of CJEU case law on cooperative agreements: the internal market rules (1.2.) and freedom of services (1.3.).

1.1. Relevant EU framework

A public authority acts in the general public interest. It daily takes decisions and actions to safeguard these interests.[379] Most often these actions and decisions also have legal

377 Case C-158/96, *Raymond Kohll v. Union des caisses de maladie* [1998] *ECR* I-1931.

378 The notion 'government contract' refers to the range of contracts concluded by public authorities with an independent legal person.

379 The present study only concerns individual decisions taken by a public authority.

repercussions. Some of the consequences may be economic in nature, and may indeed have an impact on the market itself. Where a decision or action of a public authority has an impact on the operation of the economic market, EU law has to be considered, given that a key objective of the EU is the accomplishment of an internal market where goods and services are freely provided across national borders. The impact of EU law on decisions of public authorities is continuously growing.[380]

A decision of a public authority to conclude a contract (public contract, service concession) is a decision that a public authority may take in the general public interest. In absolute terms both internal market rules and the rules of competition may be applied: the decision may either hinder free movement or distort competition between private entities – for example, by creating a monopoly.[381] Especially important for the research is to know which of the two areas of EU law constitutes the broader framework for the public procurement Directives. Indeed, if general EU law can provide an explanation for CJEU case law on cooperative agreements, similarly this must be sought within this framework.

It is generally accepted that public procurement Directives are based on the internal market rules[382] and that the Directives 'are in essence a concrete expression of several fundamental freedoms relating to the internal market'.[383] The Directives are not directly related to competition law.[384] More specifically, the Directives are based on the rules on free movement (see also chapter 2).[385] The objective of the Directives is to facilitate the free movement of goods and services.[386] The reason the public procurement Directives exist is to remove the barriers in public markets, a corollary of removing trade barriers. Internal market rules aim in general to prohibit State measures that hinder free trade. Procurement is one of the important barriers to trade, taking into account its economic importance and the preferences of public authorities for national industry.[387]

CJEU case law on cooperative agreements concerns decisions taken by a public authority to cooperate with another public authority and the extent to which such a decision is

380 See C. Harlow and R. Rawlings, *Law and administration* (Cambridge: Cambridge University Press, 2009), pp. 89–92: the spill-over effect.

381 Regarding EU competition law on public contracts see C. Munro, 'Competition law and public procurement: two sides of the same coin?' (*PPLR*, 2006), pp. 352 et seq.; P.-A. Trepte, 'Public procurement and the Community competition rules' (*PPLR*, 1993), pp. 93–114.

382 S. Arrowsmith, *The law of Public and Utilities Procurement* (London: Sweet and Maxwell, 2005), p. 126; S.E. Hjelmborg, P.S. Jacobsen and S.T. Poulsen, *Public procurement* law (Copenhagen: Djøf Publishing, 2006), p. 35; B.J. Drijber and H. Stergiou, 'Public procurement law and Internal market law' (*CMLR*, 2008), p. 805.

383 J. Wolfswinkel, 'The allocation of a Limited Number of Authorisations' (*Review of European Administrative Law*, 2010), pp. 74–75.

384 Opinion Adv. Gen. Stix-Hackl, Case C-274/02, *Sintesi SpA v Autorità per la Vigilanza sui Lavori Pubblici*, [2004] ECR I-09215 at [30].

385 G.S. Olykke, 'How does the Court of Justice of the European Union pursue competition concerns in a public procurement context?' (*PPLR*, 2011), p. 180.

386 Opinion Adv. Gen. Trstenjak Case C-503/04, *Commission v. Germany* [2007] *ECR* I-6153, at [76].

387 See for example Case 45/87, *Commission v. Ireland ("Dundalk")* [1988] *ECR* 4929.

governed by EU law. In this situation it is assumed *a priori* that the decision is not taken by a private undertaking but that it is a public action, and, as such, falls within the scope of the EU rules on free movement. Chapter 3 makes clear that the scope of the thesis is confined to public authorities. It is part of the essence of public authorities that they fundamentally do not engage in commercial activities. An undertaking is an entity engaged in an economic activity.[388] The notion of undertaking determines the applicability of EU competition law. Competition law is mostly applicable to actions and decisions taken by undertakings. However, such actions and decisions do not come within the scope of the book.

1.2. *Internal market*[389]

The realisation of an internal market, ensuring the free movement of goods, persons, services and capital amongst the various EU Member States, was, and essentially remains, the main objective of the European Union. This emphasises the economic objective of the EU. This objective is the basis for the case law in which the Court of Justice has recognised the EU as a union based on the rule of law.[390] In this sense, EU law should be applied only when in a situation, an action, or a decision might clash with the EU objectives.

The economic goals of the EU are now stated in article 3.2. TEU: 'The Union shall establish an internal market. It shall work for the sustainable development of Europe based on balanced economic growth and price stability, a highly competitive social market economy, aiming at full employment and social progress, and a high level of protection and improvement of the quality of the environment. It shall promote scientific and technological progress'. In contrast to the previous versions of the Treaty, the establishment of an internal market[391] is no longer merely a means to meet the goals of the European Union, but has become a goal in itself. The cornerstones of this internal market are the fundamental freedoms.

The provisions regarding these goals do not in themselves create any subjective rights nor do they impose any duties on the Member States.[392] The provisions, however, are a cardinal point of reference for interpreting the substantive provisions of the Treaty on the European Union (TEU) and the Treaty on the Functioning of the European Union

388 Case C-41/90, *Höfner and Elsner v. Macrotron* [1991] *ECR* I-1979, at [21].

389 Some general books on the internal market rules: C. Barnard and J. Scott (eds.), *The Law of the Single European Market: Unpacking the Premises* (Oxford/Portland: Hart Publishing, 2002); N.N. Shiubhne (ed.), *Regulating the Internal Market* (Cheltenham/Northampton: Edward Elgar Publishing, 2006); C. Barnard, *The Substantive Law of the EU*, 4th edn (Oxford: OUP, 2013).

390 L. Azoulai, *The forms and forces of European legal integration* (EUI Working Papers, 2011/06), http://papers.ssrn.com/sol3/papers.cfm?abstract_id=1899484, pp. 2–3.

391 This term entered EU law mainly via the White Paper *Completing the Internal Market*, COM(85) 310 final.

392 Case C-339/89, *Alsthom Atlantique SA v. Compagnie de construction mécanique Sulzer SA* [1991] *ECR* I-00107; Case C-9/99, *Echirolles Distribution SA v. Association du Dauphiné and Others* [2000] *ECR* I-8207.

(TFEU) (e.g. the rules of free movement)[393] and of the provisions of the EU directives. The objectives help determine how and to what extent a public authority needs to guarantee free movement within the European Union. (teleological interpretation[394]). The CJEU also used a teleological interpretation in its case law on cooperative agreements between public authorities.[395]

The TFEU contains a large number of provisions that should guarantee the free movement of goods, persons, services and capital, the so-called fundamental freedoms. They have to be considered as constitutional Union rights.[396] The CJEU uses a teleological interpretation to define the scope of those rights. The rights must achieve their full effect ('effet utile'). The CJEU seeks through the notions used in the Treaties (e.g. Member State or restriction) or in directives (e.g. public procurement Directives: public authority or contract) to identify as many persons and situations that jeopardize the realisation of the internal market. The realisation of free movement is one of the basic requisites for the ultimate achievement of an internal market. This is still an ongoing process. Free trade should in the end lead to comparative advantage and economies of scale.

The free movement provisions are aimed at removing barriers between Member States: 'The market freedoms are traditionally considered to have an identity of aim: to contribute to the completion and functioning of the internal market through the elimination of obstacles to economic free movement between Member States and the creation of an area without internal frontiers in which the free movement of goods, persons, services and capital is ensured'.[397]

A key element in the realisation of this free movement is the principle of non-discrimination on the ground of nationality (Art. 18 TFEU). By virtue of this principle, every restriction on free movement based on nationality is *a priori* prohibited. For one thing this guarantees equal treatment for all European citizens: 'it requires that persons in a situation governed by Community law be placed on a completely equal footing with nationals of the member state'.[398] This principle is less important for matters of public contracts, because Articles 34, 49 and 56 TFEU, which are the bedrock for public procurement Directives and the principle of equal treatment applicable to public contracts and service concessions, contain similar provisions that exclude discriminative behaviour.

393 M. Fallon, *Droit matériel général de Union européenne* (Bruxelles: Bruylant, 2002), p. 17 with reference to case C-78/90, *Compagnie Commerciale de l'Ouest and others v. Receveur Principal des Douanes de La Pallice Port* [1992] *ECR* I-1847; Case C-260/89, *Elliniki Radiophonia Tiléorassi AE and Panellinia Omospondia Syllogon Prossopikou v. Dimotiki Etairia Pliroforissis and Sotirios Kouvelas and Nicolaos Avdellas and others* [1991] *ECR* I-02925.

394 See on this notion Chapter 3.

395 See Chapter 5.

396 J. Baquero-Cruz, *Between Competition and Free Movement the Economic Constitutional Law of the European Community* (London: Hart Publishing, 2002), p. 81.

397 P. Caro de Sousa, 'Catch me if you can? The Market Freedoms Ever-expanding Outer Limits' (*EJLS*, 2011), p. 167.

398 Case 186/87, *Ian Willam Cowan v. Trésor public* [1989] *ECR* 195, at [219].

Public procurement Directives are based on and include concrete applications of, in particular, the TFEU dispositions on the free movement of goods and on free movement of services.[399] In essence, the Directives are above all 'a concrete expression of … the free provision of services'.[400] This thesis is concerned with how public authorities organise and manage their public service tasks. Consequently, the thesis is above all interested in the provision of services; hence, it is focussed exclusively on the freedom of services (see section 1.3.).

Chapter 2 demonstrated that two objectives underlie the public procurement Directives: the realisation of the internal market and ensuring effective competition. Before the Treaty of Lisbon the activities of the EU institutions had to ensure such effective competition (Article 3 EC). This objective disappeared in the TFEU. The objective can now only be found in Protocol n° 27 on the Internal Market and Competition[401]: 'Considering that the internal market as set out in Article 3 of the Treaty on European Union includes a system ensuring that competition is not distorted'. Legal scholars claim that this 'objective' is challenged by its disappearance in the EU treaties, although they confirm the necessity to protect effective competition in order to realise the internal market.[402] Taking into account these shifts in the EU treaties it is rather surprising that the CJEU emphasized the opening-up to undistorted competition recently as the principle objective of the EU rules in the field of public procurement.[403] Although this objective remains important in the field of public procurement, it is difficult to defend that it is the principle objective in the light of the Treaty of Lisbon.

1.3. Freedom of services[404]

Article 56 TFEU states that 'restrictions on freedom to provide services within the Community shall be prohibited in respect of nationals of Member States who are established in a State of the Community other than that of the person for whom the services are intended'. The purpose of this provision is to open the service markets in all the Member States to providers from other Member States.[405]

399 Opinion Adv. Gen. Stix-Hackl, Case C-274/02, *Sintesi SpA v Autorità per la Vigilanza sui Lavori Pubblici*, [2004] ECR I-09215 at [29].

400 B.J. Drijber and H. Stergiou, 'Public procurement law and internal market law' (*CMLR*, 2009), p. 805.

401 OJ [2010] C83/309.

402 J. Drexl, 'Competition Law as Part of the European Constitution', in A. von Bogdandy and J. Bast (eds.), *Principles of European Constitutional Law* (Munich: C.H. Beck/Oxford: Hart Publishing, 2011), pp. 664–665.

403 Case C-15/13, *Technische Universität Hamburg-Harburg, Hochschul-Informations-System GmbH v. Datenlotsen Informationssysteme GmbH* [2014] *ECR* I-00000, at [22].

404 Some general books on freedom of services: J. Snell, *Goods and Services in EC Law* (Oxford: OUP, 2002); L. Woods, *Free Movement of Goods and Services within the European Community* (Ashgate, Aldershot, 2004); V. Hatzopoulos, *Regulating Services in the European Union* (Oxford: OUP, 2012).

405 Case C-226/09, *European Commission v. Ireland* [2010] *ECR* I-11807, at [30].

The application of Article 56 TFEU is in the first instance contingent on the concept 'service'. Article 57 TFEU regards services as activities not falling under the other freedoms. This article also provides for a definition: those which are 'normally provided for remuneration'. The notion of 'service' actually refers to a specific form of the notion 'economic activity'. The two notions define one another mutually.

In the context of the free movement of services the CJEU makes use of two classic criteria to determine if there is an economic activity: (1) there must be a demand or supply of services and (2) a remuneration must be present.[406] Contracts concerning the demand or the supply of services do not concern the manufacture or supply of goods.[407] Public tasks delivered by an undertaking or a public authority to another public authority can also be considered as services. The second criterion, in particular, stirred up some debate within the case law. The Court of Justice proffered an extensive interpretation to this criterion.

The meaning originally attached to the term 'remuneration' has also undergone an extensive evolution in CJEU case law. Remuneration is normally determined by an agreement between providers and recipients of services.[408] The Court recently ruled that remuneration need not be agreed between the parties, nor does it need to be provided by the service recipient, and it can even be subject to later reimbursement by a third party.[409]

Remuneration does not imply that a payment must necessarily take place in money form. It is sufficient that the service provider receives something of equivalence in exchange.[410] Nor is an immediate payment on the part of the beneficiary necessary.[411] The service cannot be free of charge, but the provider should not necessarily make a profit.[412]

In *Ordine degli Architetti* the CJEU had to investigate whether a horizontal cooperative agreement between public authorities falls within the scope of public procurement Directives.[413] However, the CJEU first looked into whether this form of cooperation could be qualified as a public service contract. Indeed, only in that case are the aforementioned Directives applicable. A public service contract requires a contract for pecuniary interest (a remuneration) and a service. The CJEU ruled that both elements

406 O. Odudu, 'Economic activity as a limit to community law' in C. Barnard and O. Odudu, *The Outer Limits of European Union Law* (Oregon: Hart Publishing, 2009), pp. 228–229.

407 Case C-268/99, *Aldona Malgorzata Jony and Others v. Staatssecretaris van Justitie* [2001] *ECR* I-8615, at [71].

408 Case 263/86, *Belgian State v. René Humbel* [1988] *ECR* 5365, at [17].

409 P. Caro de Susa, 'Catch me if you can? The Market Freedoms Ever-expanding Outer Limits' (*EJLS*, 2011), p. 181; P. Cabral, 'The internal market and the right to cross border medical care' (*ELR*, 2004), p. 677; L. Woods, *Free Movement of Goods and Services within the European Community* (Ashgate: Aldershot, 2004), pp. 168–174.

410 Case 196/96, *Steymann v. Staatssecretaris van Justitie* [1988] *ECR* 2085.

411 Case 382/85, *Bond van Adverteerders and others v. The Netherlands* [1988] *ECR* 2085, at [16].

412 Case C-281/06, *Jundt v. Finanzamt Offenburg* [2007] *ECR* I-12231, at [32] to [33].

413 Case C-159/11, *Azienda Sanitaria Locale di Lecce, Università del Salento v. Ordine degli Ingegneri della Provincia di Lecce and Others* [2012] *ECR* I-00000.

were present. Nevertheless, the CJEU examined if this cooperative agreement, which could be defined as a public contract, did not fall outside the scope of EU law after all. Consequently, CJEU case law on cooperative agreements is not based simply on the notions of 'service' or 'remuneration'.

It also follows from Article 56 TFEU this provision is applicable only in matters concerning cross-border services. The meaning of this notion is discussed in point 4 below.

2. Applicability of EU law to State Measures

For the rules of the internal market to apply, there must exist a State measure as defined by EU case law. The notion 'State Measure' consists of two elements: Measure and State. Both terms will be briefly analysed.

The first consideration that raises the issue of the applicability of EU internal market law is, of course, that some measure has been taken. For a long time the question was raised if individual decisions (e.g. tendering decisions, the decision to cooperate with other public authorities) were also covered by this notion. It is implicitly clear from CJEU case law that the notion 'measure' receives an extensive interpretation.

Any decision or action that affects the fundamental freedoms and deters cross-border trade is covered by the notion 'measure'. It may be a directive, an individual decision,[414] or even an administrative practice. It may concern an obligation, a prohibition, a condition, or a restriction. The action needs not to have any direct influence on an economic activity. An indirect influence is sufficient.[415] Every decision taken in the context of a procurement procedure could constitute a measure.[416] The present thesis is solely interested in individual decisions, for instance, the decision to cooperate.

The thesis studies a specific decision to cooperate. This decision is taken by a public authority or a contracting authority. Chapter 3 examined the notions 'public authority' and 'contracting authority'. It was suggested that these concepts were actually derived from the concepts 'State' or 'Member State'.

To what extent do decisions of public authorities that concern the organisation of public tasks fall within the applicability of EU law? This question is linked by some scholars to Article 345 TFEU.[417] This Article reads as follows: 'The treaties shall in no way prejudice

414 Case C-244/97, *Erich Ciola v. Land Vorarlberg* [1999] *ECR* I-02517, at [32].

415 H.D. Jarass, 'A Unified Approach to the Fundamental Freedoms', in M. Andenas and W.-H. Roth (eds.), *Services and Free Movement in EU Law* (Oxford: OUP, 2002), p. 149.

416 M. Trybus, 'Public contracts in European Union Internal Market Law: Foundations and Requirements', in R. Noguellou and U. Stelkens (eds.), *Comparative law on Public Contracts* (Brussel: Bruylant, 2010), p. 90.

417 C. Boutayeb, 'Une recherche générale sur la place et les fonctions de l'intérêt général and droit communautaire' (*RTDE*, 2003), p. 593; A.L. Durviaux and N. Thirion, 'Les modes de gestion des

the rules in Member States governing the system of property ownership'. The Member States retain their competence over property ownership.

According to some legal scholars,[418] the authors of the Treaty of Rome added this provision to persuade the Member States to sign the Treaty. The provision was intended primarily to facilitate the nationalisation process of the industrial sector that made its advent in the 1950s.[419] The Member States have the right to a public sector and moreover a public sector that can intervene on the Market.[420] Article 345 TFEU is one of the provisions in the treaties, which confirm explicitly a competence of the Member States.

The principle of neutrality, as derived from Article 345 TFEU, has various implications for the competences of the public authorities in each Member State. This principle guarantees the freedom of a public authority to decide whether, when, and how it will embark upon privatisation.[421] A public authority itself decides whether an economic activity should be taken on, and if so, whether it should do so in cooperation with another public authority, or whether it should delegate this economic activity on to a third party[422]: 'A public authority which is a contracting authority has the possibility of performing the tasks conferred on it in the public interest by using its own administrative, technical, and other resources, without being obliged to call on outside entities not forming part of its own departments'.[423] In brief, the Member States themselves determine the way they intervene in the economic market and how they organise their apparatus.[424]

This provision is usually linked with the competence of Member States to organise the delivery of services of general interest.[425] By virtue of being the owner of undertakings

services publics locaux, la réglementation relative aux marchés publics et le droit communautaire' (*JT*, 2004), p. 26.

418 K. Lenaerts and K. Vanvoorden, 'The right to property in the case law of the Court of Justice of the European Communities', in H. Vandenberghe (ed.), *Property and human rights* (Brugge: Die Keure, 2006), p. 198; H. Smit and P.E. Herzog, 'Preliminary observations on article 222', in H. Smit and P.E. Herzog, *The Law of the European Community - A commentary on the EEC Treaty, Vol. 5* (New York: Mattew Bunder, 1998), at 6–216.58.

419 D. Caruso, 'Private Law and Public Stakes in European Integration: the case of Property' (*ELJ*, 2004), p. 755.

420 A. Verhoeven, 'Privatisation and EU Law: Is the European Commission 'Neutral' with Respect to Public v. Private Ownership of Companies' (*ICLQ*, 1996), p. 863.

421 *Ibidem*, p. 863.

422 M.T. Karayigit,*The notion of services of general economic interest* (*EPL*, 2009), p. 580.

423 Case C-26/03, *Stadt Halle and RPL Recyclingpark Lochau GmbH v. Arbeitsgemeinschaft Thermische Restabfall- und Energieverwertungsanlage TREA Leuna* [2005] *ECR* I-00001, at [48].

424 E. Szyszczak, *The Regulation of the State in Competitive Markets in the EU* (Oxford: Hart Publishing, 2007), p. 107.

425 C. Boutayeb, 'Une recherche générale sur la place et les fonctions de l'intérêt général and droit communautaire' (*RTDE*, 2003), p. 593; A.L. Durviaux and N. Thirion, 'Les modes de gestion des services publics locaux, la réglementation relative aux marchés publics et le droit communautaire' (*JT*, 2004), p. 26.

that perform services of general interest, a public authority is able to control the quality of the delivered public service. Public ownership is one way to organise a service of general interest. The European Union would, in accordance with Article 345 TFEU, be neutral as regards the way a public authority organises and discharges its missions of general interest. By extension, cooperative agreements between public authorities, which is one of the ways to organise or discharge public service tasks, would also be covered by the principle of neutrality.

Based on a thorough examination of the preparatory works of Article 345 TFEU, the Article itself and the place of this Article in the Treaty, most authors infer that the provision refers to all measures taken by a public authority to shape its national economic activity. The EU has to adopt a neutral attitude toward privatization and nationalisation.[426] The Commission and the European Parliament draw a similar conclusion on the basis of other legislation and interventions.[427] The principle of neutrality merely signifies that each Member State may organise as it thinks fit the system of ownership of undertakings.[428]

The Court does, however, place Article 345 TFEU within the other competences of the European Union and the objectives of the TFEU. According to the Court,[429] property in terms of competence still belongs to the Member States, but the property regimes, as they exist in every Member State, do not escape application of the fundamental rules of the TFEU. Thus, the CJEU gives a restrictive interpretation to Article 345 TFEU. What are these fundamental rules?

It is beyond the scope of the thesis to deal with each judgment of the Court that recognises such a fundamental right. Only the case law that shows any relevance to the subject of the thesis will be mentioned. Thus, the Court recognised in a whole series of judgments and rulings[430] the provisions on free movement of services and on freedom of establishment (Articles 49 and 56 TFEU) as being fundamental rules. It is based on these provisions

426 P. Leger (éd.), *Commentaire article par article des traités UE et CE* (Brussels, 2000), p. 1878; W. Devroe, 'Privatizations and community law: neutrality versus policy' (*CMLR*, 1997), p. 268; P.-C. Müller-Graff, *Gemeinsames Privatrecht in der Europäischen Gemeinschaft* (Baden-Baden: Nomos, 1993), p. 23; S. Bartels, 'Europees privaatrecht: over de bevoegdheidsverdeling tussen Unie en lidstaat met betrekking tot het eigendomsrecht' (*AA*, 1999), pp. 250–251; B. Akkermans and E. Ramaekers, 'Article 345 TFEU (ex Article 295 EC), Its Meanings and Interpretations' (*ELJ*, 2010), p. 314; D. Caruso, 'Private law and public stakes in European integration: the case of property' (*ELJ*, 2004), p. 755. See, however, V. Withofs, Artikel 345 VWEU: een rem op de Europese harmonisatie van het goederenrecht? (*TBBR*, 2013), p. 71.

427 B. Akkermans and E. Ramaekers, 'Article 345 TFEU (ex Article 295 EC), Its Meaning and Interpretation' (*ELJ*, 2010), p. 308.

428 Case C-367/98, *Commission of the European Communities v. Portuguese Republic* [2002] *ECR* I-04731, at [28].

429 Joined cases T-228/99 and T-233/99, *Westdeutsche Landesbank Girozentrale and Land Nordrhein-Westfalen v. Commission of the European Communities* [2003] *ECR* II-435, at [192]; Case C-302/97, *Klaus Konle v. Republik Österreich* [1999] *ECR* I-3099, at [38].

430 Case 182/83, *Robert Fearon & Company Limited v. Irish Land Commission* [1984] *ECR* 3677; Case C-302/97, *Klaus Konle v. Republik Österreich* [1999] *ECR* I-3099; Case C-300/01, *Doris Salzmann* [2003] *ECR* I-4899; Case C-452/01, *Margarethe Ospelt and Schlössle Weissenberg Familienstiftung* [2003] *ECR* I-9743.

that the Court of Justice derived the principle of equal treatment, a principle that requires a public authority signing a public contract or service concession contract to guarantee transparency.[431] These provisions and principles are the basis for the public procurement Directives and they oblige public authorities to organise tendering procedures. These provisions and principles are applicable even if a public authority takes a measure that concerns the organisation or management of public service tasks.

In general, the Court of Justice confirms that if public authorities decide something about their property regime, they are still bound by the rules on free movement and, thus, also implicitly by the Directives on public procurement.[432] It therefore seems logical that the Court of Justice has never referred to the Article 345 TFEU to exclude from the scope of European Union law measures with regard to the organisation of the services of public interest.

On the basis of Article 345 TFEU, the Court seems to seek a balance of powers between the EU and the Member States,[433] a balance the Court also appears to be searching for in its case law on cooperative agreements between public authorities.

The primacy of the free movement provisions in a number of national competences can be explained in yet another way. In the 1950s, some European countries decided to transfer competences to institutions that were jointly established. A common interest (peace, progress) justified this transfer. It seems logical that in such situation, when a conflict incurs, the national interest must yield to the supranational interest.[434]

It follows from the CJEU's case law that a decision to tender a public contract or a service concession falls within the meaning of 'measure'.[435] This is also the case where a public authority decides to cooperate with another public authority through a public contract or a service concession. These kinds of decisions are State measures. These decisions or measures have been taken by public authorities. A first confirmation can be found in *Commission v. Italy*[436], where the CJEU implicitly confirmed that an agreement between

431 Case C-87/94, *Commission v. Belgium (Walloon Buses)* [1996] *ECR* I-02043; Case C-275/98, *Unitron Scandinavia A/S* [1999] *ECR* 1–8305, at [31]; Case C-324/98, *Telaustria Verlags Gmbh* [2000] *ECR* I-10745.

432 Case 182/83, *Robert Fearon and Company Ltd v. The Irish Land Commission* [1984] *ECR* 3677, at [7] and [8]; Case C-367/98, *Commission v. Portugal* [2002] *ECR* I-4731, at [48]. See also Case C-483/99, *Commission v. France* [2002] *ECR* I-4781, at [44] and Case C-503/99, *Commission v. Belgium* [2002] *ECR* I-4809, at [44].

433 A. Verhoeven, 'Privatisation and EC Law: Is the European Commission 'neutral' with respect to public versus private ownership of companies?' (*ICLQ*, 1996), p. 865.

434 Cf. D. Simon, 'L'intérêt général national vu par les droits européens' (*Cah. const.*, 2006), p. 3.

435 M. Trybus, 'Public contracts in European Union Internal Market Law: Foundations and Requirements', in R. Noguellou and U. Stelkens (eds.), *Comparative law on Public Contracts* (Brussel: Bruylant, 2010), p. 90 with reference to Case C-243/89, *Commission v. Danmark (Storebaelt)* [1993] *ECR* I-2253; Case C-359/93, *Commission v. The Netherlands (UNIX)* [1995] *ECR* I-157; Case C-59/00, *Bent Mousten Vestergaard v. Spotrup Boligselkab* [2001] *ECR* I-9505.

436 Case C-3/88, *Commission v. Italy* [1989] *ECR* 04035, at [8] and [9].

a public authority and an entity entirely owned by the same public authority falls under the scope of Articles 49 and 56 TFEU and the principle of equality.

As already mentioned, the Member States originally had the competence to determine how their public authorities organise public services and the means they could use to accomplish tasks of general public interest. One of these means is cooperation with another public authority. Originally, in the relationship between State and Market in EU law, the State had priority in this field of action. Consequently, the Member States possess the authority to regulate this field.

In the European Union this national competence is embedded in the mainly economic objectives toward which the European Union strives. The legal precepts that inform the endeavour to achieve these objectives have priority over national competences. The functional interpretation given by the CJEU has the effect that the EU rules not only influence those national regulations and decisions that are economic in nature but also have an impact on regulations governing the organization and management of public services and on individual decisions taken in this regard.

Thus, by its very nature the European Union carries the greater weight and this preponderance means that the objectives of its rules and regulations are generally deferred to in all actions taken by a public authority. Moreover, through its case law, the CJEU strives to strike a permanent balance between the powers of the EU and those of the Member States. This endeavour leaves its mark on the evolution of the European Economic Constitution.[437] CJEU case law on cooperative agreements between public authorities is an example of this endeavour, which is emphasised in the thesis. The notion 'European Economic Constitution' is defined for the purpose of the thesis as 'a mere analytical tool for describing the relationship between the market and intervention in a given legal order. An economic constitution understood in these terms includes provisions and case law that are fundamental for the economic orientation of a

437 H. Armin, 'The Economic Constitution within the Internal Market', in A. von Bogdandy and J. Bast (eds.), *Principles of European Constitutional Law* (Munich: C.H. Beck/Oxford: Hart Publishing, 2011), pp. 589–629. C. Joerges, 'Unity in Diversity as Europe's Vocation and Conflicts Law as Europe's Constitutional Form', in, R. Nickel and A. Greppi (eds.), *The Changing Role of Law in the Age of Supra- and Transnational Governance* (Baden-Baden: Nomos, 2012), pp. 99–133. Joerges, Christian, 'What is left of the European Economic Constitution? A Melancholic Eulogy' (*ELR*, 2005), pp. 461–489. Joerges, Christian, and Florian Rödl, 'The 'Social Market Economy' as Europe's Social Model?', in L. Magnusson and B. Stråth (eds.), *A European Social Citizenship? Preconditions for Future Policies in Historical Light* (Brussels: Lang, 2005), pp. 125–158. Weiler, Joseph H.H., 'Does Europe Need a Constitution? Reflections on Demos, Telos and the German Maastricht Decision' (*ELR*, 1995), pp. 219–258. J. Gerber, *'Constitutionalising Economy: German neo-liberalism, Competition Law and the 'New' Europe'* (*The American Journal of Comparative Law*, Vol. 42, No.1), pp. 25–84. M. Maduro, 'Contrapunctual [sic] Law: Europe's Consitutional Pluralism in Action', in N. Walker (ed), *Sovereignty in Transition* (Oxford: Hart, 2003); M. Kumm, 'The Jurisprudence of Constitutional Conflict: Constitutional Supremacy in Europe before and after the Constitutional Treaty' (*ELJ*, 2005), p. 262.

community regardless of what their underlying philosophical concepts are and whether they are laid down in a document or derived from court cases'.[438]

In developing its case law the CJEU brought under the jurisdiction of EU law the relationship of cooperation that takes place between public authorities. The Court approached the relationship from the standpoint of the objectives and rules upon which the EU legal order rests. If such cooperation distorts or threatens to distort competition or if it hinders market access, then EU law applies (i.e. the public procurement Directives and the principle of equal treatment). In this sense, CJEU case law on cooperative agreements is a concrete example of the manner in which the Court interprets Article 345 TFEU in general. The Member States are indeed competent to regulate the organisation of their own administration, but decisions in this regard remain subject to the rules of the internal market.

However, the notion 'measure' is not decisive for placing cooperative agreements between public authorities beyond the range of applicability of EU law. Every action, every decision by a State is indeed a measure, according to EU law. Even when a public authority calls upon its own administration, it is taking a measure.

According to legal experts,[439] the CJEU case law on cooperative agreements should be understood in terms of the CJEU's mistrust of certain public authority decisions. The Court mistrusts the various devices that public authorities use to avoid the application of the public procurement Directives. Public authorities supposedly do this by creating all sorts of institutions or agreements, which then may not come under the term 'contracting authority', and hence need not comply with the provisions of the public procurement Directives. To avoid such evasions, CJEU has broadly interpreted the notions 'contracting authority' and 'body governed by public law'. The CJEU case law on cooperative agreements could be understood in the same way according to these scholars. These scholars seem to seek an explanation for this case law in the notion 'State'.

The presence of a body governed by public law and the application of the public procurement Directives on cooperative agreements between public authorities is determined in both cases by a dependency factor. The criteria (financing, control, creation of management bodies) that define this dependency for a body governed by public law and, consequently, the notion of contracting authority, are broadly interpreted by the CJEU (see chapter 3). In deference to cooperative agreements between public authorities,

438 C. Semmelmann, 'The European Union's economic constitution under the Lisbon Treaty soul-searching among lawyers shifts the focus to procedure' (*ELR*, 2010), p. 517 with reference regarding the first sentence of this quote, cf. W. Sauter, 'The Economic Constitution of the European Union' (*Col. J. Eur. L.* 2, 1998), p. 29; M. Poiares Maduro, *We the Court, The European Court of Justice and the European Economic Constitution. A Critical Reading of Article 30 of the EC Treaty* (Oxford: Hart, 1998), p. 7; A. Peters, *Theorie der Elemente der Verfassung Europas* (Duncker & Humblot, 2001), p. 124; A. Hatje, 'The Economic Constitution within the Internal Market', in A. v. Bogdandy and J. Bast (eds), *Principles of European Constitutional Law*, 2nd edn (Oxford: Hart/Beck, 2010), p. 589.

439 W. Sauter and H. Schepel, *State and Market in European Union Law* (Cambridge: Cambridge University Press, 2009), p. 55.

the dependency criteria are given a rather strict interpretation.[440] Indeed, a broad interpretation would in this case preclude precisely the application of EU law. But in both cases the criteria to determine if a situation falls within the range of applicability of EU law and the objectives that lie at the basis of EU law, i.e. the public procurement Directives, have a role in determining to what extent a situation falls within the scope of EU law.

The CJEU case law on cooperative agreements cannot be elucidated with reference to the notion of 'contracting authority' or 'body governed by public law' nor with reference to the nature of an institution subject to EU law. In the first place, the CJEU itself introduced the term 'contract' as an element in the definition of the term 'public procurement' to underpin this case law.[441] The CJEU never took the notion 'public authority' and, thus, the notion of 'State', as a starting point in this specific case law. Finally, cooperative agreements concluded between public authorities existed in France and Belgium already before the creation of the EU. There is no proof that those kinds of arrangements were or are used to circumvent the application of EU law.

It will appear that other elements than the concepts of State, measure or public authority are more likely to explain the CJEU case law on cooperative agreements between public authorities.

3. Interstate element

EU law is only applicable if the situation contains an interstate element. According to the TFEU, free movement entails the prohibition of every restriction 'between Member States'[442] and on the territory of another Member State[443]: 'that the Treaty rules governing freedom of movement and regulations adopted to implement them cannot be applied to cases that have no factor linking them with any of the situations governed by Community law and all elements of which are purely internal to a single Member State'.[444]

Any situation occurring solely within one Member State falls normally outside the scope of European Union law. A purely internal situation may be defined as a situation in which no factual element shows a connection beyond the borders of any Member State. This term is also a factor in determining the division of competences between the Member States and the European Union.

440 See Case C-26/03, *Stadt Halle und RPL Recyclingpark Lochau GmbH v. Arbeitsgemeinschaft Thermische Restabfall- und Energieverwertungsanlage TREA Leuna* [2005] *ECR* I-00001, at [46]; Case C-458/03, *Parking Brixen GmbH v. Gemeinde Brixen* [2005] *ECR* I-08585, at [64].

441 Case C-107/98, *Teckal v. Comune di Viano* [1999] *ECR* I-8121. See Chapter 4.

442 Articles 28, 30, 34, 35 and 63.1 TFEU.

443 Article 43 TFEU.

444 Cases C-64/96 and C-65/96, *Land Nordrhein-Westfalen v. Uecker and Jacquet v. Land Nordrhein-Westfalen* [1997] *ECR* I-3177, at [16]; Case C-212/06, *Government of the French Community and Walloon Government* [2008] *ECR* I-1683, at [33], and Case C-434/09, *McCarthy* [2011] *ECR* I-3375, at [45]; Joined Cases C-197/11 and C-203/11, *Eric Libert and Others v. Gouvernement flamand and All Projects & Developments NV and Others v. Vlaamse Regering* [2013] *ECR* I-00000, at [33].

A purely internal situation also bears comparison with the case law on cooperative agreements between public authorities. In the latter case, EU law is not applicable when the connection between the public or contracting authority and its subsidiary is so close that an economic activity is hardly in question when the two legal persons build up a relationship. The relationship remains in-house. In a purely internal situation, an economic activity remains within the national borders. Perhaps there is something to learn from what case law has developed regarding the notion 'purely internal situation'.

Case law on purely internal situations has undergone a significant evolution. This evolution is taken up in the first point. As regards the awarding of public and service concession contracts falling outside the scope of public procurement Directives, the Court has developed its own criterion. Namely the Court operates on a cross-border interest in order to delimit the competence of the European Union. The public procurement Directives themselves are applicable, irrespective of the presence of a cross-border element. The value of the contract determines whether this specific EU law applies. In such a situation a cross-border interest is presumed.

In *Saunders*[445] the Court of Justice referred for the first time to the notion of 'situations which are wholly internal to a Member State'. In that situation there is no European factor, according to the Court. With this criterion the Court created one of the levers to delimit the scope of European Union law, and more specifically of the provisions of free movement. Traditionally the Court has deemed it necessary that a national border would be effectively and physically crossed.[446] Obviously this is easily discernible. When all elements are situated within one Member State, European Union law regarding free movement is not applicable.[447] In *Saunders* the CJEU took a purely geographical approach. The free movement provisions do not apply to activities that have no factor linking them to any of the situations governed by EU law and/or that are confined in all aspects within a single Member State.[448]

Since *Saunders* the CJEU case law has evolved significantly. The Court confirmed in more recent case law[449] that the application of rules concerning the free movement of goods is not ruled out merely because all the elements of a certain case are situated within

445 Case 175/78, *R. v. Saunders* [1979] *ECR* 1129, at [11].

446 A. Tryfonidou, 'Reverse discrimination in purely internal situations: An incongruity in a Citizens' Europe' (*LIEI*, 2008), p. 14; M. Poiares Maduro, 'The scope of European remedies. The case of purely internal situations and reverse discrimination', in C. Kilpatrick, T. Novitz and P. Skidmore (eds), *The Future of European Remedies* (Oxford: Hart publishing, 2000), pp. 122–123.

447 See also Joined Cases C-197/11 and C-203/11, *Eric Libert and Others v. Gouvernement flamand and All Projects & Developments NV and Others v. Vlaamse Regering* [2013] *ECR* I-00000, at [33].

448 Case 20/87, *Ministère public v. André Gauchard* [1987] *ECR* 4879; Case C-198/89, *Commission of the European Communities v. Hellenic Republic* [1991] *ECR* I-00727, at [9]; Case 513/03, *Heirs of M. E. A. van Hilten-van der Heijden v. Inspecteur van de Belastingdienst/Particulieren/Ondernemingen outsideland te Heerlen* [2006] *ECR* I-10653.

449 Cases C-321/94 to C-324/94, *Christian Poucet v. Assurances Générales de France and Caisse Mutuelle Régionale du Languedoc-Roussillon and Daniel Pistre v. Caisse Autonome Nationale de Compensation*

a single Member State. In *Guimont*[450] the CJEU also stated that a preliminary question from a national court would only be rejected if it were quite obvious that the interpretation of European Union law sought bears no relation to the actual nature of the case or to the subject matter of the main action.[451] According to *Guimont*, the CJEU is also competent if the interpretation of EU law sought by the referring court may be useful to it if its national law were to require it to grant the same rights as those, which an operator of another Member State would derive from EU law in the same situation.[452] This case law has been extended to the freedom of capital,[453] the freedom of services[454] and the freedom of establishment.[455]

In a market that is slowly becoming one, it is progressively hard to draw a distinction between purely internal situations and 'European' situations. Since for the awarding of government contracts the CJEU has developed a proper criterion to delineate the division of competences between the EU and the Member States in matters of interstate trade, the notion of a 'purely internal situation' and the CJEU case law elucidating this concept are less important for the thesis. However, this particular case law also suggests that the influence of EU law is expanding to the detriment of national law.

In the context of awarding 'public contracts' (public procurement and service concessions), the Court of Justice has devised a special criterion to check whether a situation is governed by European Union law: 'cross border interest'.[456]

In *Coname*[457] the Court ruled that within the scope of the freedom of establishment and free movement of services, European Union law (i.e. the principle of equal treatment and the obligation of transparency) would be applicable only if an undertaking from one Member State was interested in providing the service for a public authority of another Member State.

de l'Assurance Vieillesse des Artisans (Cancava) [1997] *ECR* I-2343, at [44]. See also Case C-379/98, *Preussen Elektra AG v. Schleswag AG* [2001] *ECR* I-2099.

450 Case C-448/98, *Criminal proceedings against Jean-Pierre Guimont* [2000] *ECR* I-10663.

451 At [20] to [23].

452 See also Joined Cases C-357/10 and C-358/10, *Ducmo Gpa Srl, Gestione Servizi Pubblici Srl and Irtel Srl v. Comune di Baranzate and Comune di Venegono Inferiore* [2012] *ECR* I-00000, at [28]; Joined Cases C-197/11 and C-203/11, Eric Libert and Others v. Gouvernement flamand and All Projects & Developments NV and Others v. Vlaamse Regering [2013] *ECR* I-00000, at [35].

453 Joined Cases C-515/99, C-519/99, C-524/99 and C-526/99 till C-540/99, *Hans Reisch and Others v. Bürgermeister der Landeshauptstadt Salzburg and Grundverkehrsbeauftragter des Landes Salzburg and Anton Lassacher and Others v. Grundverkehrsbeauftragter des Landes Salzburg and Grundverkehrslandeskommission des Landes Salzburg* [2002] *ECR* I-2147.

454 Case C-6/01, *Associação Nacional de Operadores de Máquinas Recreativas (Anomar) and Others v. Estado português* [2003] *ECR* I-8261.

455 Case C-250/03, *Giorgio Emanuele Mauri v. Ministero della Giustizia and Commissione per gli esami di avvocato presso la Corte d'appello di Milano* [2005] *ECR* I-1267.

456 See for a recent detailed research on this topic: C.R. Hansen, *Contracts not covered or not fully covered by the Public Sector Directive* (Copenhagen: Djøf Publishing, 2012), pp. 121–158.

457 Case C-231/03, *Consorzio Aziende* Metano *(Coname) v. Comune di Cingia de' Botti* (2005) *ECR* I-7287, at [17]. For a recent application see Case C-292/12, *Ragn Sells v. Sillamäe Linnavalitsus* [2013] *ECR* I-00000.

Thus, it is sufficient that an undertaking established in another Member State might be interested in providing a service to a public authority to fall under the scope of EU law.[458]

Based on this consideration, the Court has made the following distinction in *Commission v. Ireland.*[459] If a contract clearly shows a cross-border interest, the principles of Articles 49 and 56 TFEU are to be applied. This case law has, thus, formulated a general criterion by which under European law in the future, public authorities and national courts will have to decide whether at the awarding of a public procurement contract or a service concession the principle of equal treatment and the transparency obligation should be respected.[460] The public procurement Directives have been given concrete form by virtue of this criterion providing thresholds under which the Directives are not applicable.

Recently, in addressing a preliminary question, the Court has taken the opportunity to give some guidelines on how a public authority or a national judge might verify whether there is a contract of cross-border interest.[461] The Court had to rule on the applicability of the fundamental principles of European Union law to a contract that was not above the thresholds set in the public procurement Directives. The Court ruled that cross-border interest exists in the following case: 'A works contract could, for example, be of such cross-border interest because of its estimated value in conjunction with its technical complexity or the fact that the works are to be located in a place which is likely to attract the interest of foreign operators'.[462]

Furthermore, the Court mentioned objective criteria that could be set at a national or local level to quantify in clear terms the cross-border interest. According to the Court, such criteria could, for example, be the significant size of the sum being paid for that contract combined with the place of execution of the works, or the modest economic value of the contract in question. The Court, however, added that 'in certain cases, account must be taken of the fact that the borders straddle conurbations which are situated in the territory of different Member States and that, in those circumstances, even low-value contracts may be of certain cross-border interest'.[463]

The following criteria can be distinguished for differentiating cross-border traffic: the location where the contract has to be performed, financial value of the contract, the economic interest of the contract for an undertaking and the technical characteristics of the agreement.[464]

458 Case C-458/03, *Parking Brixen GmbH v. Gemeinde Brixen* [2005] *ECR* I-08585, at [55].

459 Case C-507/03, *Commission of the European Communities v. Ireland* [2007] *ECR* I-09777, at [29].

460 See more recently also Case C-412/04, *Commission of the European Communities v. Italian Republic* [2008] *ECR* I-00619, at [66].

461 Joined cases C-147/06 and C-148/06, *SECAP SpA and Santorso Soc. coop. arl v. Comune di Torino* [2008] *ECR* I-03565.

462 At [24].

463 At [31].

464 Case C-347/06, *ASM Brescia SpA v. Comune di Rodengo Saiano* [2008] *ECR* I-05641, at [62]; Case C-221/12, *NV Belgacom v. Interkommunale voor Teledistributie van het Gewest Antwerpen (Integan),*

On the basis of CJEU case law concerning the element 'cross border interest', it is clear that the CJEU applies a broad interpretation to the concept of 'intra-Union trade'. According to this interpretation, the Court goes further than the case law on cooperative agreements. The evolution of CJEU case law on 'intra-Union trade' implicates that there are few situations left that are purely internal. The evolution of CJEU case law on cooperative agreements broadened the situations that are internal. The difference between the CJEU case law on cross-border interest and on cooperative agreements is that in a purely internal situation, the CJEU just checks whether all relevant elements of a situation or of an activity can be confined in one single Member State.[465] This category of case law examines, according to the Court, if a particular situation is of cross-border importance and inquires if foreign companies might be interested in providing services.[466] Hypothetically, in that situation the State measure can have an influence on the provision of an economic activity. The absence of the 'intra trade' element explains the non-application of EU law. In the context of CJEU case law on cooperative agreements, EU law does not apply because the State measure does not affect the provision of an economic activity. It has no effect on free competition regardless of whether the situation is purely internal or not. The nature of the relationship precludes a market interest. The cross-border element is not relevant.

4. Restriction

One of the most important aspects of the realisation of the internal market is to ensure that everything (goods, persons, services and capital) moves freely between the Member States of the European Union. Free movement must be guaranteed. As far as this thesis is concerned, this means that in principle public markets should be open to providers from other Member States. This assurance of free movement between the Member States is a key element in the effective realisation of the internal market.[467] Therefore, EU intervention is necessary only when an action or decision (i.e. a State measure) imperils the realisation of the internal market.

A situation is of relevance for EU law when it threatens to hinder free movement, which by extension poses a risk to the realisation of the internal market. Is a state measure a restriction[468] to free trade?

Intermedia, West-Vlaamse Energie- en Teledistributiemaatschappij (WVEM), Provinciale Brabantse Energiemaatschappij CVBA (PBE) [2013] *ECR* I-00000, at [29]; Case C-388/12, *Comune di Ancona v. Regione Marche* [2013] *ECR* I-00000, at [51].

465 Joined Cases C-197/11 and C-203/11, *Eric Libert and Others v. Gouvernement flamand and All Projects & Developments NV and Others v. Vlaamse Regering* [2013] *ECR* I-00000, at [33].

466 Case C-458/03, *Parking Brixen GmbH v. Gemeinde Brixen* [2005] *ECR* I-08585, at [55].

467 Case 355/85, *Driancourt v. Cognet* [1986] *ECR* 3231; Case 98/86, *Ministère public v. Arthur Mathot* [1987] *ECR* 809.

468 See on this notion A. Tryfonidou, 'What can the Court's response to reverse discrimination and purely internal situations contribute to our understanding of the relationship between the 'restriction' and 'discrimination' concepts in EU free movement law?', www.jus.uio.no/ifp/forskning/prosjekter/markedsstaten/arrangementer/2011/free-movement-oslo/speakers-papers/tryfonidou.pdf, pp. 7 et seq.

First this section shall explore the question of when a State measure contains some hindrance to interstate trade. Central to this question is the notion of 'market access'. (4.1.) In regard to the tendering of public contracts and service concessions, the CJEU has recognised a number of specific principles designed to secure market access. (4.2.) After this section the question arises to what extent the CJEU case law on cooperative agreements can be explained by the concept of restriction and the interpretation given to it by the CJEU. (4.3.)

4.1. Market access

The Court of Justice has ruled often on the meaning of 'restriction' or 'obstacle' in the context of the application of the fundamental freedoms. This case law has evolved over time and has not always been unequivocal but depended on which of the four fundamental freedoms (persons, goods, services, and capital) the Court was called upon to adjudicate. Legal scholars have sought to find some consistent thread running through the case law that would serve to determine when EU law is applicable. This continuous thread perhaps also has some bearing on CJEU case law on cooperative agreements.

Only a State measure that entails a restriction to free movement falls under the scope of EU law. How the term 'restriction' is understood will determine the applicability of EU law - insofar as the other conditions requisite for rendering this law applicable (e.g. no internal situation) are present. How the concept of 'restriction' is interpreted also says something about how far economic integration has advanced. In this section the thesis explores the meaning of this term and examines to what extent it is relevant to the central theme.

The provisions concerning free movement may be read in two ways. Either that only State measures of a discriminatory nature against imports from another Member State can be regarded as hindering free trade (restrictive interpretation) or that all State measures can be regarded as hindering free trade (broad interpretation).[469] Discriminatory measures are exclusively concerned with the criterion 'nationality'.

In *Dassonville*[470] the CJEU choose the second option: '*All trading rules* enacted by Member States that are capable of hindering, directly or indirectly, actually or potentially, intra-Community trade are to be considered as measures having an effect equivalent to quantitative restrictions'.[471] In *Van Tiggele*[472] and *Cassis de Dijon*[473] the Court added to this that a measure has an equivalent effect prohibited by Article 30 EC even if the rules apply without distinction to all products.

469 Cf. J. Snell, *Goods and Services in EC Law* (Oxford: OUP, 2002), p. 2; C. Barnard, *The substantive Law of the EU* (Oxford: OUP, 2010), pp. 17–29.

470 Case 8/74, *Procureur du Roi v. Dassonville* [1974] *ECR* 837.

471 At [5].

472 Case 82/77, *Public Prosecutor of the Kingdom of the Netherlands v. Jacobus Philippus van Tiggele* [1978] *ECR* 837, at [5].

473 Case 120/78, *Rewe v. Bundesmonopolverwaltung für Bramtwein* [1978] *ECR* 649.

The Court confirmed and applied the *Dassonville* doctrine to the free movement of services: '*all requirements* imposed on the person providing the service by reason, in particular, of his nationality or of the fact that he does not habitually reside in the State where the service is provided, which do not apply to persons established within the national territory or which may prevent or otherwise obstruct the activities of the person providing the service'.[474] Henceforth the Court seemed to favour a uniform principle for all freedoms. The free movement of persons, goods, services and capital concerns 'not only the elimination of all discrimination against a person... on the grounds of his nationality but also the abolition of any restriction, even if it applies without distinction to national providers... and to those of other Member States, when it is liable to prohibit or otherwise impede the activities of a provider... established in another Member State where he lawfully provides similar services'.[475]

From the moment the CJEU started to treat discriminatory and non-discriminatory measures equally, this difference could no longer determine the applicability of EU law. Consequently another criterion was needed to provide clarity. In any event, the difference between a discriminatory and a non-discriminatory measure could not explain the CJEU case law on cooperative agreements. These agreements are not excluded from the scope of EU law because they discriminate foreign undertakings.

The CJEU case law contains a new criterion to discover whether a restriction to free trade is present, which is known as the 'market access' criterion.

In *Säger*,[476] cited earlier on and later reaffirmed in *Gebhard*,[477] the Court deemed that a restriction may be present 'when it is liable to prohibit or otherwise impede the activities of a provider... established in another Member State where he lawfully provides similar services'. However, this consideration says nothing explicit about 'market access'. *Keck and Mitthourd*[478] seems to be the first case where the Court has used this notion: 'Provided that those conditions are fulfilled, the application of such rules to the sale of products from another Member State meeting the requirements laid down by that State is not by nature such as *to prevent* their *access to the market* or *to impede access* any more than it impedes the access of domestic products. Such rules therefore fall outside the scope of Article 30 of the Treaty'. As regards freedom of services, the notion 'market

474 Case 33/74, *Johannes Henricus Maria van Binsbergen v. Bestuur van de Bedrijfsvereniging voor de Metaalnijverheid* [1974] *ECR* 1299, at [10].

475 Case C-76/90, *Manfred Säger v. Dennemeyer & Co. Ltd* [1991] *ECR* I-4221, at [12]. See also Case C-55/94, *Reinhard Gebhard v. Consiglio dell'Ordine degli Avvocati a Procuration de Milano* [1995] *ECR* I-4165, at [37]; Case C415/93, *Union Royale des Sociétés de Football Association v. Bosman* [1995] *ECR* I-4921; Case C-381/93, *Alpine Investments v. Minister van Financiën* [1995] *ECR* I-1141.

476 Case C-76/90, *Manfred Säger v. Dennemeyer & Co. Ltd* [1991] *ECR* I-4221.

477 Case C-55/94, *Reinhard Gebhard v. Consiglio dell'Ordine degli Avvocati a Procuration de Milano* [1995] *ECR* I-4165.

478 Cases C-267/91 and C-268/91, *Criminal proceedings v. Bernard Keck and Daniel Mithouard* [1993] *ECR* I-6097, at [17].

access' is clearly taken up for the first time in *Alpine Investments*[479]: 'that the application of such provisions is not such as to prevent access by the latter to the market of the importing Member State or to impede such access more than it impedes access by domestic products'.[480] This phraseology later found its way naturally into CJEU case law. Does this actually mean that 'market access' is the fundamental criterion to determine whether a restriction exists?

Two views are defended. One side of legal scholars[481] defends the view that the market access test is the ultimate criterion that determines whether a breach of the fundamental rules concerning free movement has occurred. Measures fall within the scope of EU law if they could hinder access to a relevant market. A number of Advocate Generals also think along the same lines.[482] However, some other legal scholars are not convinced that this criterion can hold up.[483]

On the basis of the case law in question, the market access criterion seems a good choice for clarifying most of the case law handed down by the CJEU in matters concerning State measures hindering free movement: 'There is one guiding principle which seems to provide an appropriate test: That principle is that all enterprises that engage in a legitimate economic activity in a Member State should have unfettered access to the whole of the Community market, unless there is a valid reason for denying them full access to a part of that market'.[484, 485]

As per the freedom of goods, the Court procrastinated to apply the market access criterion. Only in 2009, in the *Commission v. Italy*[486] and *Mickelsson*[487] cases did the Court apply this criterion in the context of the free movement of goods. Thus, it appears that a similar criterion is emerging in CJEU case law. The notion 'restriction' covers measures taken by a Member State, which, although applicable without distinction, affect access to the market for enterprises from other Member States and so hinder intra-Community trade.

479 Case C-384/93, *Alpine Investments v. Minister van Financiën* [1995] *ECR* I-1141.

480 At [37].

481 See A. Tryfonidou, 'Further steps on the road to convergence among the market freedoms' (*ELR*, 2010), pp. 47–51.

482 Opinion of A.G. Maduro in joined cases C-158/04 and C-159/04, *Alfa Vita Vassilopoulos AE and Carrefour Marinopoulos AE v. Elliniko Dimosio and Nomarchiaki Aftodioikisi Ioanninon* [2006] *ECR* I-08135, at [45]; Opinion of AG Bot in Case C-110/05, *Commission of the European Communities v. Italian Republic* [2009] *ECR* I-519, at [108] to [138]; Opinion of AG Trstenjak in Case C-205/07, *Lodewijk Gysbrechts and Santurel Inter BVBA* [2008] *ECR* I-09947, at [59] to [61].

483 See E. Spaventa, 'Leaving Keck behind? The Free Movement of Good after the rulings in commission v. Italy and Michelsson and Roos' (*ELR*, 2009), p. 929; J. Snell, 'The notion of Market access: a concept or a Slogan?' (*CMLR*, 2010), pp. 448–449.

484 Opinion of Advocate General Jacobs to Case C-412/93, *Société d'Importation Edouard Leclerc-Siplec v. TF1 Publicité SA and M6 Publicité SA* [1995] *ECR* I-179, at [41].

485 See for a recent affirmation concerning the market access criterion: C. Barnard, *The substantive law of the EU* (Oxford: OUP, 2013), pp. 18–25.

486 Case C-518/06, *Commission* v. *Italy* [2009] *ECR* I-3491.

487 Case C-142/05, *Mickelsson and Roos* [2009] *ECR* I-4273.

The applicability of the fundamental freedoms is no longer determined solely by the nature of the measure, but primarily by the success of an undertaking in attaining access to a specific market. The purpose of the provisions regarding the fundamental freedoms decides whether or not these provisions apply to a particular situation.

4.2. Principles of government contract law[488]

The public procurement Directives are aimed at guaranteeing free access and promoting competition via harmonisation of the diverse national legislations and to this end the CJEU imposed certain obligations with regard to the award of a contract: specifically, the obligation of non-discrimination, the obligation of equal treatment and the obligation of transparency.[489] The provisions of public procurement Directives are likewise interpreted and complemented on the basis of these obligations. The same principles have been recognised by the CJEU to apply to service concessions on the basis of the TFEU provisions on free movement.

These principles help ensure undistorted market access for public procurement markets and service concession markets. They are applicable only insofar as market access can be distorted by a specific situation. CJEU case law on cooperative agreements defines when such a distortion is present or not in two specific situations. (See chapter 5)

4.2.1. Equal treatment

Equality is one of the basic cornerstones of the internal market. However, this principle is not simply a milepost on the way toward the achievement of economic union, but it has also contributed to the genesis of the European Union legal order. It is a democratic guarantee that European institutions and the Member States have put in place to ensure that no unjustified distinctions are drawn. This is also why the CJEU deems the general principle of equality to be a general principle of constitutional law.[490]

In accordance with the principle of equality, equal circumstances may not be treated unequally or unequal circumstances may not be treated equally, unless this is justified objectively[491]: 'Discrimination in substance would consist in treating either similar

488 See for recent studies: C.R. Hansen, *Contracts not covered or not fully covered* (Copenhagen: Djøf publishing, 2012), pp. 51–66; S. de Mars, 'The limits of general principles: a procurement case study' (*ELR*, 2013), pp. 316–334.

489 Case C-599/10, *SAG ELV Slovensko a.s., FELA Management AG, ASCOM (Schweiz) AG, Asseco Central Europe a.s., TESLA Stropkov a.s., Autostrade per l'Italia SpA, EFKON AG, Stalexport Autostrady SA v. Úrad pre verejné obstarávanie* [2012] *ECR* I-00000.

490 Case C-162/99, *Commission of the European Communities v. Italian Republic* [2001] *ECR* I-00541, at [23].

491 See for public procurement: Joined cases C-31/03 and C-34/03, *Fabricom SA v. Belgian State* [2005] *ECR* I-1559, at [27];Case C-336/12, *Ministeriet for Forskning, Innovation og Videregående Uddannelser v. Manova A/S* [2013] *ECR* I-00000, at [30]; Case T-289/09, 20 September 2011, *Evropaïki Dynamiki –*

situations differently or different situations identically'.[492] Discrimination or inequality cannot arise in legal situations that are not comparable.[493] If the Court establishes that an inequality is nevertheless present, it will then explore whether the given differences may not be justified in the particular case in the light of the objective served by the provisions in question.[494] The principle of non-discrimination on grounds of nationality (Article 18 TFEU) is merely an expression of this more general principle of equal treatment.[495]

Equal treatment in the awarding of contracts concluded by public authorities aims at achieving a single internal market: 'the application of the principle of equal treatment to public procurement procedures does not constitute an end in itself, but must be viewed in the light of the aims that it is intended to achieve'.[496] Equal treatment assures interested undertakings established in other Member States that they will have the same opportunity to conclude the contract. It ensures a degree of competitiveness.

A public authority must treat undertakings from another Member State equally, a responsibility flowing from the principle of non-discrimination on grounds of nationality. This principle of non-discrimination was affirmed by the CJEU (i.e. without reference to public procurement Directives) in two milestone decisions: *Unitron Scandinavia*[497] and *Telaustria Verlag*.[498]

In an Interpretative Communication of the European Commission, dated April 12, 2000 on concessions, the Commission affirmed the principle of equal treatment.[499] According to the Commission, this principle follows from the principle of non-discrimination on grounds of nationality and from the fundamental freedoms, and is also applicable to situations other than public procurement, such as concessions. In *Parking Brixen*[500] the CJEU stated that public authorities concluding service concessions must comply with

Proigmena Systimata Tilepikoinonion Pliroforikis kai Tilematikis AE v. Europese Commissie [2011] *ECR* II-0000.

492 Case 13/63, *Italian Republic v. Commission of the European Economic Community* [1963] *ECR* 00165, at [4].

493 Case 22/67, *Fonds national de retraite des ouvriers mineurs v. Giovanni Mura* [1977] *ECR* 1699, at [9] tot [10].

494 K. Lengertz, 'L'égalité de traitement et droit communautaire' (*Cah.dr.eur.*, 1991), p. 21.

495 Case 810/79, *Peter Uberschär v. Bundesversicherungsanstalt für Angestellte* [1980] *ECR* 2747, at [16].

496 Joined cases C-31/03 and C-34/03, *Fabricom SA v. Belgian State* [2005] *ECR* I-1559, at [29]; Case C-336/12, *Ministeriet for Forskning, Innovation og Videregående Uddannelser v. Manova A/S* [2013] *ECR* I-00000, at [30].

497 Case C-275/98, *Unitron Scandinavia A/S and 3-S A/S, Danske Svineproducenters Serviceselskab v. Ministeriet for Fødevarer, Landbrug og Fiskeri* [1999] *ECR* I-08291.

498 Case C-324/98, *Telaustria Verlags GmbH and Telefonadress GmbH v. Telekom Austria AG, joined party: Herold Business Data AG* [2000] *ECR* I-10745.

499 OJ [2000] C 121/2.

500 Case C-458/03, *Parking Brixen GmbH v. Gemeinde Brixen and Stadtwerke Brixen AG* [2005] *ECR* I-08585.

the principle of non-discrimination and the principle of equal treatment.[501] This last principle applies regardless of nationality.[502]

In particular, in the context of the public procurement Directives, the Court confirmed that the principle of equal treatment of tenderers aims at the promotion of a healthy and purposeful competition among firms participating in the public tendering procedure. According to the CJEU this principle implies that tenderers must be in a position of equality both when they formulate their tenders and when the adjudicating authority is assessing those tenders.[503]

4.2.2. Transparency

In *Telaustria Verlag* the CJEU acknowledged for the first time, on the basis of a number of provisions from the EU Treaty, that when a public authority awards a public service concession it must comply with the obligation of transparency.[504] In *Parking Brixen* the CJEU summed up the basic consequences of the obligation of transparency.[505] The obligation of transparency that is imposed on the public authority consists of ensuring, for the benefit of any potential tenderer, a degree of advertising sufficient to enable the service concession to be opened up to competition and the impartiality of procurement procedures to be reviewed.

The obligation of transparency on the basis of the public procurement Directives appears for the first time in *Beentjes*.[506] Although the Court did not explicitly mention an obligation of transparency it does affirm that a contracting authority 'must provide adequate information on the terms and applicable to any tender offer'.[507]

The Walloon buses case marks the first time that an obligation of transparency and even a principle of transparency flowing from the preambles of Directive 90/531 pertaining to

501 At [46]. Case C-410/04, *Associazione Nazionale Autotrasporto Viaggiatori (ANAV) v. Comune di Bari and AMTAB Servizio SpA* [2006] *ECR* I-03303, at [20]; Case 196/08, *Acoset SpA v. Conferenza Sindaci e Presidenza Prov. Reg. ATO Idrico Ragusa and Others* [2009] *ECR* I-09913, at [48].

502 Critised by S. Arrowsmith and P. Kunzlik, 'EC regulation of public procurement', in S. Arrowsmith and P. Kunzlik, *Social and environmental Policies in EC Procurement Law* (Cambridge: Cambridge University Press, 2009), p. 86.

503 Case C-19/00, *SIAC Construction Ltd v. County Council of the County of* Mayo [2001] *ECR* I-07725; Case C-470/99, *Universale-Bau AG and Bietergemeinschaft: Hinteregger & Söhne Bauges.mbH Salzburg, ÖSTÜ-STETTIN Hoch- und Tiefbau GmbH* [2002] *ECR* I-11617, at [93]; T-50/05, *Evropaïki Dynamiki – Proigmena Systimata Tilepikoinonion Pliroforikis kai Tilematikis AE v. European Commission* [2010] *ECR* II-01071, at [56].

504 Case C-324/98, *Telaustria Verlags GmbH and Telefonadress GmbH v. Telekom Austria AG, joined party: Herold Business Data AG* [2000] *ECR* I-10745.

505 Case C-458/03, *Parking Brixen GmbH v. Gemeinde Brixen and Stadtwerke Brixen AG* [2005] *ECR* I-08585, *at* [49]; see also Case C-410/04, *Associazione Nazionale Autotrasporto Viaggiatori (ANAV) v. Comune di Bari and AMTAB Servizio SpA* [2006] *ECR* I-03303, at [21].

506 Case C-31/87, *Gebroeders Beentjes BV v. the Netherlands* [1988] *ECR* 4635.

507 At [21].

utility sectors were stated in clear language. In one of the preambles, contracting authorities are enjoined to guarantee a minimum of transparency in awarding contracts. The Court considered on this basis: 'Furthermore, the 33rd recital in the preamble shows that the Directive aims to ensure a minimum level of transparency in the award of the contracts to which it applies. The procedure for comparing tenders therefore had to comply at every stage with both the principle of the equal treatment of tenderers and the *principle of transparency* so as to afford equality of opportunity to all tenderers when formulating their tenders'.[508]

According CJEU case law an obligation to transparency implies for every contracting authority 'that sufficient information must be guaranteed to every potential tenderer, so that the services market is always open to competition and the tendering procedures can be tested for impartiality'.[509] The obligation of transparency must ensure 'that the principle of equal treatment of tenderers, with which every tendering procedure governed by the Directive must comply, is taken into account'.[510]

The principle of transparency entails that all conditions and terms of the award procedure be clearly, precisely, and unambiguously worded in the procurement notice or in the contractual conditions. This allows all reasonably well-informed tenderers to know the exact scope of the award. It enables the tenderers, to interpret the contractual conditions in the same way. Finally, the contracting authority is able to verify whether the bids meet the award criteria.[511]

In the context of the public procurement Directives, the obligation of transparency and the principle of equal treatment have become the leading principle applied by the CJEU when filling lacunae in the Directives and interpreting unclear provisions.

4.3. *Cooperative agreements between public authorities*

Equal treatment in public procurement is intended to afford equality of opportunity to all tenders.[512] This applies to service concessions as well. All tenderers must have equal opportunity to enter a particular market (i.e. public market). The idea of equal treatment is merely another expression of the objective of free market access. However, free market access is only guaranteed if operators are in a like situation or when there is a relevant market. If there is a difference between two situations, this can clarify whether or not EU law is applicable.

508 Case C-87/94, *Commission of the European Communities v. Kingdom of Belgium* [1996] *ECR* I-2043, at [54].

509 Case C-470/99, *Universale-Bau AG and Bietergemeinschaft: Hinteregger & Söhne Bauges GmbH Salzburg, ÖSTÜ-STETTIN Hoch- und Tiefbau GmbH* [2002] *ECR* I-11617, at [92].

510 Case C-421/01, *Traunfellner GmbH v. Österreichische Autobahnen- und Schnellstraßen-Finanzierungs-AG* [2003] *ECR* I-11941, at [29].

511 Case C-368/10, *Commission v. Netherlands* [2012] *ECR* I-00000, at [88].

512 Case 87/94, *Commission v. Belgium* [1996] *ECR* I-2043, at [33] and [54].

According to the thesis, *Parking Brixen*[513] differentiates clearly both situations, where the application or non-applicability of EU law on cooperative agreements may be ascertained: 'in the field of public procurement and public service concessions, the principle of equal treatment and the specific expressions of that principle, namely the prohibition on discrimination on grounds of nationality and Articles 43 EC and 49 EC,[514] are to be applied in cases where a public authority entrusts the supply of economic activities to a third party. By contrast, it is not appropriate to apply the Community rules on public procurement or public service concessions in cases where a public authority performs tasks in the public interest for which it is responsible by its own administrative, technical and other means, without calling upon external entities'.[515]

The CJEU equates the second situation in *Parking Brixen* with a situation that, according to *Teckal* case law, falls outside the range of applicability of EU law[516] and also other forms of cooperative agreements between authorities.[517] A comparable idea is discernible in *Sporting Exchange*.[518] The obligation of transparency, and thus EU law, applies if a Member State allows an operator to carry on an economic activity.[519] Effects on the market will determine whether a particular situation is subject to EU law, i.e. the principle of equal treatment or public procurement Directives. If a state measure advantages an economic activity, it could distort free competition or hinder free trade. This is different if a public authority carries out by itself a public service task or carries it out jointly with other public authorities without the intervention of an undertaking.

Thus the CJEU distinguishes between two different situations: in the one, EU law is applicable, in the other it is not. Further, application of EU law in the second situation could lead to an inequality. Thus, the principle of equality can be a primary explanation for CJEU case law on cooperative agreements. Two considerations would seem to account elements for the difference in treatment: 1) the object of the state measure and 2) the nature of the executor of the task (whether there is a third party or not).

The object of a measure is one of the points Hatzopoulos highlights to determine whether an economic activity is present and therefore EU law must be applied.[520] According to Hatzopoulos certain measures, and thus also State measures, are exempt from the application of EU law when they are alien to the regulation of an economic activity.

513 Case C-458/03, *Parking Brixen GmbH v. Gemeinde Brixen and Stadtwerke Brixen AG* [2005] *ECR* I-08585.
514 Now Articles 49 and 56 TFEU.
515 At [61].
516 At [62].
517 Case C-480/06, *Commission of the European Communities v. Federal Republic of Germany* [2009] *ECR* I-04747, at [46] to [47].
518 Case C-203/08, *Sporting Exchange Ltd v. Minister van Justitie* [2010] *ECR* I-04695.
519 At [47].
520 V. Hatzopoulos, *Regulating Services in the European Union* (Oxford: OUP, 2012), pp. 78–83.

He links the CJEU case law on cooperative agreements to this aspect. According to Hatzopoulos, measures whereby public authorities cooperate with other public authorities on an institutional or contractual level to meet their obligations (services of general interest) *vis-a-vis* citizens should not be ensnared by public procurement rules[521] and, thus, the principle of equality. These measures are intended to subserve an objective of general interest and they are necessary to achieve these objectives. They have nothing to do with an economic activity. In order to situate CJEU case law on cooperative agreements within the Court's case law he refers to two cases.

In *Deliège*[522] the CJEU intervened in a case where a Belgian judoka sought an order requiring the Belgian Sport Federations to take the appropriate steps to allow her to attend certain international tournaments and she brought an action seeking a ruling that the Belgian selection system for international tournaments is unlawful. The CJEU had to examine whether certain rules and systems of the Belgian sports federations[523] were not in conflict with the free movement of persons and services. In the first place it had to weigh whether an economic activity was present. The Court proposed that this could be the case even when it is only a question of the performance of a sport. Assuming that an economic activity existed, the Court had to examine whether such measures by a sports federation also constituted a restriction. The CJEU considers that the restriction in the case was 'a limitation inherent to the conduct of an international high-level sports event'.[524] Such rules may not in themselves be regarded as constituting a restriction on the freedom to provide services, prohibited by Article 56 TFEU.

Deliège builds on a number of considerations from *Donà*.[525] The provisions concerning free movement of persons and services prohibit no measures that exclude certain persons insofar as this is based on reasons that are not economic in nature and that are of sporting (non economic) interest only.[526] The restriction must remain limited to its proper objectives.[527]

The second case, this time examined by the General Court, is *Meca-Medina*.[528] In this case, the Court had to defer to decisions taken by anti-doping organisations, in which two athletes were barred for a specified time. This raised the question, *inter alia*, of whether this amounted to an obstruction of free movement. The Court reasoned: 'Such

521 *Ibidem* p. 81.

522 Joined cases C-51/96 and C-191/97, *Christelle Deliège v. Ligue francophone de judo et disciplines associées ASBL, Ligue belge de judo ASBL, Union européenne de judo and François Pacquée* [2000] *ECR* I-2549.

523 In this case, it is a matter of the rules of selection that limit the number of participants in such tournaments.

524 Joined cases C-51/96 and C-191/97, *Christelle Deliège v. Ligue francophone de judo et disciplines associées ASBL, Ligue belge de judo ASBL, Union européenne de judo and François Pacquée* [2000] *ECR* I-2549, at [64].

525 Case 13/76, *Gaetano Donà v. Mario Mantero* [1976] *ECR* 1333.

526 At [14].

527 At [76].

528 Case T-313/02, *Meca-Medina and Majcen v. Commission* [2004] *ECR* II-3291.

regulations, which relate to the particular nature and context of sporting events, are inherent in the organisation and proper conduct of sporting competition and cannot be regarded as constituting a restriction on the Community rules on the freedom of movement of workers and the freedom to provide services. In that context, it has been held that the rules on the composition of national teams, or the rules relating to the selection by sports federations of those of their members who may participate in high-level international competitions constitute purely sporting rules which therefore, by their nature, fall outside the scope of Articles 39 EC and 49 EC'.[529] By their very nature such rules fall outside the scope of EU law.

In *Deliège* and *Meca-Medina* a measure was taken which precludes free movement. However, according to the CJEU the measure cannot be considered as a restriction. In each of these cases the measure had another aim than an economic one. The measure concerned the organisation of the sport federation. This federation took a measure in the two cases to ensure the preservation of its own interests. These measures do not disadvantage a European citizen, because the specific citizen is not placed in the same situation as his competitors. The specific citizen has infringed a regulation of its organization. That is the reason why he cannot move freely.

Public authorities apply measures or take decisions that concern the general public interest. The decision of a public authority to cooperate with another public authority could constitute a restriction. If these measures solely subserve the general interest, and are necessary for this, they fall beyond the scope of EU law.

According to *Donà* and *Deliège*, there is no hindrance to access of the market if a decision-making institution applies a measure that is based on reasons that are not economic in nature and pursue the specific interest represented by the institution. In other words, if a public authority cooperates with another public authority and this is justified solely in terms of the objectives such a public authority pursues, i.e. objectives of general interest, there is no restriction and hence EU law is not applicable.

In *Commission v. Germany*[530] (horizontal cooperative agreement) the CJEU considered: 'such cooperation between public authorities does not undermine the principal objective of the Community rules on public procurement, that is, the free movement of services and the opening-up of undistorted competition in all the Member States, where implementation of that cooperation is governed solely by considerations and requirements relating to the pursuit of objectives in the public interest'.[531] The *Teckal* criteria formalise (in the context of a vertical cooperative agreement) the idea that a particular measure falls outside EU law if it strives for objectives in the public interest.

529 At [41].

530 Case C-480/06, *Commission of the European Communities v. Federal Republic of Germany* [2009] *ECR* I-04747.

531 At [47].

The Court seems to make this link in *Stadt Halle*.[532] The relationship between a public authority and its departments is *in itself* contingent on requirements and considerations proper to the pursuit of objectives in the public interest. The *Teckal* relation is in the same vein.

Through the interpretation of the public procurement Directives the CJEU expresses a more general idea of EU law, taking into account the fact that directives in themselves only clarify the rights already granted by the EU Treaties.[533] When public authorities cooperate to organise or manage their public services, the restriction to trade or to free competition is inherent to the conduct of a public authority. This kind of 'State' measures concerns an internal situation within a public authority. The aim of such a measure is to organise better its proper administration in order to improve the provision of services of general interest. It seems to express the idea that public authorities in different Member States are free to organise their public service and that Member States are competent to make regulations in this regard.

Beyond the context of 'general interest', in which the measure is situated, the CJEU case law on cooperative agreements also requires that private undertakings not be given an advantage. This criterion, however, externalises the same idea. If not a single private undertaking receives an advantage, free competition is also not distorted and in this sense the measure has no economic consequences.

CJEU case law on cooperative agreements can consequently be elucidated in terms of the concept of 'restriction' and in terms of the object of the restriction. In some situations the object of the restriction has no influence on the market and will not distort competition. On the grounds of the principle of equality such situations cannot fall within the scope of EU law.

According to Article 345 TFEU Member States are free how to regulate the organisation of public tasks. In the same line of thinking public authorities are free to organize these tasks. They have the freedom to discharge the tasks with their own administration. This justifies, according to the CJEU, why cooperative agreements under certain conditions do not fall under the scope of EU (public procurement) law.[534] Apparently, the CJEU presumes that the choice for an in house-provision has no effect on the market and that every situation that is similar to such provision does not have that effect. The criteria that the CJEU developed to exclude certain cooperative agreements between public authorities out of the scope of EU law must reflect this similarity. That is why these criteria have to be strictly interpreted.

532 Case C-26/03, *Stadt Halle and RPL Recyclingpark Lochau GmbH v. Arbeitsgemeinschaft Thermische Restabfall- und Energieverwertungsanlage TREA Leuna* [2005] *ECR* I-00001, at [49] and [50].

533 See Case 2/74, *Reyners v. Belgium* [1974] *ECR* 631.

534 Case C-15/13, *Technische Universität Hamburg-Harburg, Hochschul-Informations-System GmbH v. Datenlotsen Informationssysteme GmbH* [2014] *ECR* I-00000, at [25].

5. Justifications[535]

A number of factors of general interest allow a State not to observe the principles underpinning the fundamental freedoms when it takes a measure with cross-border effect. There is a difference between derogations provided *expressis verbis* in the TFEU and the mandatory requirements affirmed by the CJEU in its case law.

Articles 51, 52 and 62 TFEU provide a number of hypothetical situations where a State need not maintain the fundamental freedoms and, thus, the principles derived from them as well. The list provided by the TFEU is exhaustive[536] and the derogations have to be interpreted strictly.[537]

A State can limit the free movement of services to protect public order, public safety and public health (Article 62 TFEU). Directive 2004/38/EC of the European Parliament and of the Council of 29 April 2004 on the right of citizens of the Union and their family members to move and reside freely within the territory of the Member States (CRD) further develops this regime of exception.[538] Measures for protecting public order and safety may be decided solely by virtue of the personal characteristics of those concerned.[539] A subject, for instance, can be rejected merely if the presence or behaviour of the party concerned poses a real and sufficient threat[540] to a fundamental interest of the commonweal.[541] However, the thesis does not go more deeply into the extensive case law on derogations as this is beyond the scope of this thesis.

Over the years, the Court of Justice has also adduced a number of additional reasons to justify a restriction on a fundamental freedom in addition to those given in the TFEU.

In the seminal case *Vanbinsbergen*, the Court ruled that departures from the principle of free movement of services were possible '*where they have as their purpose the application of professional rules justified by the general good*'.[542] In the other seminal case *Cassis de Dijon* the Court went further down this route regarding the free movement of goods: 'obstacles to movement within the Community resulting from disparities between the national laws relating to marketing of the products in question must be accepted in so far as those provisions may be recognised as being necessary in order to satisfy mandatory

535 C. Barnard, 'Derogations, Justifications and the Four Freedoms: Is State Interest Really Protected?', in C. Barnard and O. Odudu (eds.), *The Outer Limits of European Union Law* (Oregon: Hart Publishing, 2009), pp. 273–315.

536 Case C-17/92, *Federación de Distribuidores Cinematográficos v. Estado Español en Unión de Productores de Cine y Televisión* [1993] *ECR* I-02239, at [20]; Case 388/01, *Commission v. Italy* [2003] *ECR* I-00721, at [20].

537 Case C-441/02, *Commission v. Germany* [2006] *ECR* I-3449, at [32] to [35].

538 *OJ* [2004] L 158/77.

539 Art. 27(2) CRD. See also Case 41/74, *Yvonne van Duyn v. Home Office* [1974] *ECR* 1337.

540 Case 36/75, *Roland Rutili v. Ministre de l'intérieur* [1975] *ECR* 01219, at [28].

541 Case 30/77, *Régina v. Pierre Bouchereau* [1977] *ECR* 01999, at [35].

542 Case 33/74, *Johannes Henricus Maria van Binsbergen v. Bestuur van de Bedrijfsvereniging voor de Metaalnijverheid* [1974] *ECR* 1299, at [12].

requirements relating in particular to the effectiveness of fiscal supervision, the protection of commercial transactions and the defence of the consumer'.[543]

The CJEU accepts a mandatory requirement if four conditions are met:[544]

- A measure must be applied in a non-discriminatory manner;
- A measure must be justified by the imperative requirement of serving the general interest;
- The measure had to be suitable for securing the attainment of the objective, which they pursued;
- The measure could not go beyond what beyond what was necessary to attain it.

Legal doctrine has divided the mandatory requirements into four categories: 1) the protection of third parties, 2) civil liberties, 3) the need to prevent distortions in the market and 4) the preservation of public order.[545] In this context, the Court of Justice tends to have a critical eye to the mandatory requirements used by public authorities.

In respect of the application of public procurement Directives and the principle of equal treatment, the Court has already had several occasions to investigate whether or not a Member State could not invoke a derogation or mandatory requirement to avoid a competitive tendering procedure.

In *Coname*[546] the CJEU for the first time openly conceded that there are 'objective circumstances' that could justify that the award of a public contract or service concession could be exempted from the application of EU law. The Court did not explain the notion 'objective circumstances'. In *Commission v. Italy*,[547] the Court proffered 'reasons of overriding general interest' giving the following example: 'the objectives of consumer protection and the prevention of both fraud and incitement to squander on gaming, as well as the general need to preserve public order'. This is in accord with a number of mandatory requirements as explained above. *ASM Brescia*[548] added an example to the issue of 'objective circumstances': the necessity of complying with the principle of legal certainty.

One may now ask if 'reasons of overriding general interest' and 'objective circumstances' are essentially the same thing. The CJEU recently answered this question affirmatively.[549]

543 Case 120/78, *Rewe v. Bundesmonopolverwaltung für Bramtwein* [1978] *ECR* 649, at [8].

544 Case C-55/94, *Reinhard Gebhard v. Consiglio dell'Ordine degli Avvocati a Procuration de Milano* [1995] *ECR* I-4165, at [17].

545 C. Barnard, 'Derogations, Justifications and the Four Freedoms: Is State Interest Really Protected?', in C. Barnard and O. Odudu (eds.), *The Outer Limits of European Union Law* (Oregon: Hart Publishing, 2009), pp. 277–278.

546 Case C-231/03, *Consorzio Aziende* Metano *(Coname) v. Comune di Cingia de' Botti* [2005] *ECR* I-7287, at [19].

547 Case C-240/06, *Commission v. Italy* [2007] *ECR* I-09413, at [26] and [27].

548 Case C-347/06, *ASM Brescia SpA v. Comune di Rodengo Saiano* [2008] *ECR* I-5641, at [64].

549 Case C-221/12, *Belgacom NV v. Interkommunale voor Teledistributie van het Gewest Antwerpen (INTEGAN) and Others* [2013] *ECR* I-00000, at [38].

The EU rules on derogations and mandatory requirements are not relevant for the thesis. The presumption in the thesis is that the case law on cooperative agreements between public authorities does not create a derogation from the applicability of EU law. This case law excludes such situations from the scope of EU law. Both categories of law, however, have as a characteristic that they balance values of market integration against other values. The CJEU case law on cooperative agreements could be seen as CJEU protection of certain social values. The freedom to organise the deliverance of public tasks could be in favour of the citizen who needs to have access to the public task.

6. General conclusions

Chapter 5 endeavours to show that in certain situations cooperative agreements between public authorities fall out of the scope of EU law. This follows from the CJEU interpretation of public procurement Directives and the principle of equality. In its case law the CJEU has developed its own criteria to exclude this kind of cooperation from EU law. In this chapter the thesis examines how the application of EU law to cooperative agreements between public authorities can be explained.

The thesis submits that CJEU case law on cooperative agreements has to be explained in terms of the internal market rules. Public procurement Directives are rooted in these rules and more specifically in the rules on the fundamental freedoms. These rules are relevant when certain conditions of applicability have been met. Consequently, the question of how EU law is applicable to cooperative agreements between public authorities must be answered in terms of these conditions of applicability and any exceptions thereto.

The following conditions determine the applicability of the rules on the fundamental freedoms and are of relevance for the thesis: the presence of a State measure, interstate trade, and a restriction. At the core of any cooperative agreement between public authorities is invariably a decision of a public authority. This kind of decision (the decision to cooperate) must be considered a State measure. As a state measure, the decision to cooperate falls under the scope of EU law.

Since any cooperative agreement between public authorities is premised on a State measure, this condition does not determine whether such cooperation falls inside or outside the scope of EU law. If cooperative agreements between public authorities fall outside the scope of EU law, that is because neither domestic nor foreign undertakings are interested in the task, or in other words, because the contract is of no economic interest. Hence the presence or absence of an inter-State element plays no role in determining whether EU law on cooperative agreements is applicable.

The CJEU case law on cooperative agreements can not be considered a derogation to the applicability of EU law, because this case law concerns precisely the criteria that exclude such a situation from the applicability of EU law.

The 'principle of equality' and the concept of 'restriction' are presumably relevant. When economic operators are not concerned by or interested in the conclusion of an agreement (i.e. between public authorities) the State measure (decision to cooperate) can also not restrict market access. If the State measure is meant only to accomplish public service tasks without thereby disadvantaging a private initiative or firm, then there is no restriction. Consequently, EU law is not applicable.

A difference in the situation may arise when a public authority cooperates either to ensure its own public service tasks or to entrust the provision of an economic activity. When the first kind of cooperation is governed solely by considerations of general interest and a private initiative is not involved, free competition cannot be distorted. In fact, the situation stays 'in house'. This justifies the exclusion from the scope of EU law. In that case private undertakings will not be interested in market access. This is different from a situation where the provision of an economic activity is entrusted. In that case a private undertaking will want to conclude a contract with the public authority. As a consequence, in this situation the public authorities will have to give all interested undertakings an equal chance to conclude the contract. Market access may in this case not be restricted. The purpose of the measure determines whether a restriction or an unequal situation exists. According to the thesis it is here that CJEU case law on cooperative agreements could have its foundation.

Chapter 5

COOPERATIVE AGREEMENTS BETWEEN PUBLIC AUTHORITIES: OUTSIDE THE SCOPE OF EU LAW?

Since the emergence of the nation state (18th and 19th centuries) in Western Europe, public service tasks have essentially been carried out by the following public authorities: central and local government. They have normally used their own resources to deliver these services. The thesis refers to this practice as 'in-house provision'. However, it did not exclude the use of contracts by public authorities. As already explained in chapter 1, the complexity of society and increasing demands of citizens made a centralised organization of public administration and in house-provision of public service tasks increasingly more difficult.

The 1980s in Britain saw the emergence of the idea of 'New Public Management'[550] (NPM) as a way to achieve efficient and cost-effective management of public service tasks. In effect, the 'New Public Management' gave a new twist to the way public authorities organise or manage their public service tasks. There was 'a transition from traditional bureaucratic methods and structures in favour of market-based and business-like regimes of public service'.[551] Subsequently, these changes were gradually instituted in the majority of European countries as well. The creation of agencies and non-departmental bodies was among those changes.[552] In addition, public authorities were increasingly using contracts to provide public services.[553] Sometimes public authorities have needed to cooperate with third parties to ensure complete and cost effective delivery of public services; that is, tasks of public interest. They outsourced public service tasks. In-house provision and outsourcing are the *summa divisio* of how a public authority organises and manages the delivery of public service tasks.

550 O.E. Hughes, *Public management and Administration: an Introduction* (Basingstoke: Palgrave Macmillan, 2003); D. Oliver and G. Drewry, *Public Service Reforms: Issues of Accountability and Public Law* (London: Pinter, 1996); J. Stewart and K. Walsh, 'Change in The Managemenet of Public Services' (*Public Administration*, 1992), pp. 499 et seq.

551 C.M. Donelly, *Delegation of governmental power to private parties* (Oxford: OUP, 2007), p. 62.

552 See P. Craig, *Administrative law* (London: Sweet and Maxwell, 2012), pp. 75–106.

553 On the relation between New public contracting and New public management see: P. Vincent-Jones, *The new public contracting* (Oxford: Oxford University Press, 2006), pp. 43–49.

Local authorities, in particular, are faced with the fact that they are no longer able to fulfil their public service(s) on their own. One of the possibilities to tackle this problem is cooperation: 'To tackle the many traditional and new tasks of municipalities – and local authorities in general – is, particularly in times of restricted budgets, not always easy, especially for smaller authorities. In addition, many tasks, in particular in the areas of environment and transport are not confined to the municipality. Conversely, inter-municipal cooperation without calling on private capital is owing to its synergistic effects a method used in Member States for performing public functions in an efficient and cost-effective manner'.[554]

A public authority may then, for example appeal to other public authorities in such a context. Therefore, public authorities cooperate and share services.[555] Cooperation between public authorities is one of the ways that a public authority organises and discharges its public service tasks.[556] Public authorities cooperate in different ways. The thesis is only interested in cooperation based on an agreement. Two kinds of agreements must be distinguished: either the public authorities create jointly a new independent legal person and delegate the public service or task to the subsidiary they control (institutional or vertical cooperation), or there is cooperation in the form of a contract between public authorities (contractual or horizontal cooperation). Vertical cooperation refers to what in the thesis is referred to as 'quasi-in-house'[557] relations. In both cases, the following distinction can be made: either the operator called upon is fully public owned or it is not. This distinction has had a fundamental influence on how the application of EU law to vertical and horizontal cooperative agreements was approached. The following examination of the CJEU law will make this clear. (See sections 2 and 3)

As seen in chapter 4, under EU law the manner in which a public authority organises its public service tasks is normally within the scope of the competence of the Member States. Accordingly, Advocate General La Pergola considered in his Opinion *BFI*[558]: 'The question of a public authority's freedom to organise itself in the way best suited to meet the community's requirements need not, I think, detain us. The organizational arrangements chosen by a public authority must not allow the application of provisions designed to govern the quite different and well-defined situation in which a private individual provides a service for a public authority in return for remuneration. This is

554 Opinion Adv. Gen. Trstenjak under Case C-324/07, *Coditel Brabant SA v. Commune d'Uccle et Région Bruxelles-Capital* [2008] *ECR* I-8457, at [87].

555 The Scottish procurement directorate gives the following definition to 'shared services': *Shared Services in this context means the provision of services from one public body to one or more others either directly (through a lead authority) or via a delivery vehicle (such as a special purpose vehicle)* (www.scotland.gov.uk/Resource/Doc/1265/0054682.pdf).

556 D. Casalini, 'Beyond EU Law: the New "Public House"', in G.S.Olykke, C.R. Hansen and C.D. Tvarno, *EU Public procurement – Modernisation, Growth and Innovation* (Copenhagen: Djøf Publishing, 2011), p. 153.

557 The CJEU exempts contracts concluded between public authorities from the scope of EU law, which concern situations similar (quasi) to in-house provision.

558 Opinion of La Pergola, case 360/96, *Gemeente Arnhem and Gemeente Rheden v. BFI Holding BV* [1998] *ECR* I-06821, at [37].

clear from the wording of the Directive'.[559] However, the thesis examines the extent to which the public procurement Directives or the EU principle of equal treatment may influence the manner in which these issues are resolved and, thus, impinge upon the scope of the competences of Member States. The impact of EU public procurement law on contractual relationships between public authorities is an important topic, as is evident from the fact that the European Commission dedicated a working paper to this topic in 2011.[560]

Each decision of a public authority, as well as the decision to cooperate, is a 'State measure' that could hinder trade or distort competition and to that extent EU law has a bearing. As for the organisation or management of public service tasks, the CJEU has always sought to take into account the influence of EU on the various ways public authorities organise and manage their public service tasks.

This thesis is also of relevance for the division of powers between EU and the Member States. Indeed, in its case law on cooperative agreements the CJEU has always sought to balance the 'Member States' freedom to organise their own public services against the EU goals of opening up the market and ensuring equal competition'.[561] This emphasises the constitutional importance of the research.

This chapter will begin by briefly examining the extent to which EU law is applicable to the organisation or management of public service tasks. A distinction will be made in this regard between in-house provision and cooperation between public authorities. (1.) Next, the chapter delves deeper into cooperative agreements between public authorities. A distinction has to be made between vertical or institutional cooperative agreements (2.) and horizontal or contractual cooperative agreements (3.). The CJEU has recently made clear that both forms of cooperative agreements are object of a different case law.[562] It states that for both forms of cooperation there are other criteria that may be applied to keep them from falling out of the scope of EU law. Although the CJEU case law seems to distinguish three kinds of situations that could be excluded from the scope of EU law (in house, vertical and horizontal cooperative agreements), the present chapter tries to find a common explanation for this exclusion.

Late in 2011 the EU Commission signalled the need for a revision of the existing public procurement Directives. Accordingly, a need was now also felt for a Directive on service concessions. In chapter 2 the thesis explained certain Member States (e.g. France) opposed to the creation of specific directives on services concessions in previous reforms of the public procurement Directives. The new Directives, approved by European

559 At [37].

560 Commission Staff Working Paper concerning the application of EU public procurement law to relations between contracting authorities ('public-public cooperation') SEC(2011) 1169 final.

561 J. Wiggen, 'Public procurement rules and cooperation between public sector entities: the limits of the in-house doctrine under EU procurement law' (PPLR, 2011), p. 158.

562 Case C-159/11, *Azienda Sanitaria Locale di Lecce, Università del Salento v. Ordine degli Ingegneri della Provincia di Lecce and Others* [2012] *ECR* I-00000, at [31] to [34].

Parliament in January and February 2014 and published in the Official Journal of the European Union on 28 March 2014, now also include detailed provisions on their applicability to cooperative agreements between public authorities. The thesis will look into these new provisions. (4.)

1. Applicability of EU law

The chapter clarifies to what extent EU law is applicable to the organisation or management of public service tasks. Four areas may be distinguished: 1) in-house provision, 2) cooperation between public authorities, 3) a contract with a private undertaking and 4) transfer of a public service task. When a public authority engages a private undertaking to organise or discharge its public service tasks, it is clear that EU law applies insofar as an interstate element is present. In this situation, the public authority concludes a contract with an operator executing an economic activity. Hence, the thesis will not investigate the latter situation, even though it is doubtlessly influenced by EU law; likewise with the situation where a public authority delegates its competence to manage a public service task to a third person: In this case there is indeed no cooperation, instead, the public authority takes a decision unilaterally. This then leaves only the first two situations.

1.1. In-house provision

Public authorities primarily make use of their own services to accomplish their public service tasks. In this situation the public authority does not consult the market. The question arises whether EU law governs such a situation.

In *Stadt Halle*[563] the CJEU delivered a preliminary ruling on the applicability of public procurement Directives to such a situation. To answer this question the Court makes a fundamental distinction between the situation where a public authority uses its own departments to accomplish a task from the situation where the public authority takes recourse to a third party. In the first situation the Court ruled as follows: a public authority 'has the possibility of performing the tasks conferred on it in the public interest by using its own administrative, technical or other resources, without being obliged to call on outside entities not forming part of its own departments'.[564] Cosmas confirmed already in its Opinion prior to *Teckal* that EU law does not require public authorities to observe the procedure that ensures effective competition between interested parties, if where those public authorities wish to discharge the public service tasks with their own administration.[565] In-house provision is not subject to public procurement Directives.

563 Case C-26/03, *Stadt Halle and RPL Recyclingpark Lochau GmbH. v. Arbeitsgemeinschaft Thermische Restabfall- und Energieverwertungsanlage TREA Leuna* [2005] *ECR* I-00001.

564 At [48].

565 Opinion of G. Cosmas, case C-107/98, *Teckal Srl v. Comune di Viano* [1999] *ECR* I-8121, at [54].

However, it follows from *Teckal*[566] that the situation whereby a public authority has recourse to a third party is, in principle, subject to public procurement Directives.

As such the Court confirmed a wide set opinion in the continental law systems.[567] If a public authority takes recourse to its own resources, it does not sign a contract: 'In such a case, there can be no question of a contract for pecuniary interest concluded with an entity legally distinct from the contracting authority'.[568] In this case there are no two different wills. Procuring entities are not obliged in all situations to apply EU rules concerning public procurements.

In *Coditel Brabant*[569] the Court makes this assessment regarding in-house provision separately from the question of whether *a contract for pecuniary interest concluded with an entity legally distinct from the contracting authority* exists. *Coditel Brabant* concerned a service concession, a contract not subject to the public procurement Directives. Nevertheless, the Court considered: 'a public authority has the possibility of performing the public interest tasks conferred on it by using its own administrative, technical and other resources, without being obliged to call on outside entities not forming part of its own departments'.[570] Even where a relationship may be regarded as a service concession if two independent wills would be present, an in-house provision falls outside the scope of EU law. The principle of equality does not apply.

The Court reaffirmed this in *Commission v. Germany*,[571] where the competence of the Member States over in-house arrangements appears to rest on the postulate that free movement of services is not thereby hindered and that free competition is not distorted.[572] Chapter 4 defends the point that the hindering of market access or the distortion of competition determines mostly whether EU law is applicable on cooperative agreements between public authorities. According to *Deliège*[573] one could argue that the decision to call on its own departments is a measure inherent to the conduct of a public authority in respect of its own organisation and, as such, it does not affect the market.[574] With regard to the principle of equality, neither situation is comparable and, thus, the same legal rules do not apply.

566 Case C-107/98, *Teckal v. Comune di Viano* [1999] *ECR* I-8121.

567 Ph. Flamme and M.-A. Flamme, *Les marchés publics de services et la coordination de leurs procédures de passation* (*RMCUE*, 1993), p. 157, nr. 16; M. Mensi, *L'ouverture à la concurrence des marchés publics de services* (*RMCUE*, 1993), p. 67.

568 Case C-26/03, *Stadt Halle and RPL Recyclingpark Lochau GmbH. v. Arbeitsgemeinschaft Thermische Restabfall- und Energieverwertungsanlage TREA Leuna* [2005] *ECR* I-00001, at [48].

569 Case C-324/07, *Commune d'Uccle et Région Bruxelles-Capital* [2008] *ECR* I-08457.

570 At [48].

571 Case C-480/06, *Commission v. Germany* [2009] *ECR* I-04747.

572 At [45] and [47].

573 Joined cases C-51/96 and C-191/97, *Christelle Deliège v. Ligue francophone de judo et disciplines associées ASBL, Ligue belge de judo ASBL, Union européenne de judo and François Pacquée* [2000] *ECR* I-2549.

574 See chapter 4.

In doing this, the Court relies on an important criterion of demarcation regarding the distribution of powers between the EU and its Member States. The CJEU makes a choice of constitutional import in *Stadt Halle*, *Coditel Brabant* and in *Commission v. Germany*. If a public authority has its own services to carry out a task, it need not apply EU law. It is not required to set up an awarding procedure.

The CJEU leaves public authorities a free choice regarding how a public authority organises its public service tasks and whether the task will be carried out by its own services. In both cases the decision is left to the discretionary powers of the Member States and not to the EU. This also implies that the Member States (and not the EU) are empowered in this area to exercise regulatory powers.[575] The constitutional option appears to rest on the economic objectives inherent to the European Union. In this sense this case law is part of the European Economic Constitution (see on this concept chapter 4).

As it will be explained in chapter 6, in England, public authorities were obliged in the 1980s to outsource tasks even when they wished to have these tasks carried out by their own departments. This is called 'compulsory competitive tendering'. Again, according to EU law this is a policy choice the Member States can make. Indeed, this belongs, according to *Stadt Halle*,[576] to their sphere of competence. EU Law does not stipulate in this situation that a general obligation exists for Member States to resort to the market.[577]

Therefore EU law has no influence on in-house provision. Each of the Member States is free to regulate this situation as it sees fit. The following section of this chapter investigates the extent to which this also holds true when a public authority cooperates with another public authority (vertical or horizontal).

1.2. Cooperative agreements

The present section addresses three questions: 1) The first question that arises is whether the public procurement Directives or the principle of equality are at all applicable to cooperative agreements between public authorities (1.2.1.), 2) the second question concerns the kind of cooperation between public authorities to which CJEU case law is applicable (1.2.2.) and 3) the third question explores whether EU law itself explicitly provides for exceptions to its applicability in such circumstances (1.2.3.).

575 See also the European Communication on Public private partnerships and Community Law on Public Contracts and Concessions, COM(2005) 569 final.

576 C-26/03, *Stadt Halle and RPL Recyclingpark Lochau GmbH. v. Arbeitsgemeinschaft Thermische Restabfall- und Energieverwertungsanlage TREA Leuna* [2005] *ECR* I-00001.

577 A. Sanchez Graells, *Public Procurement and the EU Competition Rules* (London: Hart Publishing, 2011), pp. 232–234.

1.2.1. Under the scope of EU law?

In chapter 4 the thesis demonstrated that the decision to cooperate with another public authority constitutes a state measure. In this capacity such a decision can well fall within the scope of applicability of the fundamental freedom rules and the principle of equality. However, the applicability of EU law to cooperative agreements between public authorities raises a problem in the context of public procurement Directives. The Directives describe very precisely their area of applicability. But does this tell us anything about cooperative agreements between public authorities?

A legislative act could address a particular situation in two ways: either it remarks explicitly about its own applicability to the situation, or it contains a provision that exempts a situation from the applicability of the legislative act. (see section 1.2.3.) The present section explores to what extent the public procurement Directives contain a provision in one or the other of these two senses that is relevant to cooperative agreements between public authorities. Before the adoption of Directive 2004/17/EC and Directive 2004/18/EC, it was not very clear whether cooperative agreements between public authorities would fall within the scope of public procurement regulations.

In some EU Member States the applicability of public procurement Directives on cooperative agreements between public authorities was originally not as evident as it seems today.[578] Chapter 6, which examines the French legal system with regard to cooperative agreements between public authorities, makes clear that in France the 'Conseil d'État'[579] (Council of State) has long shielded such cooperation from application of the French legislation on the awarding of public contracts.[580]

One could argue that the public procurement Directives or the principles of equality and transparency are only applicable when a public authority turns to the private sector.[581] German scholars defended until recently that the public procurement Directives must be confined to 'public entities buying from or cooperating with the private sector and hence opening up competition'.[582] This point of view was still shared by Advocate General La

578 M. Burgi, 'In-House' Providing in Germany', in M. Comba and S. Treumer (eds.), *The In-House Providing in European Law* (Copenhagen: Djøf Publishing, 2010), pp. 79–80: *"cooperation between purely public entities is a question of the member states organizational sovereignity only, in which the EU lacks competence to infere"*.

579 The 'Conseil d'État' is the High Administrative Court in France.

580 In France: F. Moderne, 'La concurrence des services techniques de l'Etat et des techniciens privés auprès des collectivités locales' (*RD.imm.*, 1982), p. 467; F. Raynaud en P. Tombeur, 'Chronique générale de jurisprudence administrative française' (*AJDA*, 1998), p. 557. The French Council of State has approved the applicaton of the public procurement rules on contracts between public bodies in the decision Communauté de communes du Piémont de Barr: C.E.fr., Communauté de communes du Piémont de Barr, nr. 188.239 (*AJDA*, 1998), p. 553, with observations from F. Raynaud en P. Tombeur.

581 A.L. Durviaux, 'Les relations in-house: un pas de plus dans une direction délicate' (*BJCP*, 2007), p. 22.

582 M. Burgi, 'In House Providing in Germany", in M. Comba and S. Treumer (eds.), *The In-house Providing in European Law*, Copenhagen (Copenhagen: Djøf Publishing, 2010), p. 79.

Pergola in its Opinion to *BFI*.[583] In his view the Directives only apply to players active on the market. A public authority normally seeks solely to benefit the general interest, i.e. an activity that is not bound by market principles. Thus, if a public authority seeks the help of another public authority, it would not endanger the free market.

However, Article 1(c) of Directive 92/50/EEC[584] provided that: 'service provider shall mean any natural or legal person, *including a public body*,[585] which offers services'. For the first time a potential indication that public procurement regulations apply to cooperative agreements between public authorities was included in the relevant Directives.

The provisions of Directive 2004/17/EC and Directive 2004/18/EC contain sufficient grounds to infer that cooperative agreements between public authorities fall within their scope. For instance, Recital 4 in the Preamble to Directive 2004/18/EC makes it clear that a body governed by public law can participate as a tenderer. Paragraph 1 of Article 4 of the Directive 2004/18/EC does not take into account the public or private nature of the tenderer in regard to the application of the public procurement regime.[586] Article 1(7) Directive 2004/17/EC and Article 1(8) of Directive 2004/18/EC include for every kind of public contracts a public entity as a possible contractor.

Thus, these Directives are clear as to their applicability to cooperative agreements between public authorities. However, these Directives do not include any special provision defining whether these kinds of agreements fall within the scope of the Directives.

This is rather surprising insofar as the aim of the European Commission in drafting Directive 2004/17/EC and Directive 2004/18/EC was to clarify the existing rules, especially for situations where issues were difficult to resolve through an interpretation of the provisions.[587] Thus, the Commission also made an attempt to include a provision to cover the more specific quasi-in-house provision of public service tasks as confirmed in *Teckal*,[588] which focused on vertical cooperative agreements between public authorities[589]: 'This Directive shall not apply to public contracts awarded by a contracting authority to a legally distinct entity owned exclusively by that contracting authority, if the entity concerned does not have autonomous decision-making powers in relation to the contracting authority on account of the latter exercising over that entity a control

583 See Opinion of La Pergola, case 360/96, *Gemeente Arnhem and Gemeente Rheden v. BFI Holding BV* [1998] *ECR* I-06821, at [37].

584 Directive 92/50/EEC of 18 June 1993 '*Relating to the coordination of procedures for the award of public service contracts*', OJ 1992 L 209, 1–24.

585 Emphasised by the author.

586 Case C-305/08, *Consorzio Nazionale Interuniversitario per le Scienze del Mare (CoNISMA) v. Regione Marche* [2009] *ECR* I-12129, at [31].

587 Commission communication XV/5500/98/EN, 11 March 1998, 4.

588 Case C-107/98, *Teckal v. Comune di Viano* [1999] *ECR* I-8121.

589 COM (2002) 26, 6 May 2002.

which is similar to that which it exercises over its own departments; [and] the entity carries out all its activities with the contracting authority which owns it' (Article 19(a)). But within the Council, the Member States could not agree on a definition of quasi-in-house.[590] They left it to the CJEU to further elaborate the scope in its case law.

As it will be evident in section 4, the recently approved Directives on public procurement and services concessions[591] by the European Parliament contain provisions that address both vertical and horizontal cooperative agreements between public authorities (see 4).

Since 1999 the CJEU concluded in several cases that cooperative agreements between public authorities also fell within the scope of public procurement Directives. This confirms that the Directives adopted before 2004 contain provisions leading to the conclusion that cooperative agreements between public authorities fall under their scope.

In *Teckal*[592] the CJEU acknowledged for the first time the applicability of public procurement Directives to cooperative agreements between public authorities. Indeed, the Court held that the Directives are applicable to a contract between a municipality (contracting authority) and one other body, 'whether or not that entity is itself a contracting authority'.[593] The qualification of 'contractor' is not important for determining the applicability of the public procurement regime. However, Advocate General La Pergola took a different view. According to his Opinion in *BFI*[594] public contracts between public bodies could be excluded from the scope of public procurement Directives. This Opinion could be defended because the Directives did not provide any disposition on this subject.

In *ARGE*[595] the CJEU confirmed that the public procurement Directives authorise the participation of public bodies in an award procedure for a public procurement contract.[596] A public authority could be a contracting party. The next step confirming the applicability of the public procurement regime to a contract between two public bodies (or cooperative agreement between public authorities) was a small one.

The CJEU was clearer in a case decided in 2005.[597] The Spanish law on public procurement excluded from its scope cooperation agreements between the State authorities, on the

590 Position of the Council CSL110 29/3/02 of March 2003.

591 Proposal of the European Commission for a directive of the European Parliament and the Council on the award of concession contracts, COM (2011)897 final.

592 Case C-107/98, *Teckal v. Comune di Viano* [1999] *ECR* I-8121.

593 At [51]. See also Case C-94/99, *Arge Gewässerschutz* (2000) *ECR* I-11037, at [40]; Case C-480/06, *Commission v. Germany* [2009] *ECR* I-04747, at [33].

594 Opinion of La Pergola, case 360/96, *Gemeente Arnhem and Gemeente Rheden v. BFI Holding BV* [1998] *ECR* I-06821, at [37].

595 C-94/99, *ARGE Gewässerschutz v. Bundesministerium für Land- und Forstwirtschaft* [2002] *ECR* I-11037.

596 At [28].

597 Case C-84/03, *Commission v. Spain* [2005] *ECR* I-00139.

one hand, and the Social Security, autonomous communities, local bodies, their autonomous bodies and any other public body, on the other hand, or between these bodies'. The Commission alleged that the Kingdom of Spain had excluded from the codified law cooperative agreements concluded between bodies governed by public law, although those agreements may constitute public contracts for the purpose of Directives 93/36/EEC and 93/37/EEC. In accordance with Article 1(a) of Directive 93/36/EEC, it is sufficient, in principle, if the contract was concluded between a local authority and a person legally distinct from it. This approach must also be applied to inter-administrative agreements, according to the CJEU. Agreements between public authorities cannot be excluded, *a priori*, from the scope of the public procurement Directives.[598]

Finally, the CJEU decided in *CoNISMa*[599] as follows: 'It therefore follows from both Community rules and the Court's case-law that any person or entity which, in the light of the conditions laid down in a contract notice, believes that it is capable of carrying out the contract, either directly or by using subcontractors, is eligible to submit a tender or put itself forward as a candidate, regardless of whether it is governed by public law or private law, whether it is active as a matter of course on the market or only on an occasional basis and whether or not it is subsidised by public funds'.[600] The nature of the economic operator or of the contracting partner is irrelevant to the application of the public procurement Directives. The CJEU based the above judgement on one of the fundamental principles of the Directives; namely, the widest possible opening to competition. This is in the interest of all parties, public authorities and undertakings.

It therefore follows from the Court's case law that also cooperative agreements between public authorities could possibly fall within the scope of Directives 2004/17/EC or 2004/18/EC. The CJEU based the applicability of the Directives to cooperative agreements on a formal element, i.e. the presence of a contract. However, *Conisma* proves that a functional explanation is present. A public authority acting as an economic operator has to be exposed to an equal treatment as a private operator to ensure free competition. Once the application of the Directives affirmed the risk existed that if a public authority outsourced its services by contract the public procurement regime or the principles of equality and transparency always must be applied even if the contract partner is a public authority. The Directives provide for only one exception that, moreover, is subject to strict conditions (see 1.2.3.) Since at issue is an exception, these conditions receive a strict interpretation.

This would restrict enormously the possibilities of a public authority to seek help outside its own departments. In the last two decades the CJEU, expressing itself on this problem, has created distinct case law on the subject to limit the application of EU law to these situations (see 2. and 3.) Thus the Court of Justice thereby assumed the role of European lawmaker and this in turn raised the question of the democratic legitimacy of the case law.

598 At [40].

599 Case C-305/08, *Consorzio Nazionale Interuniversitario per le Scienze del Mare (CoNISMA) v. Regione Marche* [2009] *ECR* I-12229.

600 At [42].

1.2.2. Kind of cooperation

The CJEU had to consider in *Teckal*[601] a situation that in principle came within the scope of EU law. The preliminary question in *Teckal* concerned the interpretation of the public procurement Directives. The CJEU confirmed the applicability of the Directives on cooperative agreements between public authorities (see 1.2.1.) However, is this case law really transposable to other agreements concluded between public authorities? In several cases the CJEU has given an explicit answer.

In *Parking Brixen*[602] and other case law, the CJEU excluded the obligation of transparency in service concessions if the public authority providing the concession exercises over the subsidiary a control similar to that it exercises over its own departments and this concession holder also performs the greater part of its activities on behalf of the body (or bodies) that it control(s). The Court thereby affirms that EU law is applicable if a service concession is concluded between two or more public authorities.[603]

Accordingly, the CJEU has also repeatedly reaffirmed that if the value of a contract is under the threshold set under EU public procurement rules it has no effect on the applicability of the *Teckal* case law.[604]

Thus far our analysis has concerned only the scope of applicability of vertical cooperative agreements. But is it also valid for horizontal cooperative agreements?

Commission v. Germany[605] and *Ordine degli Ingegneri*[606] concern a public contract falling under the scope of the public procurement Directives. These are the two leading cases introducing a new situation (horizontal cooperative agreements between public authorities) that falls out of the scope of EU law. The next issue to be considered is whether this case law can be applied to a service concession. *Parking Brixen*[607] is the relevant case to answer this question.

In this last case the CJEU had to examine if a public service concession must be put out to competition in a similar manner to a public procurement contract. The Court confirmed that a service concession does not fall within the scope of the public

601 Case C-107/98, *Teckal v. Comune di Viano* [1999] *ECR* I-8121.

602 Case C-458/03, *Parking Brixen GmbH v. Gemeinde Brixen* [2005] *ECR* I-08585, at [62]; Case C-410/04, *Associazione Nazionale Autotrasporto Viaggiatori (ANAV)* [2006] *ECR* I-3303, at [24].

603 See also Case C-324/07, *Commune d'Uccle et Région Bruxelles-Capital* [2008] *ECR* I-08457.

604 Case C-573/07, *Sea Srl v. Comune di Ponte Nassa* [2009] *ECR* I-08127, at [35]; Joined cases C-182/11 and C-183/11, *Econord SpA v. Comuni di Cagno, Comune di Varese, Comune di Solbiate* [2012] *ECR* I-00000, at [26].

605 Case C-480/06, *Commission of the European Communities v. Federal Republic of Germany* [2009] *ECR* I-04747.

606 Case C-159/11, *Azienda Sanitaria Locale di Lecce, Università del Salento v. Ordine degli Ingegneri della Provincia di Lecce and Others* [2012] *ECR* I-00000.

607 Case C-458/03, *Parking Brixen GmbH v. Gemeinde Brixen* [2005] *ECR* I-08585.

procurement Directives. Irrespective of this ruling these contracts are, according to the Court, obliged to comply with the fundamental rules of the TFEU. Thus, public service concessions are bound by EU law. Likewise, the considerations developed in *Teckal*[608] and in *Stadt Halle*[609] regarding quasi-in-house and in-house situations are transposable to the interpretation and application of Treaty provisions and to the principles that relate to service concessions.

There is no reason why the CJEU analysis on horizontal cooperative agreements should not be transposable to a (public) service concession. The Court also makes this clear in *Ordine degli Ingegneri*: 'However, the fact that the contract at issue in the main proceedings is capable of falling, as the case may be, either under Directive 2004/18 or the fundamental rules and general principles of the FEU Treaty does not affect the answer to be given to the question posed. The criteria laid down in the case law of the Court in order to determine whether an invitation to tender is mandatory are relevant both with regard to the interpretation of that Directive and with regard to the interpretation of those rules and principles of the FEU Treaty'.[610] This consideration also proves that the CJEU case law on horizontal cooperative agreements also applies to contracts below EU thresholds.

More generally, in *Parking Brixen* the Court established that the *Teckal* criteria apply every time a public authority charges a third party with the execution of an economic activity.[611] Thus the CJEU seems to be saying that these criteria can be applied to all kinds of contracts concluded between public authorities. Already elsewhere, it was argued that the principle of equal treatment and the obligation to transparency are applicable to all kinds of contracts concluded between public authorities.[612] Hence, if this principle is to be observed, exceptions to its application must also be applicable to these contracts.[613]

The same reasoning could also be applied to unilateral relations between public authorities. Several times the CJEU has confirmed that public authorities, which grant unilateral advantages to economic operators, are bound by the fundamental rules of the Treaties, including in particular Articles 49 and 56 TFEU, the principles of equal treatment and of non-discrimination on grounds of nationality and the consequent obligation of transparency.[614] Exemptions to the applicability of these principles should apply in the same manner.

608 Case C-107/98, *Teckal v. Comune di Viano* [1999] *ECR* I-8121.

609 Case C-26/03, *Stadt Halle and RPL Recyclingpark Lochau GmbH v. Arbeitsgemeinschaft Thermische Restabfall- und Energieverwertungsanlage TREA Leuna* [2005] *ECR* I-00001.

610 At [24].

611 Case C-458/03, *Parking Brixen GmbH v. Gemeinde Brixen* [2005] *ECR* I-08585, at [61].

612 K. Wauters, *Overheidsovereenkomsten en rechtsbescherming* (Antwerpen: Intersentia, 2009), pp. 75–78.

613 See Case C-573/07, *Sea Srl v. Comune di Ponte Nassa* [2009] *ECR* I-08127, at [35] to [37]; Case C-159/11, *Azienda Sanitaria Locale di Lecce, Università del Salento v. Ordine degli Ingegneri della Provincia di Lecce and Others* [2012] *ECR* I-00000, at [24].

614 Case C-203/08, *Sporting Exchange* [2010] *ECR* I-4695, at [39]; Case C-64/08, *Engelmann* [2010] *ECR* I-08219, at [49]; Joined Cases C-72/10 and C-77/10 *Costa and Cifone* [2012] *ECR* I-0000, at [54]; Joined

1.2.3. Exclusion

Directive 2004/18/EC provides one explicit exception to the applicability of the public procurement regime to cooperative agreements between public authorities.

Article 18 of Directive 2004/18/EC[615] stipulates: 'This Directive shall not apply to public service contracts awarded by a contracting authority to another contracting authority or to an association of contracting authorities on the basis of an exclusive right which they enjoy pursuant to a published law, regulation or administrative provision which is compatible with the Treaty'.[616]

Article 18 addresses specifically a situation where a public authority cooperates with another public authority. However, the cooperation is based exclusively on the acknowledgement of an exclusive right. In such a situation an award procedure is not necessary, according to Article 18 because the Directives do not apply. The granting of an exclusive right excludes every other competitor.[617] As a preliminary observation one should bear in mind that the mentioned exception excludes the EU internal market rules, which are fundamental in the European Union, and it should be interpreted strictly inasmuch as it is an exception.[618] This provision has been considered by the CJEU on three occasions.

In *BFI*[619] the CJEU had to examine a situation where two Dutch towns established a company that would provide waste disposal services for the two towns. These services had been allotted without any tendering procedure. The Dutch court thought such an award could fall within the scope of Article 6 of Directive 92/50/CEE. According to the Dutch court the only problem was whether the company was a contracting authority. The CJEU examined this issue thoroughly and by implication acknowledged that this was a major condition for the applicability of Article 6. Furthermore the CJEU found it essential that the exclusive right be pursuant to a published law, regulation or administrative provision, thus confirming the second condition on which applicability of Article 18 of Directive 2004/18/EC depends.

The *Teckal*[620] ruling also had a bearing on the interpretation of the scope of Article 6 of Directive 92/50/EEC. The question arose whether this article could be applied to a public

Cases C-186/11 and C-209/11 *Stanleybet International Ltd, William Hill Organization Ltd, William Hill Plc, Sportingbet plc v. Ypourgos Oikonomias kai Oikonomikon, Ypourgos Politismou* [2013] *ECR* I-0000, at [47].

615 Previous Article 6 directive 92/50/EEC of 18 June 1992 relating to coordination of procedures for the award of public service contracts.

616 See also Art. 23 of directive 2004/17/EC.

617 R. Caranta, 'The In-House Providing: The Law as it Stands in the EU', in M. Comba and S. Treumer (eds.), *The In-House Providing in European Law* (Copenhagen: Djøf Publishing, 2010), p. 15.

618 Case C-26/03, *Stadt Halle and RPL Recyclingpark Lochau GmbH. v. Arbeitsgemeinschaft Thermische Restabfall- und Energieverwertungsanlage TREA Leuna* [2005] *ECR* I-00001, at [46].

619 Case C-360/96, *Gemeente Arnhem and Gemeente Rheden v. BFI Holding BV* [1998] *ECR* I-6821.

620 Case C-107/98, *Teckal v. Comune di Viano* [1999] *ECR* I-8121.

supply contract. The CJEU answered in the negative and thus restricted the range of applicability of the Article. Article 6 concerns only public service contracts. There is no explanation for this difference to be found in the Directives themselves and the lack of explanation is confirmed by the CJEU in *Teckal*. The interpretation in *Teckal* was the starting point for the CJEU to create an autonomous exemption to the application of public procurement rules to the several kinds of public contracts (work, service and supply). Since the Directives at that time contained no provision comparable to Article 6 for public work contracts and public supply contracts, the CJEU began a quest for a general exception system for when public authorities cooperate. The quasi-in-house case law has its origins here.

Finally a Spanish Court submitted a preliminary question to the CJEU as to the applicability of the public procurement regime to reserved and non-reserved postal services awarded to Correos without a public call for tenders.[621] Reserved postal services are not subject to competition since no other economic operator is authorised to offer those services. As to the non-reserved postal services the CJEU examined whether the exemption provided by Article 6 of Directive 92/50/EEC might not be applicable. Based on its previous case law the Court recognised three conditions for application of Article 6: (1) the article applies only to public services, (2) the public authority grants an exclusive right and (3) the granting must be compatible with the Treaty (TFEU). These conditions are cumulative.

Conferring an exclusive right to provide non-reserved postal services would contradict the objectives and provisions of Directive 97/67/EC 'on common rules for the development of the internal market of Community postal services and the improvement of quality of service'[622], which aims to establish gradual and controlled liberalisation in the postal sector.[623] It would not be compatible with the Treaty provisions to grant in such a situation an exclusive right to a contractor.

This case law presents an extremely restrictive interpretation of Article 6 (and Article 18 of Directive 2004/18/CE). A contracting authority can directly award a contract to another public body only under the strict conditions laid down in the Directive.[624] This provision could not be used to effect a broader derogation to the public procurement regime in situations where a public authority seeks cooperation with a distinct legal body that does not 'play on the market'. Consequently, the CJEU had to look for other criteria whereby other cooperative agreements between public authorities could be removed from within the scope of public procurement Directives and EU law in general. The criteria will be examined below.

621 Case C-220/06, *Asociación Profesional de Empresas de Reparto y Manipulado de Correspondencia* [2007] *ECR* I-12175.

622 OJ 1998 L 15.

623 Case C-220/06, *Asociación Profesional de Empresas de Reparto y Manipulado de Correspondencia* [2007] *ECR* I-12175, at [67].

624 Case C-220/05, *Jean Auroux and Others v. Commune de Roanne* [2007] *ECR* I-389, at [59].

2. Institutional or vertical cooperative agreements

This section examines under what condition vertical cooperative agreements between public authorities fall beyond the scope of EU law. First, the thesis examines broadly the origins of the CJEU case law (2.1.). Next it explains the two criteria employed by the CJEU to place vertical cooperative agreements beyond the applicability of EU law: the control criterion (2.2.) and the activities criterion (2.3.).

2.1. *Origins of the case law*

In order to accomplish tasks of general interest more efficiently and less expensively, public authorities may establish an independent legal entity on their own (unilateral decision) or together with private partners or with other public authorities (contract). These separate legal entities perform tasks either directly for the benefit of the public authority, which is member of the separate legal entity (public contract) or they themselves perform a task of general interest on behalf of one or more of the member(s) (service concession). One question that arises in the thesis is whether and when cooperative agreements between public authorities fall outside the scope of TFEU and of public procurement Directives.

Between the 1970s and the 1990s the CJEU did not have to examine these kinds of issues with regard to the public procurement Directives and the TFEU. Early on, in a 1998 communication entitled 'Public procurement in the European Union', the European Commission laid down that an agreement 'awarded within the public administration, for example between a central and local administration or between an administration and a company wholly owned by it' could constitute an 'in house'- provision.[625] The presence of a third party does not, according to the Commission, always mean that public procurement Directives are applicable. But the Commission is wrong to use the term 'in-house' in this situation. The examples it gives are more like quasi in-house situations. It is this kind of situation the CJEU had to deal with in *Teckal.*[626]

Teckal was the first case where the CJEU ruled on the subject. As discussed earlier, the CJEU confirmed the applicability of EU law to cooperative agreements between public authorities in this matter. Accordingly in this case the CJEU has also developed for the first time criteria such that under certain circumstances cooperative agreements between public authorities lie beyond the scope of EU law. Since *Teckal* lies at the origin of CJEU case law on cooperative agreements it deserves a more extended treatment.

In *Teckal* the CJEU had to rule on a contract placed by the municipal Council of Viano in Italy and concluded with a consortium of municipalities, called AGAC, of which Viano itself was a member (vertical cooperation). The AGAC consortium had been set up

625 COM(98)143final.

626 Case C-107/98, *Teckal v. Comune di Viano* [1999] *ECR* I-8121.

by several municipalities, including Viano, to manage energy and environmental services. The Viano Council entrusted to AGAC the management of heating installations in municipal buildings, together with the supply of fuel to those buildings. The Council failed to hold any competitive tendering procedure involving third parties. *Teckal*, being a private company active in the supply of heating products and services, alleged that the Council, before placing the contract with AGAC, should have followed the tendering procedures for public contracts required under the public procurement directives.

The applicability of the tendering procedures set out in the public procurement Directives is dependent on how the term 'public contract' is construed. If the agreement between the municipality of Viano and AGAC can be classified as a public contract, the Directives are applicable. The CJEU stated it was for the national court to determine whether the relationship between the municipality of Viano and AGAC constituted a public contract and, in particular, whether there had been an agreement between two separate entities. The role of the CJEU is simply to provide an interpretation for EU law, i.e. public procurement Directives.

To resolve the issue of the applicability of public procurement Directives the CJEU suggested the national judge to proceed from the concept 'contract' as an element of the definition of the term 'public contract'. According to Advocate General Cosmas a contract exists if there is 'a concordance of wills between two different persons, the contracting authority and the supplier, and, second, the commercial relationship that is created consists in the supply of a product for pecuniary remuneration'.[627] The contract is a synallagmatic act. The CJEU noted that it is sufficient in principle if the contract was concluded between, on the one hand, a local authority and, on the other, a person legally distinct from that local authority to apply the public procurement Directives. The CJEU thus appears to follow the reasoning of the Advocate General in its Opinion. In opting for the concept of 'contract' as a starting point to examine the applicability of the public procurement Directives on cooperative agreements between public authorities the CJEU has elected a notion of EU law. This implies that this concept has an autonomous meaning and that will be broadly interpreted (See chapter 3).

The CJEU could have limited itself to the affirmation that a contract is present and then conclude that public procurement rules must be applied. Instead, it considered that cooperative agreements between public authorities under certain circumstances fall outside the scope of EU law, possibly realising that otherwise public authorities in several Member States would be extensively limited in their freedom to organise their public service. In several continental countries cooperation between public authorities is governed by administrative law. The freedom of a public authority to organise its own public services is one of the leading principles of this law.

The CJEU had to find a criterion or criteria that would exclude from the scope of public procurement Directives arrangements where two different persons cooperate. As already

[627] Opinion of G. Cosmas, case C-107/98, *Teckal Srl v. Comune di Viano* [1999] *ECR* I-8121, at [52].

noted the public procurement Directives contain only one exception to their application on cooperation between public authorities, which is Article 18 of Directive 2004/18/EC (former Article 6 of Directive 92/50/EEC). This exception was not applicable in *Teckal*. The CJEU had to create a new exception or exemption. As such the Court could not adopt a formal criterion but instead had to find a more flexible one. A formal criterion exclusively based on a classical interpretation of the concept of contract (the presence of two independent legal persons) invariably leads to the conclusion that the public procurement regime applies. (see chapter 6 on the French system)

The CJEU seems to have taken inspiration from a number of Opinions of several Advocate Generals to create its innovative case law on vertical cooperative agreements. In *BFI*[628] two Dutch municipalities, Arnhem and Rheden, decided to reorganise the way in which they fulfilled their obligations in regard to the collection and disposal of household waste. They therefore decided jointly to create a limited company ('ARA Holding BV') where this new entity would carry out these tasks on their behalf. Advocate General La Pergola concluded that ARA was still an organ of the participating municipalities in a broad and indirect sense.[629] According to him there is only a form of inter-departmental delegation involved. In order to designate ARA as an organ, the Advocate General refers to the financial ties and to the composition of management board. These elements will reappear later in CJEU rulings to determine whether a contracting authority exercises control over the provider similar to that which it exercises over its own departments.[630] Even if the executor of a task has third-party status, this does not necessarily mean that a contract is present. In some circumstances (sufficient control) the 'third party' is still a part of the public administration and thus the situation must be regarded as 'in-house'.

In *RI.SAN*[631] Advocate General Alber dealt extensively with *quasi-in-house* arrangements. By decision of the municipal council of 19 March 1996, the Municipality of Ischia formed a mixed-capital limited company to run the solid urban waste collection service. Advocate General Alber confirmed that the public procurement Directives do not cover in-house services provided by part of the same public administration. In that case there is no third party entrusted with providing the service.[632] He also looked at the situation in which a public authority appeals to another public authority of which it holds a part. According to Alber the fact that the other public authority is a private company does not per se preclude it from being part of the public administration. The third party must be classified in according to a functional interpretation.[633] The CJEU, however, concluded

628 Case C-360/96, *Gemeente Arnhem and Gemeente Rheden v. BFI Holding* [1998] *ECR* I-6821.

629 Opinion of A. La Pergola case C-360/96, *Gemeente Arnhem and Gemeente Rheden v. BFI Holding BV* [1998] *ECR* I-06821, at [36].

630 See Case C-107/98, *Teckal v. Comune di Viano* [1999] *ECR* I-8121.

631 Opinion of S. Alber case C-108/98, *RI.SAN. Srl v. Comune di Ischia, Italia Lavoro SpA and Ischia Ambiente SpA* [2000] *ECR* I-05219.

632 At [50].

633 At [52].

otherwise in its case law.[634] The degree of influence exercised by the public administration over the company is decisive. If one can establish both financial and organizational interconnections between Ischia and Ischia Ambiente, then the services can be qualified as an in-house service.[635]

The first *Teckal* criterion, the control criterion (which will be discussed below), is already evident in these two Opinions. Fundamental to the possible application of the public procurement regime is the state of dependency of the new constituted 'company'. Legal autonomy is of no importance.

In *Teckal* the contracting authority did not have recourse to its own resources, but to a third party. In order to decide if a third party was present, the Advocate General looked at the kind of control that the public authority has over third persons and to whom the particular third party provides services. As regards this control, the Advocate General seems to use a rather formal approach based on administrative law, as it exists in certain continental legal systems (e.g. Belgium and France). He refers to a 'hierarchical control' and a 'kind of control which an entity exercises over an internal body'.[636] The fact that AGAC provides services to private or public bodies that are not members of a cooperative venture seems to be one of the factors in the Advocate General's conclusion that AGAC cannot be regarded as a quasi-in-house situation.[637] Thus, for the first time the second *Teckal* criterion (activities) also appears in the reasoning on the legal status of a possible in-house provision.

According to the Court, the new exemption to application of the public procurement rules would be present where 'the local authority exercises over the person concerned a control which is similar to that which it exercises over its own departments and, at the same time, that person carries out the essential part of its activities with the controlling local authority or authorities'.[638] The use of the term 'departments' derives from the original reason for setting up autonomous bodies, which was to manage public services outside the administration.

The CJEU proposed two criteria to exempt an arrangement between two public bodies (or cooperative agreements between contracting authorities) from the public procurement regime: first there must be a control that is similar to that which it exercises over its own departments and, secondly, the carrying out of the essential part of the activities with the controlling authority or authorities. These are the so-called '*Teckal* criteria' (control and activities). Both criteria express the idea of (in)dependency.[639] Are the two wills independent and thus are we in the presence of a contract? These two substantial criteria

634 See Case C-26/03, *Stadt Halle and RPL Recyclingpark Lochau GmbH v. Arbeitsgemeinschaft Thermische Restabfall- und Energieverwertungsanlage TREA Leuna* [2005] *ECR* I-00001, at [49].

635 At [53] and [54].

636 Opinion of G. Cosmas, case C-107/98, *Teckal Srl v. Comune di Viano* [1999] *ECR* I-8121, at [61].

637 At [62].

638 Case C-107/98, *Teckal v. Comune di Viano* [1999] *ECR* I-8121at [50].

639 J.-M. Peyrical, 'Que reste-t-il du in house?' (*RFDA*, 2005), p. 956.

make it possible to distinguish two situations: a vertical cooperative agreement falling inside or outside the scope of EU law. Whenever the two *Teckal* criteria are met, the situation is comparable to in house-provision. The principle of equality requires that the two situations be treated equally and thus that both are beyond the reach of EU law.

The *Teckal* criteria are of a cumulative nature.[640] The two criteria must be met 'at the same time'.[641] In his Opinion prior to the *ARGE* case, Advocate General Leger gives an explanation to the necessity of these two criteria: 'the principle set out in that judgement (*Teckal*) is based on the criterion that the operator is independent. An entity is not necessarily deprived of freedom of action simply because the decisions affecting it are taken by the local authority that controls it, if it is able to carry out a substantial part of its economic activity for other operators. However, the entity must be considered to be wholly linked to the controlling authority if, in addition, the organisational relationship between the authority and the entity in question is coupled with the fact that the latter provides its services more or less exclusively to the authority. Such circumstances show that the local authority intends to use the services not just for public purposes but also, and principally, for its own benefit'.[642]

In *Teckal* the CJEU did not give any further explanation in respect of the criteria. It seems that the Court left it to the national courts to concretise the *Teckal* criteria. This raises the question of on what basis does the CJEU provide these two new criteria. After all, nothing comes from nothing. The Court nowhere refers to relevant European directives or to earlier case law. Instead, as indicated above, certain aspects of the criteria already found expression in Opinions of Advocate Generals. On the basis of these opinions, some legal scholars think that Italian law is at the origins of these criteria.[643]

The two criteria are in themselves formal and based on public law, but are to be interpreted in a functional manner.[644] The big difference with other CJEU case law is that this functional interpretation reduces the influence of EU law on national law. Regarding the first criteria the CJEU could not speak about a full or identical control because in such circumstances it was obvious that the public procurement Directives did not apply.[645] In the presence of full control, one cannot identify two different wills. This explains why the Court used the word 'similar' in *Teckal*. The situation, to which the Court refers, is

640 P. Delvolve, 'Marchés publics: les critères des 'contrats-maison' (*RDUE*, 2002), p. 55; P. Nihoul, 'Les marches publics dans l'Union européenne (2003–2005)' (*JDE*, 2006), p. 270; C. Dubois, 'To be or not to be 'In house'? Observations relatives à l'exception 'In house' après l'arrêt Carbotermo' (*CDPK*, 2007), p. 219.

641 Case C-107/98, *Teckal v. Comune di Viano* [1999] *ECR* I-8121, at [50].

642 Opinion Advocate General Léger C-94/99, *ARGE Gewässerschutz v. Bundesministerium für Land- und Forstwirtschaft* [2002] *ECR* I-11037, at [73] and [74].

643 M. Comba, 'In-House Providing in Italy: the circulation of a model', in M. Comba and S. Treumer (Eds.), *The In-house providing in European law* (Copenhagen: Djøf Publishing, 2010), pp. 101–103.

644 See also Opinion Advocate General Stix-Hackl case C-26/03, *Stadt Halle and RPL Recyclingpark Lochau GmbH v. Arbeitsgemeinschaft Thermische Restabfall- und Energieverwertungsanlage TREA Leuna* [2005] *ECR* I-00001, at [65].

645 D. Deom, 'Quel avenir pour le service public local à l'heure européenne' (*Mouv.comm.*, 2004), p. 464.

comparable to a real in house-relation, yet it is not the same. For that reason, one should describe the *Teckal* case law as *quasi-in-house.*

It appears that the Court has avoided the possible risk that all agreements concluded by public authorities would fall under the public procurement regime, even agreements concluded with related public bodies.[646] The Court here behaves as legislator, and from a democratic perspective this must be criticised. However, the Court is rather creating a rule specifying precisely where EU law may not be applied and, in particular, in a situation where the Directives seem to imply the opposite. This interpretation consequently seems to favour the Member States. For once the Court is not extending applicability of EU law but is instead providing an instrument whereby the applicability of EU law can be limited.

The question that then arises is whether it was wise for the Court to establish such criteria in the first ruling where the question arose about the applicability of EU law to vertical cooperative agreements. The Court seems itself to have answered this question implicitly in the negative when issuing its first ruling[647] in regard to a horizontal cooperative association. The Court seems to have deliberately not yet spelled out any criteria in that ruling. Furthermore, the two *Teckal* criteria are strictly formal criteria that in part hinder a functional interpretation. Thus it required an entire evolution of CJEU case law to arrive at an interpretation that provides more freedom to public authorities to organise their own public services. The thesis purports to argue that it would have been better if the CJEU, as in *Deliege*[648] had applied a completely functional construction on the public procurement Directives; the result would have been the same.

In *Teckal* the Court attempts with the concept 'contract' to find a solution to the problem of the applicability of the public procurement Directives to cooperative agreements between public authorities. The reasoning seems to be that if certain criteria are met, there are not two expressions of will and hence there is also no contract. Some authors believe that the CJEU case law on cooperative agreements still takes the concept 'contract' as a starting point.[649] The ruling in *RI.SAN*[650] seems to contradict this statement. In this ruling the CJEU found it of no importance if a contract was present to apply the free movement rules.[651] In *Parking Brixen,*[652] however, the Court seems to deny that quasi-in-house case law is based on the concept 'contract'. This notion is not relevant for the

646 Y.-R. Guillou, 'L'exonération des relations 'in house' du régime des marches publics' (*ACCP* 32,2004), p. 72.

647 Case C-480/06, *Commission of the European Communities v. Federal Republic of Germany* [2009] *ECR* I-04747.

648 Joined cases C-51/96 and C-191/97, *Christelle Deliège v. Ligue francophone de judo et disciplines associées ASBL, Ligue belge de judo ASBL, Union européenne de judo and François Pacquée* [2000] *ECR* I-2549.

649 J. Wiggen, 'Public procurement rules and cooperation between public sector entities: the limits of the in-house doctrine under EU procurement law' (*PPLR*, 2011), pp. 157 et s.

650 Case C-108/98, *RI.SAN. Srl v. Comune di Ischia, Italia Lavoro SpA and Ischia Ambiente SpA* [2000] *ECR* I-05219.

651 At [20].

652 Case C-458/03, *Parking Brixen GmbH v. Gemeinde Brixen* [2005] *ECR* I-08585, at [60].

applicability of the principles of equal treatment and transparency to the awarding of a service concession. Consequently the concept 'contract' may likewise not be relevant for placing the same situation beyond the scope of these provisions and these principles. According to this thesis, the CJEU case law proves that the notion 'contract' is not able to explain why vertical and horizontal cooperative agreements under certain circumstances fall out of the scope of EU law.

By opting for this notion of 'contract' as a primary premise, the CJEU likewise bound itself to its case law in which the concept of 'public contract' is interpreted broadly in order to place as many arrangements as possible under the jurisdiction of the Directives. This choice is also decisive for the interpretation the Court would give to the two criteria that were designed precisely in *Teckal* to create an exception to the applicability of the Directives. This necessarily had to lead to a strict interpretation. But this was still not enough to affect a real balance between, on the one hand, the competence of the Member States to regulate the organisation of their public service tasks and the competence of the EU on the other.

For a long time public authorities had to wait for further elaboration of the two *Teckal* criteria. However, the CJEU, since 2005, has had in several opportunities to provide further explanation on the two *Teckal* criteria.

2.2. *The control criterion*

In the first place the CJEU ruled in *Teckal* that a public authority must have a control over the third party similar to that which it exercises over its own departments, for a cooperative agreement to fall beyond the reach of EU law. Most of the Court's case law is concerned with this criterion. It is the most controversial criterion and it is also the one that is most difficult to interpret. As mentioned above the CJEU did not explain in *Teckal* what it meant by exercising over another person a control that is similar to that which a public authority exercises over its own departments. Before 2005, the CJEU did not have the opportunity to clarify the control criterion.[653]

What kinds of elements are important to determine whether a public authority has the necessary control to equate it to that it exercises over its own departments? In their Opinions preceding *ARGE* and *Stadt Halle* Advocates General Leger and Stix-Hackl took the opportunity to explain their view on the control criterion. According to Leger it is for the national court to consider in detail the evidence available.[654] Leger did not provide any concrete examples on how to check the sufficiency of the control. But Stix-Hackl tried to find a definition at European level. In general she considered that it was not enough to make a purely abstract assessment based on the legal form chosen for the

[653] It is with *Stadt Halle* the CJEU made its first finding explaining the control criterion: Case C-26/03, *Stadt Halle and RPL Recyclingpark Lochau GmbH v. Arbeitsgemeinschaft Thermische Restabfall- und Energieverwertungsanlage TREA Leuna* [2005] *ECR* I-00001.

[654] Opinion Advocate General Leger C-94/99, *ARGE Gewässerschutz v. Bundesministerium für Land- und Forstwirtschaft* [2002] *ECR* I-11037, at [60 et seq.].

entity over which control is exercised. Provisions governing the specific situation would be decisive.[655]

The 'control' question arises in three different situations, which Advocate General Stix-Hackl distinguished in her Opinion to *Stadt Halle*: (1) awards to wholly owned companies, owned 100% by the contracting authority or entities which may be equated with that public authority; (2) awards to joint public companies whose shares are held by a number of contracting authorities; (3) and awards to semi-public companies, in which genuinely private parties hold a stake.[656] According to the thesis a distinction may be drawn on the basis of case law between two situations: either the third party consists of at least one private undertaking as shareholder (private input) or, the only or all shareholder(s) are public authorities (public input). For both situations CJEU case law is available. This case law will be examined in this Section. Next, the Section will look into whether it is enough for the various shareholders of an entity to exercise jointly control over it.

2.2.1. Private input

Since the 1980s public authorities all over Europe have evaluated alternative models of financing and operating national and regional public infrastructure. Public Private Partnerships (PPP) were increasingly used.[657] Given the economic crisis, public authorities do not always have the finances to complete complex tasks. PPP is a modern way to manage public tasks. Private partners not only provide a service to a public authority, but they also participate in several kinds of risks of the public authority. The European Commission also saw the importance of PPPs, and accordingly, has issued a number of diverse guidelines of relevance to these matters.[658]

A number of public authorities saw in *Teckal* a means to set up PPPs as a way of escaping the public procurement rules.[659] It would follow that all cooperative agreements between public authorities themselves lie beyond the scope of public procurement Directives even if a public authority contains a private shareholder – provided, of course, that the two *Teckal* criteria are met. Indeed the Court did not specify in *Teckal* what kind of shareholders the operator, executing the contract, had to be composed of.

[655] Opinion Advocate General Stix-Hackl case C-26/03, *Stadt Halle and RPL Recyclingpark Lochau GmbH v. Arbeitsgemeinschaft Thermische Restabfall- und Energieverwertungsanlage TREA Leuna* [2005] *ECR* I-00001, at [65].

[656] Opinion Advocate general Stix-Hackl case C-26/03, *Stadt Halle and RPL Recyclingpark Lochau GmbH v. Arbeitsgemeinschaft Thermische Restabfall- und Energieverwertungsanlage TREA Leuna* [2005] *ECR* I-00001, at [58].

[657] See S. Arrowsmith, 'Public Private Partnerships and the European Procurement Rules: EU Policies in conflict?' (*CMLR*, 2000), pp. 709 et s.

[658] COM(2005) 569 of November 15, 2005; Commission Interpretative Communication COM(2007) 6661 of February 5, 2008.

[659] See K. Weltzien, 'Avoiding the Procurement Rules by Awarding Contracts to an In house Entity: the Scope of the Procurement Directives in the Classical Secto' (*PPLR*, 2005), p. 251.

In light of the growing use of PPP it is useful to question whether the assignment of tasks by a public authority to a legal person created separately by a public authority with a private shareholder is not also subject to public procurement Directives. Are such entities able to benefit from the exemption created by the Court in *Teckal*, or more specifically, in such a situation is control exercised in a form similar to the exercise of control over one's own services? These questions also implicitly contain the question of to what extent the element of 'capital' is important for meeting the first *Teckal* criterion? Considering the economic importance of PPP and the knowledge that the application of public procurement Directives entails ancillary costs, energy and time the answer to this question was of major practical importance.

At the beginning of 2005 the CJEU examined this in *Stadt Halle*.[660] The Court had to deal with a situation where a public authority (the city of Halle) awarded a contract for waste disposal to a company (RPL Lochau), 75.1% owned by the public authority and the remaining 24.9% by a private limited liability company (private input). The contract was awarded without any competitive procedure. Thus, the public authority did not apply EU law (public procurement Directives).

The situation as described in the documents submitted to the Court was not an internal relationship. As the public authority and the supplier were not participating in a real in-house situation the CJEU had recourse to *Teckal*.[661] In the *Teckal* case the distinct entity was wholly owned by the contracting authority but in *Stadt Halle* there was a significant amount of private capital in the ownership of the supplier. According to the Court the participation, *even as a minority*, of a private undertaking in the capital of a company in which the particular contracting authority is also a participant, excludes the possibility of that contracting authority exercising control over that company similar to the control it exercises over its own departments.[662] The Court created a presumption. Private participation excludes the application of the *Teckal* solution.

The Court thus took a different view from Advocate General Stix-Hackl who considered that the level of a public contracting authority's shareholding cannot be the only critical factor and that the *Teckal* criteria must be extended to apply not only to wholly owned companies but also to semi-public companies.[663] In her Opinion the Advocate General advanced some notions to help to determine control, notions that the CJEU would use in its later case law: supervisory powers, namely a comprehensive control on strategic market decisions, and individual management decisions.[664]

660 Case C-26/03, *Stadt Halle and RPL Recyclingpark Lochau GmbH v. Arbeitsgemeinschaft Thermische Restabfall- und Energieverwertungsanlage TREA Leuna* [2005] *ECR* I-00001.

661 Case C-107/98, *Teckal v. Comune di Viano* [1999] *ECR* I-8121.

662 At [49].

663 Opinion Advocate General Stix-Hackl case C-26/03, *Stadt Halle and RPL Recyclingpark Lochau GmbH v. Arbeitsgemeinschaft Thermische Restabfall- und Energieverwertungsanlage TREA Leuna* [2005] *ECR* I-00001, at [70].

664 At [78].

The CJEU advanced two reasons for its finding. First, the relationship between a public authority and its own departments is fully governed by public interest considerations whilst private capital investment in an undertaking follows private interest considerations. Second, the award of a public contract to a semi-public company without calling for tenders would interfere with the objectives of undistorted competition and equal treatment, in particular because 'such a procedure would offer a private undertaking an advantage over its competitors'.[665] It is the last consideration that convinced legal scholars to approve the ruling: 'Any other position would amount to an elusion of the principles of transparency and open and fair competition'.[666]

The Court primarily looks at the relationship between the contracting authority and its departments or its subsidiaries. The aim of the relationship (or the measure) influences the application of EU law. If the relationship is governed by considerations and requirements proper to the pursuit of objectives in the public interest, EU law is then less likely to be applicable.

Second, the Court based its ruling on the objectives of the public procurement Directives, which are also linked to goals of the internal market: the objective of free and undistorted competition and the principle of equal treatment. Insofar as a situation created by a public authority favours a private company, the application of EU law is relevant. At this point the 'market access' criterion becomes a relevant consideration. If a State measure (decision to cooperate) prevents or makes extremely difficult access by companies to the national market there is a violation of the principle of equality. In that situation it distorts competition.

This reinforces the opinion of Hatzopoulos that the object of a measure influences the presence of an economic activity and hence EU law would be applicable.[667] In *Deliège*[668] the CJEU assumed that a restriction to the fundamental freedoms falls outside the scope of EU law if this limitation is inherent to the conduct of the State (i.e. a national sport federation) (see chapter 4). One could argue that the presence of a private undertaking confirms the economic object of the State measure (i.e. the decision to cooperate).

Although the Court seemed to consider *Teckal* as an exception to the application of the public procurement Directives, *Stadt Halle*'s ruling[669] appeared to consider otherwise. In the case of a purely in-house situation a contracting authority is not required to apply

665 Case C-26/03, *Stadt Halle and RPL Recyclingpark Lochau GmbH v. Arbeitsgemeinschaft Thermische Restabfall- und Energieverwertungsanlage TREA Leuna* [2005] *ECR* I-00001, at [51].

666 R. Caranta, 'The In-House Providing: The Law as it Stands in the EU', in M. Comba and S. Treumer (eds.), *The In-House Providing in European Law* (Copenhagen: Djöf Publishing, 2010), p. 22.

667 V. Hatzopoulos, *Regulating Services in the European Union* (Oxford: Oxford University Press, 2012), pp. 78–83.

668 Joined cases C-51/96 and C-191/97, *Christelle Deliège v. Ligue francophone de judo et disciplines associées ASBL, Ligue belge de judo ASBL, Union européenne de judo and François Pacquée* [2000] *ECR* I-2549.

669 Case C-26/03, *Stadt Halle and RPL Recyclingpark Lochau GmbH v. Arbeitsgemeinschaft Thermische Restabfall- und Energieverwertungsanlage TREA Leuna* [2005] *ECR* I-00001, at [48] and [49].

the public procurement Directives. The Court added that a call for tenders is also not mandatory in other circumstances. Thus, the Court referred to the quasi-in-house situation and it seems that this situation also falls outside the scope of European Union law and more specifically of the public procurement Directives.

In *Mödling*[670] the Court adds that the contribution of private capital pursues other objectives. In using the expression 'other objectives', the Court meant economic objectives or objectives that are not of general public interest. The nature of the capital of which company is composed, also determines the economic nature of the relationship between a contracting authority and a third party and thus the applicability of the public procurement Directives and EU law in general.

With these considerations the CJEU gave a more restrictive interpretation to the concept of control than it is used to do in competition cases: 'Thus, the fact that the contracting authority has a majority holding in the capital of its subsidiary, the fact that it exercises the majority of the voting rights and the fact that it appoints the majority of the members of the subsidiary's managerial bodies may – together with any agreements between the members – combine to support the conclusion as to the existence of control within the meaning of competition law and make the subsidiary a public undertaking within the meaning of Article 86(1) EC; such considerations are not sufficient, however, to support the assumption of a – more extensive – control similar to that which it exercises over its own departments'.[671] It also seems to go further than the dependency relation requires qualifying a legal person as a body governed by public law (See chapter 3). For there to be a dependency it is sufficient, for instance, that it be demonstrated that the legal person is for the most part financed by a public authority or several public authorities. This consequently does not rule out the presence of a private shareholder.

The *Stadt Halle*'s ruling can be found in more brief considerations in *Coname,*[672] *ANAV,*[673] *Agusta*[674] and *Coditel Brabant*[675]: in so far as the enterprise is a company that is open, even in part, to private capital, that fact precludes it from being regarded as a structure for the 'in-house' management of a public service on behalf of the controlling local authority. As a result, the mere existence of a private shareholder in an enterprise precludes an *a priori* application of the quasi in-house exemption.[676]

670 Case C-29/04, *Commission of the European Communities v. Republic of Austria* [2005] *ECR* I-9705, at [47].

671 Opinion of J. Kokott Case C-458/03, *Parking Brixen GmbH v. Gemeinde Brixen* [2005] *ECR* I-08585, at [52].

672 Case C-231/03, *Coname* [2005] *ECR* I-7287.

673 Case C-410/04, *Associazione Nazionale Autotrasporto Viaggiatori (ANAV)* [2006] *ECR* I-3303.

674 Case C-337/05, *Commission v. Italy* [2008] *ECR* I-02173.

675 Case C-324/07, *Commune d'Uccle et Région Bruxelles-Capital* [2008] *ECR* I-08457.

676 F. Avarkoti, 'The application of EU Public Procurement Rules to "In-house" Arrangements' (*PPLR*, 2007), p. 28. See also case C-324/07, *Commune d'Uccle et Région Bruxelles-Capitale* [2008] *ECR*, I-08457, at [30].

Thus public private partnerships, embracing the recourse of the public authority for resources to the private partner, will always fall within the scope of Directive 2004/18/EC. This shows the influence EU law has on the choices of a public authority for organising its public tasks. If a public authority chooses to do this via a PPP, its freedom of contract is limited. Indeed, the choice of contract partner is restrained by certain principles and the award procedures are provided in the public procurement Directives. The CJEU emphasizes the restrictive character of the quasi-in-house case law.[677] This case law must not be understood in a broad sense. The choice of how a public authority has to organise its own public services is thus limited.

Thus in *Stadt Halle* the CJEU makes a second constitutional choice. Whenever a public authority chooses to allow its public service tasks to be carried out by an entity in which private capital is involved, such a situation falls within the competence of the EU.

Once the presence of private capital in an undertaking is established, that completes a task for a public authority, was sufficient to confirm that the agreement with this public authority fell under the public procurement Directives, another question arises as to the relevant point in the public procurement procedure the consideration of private capital should be determined.

In *Mödling*[678] the CJEU gave its answer to this question. It is generally appropriate to consider the public authority's possible obligation to set up a public tendering procedure in the context of the circumstances prevailing on the date on which the particular public contract is awarded. Private capital must consequently be deemed to be present at the same moment the contract is awarded. But the particular circumstances of a case could, according to the Court, require that events occurring subsequently be taken into account.[679] In the specific case there were reasons to give consideration to facts that occurred after the contract was awarded so that the control criterion is met.

According to the Court, *Mödling* has to be considered an exceptional ruling.[680] Normally, the actual date on which the public contract is awarded determines whether the provisions of the public procurement Directives must be applied. Only in very special circumstances must the public authority take into account events that took place after the contract has been awarded. Such is obviously the case where a public authority seeks to avoid the application of tendering procedures. In *Sea*, the Court confirms the presence of special circumstances 'when shares in the contracting company, previously wholly

677 Case C-26/03, *Stadt Halle and RPL Recyclingpark Lochau GmbH v. Arbeitsgemeinschaft Thermische Restabfall- und Energieverwertungsanlage TREA Leuna* [2005] *ECR* I-00001.

678 Case C-29/04, *Commission of the European Communities v. Republic of Austria* [2005] *ECR* I-09705, at [47].

679 At [39].

680 Case C-371/05, *Commission of the European Communities v. Italian Republic* [2008] *ECR* I-00110, at [30].

owned by the contracting authority, are transferred to a private undertaking shortly after the contract at issue has been awarded to that company'.[681] The CJEU dismantled the artificial construction.[682]

According to the Court, the fact that a company with limited shares is also open in the future to private capital, does not *per se* negate control similar to the control a public authority exercises over its own departments. The fact that after the attribution of the contract, but still during the period for which that contract was valid, private shareholders were permitted to hold capital in that company would at that same moment be tantamount to modification of a fundamental condition of the contract, which would in turn, according to the Court, require the contract to be put out for competitive tender.[683]

2.2.2. Public input

It is understandable that the CJEU had a more restrictive view on situations where a public authority engages a semi-public enterprise if one considers the economic purposes of the European Treaties (TEU and TFEU) and of Directives 2004/17/EC and 2004/18/EC. The presence of a private undertaking as shareholder of a contracting partner can give competitive advantage if the contracting partner is chosen without an award procedure being completed on the principle of equality. Public authorities were eager to know if the Court would have the same restrictive point of view when an undertaking is fully public owned with only public capital.

This form of cooperation has been the subject of a long and on-going evolution in case law. As time passes, the CJEU seems to be applying the control criterion with more flexibility. However, one may ask whether this flexibility is an actual choice of the CJEU, rather than being caused by the *de facto* and *de jure* elements of each case.

The CJEU had two possible ways to resolve the problem of cooperative agreements between 'public-owned' public authorities. On the one hand, it could devise a presumption as it did in *Stadt Halle*[684]: namely, when a subsidiary is fully owned by public capital, the control criterion is fulfilled. On the other hand it could examine all elements of the case and decide whether on their basis a 'similar' control exists.

681 Case C-573/07, *Sea Srl v. Comune de Ponte Nossa* [2010] *ECR* I-08127, at [48].

682 See also F. Avarkioti, 'The application of EU Public Procurement Rules to 'In-house' arrangements' (*PPLR*, 2007), p. 30. In Commission v. Germany the Court advanced the same element to judge a horizontal cooperative agreements: Case C-480/06, *Commission of the European Communities v. Federal Republic of Germany* [2009] *ECR* I-04747, at [48].

683 Case C-480/06, *Commission of the European Communities v. Federal Republic of Germany* [2009] *ECR* I-04747, at [53].

684 Case C-26/03, *Stadt Halle and RPL Recyclingpark Lochau GmbH v. Arbeitsgemeinschaft Thermische Restabfall- und Energieverwertungsanlage TREA Leuna* [2005] *ECR* I-00001.

In *Parking Brixen*[685] the CJEU took the second option, as Advocate General Kokott likewise did in her Opinion[686] where she followed the strict interpretation of the first *Teckal* criterion in earlier decisions on private input.[687] A national judge must, according to the Court, take account of all the legislative provisions and relevant circumstances. From that assessment it must follow that the operator in question is under a type of control that enables the public authority to influence the operator's decisions.[688] This control must be sufficiently powerful to have decisive influence over both strategic objectives and significant decisions. In *Econord*[689] the CJEU synthesises this control as a structural and functional control. According to Econord this control has to be effective. A public authority has to prove that it complies with the first *Teckal* criterion. However, how can a public authority prove this?

In *Centro Hospitalar de Setúbal*[690] the fact that the contractor had the legal form of an association governed by private law and that it was non-profit, was irrelevant to solve the problem of the first *Teckal* criterion.[691]

The CJEU examines if a power of decisive influence is present in order to verify the control criterion. It depends on the degree of independence an operator enjoys from the public authority.[692] The independence of an operator enables it to operate independently of the public authority that has engaged it. Thus an operator may be considered to be like any other undertaking operating on the market. As a criterion, the independence of an undertaking may be construed as a factor directly associated with the objectives of the European Union; namely, free trade and free competition. If a public authority should conclude an agreement with such an independent undertaking without compliance with the principle of equality or without the tendering procedures provided in the public procurement Directives, this undertaking receives an unfair advantage over its competitors. Thus, this bears a link to the 'market access' criterion as used by the Court of Justice when adjudicating on the application of TFEU provisions on free movement. If the contracting party is market-oriented, competition is distorted since other undertakings are not given the chance to enter the market.

685 Case C-458/03, *Parking Brixen GmbH v. Gemeinde Brixen* [2005] *ECR* I-08585.

686 Opinion Advocate general Kokott Case C-458/03, *Parking Brixen GmbH v. Gemeinde Brixen* [2005] *ECR* I-08585, at [65].

687 Case C-26/03, *Stadt Halle and RPL Recyclingpark Lochau GmbH v. Arbeitsgemeinschaft Thermische Restabfall- und Energieverwertungsanlage TREA Leuna* [2005] *ECR* I-00001.

688 Case C-458/03, *Parking Brixen GmbH v. Gemeinde Brixen* [2005] *ECR* I-08585, at [65]; Case C-340/04, *Carbotermo SpA Consorzio Alisei v. Comune di Busto Arsizio AGESP SpA* [2006] *ECR* I-04137, at [36]; Case C-324/07, *Commune d'Uccle et Région Bruxelles-Capital* [2008] *ECR* I-08457, at [26].

689 Joined cases C-182/11 and C-183/11, *Econord SpA v. Comuni di Cagno, Comune di Varese, Comune di Solbiate* [2012] *ECR* I-00000, at [27].

690 Case C-574/12, *Centro Hospitalar de Setúbal EPE, Serviço de Utilização Comum dos Hospitais (SUCH) v. Eurest (Portugal) – Sociedade Europeia de Restaurantes Lda* [2014] *ECR* I-00000.

691 At [33].

692 Case C-458/03, *Parking Brixen GmbH v. Gemeinde Brixen* [2005] *ECR* I-08585, at [70].

As an illustration of the degree of independence, and thus to demonstrate that a decisive influence exists, the CJEU in its case law has placed emphasis on a number of different factors. On the basis of this case law there are mainly three factors that are important: capital, the market-oriented character and control mechanisms.[693] Once again, the CJEU provides no simple explanation as to why it considers these factors to be important or what legislation it invokes to give these factors prominence.

From *Stadt Halle* it becomes clear that the nature of the **capital** says something about the possible objectives of the operator the public authority engages in.[694] The objectives determine in part that the operator will act as an undertaking and consequently a state measure in respect of said operator could also give the operator an advantage and thus distort competition. As regards capital the Stadt Halle ruling confirmed that capital must be entirely public. But is this enough to claim it is a 'similar' control'? In *Carbotermo* the Court considers: 'The fact that the contracting authority holds, alone or together with other public authorities, all of the share capital in a successful tenderer tends to indicate, without being decisive, that that contracting authority exercises over that company a control similar to that which it exercises over its own departments'.[695] The presence of fully public owned capital suggests that control is similar. But *Coditel Brabant* shows that this is not enough to satisfy the first *Teckal* criterion. The Court considered it necessary in this case to explore still other factors of relevance.[696] It underscores the rather restrictive position of the CJEU, i.e. to keep cooperative agreements between public authorities within the scope of EU law.

For a similar control to exist in the present sense, the operator may not be **market-oriented**. In *Parking Brixen* the CJEU amasses a number of factual elements to come to the conclusion that the operator is market-oriented. The Court places particular emphasis on one item, namely, the considerable and broad powers of the administrative board to manage the operator. It shows the broad independence of the operator.[697] This element reappears in *Carbotermo*. The Court noted that the day-to-day management of the subsidiary by its board of executives was not constrained by any special supervision or veto powers enjoyed by the public authority.[698] It was also significant that the subsidiary concerned was only indirectly owned by the public authority through an intermediary holding company. This could weaken any control exercised over the subsidiary.[699] Thus, as in *Parking Brixen*, the Court looked at the measure of independence of the public

693 Case C-324/07, *Commune d'Uccle et Région Bruxelles-Capital* [2008] *ECR* I-08457, at [66]; Case C-573/07, *Sea Srl v. Comune di Ponte Nassa* [2009] *ECR* I-08127, at [29].

694 Case C-26/03, *Stadt Halle and RPL Recyclingpark Lochau GmbH v. Arbeitsgemeinschaft Thermische Restabfall- und Energieverwertungsanlage TREA Leuna* [2005] *ECR* I-00001, at [50].

695 Case C-340/04, *Carbotermo SpA Consorzio Alisei v. Comune di Busto Arsizio AGESP SpA* [2006] *ECR* I-04137, at [37].

696 Case C-324/07, *Commune d'Uccle et Région Bruxelles-Capital* [2008] *ECR* I-08457, at [33] et s.

697 Case C-458/03, *Parking Brixen GmbH v. Gemeinde Brixen* [2005] *ECR* I-08585, at [68].

698 At [38].

699 Case C-340/04, *Carbotermo SpA Consorzio Alisei v. Comune di Busto Arsizio AGESP SpA* [2006] *ECR* I-04137, at [39].

authority performing the task. Thus, if such independence is established, the public authority must be subject to competition whenever it concludes a contract with another public authority.

However, in *Coditel Brabant* the CJEU makes clear that even if an administrative board enjoys the widest powers, it cannot automatically render the operator market-oriented for all that. The operator's objectives seem also to be important. If the operator aims solely at objectives of general interest that are the same as the objectives of the public authority or authorities affiliated with it, the operator is then not market-oriented.[700] This is also the position of Hatzopoulos namely that the object of a measure is one of the elements to determine whether EU law must be applied.[701] Cooperative agreements between public authorities that aim only at objectives of public interest have no or little influence on the market.

The notion of '**control mechanisms**' is used to assess to what extent the organs of the operator are able to take independent decisions. In *Sea*[702] this was decisive in the consideration that a similar control was present. The affiliated public authorities had in this case much influence, via the organs of the operator, to make important decisions.[703] In *Econord*[704] the Court considered that it is certainly not essential that each of those public authorities should in itself have an individual power of control over that entity.[705] But each of the public authorities has to establish that it has effective control to meet the first *Teckal* criterion. A pure formal affiliation is not sufficient to exempt the public authority from putting in place a tendering procedure. It is not sufficient that a public authority holds a capital share in the entity. It must also play a role in its managing bodies.[706] In *Coditel Brabant* the Court had already ruled that control must be effective.[707] The effective control must be present on the basis of the elements capital, the market-oriented character and control mechanisms.

2.2.3. Jointly exercised control

The preceding point made clear what kind of control the CJEU expects to fulfil the first *Teckal* criterion. Another question that has arisen in the examined case law is to what extend this control has to be present in one public authority if several public authorities are affiliated to the operator with whom it cooperates.

700 Case C-324/07, *Commune d'Uccle et Région Bruxelles-Capital* [2008] *ECR* I-08457, at [37] and [38].
701 V. Hatzopoulos, *Regulating Services in the European Union* (Oxford: Oxford University Press, 2012), pp. 78–83.
702 Case C-573/07, *Sea Srl v. Comune de Ponte Nossa* [2010] *ECR* I-08127.
703 At [81 et seq].
704 Joined cases C-182/11 and C-183/11, *Econord SpA v. Comuni di Cagno, Comune di Varese, Comune di Solbiate* [2012] *ECR* I-00000.
705 At [30].
706 At [33].
707 Case C-324/07, *Commune d'Uccle et Région Bruxelles-Capital* [2008] *ECR* I-08457, at [37] and [46].

According to the CJEU in *Carbotermo*[708] control need not be exercised only by one public authority alone, but could also be exercised together with other public authorities.[709] It is this last consideration the Court used in two subsequent cases (*Asemfo*[710] and *Coditel*[711]) to temper a more restrictive interpretation of the first *Teckal* criterion. Although *Carbotermo* seems at first glance to opt for a strict interpretation of the first *Teckal* criterion, this decision left the door open to other possible ways for public authorities to cooperate without EU law being applicable.

The most important contribution concerning the jointly exercised control is found in *Coditel Brabant*.[712] Must the 'similar control' criterion be met exclusively by one public authority or is it sufficient to be met collectively, i.e. by all the public authorities together composing the operator?

The CJEU found a jointly exercised control to be sufficient. To require the control exercised by a public authority in such a case to be individual would have, according to the Court, the effect of requiring a call for competition in the majority of cases where a public authority seeks to create an entity composed of other public authorities, such as an inter-municipal cooperative association. This would be inconsistent with EU rules allowing public authorities to perform jointly the public-interest tasks conferred on them by using their own administrative, technical and other resources, without being obliged to call on outside entities not forming part of its own departments.[713] The procedure, which is used for adopting decisions, such as majority rule, is of no importance.

The answer to the question of jointly control could be considered to have been already present in *Stadt Halle* where the Court emphasised the relevancy of the fact that the contracting party of the public authority was a consortium of several contracting authorities.[714] The Court appears to confirm that the control criterion could be met if the subsidiary consists of several public authorities, even if one public authority, member of the subsidiary, does not have a complete control of it.

2.2.4. Conclusion

Vertical cooperative agreements between public authorities, even when they are entirely public-owned, could fall within the scope of EU law. This is the case when this kind of

708 Case C-340/04, *Carbotermo SpA Consorzio Alisei v. Comune di Busto Arsizio AGESP SpA* [2006] *ECR* I-04137.

709 At [57].

710 Case C-295/05, *Asociación Nacional de Empresas Forestales (Asemfo) v. Transformación Agraria SA (Tragsa)* [2007] *ECR* I-02999.

711 Case C-324/07, *Commune d'Uccle et Région Bruxelles-Capital* [2008] *ECR* I-08457.

712 At [43 et seq.].

713 At [48].

714 Case C-26/03, *Stadt Halle and RPL Recyclingpark Lochau GmbH. v. Arbeitsgemeinschaft Thermische Restabfall- und Energieverwertungsanlage TREA Leuna* [2005] *ECR* I-00001, at [47] and [49].

cooperative agreements is considered to be a public contract or service concession. In all these situations, however, there is also a possibility this kind of cooperative agreements will fall outside the scope of EU law.

A cooperative agreement between public authorities, in the form of a public contract or a service concession, lies outside the scope of EU law, when it is established that one public authority, perhaps together with other public authorities, exercises a control over the other that is similar to the control it exercises over its own departments. This criterion exposes an important form of dependency between the two public authorities. This dependency of the entity on a public authority signifies that the entity could actually not be compared with other undertakings active on the market. The operator is unable to conduct a policy on its own. The end aspired to by this cooperative agreement is also not economic in nature. It aims at objectives of general interest. Market access for the other undertakings in this situation is not threatened. Through the decision to cooperate (State measure) the situation (cooperative agreement) remains within the ambit of public administration.

Based on CJEU case law this criterion is a presumptive expression of two ideas. First, the particular situation is regulated solely by considerations and requirements appropriate to the pursuit of objectives in the public interest. Second, in the case of a 'similar control' there is no risk that competition will be distorted.

The application of EU law can be excluded where several public authorities are shareholders of the public authority that is to provide the services. Each of the participating public authorities must exercise an effective influence and they must together ensure that the public authority is not independent.

With the notion of 'control' the Court introduced a formal criterion for determining the applicability of EU law. The Court interprets this notion functionally throughout. The Court thus determines on the basis of the objectives of the internal market the power of Member States to regulate the organisation and management of public tasks.

Throughout the case law it is clear that the CJEU is always seeking a balance between, on the one hand, the competence of the EU to sustain free movement and free competition and, on the other, the competence of the Member States in regard to the organisation or the management of public service tasks. Starting from a rather formal premise, the CJEU gradually ended up with a functional interpretation of the control criterion. But it also suggests that in *Teckal* it would have been better had the Court not used formal criteria to keep cooperative agreements between public authorities outside the scope of EU law under certain conditions. This has, in our opinion, resulted in a broad interpretation of the Directives in favour of the EU. The Directives published on 28 March 2014 in the OJEU suggest that the Member States were not happy with this course of events. The Directives provide a number of corrections to this broad interpretation (See section 4 of the present chapter).

2.3. The activities criterion

2.3.1. Need for a second criterion?

The public procurement Directives and Articles 49 and 56 TFEU, together with the general principles they express, must be regarded as normative if a contract is concluded between a public authority and a person legally distinct from that public authority. The public authority needs to organise a transparent procedure to safeguard an equal treatment of the interested economic operators. The Directives and the principle of equality, however, do not apply if, in addition to the control criterion, the following condition is fulfilled: the undertaking controlled by the public authority must perform the majority of its activities with the controlling authority or authorities. According to *Teckal,*[715] compliance with the control criterion is not sufficient to exclude a vertical cooperative agreement from the scope of public procurement Directives. A second criterion has also to be met: the activities criterion.

Simply establishing the existence of structural dependence in relation to the public authority that is to award a public contract is not of itself sufficient to make the services provided by the other public authority comparable to the services that would be available to the public authority were it to use its own internal resources.[716] The presence of the 'activities' criterion is necessary to prevent a public authority from competing with other undertakings via its activities.

This second *Teckal* criterion has not been treated extensively in CJEU case law. An initial explanation is the fact that the Court always begins by checking the control criterion. Most cases considered by the Court failed this first criterion. Thus, there has been no need for the Court to check the second criterion. The application of this criterion also seems less difficult. Thus, the presence of a quasi-in-house situation depends principally on whether the first *Teckal* criterion has been met.

Carbotermo[717] explains the ratio of the second *Teckal* criterion. The fulfilment of this criterion is necessary to determine if the separate enterprise is not competing through its activities with third parties.[718] According to Advocate General Leger the ruling in *Teckal* is based on the criterion of the autonomy of the economic operator.[719] Such autonomy, however, is present if the operator is able to perform important economic activities for third parties (for the market). In that case, it is logical, according to the Advocate General, that the operator be subject to the rules of the market. However, if the operator acts

715 Case C-107/98, *Teckal v. Comune di Viano* [1999] *ECR* I-8121.

716 Opinion Advocate General Leger C-94/99, *ARGE Gewässerschutz v. Bundesministerium für Land- und Forstwirtschaft* [2002] *ECR* I-11037, at [70].

717 Case C-340/04, *Carbotermo SpA Consorzio Alisei v. Comune di Busto Arsizio AGESP SpA* [2006] *ECR* I-04137.

718 At [60].

719 Opinion Advocate General Leger C-94/99, *ARGE Gewässerschutz v. Bundesministerium für Land- und Forstwirtschaft* [2002] *ECR* I-11037, at [49] and [73].

primarily for public authorities that control it as they control their own services, there is no reason for competition.[720] Public procurement Directives endeavour to give equal chances to all parties who perform the required activities. It would be a disadvantage if one of the competitors who for a relevant part of his activities is not dependent on a public authority is certain to obtain contracts without fearing competition. Once again EU law appears to be applicable if a measure taken by the public authority might hinder the free market.

CJEU case law is primarily concerned with two issues relating to the activities criterion namely the amount of activities an operator may perform for a public authority and whether the activities be accomplished by one public authority or is it acceptable that the required activities be accomplished by the several different public authorities that make up the cooperative association?

2.3.2. Kind of activities

The CJEU had the opportunity in *Carbotermo*[721] for the first time to clarify the amount of activities required to meet the second *Teckal* criterion. In order to determine whether the necessary activities are directed to the public authority, the national court must take into account all the facts of the case, both qualitative and quantitative.[722]

The CJEU made clear the manner in which the activities criterion should be understood. An undertaking's activity must principally be devoted to a public authority and any other activities are only of marginal significance. The relevant activities of the successful undertaking are all those activities which that undertaking carries out as part of a contract awarded by the public authority, regardless of who is the beneficiary: the public authority itself or the user of the services.[723] According to Advocate General Stix-Hackl the notion 'controlling authority' can be understood in a broad sense.[724] It would not concern only direct shareholders. But this does not include activities for third parties where the shareholder would otherwise have had to perform them itself.[725] It is also irrelevant who pays the enterprise for the activities, whether it be the controlling authority or third-party users of the services provided under concessions or other legal relationships established by that authority.[726]

720 At [76].

721 Case C-340/04, *Carbotermo SpA Consorzio Alisei v. Comune di Busto Arsizio AGESP SpA* [2006] *ECR* I-04137.

722 At [64].

723 At [66].

724 Opinion Stix-Hackl C-26/03, *Stadt Halle and RPL Recyclingpark Lochau GmbH v. Arbeitsgemeinschaft Thermische Restabfall- und Energieverwertungsanlage TREA Leuna* [2005] *ECR* I-00001, at [80].

725 Case C-340/04, *Carbotermo SpA Consorzio Alisei v. Comune di Busto Arsizio AGESP SpA* [2006] *ECR* I-04137, at [82].

726 At [67].

The 'activities criterion' is applicable only to activities actually underperformed by a third operator at the conclusion of contract.[727] Potential activities that may arise afterwards are in principle not relevant.

In *Carbotermo* the CJEU looked at the turnover of the operator. In *Asemfo* the operator carried out more than 55 per cent of its activities for the Autonomous Activities and nearly 35 per cent with the State. From these considerations, the Court concluded that Tragsa carried out an essential part of its activities for the public authorities and bodies that controlled it.[728] Thus, it appears from the two mentioned CJEU cases that although the Court formally states that quantitative and qualitative elements are equally important to determine the activities criterion, the Court uses mostly quantitative elements in its analysis.

This can also be seen in *Asociacion Profesional de Empresas*.[729] In this case the Court addressed an argument of the Spanish government. The latter argued that *Correos* was required to provide services to the public authorities and that this was an exclusive right. In that case it would be an exclusive cooperation, making the condition of the 'essential activities' in any case satisfied. Despite a possible exclusive right, the Court considered that this alone cannot satisfy the condition. The second *Teckal* criterion is intended to keep the public procurement Directives, and the principles of the Treaty, applicable to relationships with companies that can compete with other companies.[730]

In *Asociacion Profesional de Empresas, Correos* there were an unspecified number of independent customers and 2000 competitors. Given the significant number of customers, Correos cannot be said to perform the essential part of its activities solely for public authorities. So another element other than a quantitative one should be taken into account. The framework within which Correos operates is also crucial.

Even today it is not clear at which stage an undertaking carries out an essential part of its activities for a public authority. Advocate General Stix-Hackl invoked in her opinion preceding *Stadt Halle*, Article 23 of Directive 2004/17/EC, which excludes contracts awarded to so-called affiliated enterprises from the scope of the Directive whose turnover-based threshold is above 80%.[731] The Advocate General is, however, not convinced by the 80% 'rule'. The Directives published on 28 March 2014 confirm the 80% threshold.[732]

727 At [83].

728 Case C-295/05, *Asociacion Nacional de Empresas Forestales (Asemfo)* [2007] *ECR* I-02999, at [63–64].

729 Case C-220/06, *Asociación Profesional de Empresas de Reparto y Manipulado de Correspondencia v. Administración General del Estado* [2007] *ECR* I-12175.

730 At [62].

731 Opinion Advocate general Stix-Hackl C-26/03, *Stadt Halle and RPL Recyclingpark Lochau GmbH. v. Arbeitsgemeinschaft Thermische Restabfall- und Energieverwertungsanlage TREA Leuna* [2005] *ECR* I-00001, at [92].

732 Article 17 of Directive 2014/23/EU; Article 12 of Directive 2014/24/EU; Article 28 of Directive 2014/25/EU.

2.3.3. Several controlling public authorities

If several public authorities hold the share capital of the successful enterprise, it may be relevant to consider whether the activities to be taken into account are those which the enterprise carries out for all the controlling public authorities or only the activities carried out for a specific public authority.

It should be borne in mind in this connection that the Court has stated that the legally distinct person in question must carry out the essential part of its activities with 'the controlling local authority or authorities'.[733] It thus envisaged the possibility that the exception provided for could apply not only in cases where a single authority controls such a legal person, but also where several public authorities do so. Where several public authorities control an enterprise, the condition relating to the essential part of its activities may be met if that enterprise carries out the essential part of its activities, not necessarily for one of the public authorities, but for all of them.[734]

Accordingly, the activities to be taken into account in the case of an enterprise controlled by one or more public authorities are those which that enterprise carries out for all the public authorities.

2.3.4. Conclusion

It would not be logical if an independent body should offer services to other operators or local authorities without being subject to legislation applicable to public contracts, when it is acting in circumstances comparable to those of a traditional economic operator. Its public origin and nature are not sufficient to mark it out from other service providers on the market if it is offering the same type of services for a similar commercial purpose. The principle of equality imposes that comparable situations must be treated equally. Free access to the market has to be guaranteed in the same way to all competitors. In regard to public contracts and service concessions public authorities have to safeguard equal treatment and transparency. This protection is not necessary if the 'operator' does not act on the market.

The service provider must carry out the essential part of its activity for the controlling public authority or authorities. Consequently, if it engages in commercial activities, the public procurement Directives and the principle of equality are applicable, unless those activities represent a marginal part of its overall activity.

733 Case C-107/98, *Teckal v. Comune di Viano* [1999] *ECR* I-8121.

734 Case C-295/05, *Asociación Nacional de Empresas Forestales (Asemfo) v. Transformación Agraria SA (Tragsa)* [2007] *ECR* I-02999 at [70].

3. Contractual or horizontal cooperative agreements

Until 2009 the CJEU only ruled on situations where public or contracting authorities were member of a separate legal entity that then provides services to one or several of these public or contracting authorities. This is to be distinguished from the situation where public or contracting authorities commit themselves to one another under a contract without becoming together part of a separate legal person (horizontal cooperative agreements). Recall that the Court has previously held that a contracting or public authority cannot exclude a contract concluded with another public or contracting authority from the scope of the public procurement Directives or the principle of equality.[735]

In the last years, the CJEU has had several times the chance to elaborate on horizontal cooperative agreements between public authorities: twice in Grand Chamber, which underscores the importance of these rulings.[736] First, this section will investigate CJEU case law (3.1.). Some relevant commentary will then follow (3.2.).

3.1. Analysis of the relevant case law

It follows from *Commission v. Germany*[737] that the particular form of a contract is not important for determining whether cooperative agreements between public authorities is subject to EU law.[738] This consideration paved the way for the CJEU to create criteria for another situation (horizontal cooperative agreement) to fall outside the scope of EU law. In *Ordine degli Ingegneri*[739] and *Piepenbrock*[740] the CJEU ruled that its case law on horizontal cooperative agreements is applicable to all kinds of public authorities, not only local authorities. The same two cases confirmed two types of contracts concluded between public authorities do not fall within the scope of EU law.

The first category of contracts is those that meet the *Teckal* criteria (vertical cooperation) and the second category involves horizontal cooperative agreements. Both categories of

735 Case C-84/03, *Commission v. Spain* [2005] *ECR* I-00139.

736 Case C-480/06, *Commission of the European Communities v. Federal Republic of Germany* [2009] *ECR* I-04747; Case C-159/11, *Azienda Sanitaria Locale di Lecce, Università del Salento v. Ordine degli Ingegneri della Provincia di Lecce and Others* [2012] *ECR* I-00000.

737 Case C-480/06, *Commission of the European Communities v. Federal Republic of Germany* [2009] *ECR* I-04747. See on this case and its implications: M.T. Karayigit, 'A new type of exemption from the EU rules on public procurement established: "in the neighbour's house" provision of public interest tasks' (*PPLR*, 2010), pp. 183–197.

738 Case C-480/06, *Commission of the European Communities v. Federal Republic of Germany* [2009] *ECR* I-04747, at [47].

739 Case C-159/11, *Azienda Sanitaria Locale di Lecce, Università del Salento v. Ordine degli Ingegneri della Provincia di Lecce and Others* [2012] *ECR* I-00000, at [31].

740 Case C-386/11, *Piepenbrock Dienstleistungen & Co. KG v. Kreis Düren* [2013] *ECR* I-00000, at [33]. See also C-564/11, *Consulta Regionale Ordine Ingegneri della Lombardia e.a. v. Comune di Pavia* [2013] *ECR*-00000, at [32]; Case C-352/12, *Consiglio Nazionale degli Ingegneri v. Comune di Castelvecchio Subequo* [2013] *ECR*-00000, at [40].

cooperation must meet a number of other criteria in order to be exempted from the application of EU law. There are, in other words, two different types of contract, each with its own, separate criteria. Hence, a contract need not necessarily meet the *Teckal* criteria to avoid being subject to EU law.

The case law on horizontal cooperative agreements indicates that the CJEU always confirms first whether a control similar to the one the public authority has over its own services exists.[741] If this is not the case, the Court in the relevant case law had the choice of either declaring EU law applicable or seeking new criteria to exclude horizontal cooperation from the scope of EU law. The Court took the second option, thus widening the competence of the Member States. This option expresses the Court's desire in certain situations to safeguard the competence of the Member States in matters concerning the organisation and management of public tasks.

Horizontal cooperative agreements fall outside the scope of EU law insofar as public authorities establish cooperation with each other aimed at ensuring that a public task that they are required to perform is in fact accomplished.[742] From the *Ordine degli Ingegneri* ruling it appears to follow that a contract signed between public authorities has at least to ensure the implementation of any task that all public authorities are required to perform.[743] This is the first criterion a horizontal cooperative agreement must meet if it is to be excluded from the scope of EU law.[744]

When a public authority enters a cooperative agreement (a state measure), there are no economic reasons involved; the decision pursues an objective that is by its nature of general interest. As with a vertical cooperative agreement, the Court has formulated no exception to the applicability of public procurement Directives. The Directives are not applicable, simply because the contract has no effect on the market. As in the *Coditel Brabant case*,[745] the various contracting authorities work together, i.e. they all provide a service and do not merely receive a service. With their jointly owned resources the participating public authorities discharge a public service task. This explains why the ruling in *Commission v. Germany* relies on *Stadt Halle*.[746] For the first time, in the latter case, the Court ruled that a public authority could revert to its own resources without resorting to a tendering procedure.

741 At [39].

742 Case C-480/06, *Commission of the European Communities v. Federal Republic of Germany* [2009] *ECR* I-04747, at [37]; Case C-159/11, *Azienda Sanitaria Locale di Lecce, Università del Salento v. Ordine degli Ingegneri della Provincia di Lecce and Others* [2012] *ECR* I-00000, at [34]; Case C-386/11, *Piepenbrock Dienstleistungen & Co. KG v. Kreis Düren* [2013] *ECR* I-00000, at [36].

743 At [37].

744 Case C-159/11, *Azienda Sanitaria Locale di Lecce, Università del Salento v. Ordine degli Ingegneri della Provincia di Lecce and Others* [2012] *ECR* I-00000, at [36].

745 Case C-324/07, *Commune d'Uccle et Région Bruxelles-Capital* [2008] *ECR* I-08457.

746 Case C-26/03, *Stadt Halle and RPL Recyclingpark Lochau GmbH v. Arbeitsgemeinschaft Thermische Restabfall- und Energieverwertungsanlage TREA Leuna* [2005] *ECR* I-00001.

Whereas the CJEU in *Commission v. Germany* undertook a detailed investigation of all aspects of the facts[747] before it in the end decided whether EU law was applicable, the *Ordine degli Ingegneri* ruling (a preliminary ruling) contained clear criteria for deciding this question. There are, according to the thesis, not five criteria as Advocate General Trstenjak proposed in his opinion in *Ordine degli Ingegneri.*[748] One criterion had already been discussed above. The two others are listed below:

- No private provider of services shall be placed in a position of advantage *vis-à-vis* competitors.
- Cooperation shall be governed solely by considerations and requirements relating to the pursuit of objectives in the public interest.[749]

These criteria are cumulative.[750] In *Commission v. Germany* the CJEU located the two last criteria within the more general framework of the objectives of public procurement Directives and EU law: 'such cooperation between public authorities does not undermine the principal objective of the Community rules on public procurement, that is, the free movement of services and the opening-up of undistorted competition in all the Member States'.[751] When the sole purpose of a measure is the fulfilment of a general interest and, moreover, not one single undertaking enjoys an advantage, market access is not hindered. EU law is not applicable to such measures.

In *Ordine degli Ingegneri* and *Piepenbrock* the CJEU tested a concrete situation against the three established criteria. The Court established that the contract contained sufficient elements showing that, in regard to at least one public authority in the cooperative association, the contract did not entail the implementation of a public task.[752] The University of Salento performed activities that in principle were also executed by engineers or architects (study of the seismic vulnerability of hospital structures). This does not constitute academic research, which the Court implicitly considered to be an activity of general interest. In *Piepenbrock* one of the public authorities performed a service (cleaning buildings) for another public authority. In that case, the cooperative agreement is not established with a view to carrying out a public task that both public authorities were required to perform.[753]

747 Case C-480/06, *Commission of the European Communities v. Federal Republic of Germany* [2009] *ECR* I-04747.

748 Opinion Advocate General Trstenjak Case C-159/11, *Azienda Sanitaria Locale di Lecce, Università del Salento v. Ordine degli Ingegneri della Provincia di Lecce and Others* [2012] *ECR* I-00000, at [66]. See also Opinion Advocate General Mengozzi Case C-15/13, *Technische Universität Hamburg-Harburg, Hochschul-Informations-System GmbH v. Datenlotsen Informationssysteme GmbH* [2014] *ECR* I-00000, at [50].

749 At [34], [35] and [40].

750 At [36]. Case C-564/11, *Consulta Regionale Ordine Ingegneri della Lombardia e.a. v. Comune di Pavia* [2013] *ECR* I-00000, at [37]; Case C-352/12, *Consiglio Nazionale degli Ingegneri contre Comune di Castelvecchio Subequo et Comune di Barisciano* [2013] *ECR* I-00000, at [45].

751 Case C-480/06, *Commission of the European Communities v. Federal Republic of Germany* [2009] *ECR* I-04747, at [47].

752 At [37].

753 Case C-386/11, *Piepenbrock Dienstleistungen & Co. KG v. Kreis Düren* [2013] *ECR* I-00000, at [39].

Second, in *Ordine degli Ingegneri* the Court observes that the University of Salento, which performs the service, may also employ third parties to do this. Consequently, a private enterprise can, according to the Court, thereby gain an advantage.[754] The Court makes the same observation in *Piepenbrock*.[755]

3.2. Comments

The CJEU has developed specific rules concerning the application of EU law to horizontal cooperative agreements between public authorities. In addition to the *Teckal* criteria, which are applicable to vertical cooperative agreements between public authorities, the Court has developed its own criteria for horizontal or contractual cooperation to exclude it from the scope of EU law. *Teckal* case law thus retains its relevance.

Case law on horizontal cooperative agreements also makes clear that the CJEU pays attention to the intrinsic competences of the Member States to organise and manage public service tasks. Where *Teckal* still in origin relies on the concept 'contract', the criteria excluding horizontal cooperative agreements from the scope of EU law do not.

In its case law the Court distinguishes between the two types of contracts (vertical – horizontal). In a vertical cooperative agreement, the measure of independence of the contracting party patently determines whether EU law is applicable. In a horizontal cooperative agreement, on the other hand, it is the purpose of the contract that is primarily decisive. The purpose of a contract must be for the accomplishment of a public task common to all the contracting parties (i.e. public authorities). No cooperative agreement may have as its purpose the performance of an activity by one public authority for another public authority. In that situation the public procurement Directives always apply. In addition, a contract must concern considerations of public interest. Clearly, commercial objectives will bring the contract within the scope of EU law.

The CJEU emphasises several criteria to exclude cooperative agreements from the scope of EU law. The first criterion states that a contract must have the aim of ensuring the accomplishment of a public task that all contracting parties are required to perform. The CJEU seems to ground this criterion in the Opinion of the Advocate General where the latter explained the concept of 'cooperation'. According to the Advocate General 'the essence of a cooperation consists in a common strategy between partners which is based on the exchange and the coordination of their respective interests'.[756]

The CJEU uses the concept 'cooperation' for the first time in *Coditel Brabant*, where it confirms the possibility for public authorities to use their own resources to perform the

754 At [38].

755 At [40].

756 Opinion Advocate General Trstenjak Case C-159/11, *Azienda Sanitaria Locale di Lecce, Università del Salento v. Ordine degli Ingegneri della Provincia di Lecce and Others* [2012] *ECR* I-00000, at [75].

public interest tasks conferred on them in cooperation with other public authorities.[757] In this case, the CJEU refers to *Asemfo,*[758] where it then takes up a situation in which a public authority essentially caries out activities to the benefit of controlling authorities. However, the last situation does not really involve cooperation for the purpose of accomplishing a common public task. The condition that the agreement aims at ensuring the accomplishment of a common public task does not appear to follow directly from the case law prefatory to *Ordine degli Ingegneri.*

This condition is too strict if from it follows that the public authorities that sign the agreement must perform a public task that is identical for all of them. In practice, situations can arise where an agreement completes a public task whereby the completion of this task fulfils a general interest that is different for the two public authorities. For example a non-profit organization could prepare meals for the patients of a hospital. The public task of the non-profit organization is the supply of meals to the sick and the public task of the hospital is to heal the sick. Both public authorities have a common general interest: health care. Is this kind of situation then excluded of the scope of EU law? The CJEU case law seems to respond to the negative.

The condition that cooperation must be guided by considerations in the general interest seems to follow from *Coditel Brabant.* This condition can be linked to the considerations of the CJEU in *Deliège*[759] (see chapter 4). Whenever a public authority takes a measure with solely its own interests in mind, there is then no economic interest and thus the objectives set down by the EU are also not challenged. Besides, *Commission v. Germany* states this explicitly. In the case where objectives of common interest guide the cooperation, the free movement of services is not compromised[760] and likewise the situation falls outside the scope of EU law.

The third criterion prohibits public authorities from placing a private provider in a position of advantage. This criterion is necessary for the same reasons as the second criterion. This criterion presupposes, according to the thesis, that the cooperative agreement has to be concluded between public authorities and that no private party participates in such a contract. In *Stadt Halle*[761] and *Coditel Brabant*[762] the Court already considered that the participation of a private party is just one element to exclude the control criterion. As such it was not considered as a separate criterion. It seems to the

[757] Case C-324/07, *Commune d'Uccle et Région Bruxelles-Capital* [2008] *ECR* I-08457, at [49].

[758] Case C-295/05, *Asociación Nacional de Empresas Forestales (Asemfo) v. Transformación Agraria SA (Tragsa)* [2007] *ECR* I-02999.

[759] Joined cases C-51/96 and C-191/97, *Christelle Deliège v. Ligue francophone de judo et disciplines associées ASBL, Ligue belge de judo ASBL, Union européenne de judo and François Pacquée* [2000] *ECR* I-2549.

[760] Case C-480/06, *Commission of the European Communities v. Federal Republic of Germany* [2009] *ECR* I-04747at [47].

[761] Case C-26/03, *Stadt Halle and RPL Recyclingpark Lochau GmbH v. Arbeitsgemeinschaft Thermische Restabfall- und Energieverwertungsanlage TREA Leuna* [2005] *ECR* I-00001.

[762] Case C-324/07, *Commune d'Uccle et Région Bruxelles-Capital* [2008] *ECR* I-08457.

thesis that the participation of a private party in a cooperative agreement places this private party *ipso facto* in a position of advantage.

In both *Ordine degli Ingegneri*[763] and *Piepenbrock*[764] rulings the CJEU establishes that in those cases the contract could enable a public authority to make use of private firms. This appears to go further than the way the Court formulated this criterion earlier in the ruling. The criterion seems to necessitate that the agreement really advantages a private partner. When the CJEU applies the criterion, it seems sufficient that the contract foresees the possibility to choose a private partner. Continuing in the same vein *Mödling*[765] formulates a criterion that could have been applied here too. According to *Mödling* when a public authority awards a contract it needs only to take into account the elements present at that stage. Future elements are relevant only in exceptional situations.

Differently from *Teckal,*[766] in *Commission v. Germany* the Court does not immediately create new criteria on the basis of which horizontal cooperative agreements could be placed beyond the scope of the public procurement Directives. Perhaps the Court did not wish to get entangled in such criteria. Indeed, such criteria narrow the Court's potential room for manoeuvre in the future. In *Teckal* the Court directly applied two formal criteria, which, moreover, seemed to be inspired by certain national legal systems. Afterwards, the Court would have had to develop an entire case law to find a place for the different kinds of vertical cooperative associations within EU law. In *Commission v. Germany*, the Court adduced several basic elements that legitimate the exclusion of a horizontal cooperative agreement from the scope of EU law.

The question arises whether criteria were necessary in order to shield all types of cooperation from the scope of EU law. If one starts with the *Teckal* criteria, it is evident that the Court was obliged by the nature of horizontal cooperative agreements to seek other criteria if it aspired to exclude this kind of cooperation. Indeed, in such a situation, a kind of control similar to control over one's own services is precluded (cf. *Commission v. Germany*, cf. *Ordine degli Ingegneri*).

Although it is preferable to have criteria against which to test a particular situation, and two kinds of criteria are necessary for vertical and horizontal cooperative agreements, they seem to express the same idea. If as a consequence of a cooperative agreement a particular entity gains a commercial advantage on the market, EU law will then be relevant. There can be no such advantage if the entity is not acting independently (control similar to that which it exercises over its own departments), and if it deals solely with tasks of general interest that are common to all members (shareholders) of the cooperative agreement. The operator will not be market-oriented.

763 Case C-159/11, *Azienda Sanitaria Locale di Lecce, Università del Salento v. Ordine degli Ingegneri della Provincia di Lecce and Others* [2012] *ECR* I-00000, at [38].

764 Case C-386/11, *Piepenbrock Dienstleistungen & Co. KG v. Kreis Düren* [2013] *ECR* I-00000, at [40].

765 Case C-29/04, *Commission of the European Communities v. Republic of Austria* [2005] *ECR* I-9705.

766 Case C-107/98, *Teckal v. Comune di Viano* [1999] *ECR* I-8121.

This case law illustrates the manner in which the CJEU tries to find a balance between the application of EU law and the latitudes available to public authorities in organising their own services.[767] The case law on cooperative agreements is based on purely economic considerations, with the implication that the fundamental principles of the internal market – with the procurement Directive being a derivative thereof – are not applicable to a situation located outside the market or to a situation based on considerations in the general interest.

4. New Directives

The case law discussed above on determining when cooperative agreements between public authorities fall within the scope of EU law was accomplished without assistance from the EU legislator: neither a directive nor a regulation was issued. The CJEU simply supplemented the content of the existing public procurement Directives opening itself to the criticism that it acted as a lawmaker.

However, in an attempt to fill a lacuna in the legislation there has been a number of initiatives on the part of European institutions to create a framework for cooperative agreements between public authorities. Heading the list is a working paper of the European Commission (see 4.1 below). This was followed by a number of new proposals for Directives including provisions that could define the position of cooperative agreements within the public procurement Directives and EU law in general. Finally, these proposals have been amended several times. The EU Parliament has approved the different Directives related to the tendering of public contracts and service concessions on 15 January 2014.[768, 769] They were published on 28 March 2014 in the OJEU. These texts and the different proposals will be briefly discussed. (5.2.)

4.1. The Commission's Working Paper[770]

The European Commission first made public its view on the applicability of the public procurement Directives to cooperation between contracting authorities in a Working Paper.[771]

767 B. Kotschy, 'Arrêts Stadt Halle, Coname et Parking Brixen' (*RDUE*, 2005), p. 849; G. Marchegiani, 'Les relations in-house et le syndrome du cheval à bascule' (*RMCUE*, 2006), p. 48; J. Wiggen, 'Public procurement rules and cooperation between public sector entities: the limits of the in-house doctrine under EU procurement law' (*PPLR*, 2011), p. 158.

768 See www.europarl.europa.eu/sides/getDoc.do?type=TA&language=EN&reference=P7-TA-2014-0025; www.europarl.europa.eu/sides/getDoc.do?type=TA&language=EN&reference=P7-TA-2014-0024; www.europarl.europa.eu/sides/getDoc.do?type=TA&language=EN&reference=P7-TA-2014-0026.

769 For a first commentary see 'Dossier: Les nouvelles directives "marchés"' (*ACCP*, 2014, n° 143) and (*ACCP*, 2014, n° 144); 'Special issue – the new EU procurement directives' (*PPLR*, 2014, Issue 3) and (*PPLR*, 2014, Issue 4).

770 See on this working paper: R. Williams, 'Public-public cooperation – *Teckal* in ractice' (*PPLR*, 2012), NA1–10.

771 Commission Staff Working Paper concerning the application of EU public procurement law to relations between contracting authorities ('public-public cooperation'), SEC(2011) 1169 final.

The intention was to give a summary of existing case law. First, the European Commission draws a distinction between procurement activities, which should benefit from open competition among economic operators, and other arrangements which contracting authorities may use to ensure the completion of their public tasks. Thus, the European Commission has confirmed the distribution of powers between the EU and the Member States on this matter. In the first case the contracting authority should apply the public procurement Directives and EU law in general, whereas in the other, EU law is not applicable. It is a reaffirmation of the *Stadt Halle* ruling.[772] A second important distinction drawn by the European Commission is between vertical and horizontal forms of cooperation. Like the Court, the Commission does not propose to apply the same criteria to exclude a particular form of cooperation from the scope of EU law. This confirms what the CJEU later on considered in *Ordine degli Ingegneri*[773] and *Piepenbrock*.[774]

The European Commission adopted the two *Teckal* criteria for vertical cooperative agreements and considered that when the criteria are met the agreement falls outside the scope of EU law. The Commission adds that the control criterion can be exercised jointly. The Commission links the *Teckal* case law with the contracting authorities' power of self-organisation. The relation between a contracting authority and its own departments is governed by considerations and requirements proper to the pursuit of objectives in the public interest. In this sense the European Commission agrees that the object of a measure is decisive as regards the applicability of EU law. In the case where the general interest is the driving force behind the action of public authorities, market access and competition are not at risk.

As regards horizontal cooperative agreements, the European Commission simply used *Commission v. Germany*[775] as a base. The position of the European Commission on this type of cooperation is that EU law does not require public authorities to use any particular form in order to carry out jointly public service tasks. The European Commission distils different conditions from the ruling in *Commission v. Germany* to place a horizontal cooperation beyond the scope of EU law: 1) only public authorities are involved in the cooperation, 2) there is no participation of private capital, 3) the character of the agreement is that of real co-operation aimed at the joint performance of a common task, as opposed to a normal public contract and 4) the cooperation is governed only by considerations relating to the public interest.

[772] Case C-26/03, *Stadt Halle and RPL Recyclingpark Lochau GmbH. v. Arbeitsgemeinschaft Thermische Restabfall- und Energieverwertungsanlage TREA Leuna* [2005] *ECR* I-00001.

[773] Case C-159/11, *Azienda Sanitaria Locale di Lecce, Università del Salento v. Ordine degli Ingegneri della Provincia di Lecce and Others* [2012] *ECR* I-00000.

[774] Case C-386/11, *Piepenbrock Dienstleistungen & Co. KG v. Kreis Düren* [2013] *ECR* I-00000.

[775] Case C-480/06, *Commission of the European Communities v. Federal Republic of Germany* [2009] *ECR* I-04747.

The Working Paper was not able to give consideration to the ruling in *Ordine degli Ingegneri*,[776] when it considered horizontal cooperative agreements. In that case the Court formulated three criteria (see above) to exclude this type of cooperation from EU law. These criteria do not fully coincide with the content of the Working Paper.

4.2. *Proposal for new Directives*[777] *and new Directives*[778]

The European Commission has prepared three new proposals for directives: two on the award of public contracts[779] and one on the award of service concessions,[780] In the considerations that preceded the proposals on public procurement the Commission makes clear that as regards public contracts there is too much legal uncertainty over the application of the public procurement Directives to cooperative agreements between public authorities.[781] The Commission tries to find a balance between the application of the procurement rules and the freedom of public authorities to decide how to organise the manner in which they discharge their public service obligations. The same train of thought is at the origins of similar provisions regarding the exclusion of some service concessions from the scope of EU law. One objective seems to predominant to exempt cooperative agreements from the scope of EU law: the cooperation can 'not result in a distortion of competition… in so far as it places a provider in a position of advantage vis-à-vis its competitors'.[782]

In the different proposals, the Commission makes a distinction between institutional/vertical and contractual/horizontal cooperative agreements, and, moreover, uses different criteria for excluding the two types of cooperation from the application of public procurement Directives. A comparable distinction is also to be found in the proposal on service concessions. Thus, the Commission confirms the distinction made in *Ordine degli Ingegneri* and *Piepenbrock* and proposes that it is applied to service concessions. This distinction was maintained in the texts approved by the EU Parliament and published in the OJEU.

776 Case C-159/11, *Azienda Sanitaria Locale di Lecce, Università del Salento v. Ordine degli Ingegneri della Provincia di Lecce and Others* [2012] *ECR* I-00000.

777 See on the proposals of the EU Commission D. Casalini, 'Beyond EU Law: the New "Public House"', in G.S. Olykke, C.R. Hansen and C.D. Tvarno, *EU Public Procurement – Modernisation, Growth and Innovation* (Copenhagen: Djøf Publishing, 2011), pp. 151–178.

778 See the first commentaries on the new dispositions: L. Richer, 'Les contrats entre entités du secteur public' (*ACCP*, 2014, n° 143), pp. 31–35; J. Wiggen, 'Directive 2014/24/EU: the new provision on co-operation in the public sector' (*PPLR*, 2014), pp. 83–93; G. Clamour, 'Marchés et concessions "entre entités dans le secteur public"' (*CMP* 6, 2014).

779 Proposal for a directive of the European Parliament and of the Council on procurement by entities operating in the water, energy, transport and postal services sectors, December 2011, 20 COM(2011) 895 final; Proposal for a directive of the European Parliament and of the Council on public procurement, December 2011, 20 COM(2011) 896 final.

780 Proposal for a directive of the European Parliament and of the Council on the award of concession contracts, December 2011, 20 COM(2011) 897 final.

781 Consideration 14.

782 Directive 2014/24/EU, consideration 31. See also consideration 38 of Directive 2014/25/EU.

4.2.1. Vertical cooperative agreements

Article 12 of Directive 2014/24/EU[783] reads as follows:

> '1. A public contract awarded by a contracting authority to a legal person governed by private or public law shall fall outside the scope of this Directive where all of the following conditions are fulfilled:
>
> (a) the contracting authority exercises over the legal person concerned a control, which is similar to that which it exercises over its own departments;
> (b) more than 80% of the activities of the controlled legal person are carried out in the performance of tasks entrusted to it by the controlling contracting authority or by other legal persons controlled by that contracting authority; and
> (c) there is no direct private capital participation in the controlled legal person with the exception of non- controlling and non-blocking forms of private capital participation required by national legislative provisions, in conformity with the Treaties, which do not exert a decisive influence on the controlled legal person.
>
> A contracting authority shall be deemed to exercise over a legal person a control similar to that which it exercises over its own departments within the meaning of point (a) of the first subparagraph where it exercises a decisive influence over both strategic objectives and significant decisions of the controlled legal person. Such control may also be exercised by another legal person, which is itself controlled in the same way by the contracting authority.
>
> 2. Paragraph 1 also applies where a controlled legal person which is a contracting authority awards a contract to its controlling contracting authority, or to another legal person controlled by the same contracting authority, provided that there is no direct private capital participation in the legal person being awarded the public contract with the exception of non-controlling and non-blocking forms of private capital participation required by national legislative provisions, in conformity with the Treaties, which do not exert a decisive influence on the controlled legal person.
>
> 3. A contracting authority, which does not exercise over a legal person governed by private or public law control within the meaning of paragraph 1, may nevertheless award a public contract to that legal person without applying this Directive where all of the following conditions are fulfilled.
>
> (a) the contracting authority exercises jointly with other contracting authorities a control over that legal person which is similar to that which they exercise over their own departments;
> (b) more than 80% of the activities of that legal person are carried out in the performance of tasks entrusted to it by the controlling contracting authorities or by other legal persons controlled by the same contracting authorities; and

[783] See also Article 17 Directive 2014/23/EU and Article 28 Directive 2014/25/EU.

(c) there is no direct private capital participation in the controlled legal person with the exception of non- controlling and non-blocking forms of private capital participation required by national legislative provisions, in conformity with the Treaties, which do not exert a decisive influence on the controlled legal person.

For the purposes of point (a) of the first subparagraph, contracting authorities exercise joint control over a legal person where all of the following conditions are fulfilled:

(i) the decision-making bodies of the controlled legal person are composed of representatives of all participating contracting authorities. Individual representatives may represent several or all of the participating contracting authorities;
(ii) those contracting authorities are able to jointly exert decisive influence over the strategic objectives and significant decisions of the controlled legal person; and
(iii) the controlled legal person does not pursue any interests that are contrary to those of the controlling contracting authorities'.

The Directives would seem to make clear that the notion 'contract' is not important for determining the applicability of EU law to vertical cooperation arrangements between public authorities. Indeed, it presupposes precisely that these arrangements are excluded from the scope of EU law even if a contract is present. What is more, the texts approved by the European Parliament, in difference with the Commission proposals, replace the notion 'contract' by the notion 'public contract'. This seems to imply that even if all the elements needed to regard a cooperative agreement as a public contract are present EU law may still not be applicable.

A public authority shall be deemed to exercise over a legal person a control similar to that which it exercises over its own departments where it exercises a decisive influence over both strategic objectives and significant decisions of the controlled legal person. The compromise text agreed between representatives of the European Council and the European Parliament (hereafter 'the Compromise text')[784] added that the control may also be exercised by another legal person that is itself controlled in the same way by the contracting authority. This seems to alter the position of the CJEU in *Carbotermo*. The CJEU considered in this ruling that when the subsidiary concerned was only indirectly owned by the public authority through an intermediary holding company, this could weaken any control exercised over the subsidiary.[785] It seems that the CJEU in its case law excludes any kind of indirect control. EU Parliament maintained this modification in the approved texts.

In comparison with CJEU case law the Commission has added in its proposals that the subsidiary must carry out at least 90% of its activities on behalf of the controlling

784 Proposal for a directive of the European Parliament and of the Council on public procurement, 2011/0438(COD), www.europarl.europa.eu/document/activities/cont/201309/20130913ATT71292/20130913ATT71292EN.pdf.

785 Case C-340/04, *Carbotermo SpA Consorzio Alisei v. Comune di Busto Arsizio AGESP SpA* [2006] *ECR* I-04137, at [39].

authorities. The aforementioned case law refers solely to an essential part of the activities. The published texts provide that 80% of the activities must be carried out on behalf of the controlling authorities. This corresponds to the percentage advanced by Advocate general Stix-Hackl.[786]

The third criterion on private participation has been significantly altered by the Compromise text: 'there is no direct private capital participation in the controlled legal person with the exception of non-controlling and non-blocking forms of private capital participation required by applicable national legislative provisions, in conformity with the Treaties, which do not exert a decisive influence on the controlled legal person'. This text, also approved by the EU Parliament, changes fundamentally the CJEU case law. *Stadt Halle* affirmed that the participation, *even as a minority*, of a private undertaking in the capital of a company in which the particular contracting authority is also a participant precludes in any event the possibility of the contracting authority exercising be deemed to have control over that company similar to the control it exercises over its own departments.[787] Private participation is allowed but it has to be required by applicable national legislative provisions.

In the case of joint control the Directives contain a number of ancillary conditions. The following cumulative conditions must be fulfilled:

(a) the decision-making bodies of the controlled legal person are composed of representatives of all participating contracting authorities;
(b) the contracting authorities are able to exert jointly decisive influence over the strategic objectives and significant decisions of the controlled legal person;
(c) the controlled legal person does not pursue any interests which are distinct from that of the public authorities affiliated to it;
(d) the controlled legal person does not extract any gain other than the reimbursement of actual costs from public contracts with the contracting authorities.

Most of these conditions are based on *Coditel Brabant*.[788] Only in the aforementioned ruling has the Court made a factual analysis on a basis which in the end decided that EU law did not need to apply, because the subsidiary was not sufficiently independent and was not market-oriented. One condition is not explicitly stated in the Directives; namely, the holding of capital, but it follows from the third general condition that there may be no private participation. The powers of the organs of the subsidiary are not directly taken into account. The last condition has not been retained in the Compromise text. This seems logical. This criterion could not be found in *Coditel Brabant*. Moreover, this is an element of the definition of the notion 'public contract'. In *Ordine degli Ingegneri*, the

[786] Opinion Advocate general Stix-Hackl C-26/03, *Stadt Halle and RPL Recyclingpark Lochau GmbH. v. Arbeitsgemeinschaft Thermische Restabfall- und Energieverwertungsanlage TREA Leuna* [2005] *ECR* I-00001, at [92].

[787] At [49].

[788] Case C-324/07, *Commune d'Uccle et Région Bruxelles-Capital* [2008] *ECR* I-08457.

CJEU considered that a contract cannot fall outside the concept of public contract merely because the remuneration remains limited to the reimbursement of the expenditure incurred to provide the agreed service.[789]

Coditel Brabant concerned a service concession. The Commission transposed in its proposals these conditions to a public contract and the adopted Directives confirm this. These proposals demonstrate the interchangeability of the case law.

The new provisions set out in the new Directives provide also an exclusion from the scope of EU law when a subsidiary, which is a contracting authority, awards a contract to one of the controlling public authorities or to another legal person controlled by the same contracting authority. This is proposed on condition that there is no private participation in the legal person being awarded the public contract. Here the adopted texts diverge from existing case law and especially from the spirit. The case law only provides an exclusion when a controlling authority awards a contract to its subsidiary. It is evident that the new Directives wish to allow the Member States to retain more powers than might follow from CJEU case law.

4.2.2. Horizontal cooperative agreements

In order to shield a horizontal cooperative agreement from the scope of EU law Article 11(4) of the proposed Directives on public procurement and Article 11(4) of the proposed Directive on service concessions provide as follows:

'An agreement concluded between two or more contracting authorities shall not be deemed to be a public contract within the meaning of Article 2(6) of this Directive where the following cumulative conditions are fulfilled:

(a) the agreement establishes a genuine cooperation between the participating contracting authorities aimed at carrying out jointly their public service tasks and involving mutual rights and obligations of the parties;
(b) the agreement is governed only by considerations relating to the public interest;
(c) the participating contracting authorities do not perform on the open market more than 10% of the turnover of their activities that are relevant in the context of the agreement;
(d) the agreement does not involve financial transfers between the participating contracting authorities, other than those tantamount to a reimbursement for actual costs of works, services or supplies;
(e) there is no private participation in any of the contracting authorities involved.'

[789] Case C-159/11, *Azienda Sanitaria Locale di Lecce, Università del Salento v. Ordine degli Ingegneri della Provincia di Lecce and Others* [2012] *ECR* I-00000, at [29].

The first part of the first condition seems to be congruent with the first criterion set down in *Ordine degli Ingegneri*.[790] This criterion requires that cooperative agreements between public authorities should have as its purpose an assurance of completion of a public task that they all must perform. Whether a contract involves the mutual rights and obligations of the parties seems a superfluous consideration. If there are no mutual rights or obligations, there is also no contract. This consideration is implicit in the definition of the term 'public contract'.

The second criterion seems to add nothing new to the criteria established in *Ordine degli Ingegneri*. There is one semantic difference. The CJEU case law requires that 'the implementation of' the cooperation is guided solely by considerations and requirements related to the public interest. According to the proposed directives, the 'agreement' is guided by this sort of consideration. However, this difference seems of no consequence given the implementation of a contract concerns the object of the contract, which is one of the important aspects for deciding that a contract exists.

The third criterion is at variance with one of the criteria established by the CJEU on vertical cooperation. This condition is associated with the second *Teckal* criterion (activities), which the CJEU recently ruled not to be applicable to horizontal cooperation. It is surprising this criterion has been added inasmuch as it limits the possibilities for public authorities to cooperate.

The fourth criterion was taken from *Commission v. Germany*. Only financial transfers that cover costs may take place between cooperating public authorities. This condition cannot be found in *Ordine degli Ingegneri*. Thus, the CJEU considered that this criterion is not relevant (see above).

The last condition is a reaffirmation of the third criterion in *Ordine degli Ingegneri*. It is, moreover, the only condition that is the same as for vertical cooperation. The presence of a private undertaking in the cooperation may bring an advantage for the latter, which poses a risk to free competition. Consequently EU law is to be applied. Public-private partnerships therefore would be subject to EU law insofar as they may be construed to be a public contract or a service concession.

The European Parliament approved texts provide in Article 12.4 the following provision applicable to horizontal cooperative agreements:

'A contract concluded exclusively between two or more contracting authorities shall fall outside the scope of this Directive where the following cumulative conditions are fulfilled:

(a) the contract establishes or implements a cooperation between the participating contracting authorities with the aim of ensuring that public services they have

[790] Case C-159/11, *Azienda Sanitaria Locale di Lecce, Università del Salento v. Ordine degli Ingegneri della Provincia di Lecce and Others* [2012] *ECR* I-00000, at [34].

to perform are provided with a view to achieving objectives they have in common;
(b) the implementation of that cooperation is governed solely by considerations relating to the public interest;
(c) the participating contracting authorities perform on the open market less than 20% of the activities concerned by the cooperation'.

In contrast to the proposed Directives from the Commission, the adopted Directives clearly state that under the conditions laid down in the cited text horizontal cooperative agreements fall outside the scope of EU law. The Commission's proposal still considered that if the criteria mentioned in Article 11(2) are fulfilled the agreement concluded between public authorities is not a public contract, thus applying the *Teckal* ruling. The approved texts clearly confirm that even when such cooperation is a (public) contract, under certain conditions it falls beyond the scope of EU law. This confirms what the present thesis defended earlier on, namely that the notion 'public contract' is not relevant to CJEU case law on cooperative agreements. Unlike vertical cooperative agreement the text on horizontal cooperative agreements takes the notion of 'contract' as a premise, and not the notion 'public contract'.

The first criterion to exclude horizontal cooperative agreements from the scope of EU law differs slightly from the criteria provided in *Ordine degli Ingegneri*. The text provides that cooperation has to ensure that public services required of the public authorities are provided with a view to achieving *objectives* they have in common. The CJEU ruled that a cooperation arrangement between public authorities has to ensure that a public *task* that all public authorities are required to perform has been completed. The final text seems to give more freedom to a public authority to organise its public service tasks.

The text confirms the third criterion, but raises the percentage of activities that a participating authority can perform on the market. The text omits the fourth criterion from the proposal so that the approved Directive seems to accommodate to the *Ordine degli Ingegneri*-ruling. More surprisingly the criterion on private participation was not taken. This is the most important modification in respect of the Commission proposals and CJEU case law. Private participation has always been regarded as a sign that competition could be distorted. Apparently, the European Parliament and the European Council agreed that this is not always the case.

4.2.3. Conclusion

The provisions on cooperative agreements in the new Directives create legal certainty. The CJEU case law created a lot of uncertainty in different Member States as to how and to what extent cooperative agreements could be used to organise or discharge public tasks without the necessity of a tendering procedure. Broadly, the provisions of the new Directives confirm the CJEU case law. However, the new dispositions also contain several remarkable modifications to the existing CJEU case law broadening the possibilities for public authorities to cooperate without a duty to consult the market.

These provisions, however, are only applicable to public contracts and service concessions above the EU thresholds. The CJEU confirmed in its case law that the *Teckal* criteria also apply to these contracts below the EU thresholds.[791] Thus, the CJEU case law examined in the present chapter retains its importance for the future.

5. State and market

The starting point of the division of powers between the European Union (market liberalisation) and the Member State (institutional autonomy) regarding 'services of general interest' is quite straight forward. In principle, Member States are responsible and competent for the definition and the interpretation of the concept 'services of general interest', for the organization and for the use of these services.[792]

However, the CJEU gives a functional interpretation to the general rules on the allocation of competences.[793] The European Union is still considered mostly as pursuing economic objectives (internal market, free competition). Any national measure that would imply a violation of these objectives may be found to be incompatible with EU law. As Koen Lenaerts puts it: 'Once there is a cross border element or link that triggers the application of the substantive law of the EU, no area of national law – not even areas traditionally reserved to the Member States – remains a safe haven'.[794] Therefore, even national measures concerning the definition, the organisation and the use of services of general interest may still be subject to the test of compatibility with EU law especially when such measures have an impact on the freedom of movement. This division of competences should be applied taking into account the principle of subsidiarity. This means that European institutions can only regulate when they are better placed then the Member States to achieve a certain goal.[795]

It will become apparent in Chapter 6 that the concept of 'public service(s)' and the way they are organised, are shaped by the legal system in which they develop. They are an

791 See Case C-573/07, *Sea Srl v. Comune di Ponte Nassa* [2009] *ECR* I-08127, at [35]; Joined cases C-182/11 and C-183/11, *Econord SpA v. Comuni di Cagno, Comune di Varese, Comune di Solbiate* [2012] *ECR* I-00000, at [26].

792 Articles 1 and 2 of Protocol 26 to the Lisbon Treaty.

793 C.W.A. Timmermans, 'The basic principles', in P.J.G. Kapteyn, A.M. McDonnell, K.J.M. Mortelmans and C.W.A. Timmermans, *The Law of the European Union and the European Communities* (Alphen aan den Rijn: Kluwer Law International, 2008), p. 138.

794 K. Lenaerts, Federation and the Rule of Law. Perspectives from the European Court of Justice (Fordham Int.L.J., 2011), p. 1340.

795 O. Cotte, 'La répartition des compétences entre l'Union et ses Etats membres dans le domaine des services d'intérêt économique général', in G. Eckert, Y. Gautier, R. Kovar and D. Ritleng, *Incidences du droit communautaire sur le droit public français* (Strasbourg: Presses universitaires de Strasbourg, 2007), p. 311; M.T. Karayagit, *The Concept of Services of General Economic Interest Revisited* (*EPL*, 2009), p. 580.

expression of the way in which a society thinks of its organisation and how this is executed by the society. More specifically it deals with the way in which certain institutions (public authorities) safeguard the (national) public interest. In this sense, the thesis defends the proposition that internal market rules should only influence this evolution when they are strictly necessary for the realisation of the economic targets of the EU. The CJEU should also take this into account in its case law.

In any case, the new public procurement Directives and the concession Directive are encouraging the CJEU to consider the competences of the Member States. It has already been observed that the new Directives are returning competences to Member States, as opposed to the currently applicable Directives as interpreted by the Court. Thus, taking into account the growing Euroscepticism, the Court is well advised to give significant consideration to these national tendencies in its decisions. An overly functional interpretation of EU law seems to go against the wishes of Member States, a wish that was, after all, validated by the EU Parliament. All of this expresses a democratic wish the Court cannot ignore on the risk of being further criticized as a 'gouvernement des juges'.

It follows, for the subject of this thesis, that the criteria which determine if cooperative agreements involving the organisation or the management of public service fall within the scope of EU law, should be framed within the principle of institutional autonomy of the Member States, instead of within the framework of market principles. A less functional interpretation of the criteria will entail a larger scope of competences for the Member States, which seemed to be the wish of the Member States when the new Directives were approved.

The sense of a real Union can be achieved also by the European institutions recognizing the individuality of each Member States in certain areas. This recognition exists when the Member States remain competent in situations which are heavily intertwined with the constitutional singularity of each Member State.

6. General conclusions

Cooperation between public authorities is one of the ways a public authority organises or manages its public (service) tasks. In this context, national law normally regulates their activities. However, in certain circumstances EU law does have a role; namely, when cooperation between public authorities could be defined as a public contract or a service concession.

From the public procurement Directives it follows that, according to one exception, even when cooperation is a public contract, a tendering procedure need not be applied. This is the case if a public service contract is awarded on the basis of an exclusive right, which a subsidiary enjoys pursuant to a published law, a regulation or an administrative provision compatible with the Treaty (Article 18 of Directive 2004/18/EC). However, this provision entails merely a limited exception, strictly interpreted by the CJEU. For a more general exception, the CJEU had itself to find a solution, and it was this pursuit that engendered case law on cooperative agreements between public authorities, the central theme of the thesis.

In the first place, this case law makes clear that the way a public authority organises or manages its public tasks is not governed by EU law. Public authorities remain free to choose to manage themselves their public service tasks, to engage a third party to assume their management, or to transfer management of the public service to a third person. Second, EU law is not applicable when a public authority uses its own services to accomplish a task (in house). The internal management of a public authority has no effect on market behaviour and cannot distort competition. The economic objectives are thus not put at risk here. In this manner the CJEU has made two constitutional choices. The case law contains elements that affect the relationship between State and Market and affects the division of powers between the EU and the Member States.

From the moment a public authority engages a third person, EU law is applicable if the agreement is a public contract or a service concession or more generally when a public authority confers the provision of an economic activity to a third party. CJEU case law distinguishes two situations in this regard: vertical and horizontal cooperative agreements with a third person. In both cases, a 'market situation' arises and EU law must be applied when the third person is a private undertaking or if one shareholder of the third legal entity is a private undertaking. This is a reflection of the idea that this undertaking can gain an advantage as a consequence of the cooperation and thus competition could be distorted. On the other hand, other private undertakings will find it more difficult or even impossible to benefit from the same State measure. Their access to a particular market is hindered.

From the public procurement Directives point of view it also follows that even cooperative agreements concluded between fully publicly owned public authorities is subject to EU law. According to CJEU case law this also applies to service concessions. However, CJEU case law on vertical or horizontal cooperative agreements also provides a series of criteria that, if met, enable these kinds of agreements to fall outside the scope of EU law. The CJEU broadens the competence of the Member States to include situations that are not expressly provided for in an existing Directive. It is submitted that the CJEU has established a new demarcation in the relationship between State and the market. Via public procurement Directives the CJEU has entered onto a terrain that does not explicitly come under EU law.

According to this thesis, the criteria that the CJEU has developed to enable vertical and horizontal cooperative agreements to fall beyond the scope of EU law, is an expression of the same idea. A state measure, i.e. a decision to cooperate in the accomplishment of a public task objective, is of no relevance to EU law if it is guided solely by considerations related to the public interest and the measure does not advantage a private undertaking. EU law developed on the basis of economic objectives and is solely applicable in an economic context. Only state measures that put these objectives at risk, give rise to the application of EU law.

In the context of a vertical cooperative agreement the CJEU has developed two criteria: the control criterion and the activities criterion. Together they reflect the idea that the public authority that is called upon to carry out a task has no independence. Recently the CJEU has confirmed this view: 'that the exception concerning the in-house awards is based on an approach according to which, in such cases, the awarding public authority can be regarded as using its own resources in order to accomplish its tasks in the public interest'.[796] Thus the decision to cooperate is in these circumstances clearly to be situated in the internal organisation of public authorities and not in the market. The 'operator' cannot be considered to be market-oriented. Application of a State measure (the decision to cooperate) could give the operator an advantage over its competitors. If the operator is not market-oriented, the state measure has no effect on the market and competition is to that extent not distorted. The extent of the control and the amount of activities determine the object of a measure taken. They inform whether the measure has an economic effect and hence is of concern to EU law.

The CJEU case law on horizontal cooperative agreements is clearer in this area. Cooperation between public authorities cannot place a private operator in a position of advantage *vis-à-vis* competitors and this cooperation shall be governed solely by considerations and requirements relating to the pursuit of objectives in the public interest. However, the CJEU implicitly considered in recent case law on a vertical cooperative agreement that if the contracting parties pursue objectives of public interest, the awarding public authority may be exempted from the application EU law.[797] The target of the measure is an objective of general interest.

The analysis carried out above seems to demonstrate that the CJEU adopted an evolutionary approach to the development of the relevant case law. The CJEU interprets EU law in an extensive way so as to protect the powers of the Union even though *Teckal* already had effectively broadened the existing exemptions set out in public procurement Directives. The CJEU seems readily to acknowledge the uniqueness of certain legal systems in respect of the ways public authorities organise the delivery of their public tasks. A broader interpretation of the *Teckal* criteria (especially the control criterion) and the creation of a second set of criteria to place horizontal cooperation outside the scope of EU law, enabled Member States, under certain circumstances, to retain competence to set rules for when a public authority may cooperate with another public authority in order to organise or manage its public tasks.

Finally, the thesis also postulates that this CJEU case law on cooperative agreements implicitly applies the market access criterion in order to bring a particular situation

796 Case C-574/12, *Centro Hospitalar de Setúbal EPE, Serviço de Utilização Comum dos Hospitais (SUCH) v. Eurest (Portugal) – Sociedade Europeia de Restaurantes Lda* [2014] *ECR* I-00000 at [35].

797 At [36].

within the scope (or conversely, to shield it from) EU law. If a measure is of a nature (i.e. economic) to hinder this access, the public procurement Directives and/or the principle of equality must be applied. In the new Directives on public procurement and service concessions the EU institutions have acknowledged this idea when it approved provisions that emulate the CJEU case law. Distortion of competition seems to be the central idea that triggers the application of EU law on cooperative agreements.

In a number of points concerning cooperative agreements between public authorities the Directives recently adopted by the European Parliament contain changes of vision relating to the division of powers between the European Union and the Member States. The CJEU for the most part adopts EU law on cooperative agreements in light of the objectives of the EU, which are, namely, the realisation of an internal market and assuring free competition. In other words, the competence of the EU in matters of cooperative agreements was given a quite broad interpretation. The proposals of the European Commission were also premised on this consideration. However, the texts approved by the European Parliament marked implicitly a shift of competence from the EU to the Member States. The competence of the latter was restored in a number of situations of cooperation where under CJEU case law they no longer had it. The texts were adapted in the Parliament under the influence of the European Council. This suggests that many Member States did not approve the direction the CJEU took in its case law on cooperation between public authorities. It became clear that this was a sensitive matter that touched on the very sovereignty of the Member States.

These provisions on cooperative agreements in the new Directives could indicate that the criteria developed by the CJEU to exclude these agreements from the scope of EU law were too severe. Member States and the institutions of the EU were apparently convinced free access and undistorted competition are still protected with the new adopted provisions. It proves that these criteria are a mere expression of the balance of powers between the Market (the EU) and the State (Member States), between market integration and institutional autonomy.

The CJEU case law on cooperative agreements builds in part on the evolving European Economic Constitution and indeed more or less mirrors the relation between the market and intervention (State and Market). It plays a role in setting the economic direction of the Union; and it is a factor in determining the division of competences between the EU and the Member States. The recent Directives, approved by EU Parliament and the case law that preceded them indicate that this new distribution of competences in matters concerning cooperative agreements tends to favour the Member States. This was also apparent from the Commission's early proposals. The Member States were able to exert their influence even more forcefully in the EU Parliament and via the European Council to keep the organisation of public service tasks within their spheres of authority as far as possible.

This could reflect a more general aversion in a number of Member States towards the EU. The last EU elections saw the rise in several Member States of anti-establishment parties or Eurosceptic parties.[798] On one hand decisions are still taken by unaccountable institutions, decisions which have a significant impact on the whole society of the Member States and on the other hand the economic crisis created a clash between the northern and southern EU Member States.[799] EU citizens feel like they no longer exert an influence on the way their society is being organised. Member States expressed this feeling when they contributed to the establishment of the public procurement and concession Directives.

798 Www.economist.com/news/europe/21603034-impact-rise-anti-establishment-parties-europe-and-abroad-eurosceptic-union; www.euractiv.com/sections/eu-elections-2014/eurosceptics-make-controversial-return-eu-parliament-303242.

799 Www.ecfr.eu/page/-/ECFR79_EUROSCEPTICISM_BRIEF_AW.pdf.

Chapter 6

INFLUENCE OF EU LAW ON NATIONAL LEGAL SYSTEMS

Cooperative agreements between public authorities are the theme of this thesis. Such cooperation has existed and exists in most Member States of the European Union for a long time. This cooperation is considered in several Member States to be a typical example of the freedom of public authorities to organise their public service(s).[800] The principle of free administration by national, regional and local authorities has been confirmed in Article 2 of Directive 2014/23/EU: 'Those authorities are free to decide how best to manage the execution of works or the provision of services, to ensure in particular a high level of quality, safety and affordability, equal treatment and the promotion of universal access and of user rights in public services'. How public authorities organise their public service(s) is normally determined by national (administrative) law. In several Member States public authorities were not obliged to organise a tendering procedure or at least safeguard equal treatment when they wanted to cooperate with another public authority.

The two preceding chapters of this thesis were exclusively concerned with the potential effect of EU law on how a public authority organises and manages its public service tasks. This thesis concentrated particularly on cooperative agreements between public authorities, which can be qualified as a public contract or a service concession.

This chapter of the thesis accordingly explores the extent to which existing EU law (especially CJEU case law) influences national law in certain national legal systems. The English and French legal systems have been taken as examples. First, the choice of the two legal systems was inspired by the circumstance that they are typical examples of two different law systems that are encountered especially in Europe; namely, common law and civil law. Secondly, Reitz suggests that many of the fundamental differences among the public law systems of the world can best be understood as reflecting different types of political economy.[801] France[802] can be considered to be one of the most state-centred

800 The meaning of this concept will be explained in each of the examined legal systems: France and England.

801 J.C. Reitz, 'Political Economy as a Major Architectural Principle of Public Law' (*Tulane L. Rev.*, 2001), pp. 1121–1157.

802 Reitz saw no main differences between the French and German political economy and characterized both as state-centered political economies, where Germany is less state-centered: J.C. Reitz, 'Political Economy as a Major Architectural Principle of Public Law' (*Tulane L. Rev.*, 2001), p. 1130.

political economies in the EU and England as the most market centred political economy. This distinction could explain the different administrative law in the two countries and also justifies the examination of these two legal systems. As they are considered to be the two most opposing legal systems in Europe the other legal systems must be situated between those two systems. At first the two legal systems will be described as they existed before the CJEU case law on cooperative agreements between public authorities emerged.

The chapter first examines whether the concept of 'public service(s)' exists in each of these two legal systems and, if so, how it may be defined. This will be followed by an examination of how these services are organised or managed, taking cooperative agreements between public authorities as an example. It will be made clear how EU law and more particular the CJEU case law on cooperative agreements between public authorities, has or has not influenced the existing law in the legal systems of France and England.

This study will enable a comparison of two national systems with the case law developed by the Court of Justice, based on public procurement Directives and on the fundamental rules and principles set out in the EU treaties. In addition, the two legal systems will, where germane, be compared with one another.

1. French system

1.1. Service public

The first question to be addressed is the place of the concept *'service public'* in French public law (1.1.1). Next this section examines how the concept 'public service' is defined in French law. (1.1.2). Thirdly, this section will analyse the two criteria that determine the presence of a 'service public': namely, *'personne publique'* (1.1.3) and *'intérêt général'* (1.1.4). Finally, the section shall examine the ways a public authority organises or manages its *'service public'* (1.1.5).

1.1.1. The place of *'service public'*

The notion *of 'service public'* is a fundamental element of the French state and indeed it is one of the constitutional precepts of the state. It reflects the relationship between the State and its citizens. The establishment, administration, and maintenance of a public service create an unbreakable bond between the State and the citizens, whereby the main role of the State is ordained to be at the service of its citizens: *'L'État Providence'*.[803] All citizens have equal access to public services. This is at variance with the idea of the State as a *'puissance publique'*.

[803] See F. Moderne, 'Les transcriptions doctrinales de l'idée de service public', in F. Moderne and G. Marcou (dir.), *L'idée de service public dans le droit des états de l'Union européenne* (Paris: L'Harmattan, 2001), pp. 19–20.

The notion of 'service public' is one of the basic elements of public and administrative law in France.[804] It justifies the presence and actions of public authorities.[805] Public authorities primarily exist to look after services of general interest to the benefit of their citizens. The special powers of a public authority find their justification exclusively in the need for these services and the provision thereof.[806] The need for a public service legitimises the State and its existence.[807] Thus the concept of *'service public'* is constitutive of French public law.

The theory of *'service public'* has always been the cornerstone of French administrative law.[808] In *Blanco,*[809] the French *Conseil d'État* ruled the competence of the High Administrative Court in matters concerning the civil liability of public authorities' derivative of the concept of *'service public'*. Legal scholars used this decision to base all of French administrative law on this concept.[810] In consequence of this concept, French administrative law is a mostly autonomous branch of law. Usually other rules are applied to public authorities than those applied in the private domain. The situation is completely different in England. In the study of the English legal system, it will become clear that English common law is extensively applied to public authorities and certainly in their relationships with third parties.[811] Secondly, English public authorities think and act more market-centred.

The importance of the 'service public' in France also explains why there has been so much resistance in France in regard to CJEU case law as the thesis discussed in chapter 5. This case law was seen as an assault on the principle of French institutional autonomy. It limits the organisational freedom of public authorities.[812] Discussing the proposals for the Directives of 2014 the French Senate was opposed to the introduction of provisions on cooperative agreements between public authorities. The Senate found it to early to implement such provisions.[813] However, in chapter 3 the thesis explained that primary EU law more and more takes account of the concept of 'service of general interest'.

1.1.2. The concept of *'service public'*

In light of the importance of the concept of *'service public'*, a precise and clear definition of the concept is in order.

804 L. Duguit, *Les transformations du droit public* (éd. La mémoire du droit, 1999), p. 33; L. Janicot, 'L'identification du service public géré par une personne privée' (*RFDA*, 2008), p. 67.
805 P. Delvolvé, 'Service public et libertés publiques' (*RFDA*, 1985), p. 2.
806 R. Chapus, *Droit administratif général* (Paris: Montchrestien, 2001), p. 573.
807 P. Gonod, F. Melleray, and Ph. Yolka, *Traité de droit administratif*, T.2 (Paris: Dalloz, 2011), p. 46.
808 S. Braconnier, *Droit des services publics* (Paris: PUF, 2007), p. 105.
809 TC 8 February, 1873, Lebon, 1e suppl., 61, concl. David.
810 M. Waline, *Droit administratif* (Paris: Dalloz, 2010), p. 8; P.-L. Frier and J. Petit, *Droit administratif* (Paris: Montchrestien, 2012), p. 30.
811 See M. Waline, *Droit administratif* (Paris: Dalloz, 2010), pp. 7–8.
812 C. Pilone, 'Reflexions autour de la notion de contrat "in house"', in G. Clamour and M. Ubaud-Bergeron (eds.), *Contrats publics. Mélanges en honneur du Professeur Michel Guibal*, Vol. I (Montpellier: CREAM, 2006), pp. 716–717.
813 Www.senat.fr/leg/tas11-112.html.

Here lies the crux of the problem in France.[814] Over the years it became apparent that it is not easy to define this concept. Legislators have not as yet ventured on the creation of such a definition. Legal scholars came to the conclusion that it is a confusing, unstable and even indefinable concept.[815] The French *Conseil d'État* has developed criteria to determine what a *'service public'* is. It was eventually systematised by legal scholars. These following pages of the thesis are based on the system proposed by René Chapus[816] and adopted by Guglielmi and Koubi.[817]

The methodology chosen by Chapus has taken full account of the two categories that form the concept of *'service public'*, namely the organic public service and the functional public service[818] and evolutions within administrative law whereby public authorities look after services that are of general interest while private entities are chosen by the public authorities to look after these services of general interest.

To explain the concept of *'service public'*, Chapus starts from the following definition, taking into account the organic relationship of an activity (ties with a public authority) and the purpose of the activity: *'une activité constitue un service public quand elle est assurée ou assumée par une personne publique en vue d'un intérêt public'* [an activity constitutes a public service when it is carried out or assumed by a 'public person' with a view to public interest].[819] He broadly confirms a definition accepted by the majority of legal scholars.[820] Two elements are important: the relation to a *'personne publique'* and a need of general interest. Both elements are cumulative. The two criteria will now be examined in more detail.

1.1.3. Relation to a *'personne publique'*

A *'service public'* always manifests some connection with a *'personne publique'* (public authority). A *'personne publique'* decides whether an activity constitutes a *'service public'*.

814 The definition of this concept is not only a problem in France. See in Belgium: P.-O. de Broux, 'Historique et transformation de la notion de service public à la lumière du droit européen', in H. Dumont, P. Jadoul, B. Lombaert, F. Tulkens and S. Van Drooghenbroeck (eds.), *Le service public*, T. 1 (Brussels: La Charte, 2009), pp. 1–56.

815 P.L. Frier and J.Petit, *Précis de droit administratif* (Paris: Montchrestien, 2008), p. 179. D. Truchet, 'Label de service public et statut du service public' (*AJDA*, 1982), p. 428.

816 R.Chapus, *Droit administratif général* (Paris: Montchrestien, 2001), pp. 578 et seq.

817 G.J. Gugliemi, G. Koubi and G. Dumont, *Droit du service public* (Paris: Montchrestien, 2007), pp. 89 et seq.

818 See below for an explanation of both concepts. In an early ruling on 20 december 1935 the *Conseil d'État* set down the difference between the organic 'service public' and the functional 'service public': C.E., 20 December 1935, Etablissements Vézia (*RDP*, 1936), p. 119.

819 R. Chapus, *Droit administratif général* (Paris, Montchrestien, 2001), p. 579; Definition also cited in S. Boussard, *L'éclatement des categories de services public et la public par nature* (*RFDA*, 2008), p. 45 and P. Gonod, F. Melleray and Ph. Yolka (dir.), *Traité de droit administratif*, T.2 (Paris: Dalloz, 2011), p. 53. See also J. Waline, *Droit administratif* (Paris: LGDJ, 2010), p. 352: 'le service public correspond à la satisfaction d'un intérêt général… le service public, directement ou indirectement, relève en dernier ressort d'une autorité publique'.

820 A. de Laubadère, *Traité élémentaire de droit administrative* (Paris: Dalloz, 1953), p. 35; J.-L. de Corail, 'L'approche fonctionnelle du service public: sa réalité et ses limites' (*AJDA*, 1997), p. 20.

Thus, the creation of a *'service public'* enjoys democratic legitimacy[821] irrespective of whether the decision comes directly from the legislative power or whether the legislative power has delegated authority to the executive power. How is the term *'personne publique'* understood in France? What kind of relation is necessary?

In France three categories of *'personnes publiques'* are distinguished: the State, local authorities and *'établissements publics'* (public institutions).[822]

The State embraces all central and decentralised administration and a number of local autonomous authorities not represented by a legal person and dependent on the State. Local authorities will be regions, departments, municipalities, *'collectivités'* (communities) with special status as well as the *'collectivités d'outre-mer'* (overseas entities). Both these categories imply a community of persons who live on a specific territory.[823]

An *'établissement public'* is (a) an independent legal person (b) of public law (c) that manages a *'service public'*.[824] This person is specifically created via decentralisation by service (functional public service) to administer a specific *'service public'*. A body can be designated an *'etablissement public'* via a specific legal text. In that case no problem of qualification arises. Next, the *Conseil d'État* has developed in its case law criteria for recognising an *'établissement public'*, when the legislator has not qualified the entity: 1) whether it was established by a *'personne publique'*, 2) if its purpose is that of tending to the general interest, 3) what kind of control function the State exercises and 4) if the legal person has extraordinary powers.[825] The criteria are not cumulative, but the more criteria are met, the greater the probability that case law will designate the body as an *'établissement public'*.

The notion of *'personne publique'* shows affinities with the description in chapter 2 of the terms 'public authority' and 'body governed by public law' in EU law. It is likely that the Court of Justice, as in other cases, took inspiration from French administrative law and the case law of the French *Conseil d'État*.

In regard to the organic relationship, Chapus makes a distinction between a direct and an indirect relationship with a *'personne publique'*.

821 P. Gonod, F. Melleray and Ph. Yolka, *Traité de droit administratif*, T.2 (Paris: Dalloz, 2010), p. 60.

822 G. Vedel and P. Delvolvé, *Droit administratif* (Paris: PUF, 1988), p. 844; P.L. Frier, *Précis de droit administratif* (Paris: Montchrétien, 2004), p. 190. See also F. Lichère, *Droit des contrats publics* (Paris: Dalloz, 2005), pp. 14–15: He adds one more category, namely: *'groupements d'intérêt public'* (public interest groupings) with reference to T. confl., 14 February 2000, GIP, *Habitat et interventions sociales pour les mal logés et sans-abri*.

823 J. Waline, *Droit administratif* (Paris: Dalloz, 2012), p. 51.

824 Y. Gaudemet, *Traité de droit administratif*, T.1 (Paris: LGDJ, 2001), pp. 288–290; P.L. Frier, *Précis de droit administratif* (Paris: Montchrétien, 2004), p. 190 with reference to CE 8 February 1999, *Service départemental incendie et Secours*.

825 R. Chapus, *Droit administratif Général*, T.1 (Paris: Montchréstien, 2001), pp. 187–188.

In a direct relationship, the public authority manages public service tasks with its own resources and with its own public servants. At EU level the term used is an 'in-house' situation. This kind of situation falls outside the scope of EU law.[826] This situation is qualified in French law as an organic public service.

The relationship with the public authority can, however, be indirect, in which case the service will not be managed by the public authority itself. Another legal entity will be positioned between the public authority and the '*service public*'. However, a decision by a '*personne publique*' is still needed where a third (private) partner manages the '*service public*'. The '*personne publique*' must have ruled that a specific activity concerns the general interest and thus comes under its responsibility. But, the third partner must in real terms assume or have control of the management of the public service. This situation qualifies as a functional public service.

Within this category three subcategories may be further distinguished. The first two categories are easy to explain.[827] Regarding the first category one must look into what control a '*personne publique*' possesses. This control may, for instance, derive from statutory participation in the capital of the entity that manages the '*service public*'. If the '*personne publique*' is a majority shareholder, it is presumed that there is a full and direct connection and consequently this is a '*service public*'.[828, 829] For the second category, the relationship between public authorities and the legal entity is materialised in a contract (e.g. service concession).

If this relationship cannot be demonstrated on the strength of these objective elements, the existence of the relationship must be based on several criteria (third category), developed in the case law of the *Conseil d'État*. These elements are not of a cumulative nature. The *Conseil d'État* has indeed recognised that a private entity could be instructed to manage a public service independent of any formal contract.[830]

The latest debate over the recognition of a '*service public*' was whether the entity in question should possess prerogatives that normally belong to a public authority.[831] This question arises when a private entity is entrusted with a public task. Indeed, it is always assumed of a '*personne publique*' that it performs a public task.

826 Case C-26/03, *Stadt Halle and RPL Recyclingpark Lochau GmbH. v. Arbeitsgemeinschaft Thermische Restabfall- und Energieverwertungsanlage TREA Leuna* [2005] *ECR* I-00001.

827 S. Braconnier, *Droit des services publics* (Paris: PUF, 2007), p. 165.

828 CE 20 April 1956, Epoux Bertin, *Rec.*, 167.

829 The Court of Justice ruled in Asemfo (see chapter 5) that since a public authority holds, alone or together with other public authorities, all of the share capital in a successful tenderer this tends generally to indicate that that public authority exercises over that company a control similar to that which it exercises over its own departments. This indicates that the relationship between the public authority and the 'entity' does not subsist in a market context.

830 CE 13 May 1938, *Caisse primaire d'aide et de protection*, *Rec.* 41; CE fr. 31 July 1942, Monpeurt, *Lebon* 239; CE fr. 2 April 1943, Bouguen, *Lebon* 86; CE fr. 13 January 1961, Magnier, *Lebon* 33.

831 L. Janicot, *L'identification du service public géré par une personne privée* (*RFDA*, 2008), p. 68.

If the private entity has acquired such prerogatives of public power from a public authority, the activity managed by this private entity must be considered as a *'service public'*.[832] The situation is less clear if the entity has not acquired such prerogatives. Until the 1990s the *Conseil d'État* ruled out the existence of a *'service public'* in such circumstances.[833] Thus, the acquisition of a prerogative was necessary for the presence of a *'service public'*. A decision of 20 July 1990 saw the existence of such a prerogative for the first time as an optional criterion.[834] This was the first step to a less restrictive interpretation of the notion of *'service public'* when it is a third person that manages the public task.

This discussion seems to have come to an end in some recent decisions by the *Conseil d'État*. In a decision of 22 February 2007,[835] the *Conseil d'État* distinguished two hypotheses. In a first hypothesis, a *'service public'* exists when the entity that manages the service has the prerogatives of a public authority. According to some, this seems to be the primary principle but it should nonetheless meet two other distinct criteria: it must have been entrusted with the management of a *'service public'* and it must be subjected to control by the administration.[836] In the second hypothesis a *'service public'* exists when the public entity does not have the prerogatives of a public authority. This is the case when it is apparent by virtue of the general interest nature of its activities, its method of establishment, its organisation and how it operates, its duties and the measures used to check whether it has achieved objectives that the public authority intended the entity to fulfil in the general interest.[837] In both hypotheses, the legal entity must have been assigned a public task and the public authority must play an important role in how the entity operates.

In *Commune d'Aix-en-Provence*[838] the *Conseil d'État* upheld the presence of a public service for an activity assured by a private entity, considering that in this case a *'personne publique'* defined the tasks of the private entity, financed the entity, exercised control over it and saw to its proper functioning.

In its interpretation of the element 'personne publique' the Conseil d'Etat seems to conform its case law to the more functional interpretation of the CJEU of the concept of SGI (see chapter 3).

832 CE 13 January 1961, no. 43548, *Lebon* 32; CE 23 December 2012, no. 337396, *Conseil national de l'ordre des médecins.*

833 CE 18 June 1963, Narcy, Lebon 401.

834 CE 20 July 1990, no. 69867, Ville de Melun, Lebon 220.

835 CE 22 February 2007, *Association du personnel relevant des établissements pour inadaptés, Rec.* 92.

836 M. Long, P. Weil, G. Braibant, P. Delvolvé and B. Genevois, *Les grands arrêts de la jurisprudence administrative* (Paris: Dalloz, 2009), pp. 322–323 with reference to the CE 28 June 1963, Narcy, *Rec.* 401.

837 See also CE 20 July 1990, Ville de Melun et Association "Melun-culture-loisirs", *Rec.* 220. For a recent application see CE 6 April 2007, *Commune d'Aix-en-Provence, Rec.*155.

838 CE 6 April 2007, *Commune d'Aix en Provence* (*RFDA*, 2007), p. 812, concl. F. Séners, note J.-Cl. Douence (*AJDA*, 2007), pp.10–20, chr. F. Lenica and J. Boucher.

1.1.4. General interest

The second criterion for determining whether a *'service public'* exists has to do with the activity of the entity, i.e. whether the entity performs an activity of general interest. According to some this is the fundamental element in the definition of *'service public'*.[839] What is meant by this criterion?

Defining the term 'general interest' is no simple matter.[840] Its meaning varies over time and also in regard to its applicability by reason of place.[841] It is in continuous evolution. There are two ways to determine whether an activity is of general interest.[842]

In the first instance the State itself determines the nature of the activity, such as when the Constitution, a law or a *'personne publique'* declares an activity to be in the general interest. Secondly, the *Conseil d'État* defines certain activities as being a *'service public par nature'* (a public service by nature).[843] This option may also result in a situation where a service is designated by the State to be a *'service public'* but this designation is rejected by the *Conseil d'État*, because it is not a *'service public par nature'*. It is important here to ascertain whether an activity yields no financial benefits, or whether it serves no financial interest but serves the whole of the population.

Any type of activity can be recognised by the judge as a *'service public'*.[844] Rene Chapus drew a distinction between *'activités de plus grand service'* and *'activités de plus grand profit'*.[845] *'Activités de plus grand service'* are activities that meet a general need of the population and not the needs of the legal entity itself. There is no desire to make a profit. The *'activités de plus grand profit'* is aimed at ensuring or improving the funding of the *'activités de plus grand service'*. If this is the main purpose of the activity, a *'service public'* is present. A special exception in this respect is the management of governmental property (*concession domaniale*), which is not regarded as being a *'service public'*.[846]

It should be noted that the criteria the Court of Justice uses to exclude certain forms of cooperative agreements between public authorities from the scope of EU law (see chapter 5) are in some ways similar to the criteria that the *Conseil d'État* has developed to define the concept of *'service public'*.

839 S. Braconnier, *Droit des services publics* (Paris: PUF, 2007), p. 169.

840 See also Chapter 3 on the notion 'contracting authority'. The element 'general interest' is one of the criteria to qualify an entity as a 'contracting authority'. It was made clear that this element was also difficult to define in EU law.

841 G. Clamour, *Intérêt général et concurrence* (Paris: Dalloz, 2006), p. 162.

842 P.-L. Frier and J. Petit, *Précis de droit administratif* (Paris: Montchrestien, 2010), p. 189.

843 Zie hierover S. Boussard, 'L'éclatement des catégories de service public et la résurgence du "service public par nature' (*RFDA*, 2008), pp. 43–49.

844 See examples given by R. Chapus, *Droit administratif général* (Paris: Montchrestien, 2001), p. 582.

845 R. Chapus, *Droit administratif général* (Paris: Montchrestien, 2001), pp. 581 et seq. also reused by J. G.J. Gugliemi, G. Koubi and G. Dumont, *Droit du service public* (Paris: Montchrestien, 2007), pp. 97–98.

846 TC 24 November 1894, D. 1896 3.3; CE 3 November 1950, Com., 534.

The element 'control similar to that exercised over its own departments' is reflected in part in the organic criterion of the term *'service public'*, where a definite relationship with a *'personne publique'* is required. The criterion of 'most of the activities' is an element in the functional criterion of the concept of *'service public'*, where it suffices for an entity to create profits. Nevertheless it has not been established that the Court of Justice was inspired by French law.

1.1.5. Organisation and management of a *'service public'*

In this section a definition of the terms 'organisation' and 'management' will be considered first. Next the different ways a *'service public'* is managed will be discussed. Finally, it will be made clear in what respect a public authority in principle has free choice of all these management methods.

The case law developed by the Court of Justice regarding cooperative agreements between public authorities, which has been discussed in detail in chapter 5, affects the way public authorities are organised in the different Member States,[847] the way they organise their public service[848] or manage their public service.[849] However, in order to verify the effect, the terms 'organisation' and 'management' require clarification. What do these terms mean in French law?

The terms 'organisation and management' are frequently used interchangeably. In this thesis, the term organisation refers to the way a public authority organises itself to serve optimally the general interest. If it simply uses its own services, it creates a discrete legal person, it makes use of a third party...[850] The term 'management' refers to the way a public authority is managed. A public service can be managed in different ways – by a public authority or through a third person.

The CJEU case law on cooperative agreements influences aspects of these two elements: the free choice of organisation and management of the *'service public'*. It may then be asked: which kinds of elements are influenced and how they are influenced?

The primary subject of this study is cooperative agreements between public authorities: a public contract or a service concession may be considered forms of such cooperation. A public authority can decide that she performs the public service task by its own departments, or it may entrust the management of the public service task to a third party. This choice concerns the management of a public service, when the contract is a

847 E. Fatome and A. Menemis, 'Intérêt général, concurrence et service public' (*AJDA*, 2006), pp. 67 et seq.
848 E. Fatome and L. Richer, 'Les procédures de passation des contrats et pouvoir d'organisation du service public' (*ACCP* 12, 2002), pp. 60 et seq.
849 Belgian law: A.L. Durviaux and N. Thirion, 'Les modes de gestion des services publics locaux, la réglementation relative aux marchés publics et le droit communautaire' (*JT*, 2004), pp. 17 et seq.
850 E. Fatome and L. Richer, 'Les procédures de passation des contrats et pouvoir d'organisation du service public' (*ACCP*, 2002), p. 60.

service concession. However, the third party can also be a legal entity established by a public authority itself. If this legal entity executes the contract, the decision of the public authority has more to do with the way a public authority organises itself.[851]

In direct management the public authority prefers to discharge the '*service public*' itself. It is then said that the public service is performed *en régie*, or under public administration, i.e. the public authority not only determines the objectives, but itself performs an active role.[852] In the English system and on a European level, legal scholars use the concept of 'in-house'. A further distinction is made in French law between '*régie simple*' and '*régie directe*'.[853]

In a '*régie simple*' it is the public authority that meets needs of general interest with its own resources. None of these resources (financial, material) are separated from the public authority either *de facto* or *de jure*. In '*régie directe*' a secondary distinction is drawn between '*régie autonome*' and '*régie personnalisée*' (personalised administration). In the first case, '*régie*' implies simply a financial autonomy. In the second type of '*régie*', the administration is a separate legal person, with decision-making powers over important elements of the policy entrusted to it. This is not a real in house-situation.

A public authority can also decide to create a separate legal person, in which case private partners may or may not be members of it (vertical cooperative agreements). Accordingly, the following structures are distinguished: '*l'établissement public*' (see above), '*le groupement d'intérêt public*' (public interest group), and '*la société d'économie mixte*' (mixed economy company). Only the two latter structures are germane to this thesis. Both structures concern cooperation between different legal persons.

As it will be evident from the following section, a public authority also makes use of a contract to organise and manage its services of general interest and to do so it establishes legal relations with private partners and other public authorities. Here the relationship is a simple contractual and horizontal relationship.

The different ways of organizing the 'service public' were confirmed by the Conseil d'État in *Commune d'Aix-en-Provence*.[854]

The basic principle in regard to the organisation and management of a public service is that in France a public authority is free to choose how it wishes to organise or manage its

851 E. Fatôme and A. Menemis, 'Intérêt général, concurrence et service public' (*AJDA*, 2006), pp. 67 et seq.

852 G.J. Gugliemi and G. Koubi with G. Dumont, *Droit du service public* (Paris: Montchrestien, 2007), p. 321.

853 S. Braconnier, *Droit des services publics* (Paris: PUF, 2007), pp. 403 et seq.

854 CE 6 April 2007, *Commune d'Aix en Provence* (*RFDA*, 2007), p. 812, concl. F. Séners, note J.-Cl. Douence (*AJDA*, 2007), pp.10–20.

'service public'.[855, 856] The choice made by a public authority of how to organise its public service is regarded as an essential power belonging to a public authority.[857] A *Tribunal administratif* (administrative tribunal) recently ruled that at the moment a public authority sets about conducting and awarding a competitive procedure, it can, at any moment, put an end to that procedure and instead choose to assign the task to an entity over which it exercises decisive control.[858] The House of Lords in the United Kingdom has ruled along the same lines, where according to the Court a public authority is granted the ability to stop an awarding procedure and elects instead to get its own services to carry out the task.[859]

In the first place, free choice entails that a public authority may elect to discharge its public service itself or call on a third party to manage the service or privatise a public service.[860] In France, if a public authority chooses to employ its own departments, the *Conseil d'État* ruled long ago that no tendering procedure has to be organised by the public authority.[861] The CJEU case law on cooperative agreements has no influence on this free choice.

If a public authority calls on a third party, it must first and foremost make sure that it does not transfer the whole of its powers.[862] If the third party receives an independent task managing the public service (externalisation), the obligation to organise a competitive procedure was already accepted long ago. However, cooperation with other public authorities (mutualisation) was regarded more as an instance of the free choice a public authority enjoys to organise and manage a *'service public'*.[863] France took a completely different view when looking at cooperative agreements between public authorities in comparison with the EU. The EU pursues first and foremost economic objectives. Any measure taken by the State that endangers these objectives falls under the scope of EU law. Consequently according to EU law a public authority is not free in

855 E. Fatôme and A. Menemis, 'Concurrence et liberté d'organisation des personnes publiques: éléments d'analyse' (*AJDA*, 2006), p. 68; P.J. Frier and J. Petit, *Précis de droit administratif* (Paris, Montchrestien), p. 201. See also CE 6 April 2007, *Commune d'Aix en Provence* (*RFDA*, 2007), p. 812, concl. F. Séners, note J.-Cl. Douence (*AJDA*, 2007), pp.10–20; CE 4 March 2009, *Syndicat national des industries d'information de gaz* (*AJDA*, 2009), p. 891, note J.D. Dreyfus. This free choice has been confirmed by the CJEU in its case law (see chapter 5).

856 France never adopted a compulsory competitive tendering as was introduced in England in the 1980s. In that system local authorities were obliged to put their own administration in competition if they wanted to manage the public service task in house. See section 2.

857 J.-M. Auby, 'La notion de concession et les rapports des collectivités locales et des établissements publics, de l'électricité et du gaz dans la loi du 8 avril 1946' (*CJEG*, 1949), p. 8.

858 TA Montpellier, 23 March 2012, FADUC et Mme. Fraysse, n° 1002680 (*AJDA*, 2012), p. 1521.

859 *R.v Portsmouth City Council ex parte Peter Coles and Colwick Builders Limited and George Austin Limited* (*C.L.C.*, 1997), p. 407.

860 See also J.-D. Dreyfus, 'Externalisation et liberté d'organisation du service' (*AJDA*, 2009), pp. 1529–1534.

861 CE 26 June 1930, *Bourrageas*, Lebon 659; CE 29 April 1970, *Soc. Unipain* (*AJDA*, 1970), p. 430, concl. Braibant. See also chapter 5 on the *Stadt Halle*-ruling of the CJEU.

862 CE 17 March 1989, *Synd. psychiatre français* (*RFDA*, 1991), p. 267, concl. B. Stein.

863 O. Berthelot, 'Liberté du commerce et de l'industrie et transferts de compétences; socialisation de l'économie ou privatisation du service public' (*AJDA*, 2003), p. 707.

its choice to cooperate with another public authority.[864] Even if cooperation between public authorities could be qualified as a public contract or a service concession, the *Conseil d'État* considered until recently that the public procurement regulations and the principle of equality are not applicable (see 1.2.).

1.2. Cooperative agreements between public authorities

The section shall first give a brief historical overview of the genesis and evolution of the phenomenon of 'cooperation between public authorities' in France (1.2.1.). Next it shall examine the freedom of a public authority to choose its contract partner (1.2.2.). Third it raises the question to what extend a public authority is free to choose another public authority as contract partner (1.2.3.). Fourth it follows the evolution of the case law of the *Conseil d'État* in respect of the extent to which a public authority is free to conclude a public contract or a service concession with another public authority (1.2.4.). Finally the section explores how the French legislature has let itself be influenced by CJEU case law in that it has created new forms for a public-law legal person that will potentially fall outside the scope of EU law (1.2.5.).

1.2.1. Historical evolution

In France a public authority has different ways to organise and manage its '*service public*'. One of these ways is to cooperate with other public authorities.

Cooperation between public authorities is not a recent phenomenon in France.[865] In 1899, Hauriou already wrote: 'il devient difficile de ne pas reconnaître que la gestion … est essentiellement coopérative, comme d'ailleurs tout travail est cooperatif, après celle des administrés, après celle des fonctionnaires voilà que nous constatons la coopération des administrations elles-mêmes' [It becomes difficult not to acknowledge that management… is essentially cooperative insofar as all the work is done in cooperation. After cooperation among those administered, after cooperation of civil servants, there is now even cooperation between administrations].[866]

In the last few decades of the past century cooperation between public authorities came more and more to be viewed as one of the ways a public authority could achieve objectives of general interest, and it has been increasingly used in measure as tasks of general interest increased in number. It is one of the ways a public authority is enabled to outsource its tasks. In France as well, public authorities have increasingly used this device and continue to use it to improve their organisation of the '*service public*'.[867]

864 See also G. Eckert, 'Contrats entre personnes publiques et droit de la concurrence' (*AJDA*, 2013), p. 849.

865 J.-M. Pontier, 'Cooperation contractuelle et cooperation institutionnelle' (*Rev.Adm.*, 1994), p. 162.

866 M. Hauriou, *La gestion administrative, étude historique du droit administratif* (Paris, 1899), p. 31.

867 C. Pilone, 'Reflexions autour de la notion de contrat "in house"', in G. Clamour and M. Ubaud-Bergeron (eds.), *Contrats publics. Mélanges en honneur du Professeur Michel Guibal*, Vol. I (Montpellier: CREAM, 2006), p. 702.

Cooperation between authorities has been taking place on a contractual basis for the past 20 to 30 years, especially at the local level.

Public authorities cooperate in various ways but only contractual cooperative partnerships, horizontal and vertical, are considered in the thesis. That is why the notion of 'cooperative agreements' is used.

It has long been considered normal in France for a public authority to use the contractual approach. The second half of the twentieth century in France and in neighbouring countries as well, was marked by an increasing use of the contract in the way a public authority conducts its business.[868] The term used in France is '*l'administration contractuelle*' (the contracting authority).[869] The capacity of public authorities to conclude agreements has hardly been questioned nor has legal theory sought to elucidate the foundations of this capacity. Nevertheless, the use of a contract by public authorities is not a normal situation since in principle in French law public authorities are presumed to act unilaterally. A public authority does not allow itself to be bound by another party.[870] However, in practice public authorities have taken the liberty to operate via a contract.

In France, the capacity of a public authority to make use of the contract is associated with its quality as a legal person.[871] As a legal person, a public authority is endowed with certain powers that enable it to serve the general interest, and within the scope of these powers, public authorities can operate with a certain autonomy.[872] Its quality as a legal person empowers a public authority to act via a contract.

In France, the existence of agreements between public authorities was already apparent under the *Ancien Régime*, and recourse to such an instrument increased rapidly in the 19th century.[873] The use of the contract to formalise cooperation became more frequent

868 B. Stirn, 'La liberté contractuelle, droit fondamental en droit administratif' (*AJDA*, 1998), p. 673; L. Richer, 'La contractualisation comme technique de gestion des affaires publiques' (*AJDA*, 2003), p. 973; for a recent historical overview of the use of contract by a public authority in diverse sectors: X., 'Un recours accru au contrat pour conduire l'action publique ou édicter des normes', in *Rapport public 2008. Le contrat, mode d'action publique et de production de normes* (Paris: La Documentation Française, 2008), pp. 17–90.

869 See J. Pini, 'Autorité et contrat dans l'administration moderne en France', in *X., Annuaire Européen d'administration publique* (P.U.A., 1997), pp. 80 et seq.; C. Brechon-Moulènes, 'Liberté contractuelle des personnes publiques' (*AJDA*, 1998), p. 643; Dossier: *L'administration contractuelle* (*AJDA*, 2003); Y. Jegouzo, 'L'administration contractuelle en question', in *X., Mouvement du droit public. Mélanges en l'honneur de Franck Moderne* (Paris: Dalloz, 2004), pp. 544 et seq.

870 L. Duguit, *Les transformations du droit public* (éd. La mémoire du droit, 1913), p. 161.

871 C. Brechon-Moulènes, *Liberté contractuelle des personnes publiques* (*AJDA*, 1998), p. 644; P.-L. Frier, *Précis de droit administratif* (Paris: Montchrétien, 2004), p. 322.

872 S. Nicinski, 'Le dogme de l'autonomie de la volonté dans les contrats administratifs', in G. Clamour en M. Ubaud-Bergeron (eds), *Contrats publics, Mélanges en l'honneur du Professeur Michel Guibal*, T.I (Montpeller: CREAM, 2006), p. 49 with reference to C. Brechon-Moulènes, 'Liberté contractuelle des personnes publiques' (*AJDA*, 1998), p. 643.

873 D. Pouyaud, *Contrats entre personne publiques* (*Juris classeur Administratif*, 675), p. 3, no. 1 ff.; J.M. Peyrical, *Les contrats de prestation entre collectivités publiques* (*AJDA*, 2000), p. 582.

in the beginning of the seventies of the twentieth century.[874] In the last few years the use of a contract has been used increasingly when public authorities wished to cooperate, so that this was even referred to as an example of the generalisation of the *'procédé contractuel'*.[875]

Hence, there has been little discussion of the use of a contract by a public authority to cooperate with another public authority. However, this is not a topic that falls within the scope of the thesis. The more interesting issue is in what measure a public authority is free to call upon another public authority for the provision of a (public) service.

1.2.2. Selection of a contract partner

French administrative law bases the choice of a contract partner on the same principle as French private law: *'la 'liberté contractuelle'* [the freedom to contract]. Just as for other government contracts, legislation and case law concerning public contracts and service concessions have set conditions on the freedom a public authority has to conclude a contract with another public authority. The thesis shall explore how a *'personne publique'* in France chooses its contractual partners.

The basic criterion to be applied for determining to what extent public authorities in France freely choose a contract partner, is the principle of *'liberté contractuelle'* (contractual freedom)[876]: 'La liberté contractuelle consistera donc dans le fait que la formation du contrat sera entièrement abandonnée aux deux parties; elle sera présente à chaque moment, à chaque fase de la formation du contrat: liberté de contracter ou de ne pas contracter, liberté de choisir le type de contrat, liberté de choisir le co-contractant, liberté de déterminer le contenu du contrat' [Thus contractual freedom will be defined by the condition that the creation of a contract will be left entirely to the two parties; it will be present at each and every moment, in each phase in the creation of a contract: freedom to make a contract or not make a contract, freedom to choose the contracting party and freedom to determine the content of the contract].[877]

874 J.-F. Dreyfus, *Contribution à une théorie générale des contrats entre personnes publiques* (Paris: L'Harmattan, 1997), p. 12.

875 F. Moderne, 'L'evolution récente du droit des contrats administratifs: les conventions entre personnes publiques' (*RFDA*, 1984), p. 5; N. Poulet-Gebot Leclercq, 'La contractualisation des relations entre les personnes publiques' (*RFDA*, 1999), p. 552.

876 For a comprehensive study of this concept see: P.-Y. Gadhouin, *La liberté contractuelle dans la jurisprudence du Conseil constitutionnel* (Paris: Dalloz, 2008), p. 415.

877 C. Brechon-Moulènes, 'La liberté contractuelle des personnes publiques' (*AJDA*, 1998), p. 644: Contractual freedom implies that the creation of a contract is left entirely to the two parties; it shall be present at every moment, in every phase of the creation of the contract. Freedom to enter into a contract or not to enter into a contract, freedom to choose the type of contract, freedom to choose the contract partner, and freedom to determine the content of the contract. See also F. Llorens, 'Le recours des personnes publiques à la vente d'immeuble en l'état futur d'achèvement: une condamnation partielle' (*CJEG*, 1991), pp. 253–254.

In private law, the freedom of contract is traditionally a consequence of the principle of the autonomy of will, the capacity to create one's own law.[878] It is difficult to reconcile this principle with the principles that constitute the foundations of the actions of public authorities. Normally public authorities act unilaterally and act in the general interest. However, in France it has always been recognised that a public authority may operate on a contractual basis.

The principle of contractual freedom, as a principle of private law is, however, problematic in France when applied to '*contrats administratifs*' [administrative contracts]. This type of agreements is regarded purely as a contract of public law nature and private law is not applicable to it. To that extent the notion of autonomy of will is also out of place here. After an examination of case law and legal theory another conclusion beckons.

Until a few decades ago, it was a self-evident matter that contractual freedom was applicable to '*contrats administratifs*'.[879] On the other hand, the term 'contractual freedom' was not mentioned directly in regard to '*contrats administratifs*', which fundamentally are meant to serve the general interest of a public service.[880] The autonomy of these contracts in regard to general contract law gives rise to the application of particular set of rules and principles.

However, attention to the principle has increased exponentially in recent times. This growing importance has been linked to the increasing interest of public authorities in the contractual approach.[881] This increasing interest has ultimately produced case law in the *Cour constitutionnelle* (Constitutional Court) and the *Conseil d'État* (Council of State), both of which invoke the principle of '*liberté contractuelle*' (the principle of contractual freedom).

In the context of '*contrats administratifs*' contractual freedom is associated with the discretionary powers of public authorities.[882] A public authority enjoys a certain freedom within the limits of these powers. The highest courts in France have confirmed the contractual freedom of public authorities and considered it to be a general principle of

878 S. Nicinski, 'Le dogme de l'autonomie de la volonté dans les contrats administratifs', in G. Clamour en M. Ubaud-Bergeron (eds), *Contrats publics, Mélanges en l'honneur du Professeur Michel Guibal,* T.I (Montpeller: CREAM, 2006), Volume I, p. 45.

879 Ch. Brechon-Moulènes, 'La liberté contractuelle des personnes publiques' (*AJDA*, 1998), p. 643. see also N. Symchowisz, *Droit public des montages contractuels complexes* (Paris: Imprimerie Nationale Éditions, 2003), p. 84.

880 F.-X. Fort, 'Les aspects administratifs de la liberté contractuelle', in X., *Contrats publics. Mélanges en l'honneur du Professeur Michel Guibal, T. I* (Montpellier: CREAM, 2006), p. 30.

881 B. Stirn, *La liberté contractuelle, droit fondamentale en droit administrative* (*AJDA*, 1998), p. 673.

882 G. Péquignot, *Théorie générale du contrat administratif* (Paris: Pédone, 1945), p. 189; E. Picard, *La liberté contractuelle des personnes publiques constitue-t-elle un droit fondamental?* (*AJDA*, 1996), p. 651; S. Nicinsky, 'Le dogme de l'autonomie de la volonté dans les contrats administratifs', in *Contrats publics. Mélanges Michel Guibal*, T. I (Montpellier: CREAM, 2006), p. 49.

law and of constitutional value: *Conseil constitutionnel* (Constitutional Court)[883] and *Conseil d'État*.[884]

1.2.3. Freedom to choose a public authority as contract partner?

The question raised in this thesis is to what extent cooperative agreements between public authorities, insofar as they can be called a public contract or a service concession, may be freely concluded or whether a tendering procedure has to be organised and this under the influence of EU law. The case law of the *Conseil d'État* has undergone an entire evolution on this topic, basically influenced by the case law of the CJEU. This evolution will now be examined in detail, divided into several different periods.

It had long been assumed that, in the absence of a legal text, cooperative agreements between public authorities are not subject to any form of competitive tender. Legal theory deemed that in regard to the French public procurement legislation that this regulation 'a été conçu en fonction des relations entre les collectivités publiques et les cocontractants du secteur privé' [was construed as a function of relations between public authorities and cocontractors in the private sector].[885]

In the event, a public authority is free to choose its contract partner (i.e. another public authority).[886] Some legal scholars considered that this liberty has its origins in the freedom of a public authority to discharge their public service tasks in house.[887] This free choice is linked to the *intuitu personae* nature of certain of these agreements. Some legislation explicitly provided for the freedom of municipalities, departments and regions to conclude contracts with each other.[888] But where there any legal text in this

883 C.c. no. 2000–437, 19 December 2000; C.c. no. 2006–543, 30 November 2006. P. Delvolvé, 'Constitution et contrats publics', in *Mouvement du droit public. Mélanges Franck Moderne* (Paris: Dalloz, 2004), p. 483; L. Favoreu and L. Philip, *Les grandes décisions du Conseil Constitutionnel* (Paris: Dalloz), p. 457; A. Duffy, 'La constitutionnalisation de la liberté contractuelle' (*RDP*, 2006), pp. 1573–1584; Ph. Terneyre, *'A propos de la liberté contractuelle'* (*AJDA*, 2007), p. 1907; L. Richer, *Droit des contrats administratifs* (Paris: LGDJ, 2008), p. 138; *contra:* Ph. Guettier, *Droit des contrats administratifs* (Paris: Thémis, 2008), p. 134: According to this author, contractual freedom has no constitutional status.

884 CE *Fédération française des professionnels immobiliers et commerciaux*, 30 October 1980, *Leb.* 348; CE SA GBA Berry-Loire, 20 January 1989, Leb. 26; C.E. Société Borg Warner, 28 January 1998 (*AJDA*, 1998), p. 287. Ch. Brechon-Moulènes, 'Liberté contractuelle des personnes publiques' (*AJDA*, 1998), p. 643.

885 F. Moderne, 'La concurrence des services techniques de l'Etat et des techniciens privés auprès des collectivités locales' (*RD.imm.*, 1982), p. 467; See also F. Raynaud and P. Tombeur, 'Chronique générale de jurisprudence administrative française' (*AJDA*, 1998), p. 557; O. Berthelot, 'Liberté du commerce et de l'industrie et transferts de compétences; socialisation de l'économie ou privatisation du service public' (*AJDA*, 2003), p. 797.

886 A. de Laubadère, F. Moderne and P. Delvolvé, *Traité des contrats administratifs* (Paris: LGDJ, T.1, 1983), p. 694.

887 G. Eckert, 'La cooperation public-public, entre espoirs et inquiétudes', in *Mélanges en l'honneur du professeur Richer* (Paris: LGDJ, 2013), p. 617.

888 Articles 2, 45 and 69 I of Statute no. 82–213 of March 1982, 2. See also chapter 1 of a Decree of June 1983, 9.

first period that provided if a public contract or a service concession between public authorities was subject to competitive tender? A distinction should be drawn here between a service concession and a public contract.

As regards the '*délégation de service public*' (service concession, in 1993 the French legislature passed the 'Sapin law' (law of 29 January 1993 relative to 'la prévention de la corruption et à la transparence de la vie économique et des procédures publiques' [on the prevention of corruption and transparency in economic life and public procedures]). This law sets down specific obligations regarding transparency and competition whenever public authorities undertake a '*délégation de service public*'. However, it is a question whether these obligations also apply to cooperative agreements concluded between public authorities.

The '*Loi Sapin*' is applicable only if the contracting partner of the public authority is an undertaking. Opinions were, however, divided on whether a public authority can indeed be an enterprise. Some were of the opinion that public authorities can be considered undertakings[889] in particular, when they wish to undertake a '*délégation de service public*'.[890] Others draw a distinction between, on the one hand, the State and local authorities, and '*établissements publics*', on the other. Only the latter may be considered enterprises.[891] In 2000 one legal scholar claimed that the applicability of the principle in the Sapin Law concerning the '*délégation de service public*' enjoys general acceptance.[892] However, no relevant case law was adjudicated in this period so applicability remained uncertain.

The second type of agreement of interest is one, which under EU law, falls within the scope of the public procurement Directives. In the first period, the relevant legislation did not stipulate that agreements between public authorities were subject to the public procurement Directives. Generally it was also accepted that such contracts need not be concluded in conformity with the procedures provided with regard to the awarding of public procurement contracts.[893] By their very nature such agreements are exempted from public procurement regulations. Compliance with the rules on equal treatment in the conclusion of a public contract originally took its inspiration from solicitude to shield the interest of a public authority in its relation to private undertakings. This concern is absent when a public authority engages with another public authority.[894]

889 J.-CL. Douence, 'La dévolution contractuelle du service public local' (*Rép. Dalloz Collectivités locales*, 1995), p. 6150–12.

890 J.D. Dreyfus, *Contribution a une théorie générale des contrats entre personnes publiques* (Paris: L'Harmattan, 1997), p. 294.

891 D. Laurent and O. Rousset, 'Convention de délégation de dervice public local et loi Sapin: la transparence dans le brouillard' (*LPA*, 1994), p. 1.

892 J.D. Dreyfus, 'Actualité des contrats entre personnes publiques' (*AJDA*, 2000), p. 579.

893 L. Richer, *La qualité du cocontractant de l'administration; contrats entre collectivités publiques* (Paris: Ed. Le Moniteur, 1996), II. 220.1.7, p. 3; TA Poitiers, 16 March 1983, *Syndicat régional des entrepreneurs de travaux publics de Poitou-Charentes*, Lebon T. 779.

894 G. Eckert, 'Contrats entre personnes publiques et droit de la concurrence' (*AJDA*, 2013), p. 849.

According to some French authors the legislation on public procurement contracts is only applicable to agreements concluded between a public authority and a private service provider.[895] Chapter 5 explained that some Advocate generals thought in the same vein about EU (public procurement) law. Tendering to competition is meant first and foremost to protect the interests of public authorities.[896] Some case law simply exempted cooperation between public authorities from the ambit of applicability of French legislation on public procurement.[897]

In 1998 the *Conseil d'État* seized the opportunity to render a decision on the applicability of the principles of EU law that are the foundation of the public procurement Directives concerning cooperative agreements between public authorities.[898] In France the 'Communautés' (communities) had on basis of Article L.165–1 and 1 of the *Code des communes* the competence to enlarge and operate a sewage system as well as a water purification plant to the benefit of its municipalities (its members). A decision of 14 January 1997 from the *Communauté du Piémont de Barr* expressed the wish to entrust the management of these facilities to another public authority. No competitive tender was organised when this agreement was concluded.

First the *Conseil d'État* determined that this agreement was a public contract by virtue of the French public procurement legislation. Next the *Conseil d'État* determined that the public procurement legislation does not explicitly provide that agreements between public authorities must be considered as public contracts and are thus subject to a tendering procedure. Therefore, according to the *Conseil d'État*, the French legislation on public procurement is not applicable.

The decision to tender the relevant contract was also criticised directly on the basis of the public procurement Directives. The *Conseil d'État* based its decision on this critique and confirmed that the agreement does constitute a public contract under the [EU] public procurement Directives. According to these Directives the conclusion of such a contract is subject to prior publication and the equal treatment of interested candidates. The European legislation on public contracts makes, according to the Conseil d'État, abstraction of the nature of the service provider. The provider can be a private company or a public authority. It was established that the French national legislation in this regard was not compatible with the European Directives and thus the *Conseil d'État* applied the public procurement Directives directly.

In this decision the *Conseil d'État* abstracts from the fact that the contracting authority is a member of or is a shareholder in the service provider. Later on the CJEU in its case

[895] F. Moderne, 'Les Conventions des prestations de services entre l'Etat et les collectivités' (*EFE*, 1996), no. 29, cited by J.-D. Dreyfus, 'Actualité des contrats entre personnes publiques' (*AJDA*, 2000), p. 579.

[896] G. Eckert, 'Les contrats échappant aux règles de publicité et de mise en concurrence' (*AJDA*, 2013), p. 849.

[897] TA Poitiers, 16 March 1983, *Syndicat régional des entrepreneurs de travaux publics de Poitou-Charentes* (*Lebon T.*), p. 779.

[898] C.E. 20 May 1998, *Communauté de communes du Piémont de Barr* (*AJDA*, 1998), p. 553.

law made it clear that under certain conditions in such a situation the public procurement Directives do not apply.

In its ruling in *Communauté de Piémont de Barr* the *Conseil d'État* anticipates pronouncements of the CJEU, specifically that cooperative agreements between public authorities can under certain circumstances fall within the scope of EU law. There is no case law comparable to *Communauté de Piémont de Barr* regarding service concessions prior to the case law of the Court of Justice in regard to quasi-in-house situations.

In the 'Code des Marchés publics' of 2001 and 2004 the French legislator confirmed explicitly a public contract concluded between public authorities has to be subject to a tendering procedure.

1.2.4. Evolution case law

CJEU case law, from which it is deduced that cooperative agreements between public authorities also come under the scope of EU law in certain circumstances, and as a consequence a public authority may not freely conclude such an agreement, was highly criticised and feared in France. It was seen as a threat to national sovereignty. It challenged the national competence to create regulations that determine how a public service has to be organised. On the basis of the freedom to organise and manage a public service, as recognised in France, a public authority was also enabled to enter directly into a cooperative agreement with another public authority without organising a tendering procedure,[899] even if this cooperative agreement could be qualified as a public contract or service concession.

In *Communauté Piémont du Barr* the French *Conseil d'État* anticipated the CJEU case law and placed limits on the free choice of a public authority to organise and administer a public service. In the aftermath of *Teckal*[900] the French legislature also introduced an exception to the applicability of the public procurement Directives to cooperation between public authorities. The two *Teckal* criteria were introduced into French legislation.[901] The *Conseil d'État* deemed that the provision that set down that *Teckal* may also be applicable to a cooperative agreement between a public authority and a semi-public company does not conflict with EU law.[902] However, *Stadt Halle*[903] and subsequent CJEU case law has made it clear that the Court of Justice gives a strict interpretation to the *Teckal* criteria. The fear of a serious limitation being placed on national competence in regard to the organisation and management of a public service remained.

899 E. Fatôme and A. Menemis, 'Concurrence et liberté d'organisation des personnes publiques' (*AJDA*, 2006), p. 69.

900 Case C-107/98, *Teckal v. Comune di Viano* [1999] *ECR* I-8121.

901 Article 3 of the Decree of March 2001, 7 *'portant Code des Marchés publics'*.

902 CE 9 July 2003, *Féd. Française des entreprises gestionnaires des services, aux équipements, à l'énergie et à l'environnement et autres*, Req. N° 239879 (*CMP*, 2003), comm. 169.

903 Case C-26/03, *Stadt Halle and RPL Recyclingpark Lochau GmbH v. Arbeitsgemeinschaft Thermische Restabfall- und Energieverwertungsanlage TREA Leuna* [2005] *ECR* I-00001.

In *Commune d'Aix-en-Provence*[904] the *Conseil d'État* confirmed there is also a direct management if the statutory objective of the created entity is solely the management of the public service and insofar as public authorities or the entities creating the legal person exercise over the person concerned a control that is similar to that which it exercises over its own departments (quasi-in-house). The legal person has the possibility of engaging in additional commercial activities.[905] Thus the Conseil d'État considers an in-house provision to be equal to a situation where a public authority provides a public service task to another public authority insofar as the two *Teckal* criteria are met. However, the Conseil d'État also confirmed that the presence of a private company as a shareholder in the entity that concludes the contract imposes the application of a tendering procedure. Public authorities can also decide together to create and manage such a public service. As such the *Conseil d'État* confirms *Teckal,*[906] *Stadt Halle*[907] and *Coditel Brabant.*[908]

The *Conseil d'État* has further elaborated its case law explaining within which limits a public authority may cooperate with another public authority without respecting a competitive tendering procedure. This case law will now be discussed. No distinction will be made between vertical and horizontal cooperation because it will appear the *Conseil d'État* uses the same criterion to exclude both situations from the obligation to use a tendering procedure.

The *Conseil d'État* has issued decisions in a variety of situations on whether the relation between a public authority and a third person is or is not obliged to set up a competitive procedure. Often this has had to do with the application of the rules and regulations concerning public contracts or service concessions.

In *Commune d'Aix-en-Provence*[909] the *Conseil d'État* had to issue a decision in a case where *Commune d'Aix-en-Provence* had granted two subsidies to an association that managed the organisation of a festival. This case concerned a situation where no real cooperation was established between a public authority and a third party. In this case a private initiative was already in place and in their actions a public authority recognised this initiative to be a public service. In *Syndicat national des industries d'information de gaz*[910] the decision concerned an agreement concluded between on the one hand 11

904 CE 6 April 2007, *Commune d'Aix en Provence* (*RFDA*, 2007), p. 812, concl. F. Séners, note J.-Cl. Douence (*AJDA*, 2007), pp.10–20, chr. F. Lenica and J. Boucher.

905 Case C-573/07, *Sea Srl v. Comune di Ponte Nassa* [2009] *ECR* I-08127.

906 Case C-107/98, *Teckal v. Comune di Viano* [1999] *ECR* I-8121.

907 Case C-26/03, *Stadt Halle and RPL Recyclingpark Lochau GmbH v. Arbeitsgemeinschaft Thermische Restabfall- und Energieverwertungsanlage TREA Leuna* [2005] *ECR* I-00001.

908 Case C-324/07, *Commune d'Uccle et Région Bruxelles-Capital* [2008] *ECR* I-08457.

909 CE 6 April 2007, *Commune d'Aix en Provence* (*RFDA*, 2007), p. 812, concl. F. Séners, note J.-Cl. Douence (*AJDA*, 2007), pp.10–20, chr. F. Lenica and J. Boucher.

910 CE 4 March 2009, *Syndicat national des industries d'information de gaz* (*AJDA*, 2009), p. 891, note J.D. Dreyfus.

hospitals,[911] and on the other a hospital union. Via this agreement the two parties established a *groupement d'intérêt public* (public interest grouping) (GIP) (vertical cooperative agreement). In the particular situation it was a legal person that was responsible for the study, design, and development of an information system to support the activities and management of a hospital and secondarily for making it available to the members. In *Commune de Veyrier-du-Lac*[912] the *Conseil d'État* was obliged to rule on an agreement concluded between the *Communauté d'agglomération d'Annecy* and the *Commune de Veyrier-du-Lac* (municipality), where one of the two parties did not constitute a part of the other (horizontal cooperative agreement). The *Communauté* had been assigned by the municipality the management of its public service pertaining to the distribution of potable water. There had been no competitive tender procedure set up before this agreement was concluded.

In all three cases the *Conseil d'État* applied the same criterion to determine whether and in what manner a public authority is required to set up a competitive procedure whenever it enters into a relation with a third party. The *Conseil d'État* made the answer to this question dependent on whether a third party can be considered as an 'operator on a competitive market'.

In its case law the *Conseil d'État* has not defined the notion of 'operator on a competitive market'. It should be noted that the notion of 'operator on a competitive market' is not identical with the notion of 'operator' as used in the definition of the term 'public contract'. The presence of an operator implies in itself that the agreement must be deemed a public contract irrespective of the nature of the operator.[913] From the case law of the *Conseil d'État* it appears that this notion of 'operator on a competitive market' results in a much broader exclusion of EU law when public authorities cooperate.

The *Conseil d'État* pre-eminently uses, in *Commune d'Aix-en-Provence,* two criteria to judge whether or not a contract involves an operator on a competitive market. First, the nature of the activity and particular conditions under which the activity takes place. Second, when a private person performs a public service, this may also fall outside the scope of EU law. According to *Stadt Halle* a cooperative association with a private person is always subject to the application of EU law.[914] Hence the *Conseil d'État* goes further than that which the CJEU allows. The Conseil d'Etat presents in its case law a somewhat peculiar argument. When a public authority made use of a third person that is not market-oriented there can be no public contract or service concession. It thus follows according to the *Conseil d'État* that no tendering procedure need be organised. *The*

[911] Hospitals also must be considered public authorities in the sense of the public procurement directives. This could be derived from C-300/07, *Hans & Christophorus Oymanns GbR, Orthopädie Schuhtechnik v. AOK Rheinland/Hamburg* [2009] *ECR* I-04779.

[912] CE 3 February 2012 (*AJDA*, 2012), p. 555.

[913] Case C-305/08, *Consorzio Nazionale Interuniversitario per le Scienze del Mare (CoNISMa) v. Regione Marche* [2009] *ECR* I-12129.

[914] C-26/03, *Stadt Halle and RPL Recyclingpark Lochau GmbH v. Arbeitsgemeinschaft Thermische Restabfall- und Energieverwertungsanlage TREA Leuna* [2005] *ECR* I-00001.

Conseil d'État confuses two things, however: On the one hand there is the qualification of an agreement, but on the other there is the issue of the applicability of the public procurement Directives to this agreement. Quasi-in-house case law is concerned with the second question. In this particular case, the nature of the operator is not decisive for exclusion from EU law.

According to *Syndicat national des industries d'information de gaz* public authorities may also freely choose a separate legal person to perform a task or service in the case where the public authority exercises over the person concerned a control which is similar to that which it exercises over its own departments and, at the same time, that person carries out the essential part of its activities with the controlling public authority or authorities. This is a reiteration of the two *Teckal* criteria. In such a case, according to the *Conseil d'État,* this legal person cannot be considered an operator on a competitive market.[915] Payment to the GIP by members for the right of use alters nothing in this regard.

On the one hand, the *Conseil d'État* faithfully applies the two *Teckal* criteria to the inter-institutional form of cooperation. On the other hand, the *Conseil d'État* creates a link to its *Commune d'Aix-en-Provence* case. As the two *Teckal* criteria have been met, the created legal person is presumably not an operator on a competitive market. This likewise applies when the legal person consists of several members. When that is the case, collective control is sufficient.[916]

In *Commune de Veyrier-du-Lac* the intent of cooperation is that the public service, namely the distribution of drinking water should be operated on the whole territory of the participating authorities. Thus, the municipality as a participating authority has the benefit of more efficient facilities and equipment. The price the residents of the municipality must pay for the potable water must, on the one hand, be proportional to the amount of investments and, on the other cover the costs of production and distribution of the potable water. There are no indirect financial transfers between the public authorities. According to the *Conseil d'État* this proves the absence of an operator on a competitive market. Consequently, the agreement falls outside the scope of applicability of the French regulations concerning a '*commande publique*' [public contract]. This decision goes quite far in the application of the principles the Court of Justice has established in its case law regarding cooperative agreements between public authorities. In the case in question, at issue was a horizontal form of cooperation. None of the cooperating public authorities has any control on the other. Thus, only the CJEU case law on horizontal cooperative agreement is relevant.[917]

915 For a critique of this criterion see L. Richer, 'L'introduction de la notion d'activité économique dans le droit des contrats publics', in Conseil d'Etat, *Rapport public 2008. Le contrat, mode d'action publique et de production de normes* (Paris: EDCE, 2008), pp. 359 et seq.

916 See Case C-324/07, *Commune d'Uccle et Région Bruxelles-Capital* [2008] *ECR* I-08457.

917 See also Case C-480/06, *Commission v. Germany* [2009] *ECR* I-04747; Ordine at [33].

In CJEU case law a horizontal cooperative agreements requires that the intent of the cooperative agreement between public authorities is to ensure a public task in which all of them are required to participate.[918] In *Commune de Veyrier-du-Lac* one public authority performs a task for another public authority. The contracting authority does not itself perform any service. The public authority does not really participate in the performance of the public task. It merely pays another public authority to carry out its public task. This kind of cooperation does not seem to fulfil the criteria established by the CJEU for a horizontal cooperation. Nevertheless, the Conseil d'Etat accepted the exclusion of this situation from the application of the public procurement regulations. Finally the ruling of the *Conseil d'État* also attaches importance to the fact that money paid by the contracting authority should only cover the operator's costs. According to *Ordine degli Ingegneri*[919] this is only an adequate response to the term 'price', one of the conditions for applying EU law.

This raises the question of whether the French *Conseil d'État* has gone too far here.[920] In a Memorandum of 4 October 2011[921] the European Commission recognises that a horizontal form of cooperation lies beyond the scope of applicability of EU law only if the agreement concerns the joint accomplishment of a common task. As such the Commission opposes this kind of cooperation to a normal public contract. In a public contract there is one party that provides and another that 'pays'. Even in this last situation the French *Conseil d'État* admitted the free choice of a public authority to choose its contract partner. As such, the *Conseil d'État* is one step ahead of the CJEU.

In *Syndicat national des industries d'information de gaz* the *Conseil d'État* seems presumably to be averring that the diverse CJEU case law on vertical and horizontal cooperative agreement, respectively all have the same basic features, and the present thesis wishes to emphasise precisely this point: The third party performing the service for the public authority is not on the market, and because of this the State measure favouring cooperation with this operator can in no way be detrimental to competition. However, the criterion of 'operator on a competitive market' of the *Conseil d'État* seems to go further than CJEU case law.

This particular decision enables public authorities together to construct a legal person, which then performs services for these public authorities. Cooperation between (local)

918 Case C-159/11, *Azienda Sanitaria Locale di Lecce, Università del Salento v. Ordine degli Ingegneri della Provincia di Lecce and Others* [2012] *ECR* I-00000, at [34]; Case C-386/11, *Piepenbrock Dienstleistungen & Co. KG v. Kreis Düren* [2013] *ECR* I-00000, at [36].

919 Case C-159/11, *Azienda Sanitaria Locale di Lecce, Università del Salento v. Ordine degli Ingegneri della Provincia di Lecce and Others* [2012] *ECR* I-00000.

920 See L. Richer, 'Un contrat d'entente intercommunale n'est pas une délégation de service public' (*AJDA*, 2012), p. 558. W. Zimmer, 'Convention conclue par deux collectivités territoriales en vue d'exercer en coopération un service public' (*CMP* 5, 2012), pp. 19–20.

921 Commission Staff Working Paper concerning the application of EU public procurement law to relations between contracting authorities (public-public cooperation) SEC (2011), 1169 final.

public authorities, which is a common form of public service organisation in France, remained thus for the greater part outside the scope of EU law.

1.2.5. *Sociétés publiques locales* (local public companies)[922]

Beside the possibilities that flow from the case law of the *Conseil d'État* for public authorities to conclude cooperative agreements without having to deal with EU law, the legislature has also created a context in which certain forms of cooperative agreements between public authorities are according to it not subject to a tendering procedure.

On the basis of the law of 13 July 2006 *en matière d'engagement national pour le logement*[923] (concerning national involvement in housing) *collectivités territoriales* and their *groupements* had the possibility to participate in companies, wholly owned by them. These *sociétés publiques locales* had the competence to realise any project involving the organisation of public space. *Collectivités locales* and their *groupements* were enjoined to exercise a stricter control on these companies and these companies could only engage in activities that were to the benefit of the *collectivités territoriales* and their *groupements*.

The law no. 2010–559 of 28 May 2010 *pour le développement des sociétés publiques locales*[924] [for the development of local public authorities] for the first time enables *collectivités territoriales* (local public authorities) to manage their tasks of general interest together without the necessity to consult the market. To that end the public authority has to establish *sociétés publiques locales*.[925] The purpose of this legislation was to enable the establishment of certain companies without being subject to EU law.[926] According to some, the French legislator wanted clearly to give public authorities an instrument to circumvent public procurement Directives.[927] If this is truly the intent, then reference should be made to one of the considerations in *Commission v. Germany*: 'It must, furthermore, be stated that there is nothing in the information … to indicate that … the local authorities at issue were contriving to circumvent the rules on public procurement'.[928] An attempt to circumvent the application of EU law is one of the elements that could persuade the CJEU to find a national law or a state measure to be in conflict with EU law.

922 See S. Brameret, *Les relations des collectivités territoriales avec les sociétés d'économie mixte locales* (Paris: LGDJ, 2012), p. 254, footnote 46.

923 Law no. 2006–872 (*JORF*, 16/06/2006), p. 10622.

924 Article L 1531–1 of the *code général des collectivités locales* (*JORF*, 29/5/2010), p. 9697; see also Article L. 327–1 du code de l'urbanisme creating the possibility of a *société publique locale d'aménagement* (SPLA).

925 On 1 June 2012 the various public authorities created 70 SPL: see A. Samson-Dye, 'Irrégularité du recours à un contrat in house entre une SPLA et une collectivité très minoritaire' (*CMP*, 2013), p. 37.

926 J.-F. Auby, 'Les sociétés publiques sociales. Un outil aux contours incertains' (*RFDA*, 2012), p. 101.

927 G. Kalflèche, 'Le contrôle des collectivités sur les sociétés publiques locales faut-il rénover le in house' (*RFDA*, 2012), p. 1120.

928 C-480/06, *Commission v. Germany* [2009] *ECR* I-04747, at [48].

The establishment of such *sociétés publiques locales* falls wholly within the vertical or institutional cooperative agreements between public authorities. In that context only the *Teckal* case law[929] is relevant.

The law of 28 May 2010 enabled the establishment of *sociétés publiques locales* without it being necessary to set up a competitive tender procedure. The freedom to organise its public service seems safeguarded for these public authorities. *Sociétés publiques locales* consist wholly of capital from the *collectivités territoriales* or their *groupements*. These companies have the competence to maintain and administer any activity of general interest.[930] A company may pursue its activities only to the benefit of its shareholders and only on their territory. In this the French legislature is more restrictive than the case law of the Court of Justice requires. The Court sets only the one condition that most of the activities engaged in by the created company must be to the benefit of the parties who established it or of its shareholders (*Teckal*). Finally, *sociétés publiques locales* take the form of a *societé anonyme*.

However, the creation of a *société publique locale* is not in itself sufficient to circumvent the obligation to set up a competitive tender procedure.[931] Regarding the criterion of similar control the law of 28 May 2010 provides only that all of the SPL's capital shall be wholly in the hands of the shareholders. However, according to CJEU this creates only a presumption of similar control.[932] But if in a specific case an SPL is set up or commissioned, then in the event of dispute, it must be demonstrated that all elements are present for there to be a similar control.[933] To achieve this, when an SPL is set up, the statutes must provide for special and divergent dispositions. Merely adopting the usual dispositions in the assumption of the form of a *société publique locale* will probably not be sufficient.[934]

In a quite recent ruling the *Conseil d'État* judged that a shareholder in an SPLA does not exercise a comparable control when it has had no direct influence on the important internal decisions of the SPLA.[935] The Court was examining the statutes and the concrete operations of the SPLA. The *Conseil d'État* was looking at a situation where a minority shareholder concludes an agreement with a public authority of which it is itself a part. Where this shareholder has no direct influence on the decisions of the public authority then there can be no control such as control over one's own services. The *Conseil d'État*

929 Case C-107/98, *Teckal v. Comune di Viano* [1999] *ECR* I-8121.

930 Article L 1531–1 CGCT.

931 S. Nicinski, 'La loi du 28 mai 2010 pour le développement des sociétés publiques locales' (*AJDA*, 2010), p. 1763; S. Brameret, *Les relations des collectivités territoriales avec des sociétés d'economie mixte locales* (Paris: LGDJ, 2012), pp. 259–262.

932 Case C-340/04, *Carbotermo SpA Consorzio Alisei v. Comune di Busto Arsizio AGESP SpA* [2006] *ECR* I-04137, at [38].

933 See TA Montpellier, 23 March 2012 (*AJDA*, 2012), p. 1521; S. Brameret, *Les relations des collectivités territoriales avec les sociétés d'économie mixte locales* (Paris: LGDJ, 2012), p. 261; T. Bangui, 'L'effectivité du contrôle analogue des Sociétés publiques locales' (*CMP* 5, 2012), p. 7.

934 S. Brameret, *Les relations des collectivités territoriales avec les sociétés d'économie mixte locales* (Paris: LGDJ, 2012), p. 262.

935 C.E., 6 November 2013, Commune de Marsannay-la-Côte, n° 365079. See also CA Lyon, 7 November 2012 (*CMP*, 2013), p. 37.

confirms the Econord case.[936] As already stated, the CJEU demanded in this case an effective control on the part of the various shareholders. The *Conseil d'État* has confirmed the decision of the *Cour administrative d'Appel de Lyon.*

1.3. Conclusion

In Europe, the French legal system is a preeminent example of a legal system in which the concept of *'service public'* plays a central role in delimiting the role and the powers of a public authority. The *'service public'* is regarded as a kind of national emblem. The organisation and management of a *'service public'* belongs in principle among the prerogatives of the sovereign State. In France it was assumed that a public authority is free to choose how a *'service public'* is organised and managed.

Because of EU law, since the 1990s both the term *'service public'* and the free choice of management and organisation of a public service have been under pressure. The thesis has shown that the description of the concept *'service public'* in France is more and more convergent with the description of SGI in European Union law. The functional interpretation, in which the nature of the activity is decisive, is gaining more and more favour. On the other hand the freedom of public authorities to provide a public service task with its own administration was not influenced by CJEU case law. Member States have still the competence to regulate this situation.

According to EU law, whenever a public authority calls on a third party to maintain and administer a public service, it must guarantee equal treatment to the citizens of other Member States. Consequently, there is hypothetically no free choice. The same is true when the third party is a public authority. This cooperative agreement between public authorities, as means to organise the *'service public'*, is not free.

Ahead of the Court of Justice the *Conseil d'État* in France declared the Directives on public procurement to be applicable to agreements concluded between public authorities. Case law on cooperative agreements between public authorities is a good example of how EU law influences national administrative law. In its case law the *Conseil d'État* applies public procurement Directives directly and considers how the CJEU has interpreted these Directives. On this basis EU law has been able indirectly to influence how the *Conseil d'État* thinks in regard to the freedom to choose how a *'service public'* is organised. The *Conseil d'État* abandoned its case law where it confirmed a public authority freely chooses the public authority with which it concludes a contract.

Later the *Conseil d'État* confirmed the *Teckal* case law of the Court of Justice and even expanded it. Nevertheless, from the case law of the *Conseil d'État* it appears that in the case of cooperative agreements between public authorities the *Conseil d'État* takes into

[936] Joined cases C-182/11 and C-183/11, *Econord SpA v. Comuni di Cagno, Comune di Varese, Comune di Solbiate* [2012] *ECR* I-00000.

account CJEU case law, but that in a sense it applies this case law in its own (peculiar) way. The case law of the *Conseil d'État* still attempts to safeguard as far as possible the free choice of public authority to organise its public service and this in a way that is incompatible with the CJEU case law.

Finally, the legislature also intervened to consolidate *Teckal* case law. The legislature is seeking a regulation that would permit the local authority to cooperate without EU law being thereby applicable. However, such legislation is at the moment not conclusive so that the public authority must make sure that all the conditions of quasi-in-house (*Teckal*) case law have been met when cooperation is established.

2. The English system

This section examines the concept 'public service', the organisation of public services and the cooperation between public authorities, just as was done in the preceding section for the French legal system. The question then arises if the EU law has influenced these elements of English law. The primary focus will be on the system, as it presently exists in England. The analysis that follows is valid only for the English law system. Sometimes, the section also mentions specificities of the Scottish legal system.

2.1. Public services

This section first explores whether administrative law exists as an independent branch of law in England. Indeed, if it does not, the study of the English system is not pertinent to the present thesis. Second, this section attempts to define the concept of 'public service' according to English law.

2.1.1. Administrative law

The English legal system is very different from most continental legal systems. This is certainly the case in respect of how the law applies to public authorities.

In most continental legal systems, a clear distinction is made between public law and private law. On the continent, public authorities are governed wholly or in part by their own body of law, which is distinct from the civil law that applies to the relations between individuals. For a long time no such distinction was made in England. Administrative law did not exist as a distinctive branch of law. The decision in *O'Reilly v. Mackman*[937] marks the origin of this distinction in the English legal system.[938]

In the 19th and into the 20th century there was a certain aversion toward a growing administration. The importance as well as the number of public authorities increased in

937 [1983], 2 AC 237.

938 D. Oliver, *Common Values and the Public-Private Divide* (London: Butterworths, 1999), p. 201.

measure during the 20th century, as they were obliged to take on ever more tasks. Public authorities found themselves intervening increasingly in economic and social life. In the 1940s the role of the State expanded, providing an ever wider array of services to citizens.

For a long time in English law, the organisation and behaviour of public authorities were not considered to be a separate legal domain. Administrative law did not exist.[939] Common law by and large also applied to the behaviour of public authorities. A public authority was subject to the same law as was applicable to citizens. This originates from the fact that in England there is no such thing as administrative courts.[940] In addition, within the institution of judicial review there was considerable reluctance on the part of the court to control the actions of the administration.[941]

From the middle of the twentieth century the importance of administrative law began to grow. Indeed, one can even say there was a revolution in the significance of this branch of law: 'any judicial statement on public law made before 1950 are likely to be a misleading guide to what this law is today'.[942] From the 1960s especially, the courts began anew to allocate to administrative law a place of its own.[943]

In England there are diverse views on what is meant by the term 'administrative law': 'There is considerable diversity of opinion concerning the nature and purpose of administrative law. Description and prescription are not easily separated. For some, it is the law relating to the control of government power. Others place greater emphasis on rules designed to ensure that the administration effectively performs tasks assigned to it. Yet others see the principal objective of administrative law as ensuring governmental accountability and fostering participation by interested parties in the decision-making process'.[944] What is certain in any event is that the concept of 'public service', in contrast to the French administrative law, plays no central role in the definition of English administrative law. This perhaps explains in part why CJEU case law on cooperative agreements between public authorities has had less of an impact in England and was less questioned than in France.

2.1.2. Notion of public service

Unlike the French legal system, English administrative law has no general theory of public service. Moreover, the concept of 'public service' is unknown and the term does not shed much light on the particular uniqueness of administrative law. It is not fundamental to any justification for the existence of public authorities. The principal

939 See A.V. Dicey, *The Law of the Constitution* (1985).

940 Neither in Schotland.

941 See M. Taggart, 'Reinventing Administrative Law', in N. Bamforth and P. Leyland (eds.), *Public Law in a multi layered constitution* (Oxford: Hart Publishing, 2003), p. 312.

942 RVIRC, export Federation of Self-Employed and Small Businesses Ltd [1982] AC 617, at [649].

943 H.W.R. Wade and C.F. Forsyth, *Administrative law* (Oxford: OUP, 2009), p. 14.

944 P. Craig, *Administration Law* (London: Sweet and Maxwell, 2012), p. 3.

difference between France and England is that in France the concept of 'service public' is at the very core of administrative law. This concept constitutes the uniqueness of administrative law in France.

'Public service' is not a juridical concept in English law. In any event, it is not the equivalent of the notion 'public authority', i.e. a legal person that carries out a specified activity. The term rather refers to public servants working in a public administration.[945] The notion of 'public services' is more adequately reflective of the accomplishment of tasks of general interest on behalf of citizens.[946] Differently from in French law, the notion of 'public services' has an entirely functional significance. The nature of the activity is primordial; the nature of the legal person does not characterise the activity. In this sense, English law is fully in line with EU law, which also gives a functional meaning to the notion 'services of general interest'. All activities that serve the general interest are public services. This produces a diversified array of persons engaged in carrying out these activities.

One author defines the term 'public services' as follows: 'A more appropriate legal criteria for distinguishing public from private services is whether the existence of the service is a matter for consumer sovereignty in the market, or of authoritative public decision'.[947] The status of the financing of a person is not important for distinguishing a public service from a private activity. Moreover, the performance of a task of general interest can only take place when an explicit legal authorisation is present.[948] Such authorisation may be requested by both public authorities and private parties.

A public service does come into being only when the legislature so decides. Unlike in France, 'general interest' is not in itself sufficient to engender 'public services'. Legislation is created *ad hoc* and various rules are thereby likewise created to be applied to a public service. Police, schools, justice and the NHS are deemed to be public services.[949] There are various considerations that can help to explain the genesis of such legislatively created activities: public health, security, the public order, accessibility of vital services, consumer protection, etc.[950] Public authorities intervene if the existence of the social group has to be protected. The role of a public authority is more than simply that of providing formal institutional support.

945 D. Triantofyllou, 'Les mutations de la notion de service public en droit comparé', in *Service public et Communauté Européenne entre intérêt général et le marché* (Paris: la documentation française, 1998), p. 53.

946 J. Bell and T.P. Kennedy, 'La notion de service public au Royaume-Unie et en Irlande', in F. Moderne and G. Marcou (eds), *L'idée de service public dans le droit des états de l'Union Européenne* (Paris: l'Harmattan, 2001), p. 225.

947 I. Harden, *The Contracting State* (Buckingham: Open University Press, 1992), p. 8.

948 J. Bell and T.P. Kennedy, 'La notion de service public au Royaume-Unie et en Irlande', in F. Moderne and G.Marcou (eds), *L'idée de service public dans le droit des états de l'Union Européenne* (Paris: l'Harmattan, 2001), pp. 230–231.

949 HM Government, Open public services White Paper, p. 6, https://www.gov.uk/government/uploads/system/uploads/attachment_data/file/255288/OpenPublicServices-WhitePaper.pdf.

950 See J. Bell and T.P. Kennedy, 'La notion de service public au Royaume-Unie et en Irlande', in F. Moderne and G.Marcou (eds), *L'idée de service public dans le droit des états de l'Union Européenne* (Paris: l'Harmattan, 2001), pp. 238–243.

Sometimes the term is also to be found in the case law of the House of Lords.[951] In *Foster v. British Gas*[952] the House of Lords was called upon to rule on an alleged instance of unequal treatment of a woman in the process of retiring. The issue was whether English law was not in conflict with EU law, or more specifically, whether the British Gas Corporation fell within the scope of applicability of Directive 76/207/EEC of 6 February 1976.[953] The House of Lords posed a preliminary question *in re* to the Court of Justice. According to the Court of Justice the aforementioned Directive was applicable to 'a body, whatever its legal form, which has been made responsible, pursuant to a measure adopted by the state, for providing a public service under the control of the state and has for that purpose special powers beyond those which result from the normal rules applicable in relation between individuals, is included... among the bodies against which the provisions of a directive capable of having direct effect may be relied'.[954] Thus, via the case law of the Court of Justice the concept of 'public service' found its way into the case law of the House of Lords and thus into English law.

The House of Lords confirmed this precept and ruled that British Gas was subject to this Directive because it was a corporation that had been given exclusive control of the public gas supply and had special powers beyond those resulting from transactions between individuals.

In Scotland, the Scottish Parliament passed the Public Services Reform (Scotland) Act 20 on March 25, 2010.[955] The overarching purpose of this Bill is to help simplify and improve the landscape of Scottish public bodies, to deliver more effective, coordinated government that can better achieve its core functions for the benefit of the people of Scotland. From this Bill it would seem that in Scotland as well, the concept of 'public service" is not in itself a juridical concept. Public services are public bodies that deliver certain services to the benefit of the citizens.

2.2. *The organisation or management of public services*

Since the concept of 'public service' does not exist in English law and the term 'public services' does not refer to a legal person but to specified activities, the concepts of 'organisation' or 'management' are not particularly to the point. It is better to speak of the provision of public services. In the last half of the past century the way in which public services were provided underwent major changes in England. Under Margaret Thatcher the Government promoted the use of commercial 'techniques' and so the

951 This Court has been renamed 'Supreme Court'.

952 *Foster v. British Gas, AC* 2 (1991), pp. 206–317.

953 Council Directive 76/207/EEC of 9 February 1976 on the implementation of the principle of equal treatment for men and women as regards access to employment, vocational training and promotion, and working conditions, *OJ* [1976] L 039/40.

954 *Foster v. British Gas, AC* 2 (1991), at [20].

955 Www.legislation.gov.uk/asp/2010/8/data.pdf.

concept of value for money was developed.[956] Value for money is still an element taken into account in the provision of public services. National and local authorities apply the concept of value for money in their search for economy, efficiency and effectiveness.[957]

Vincent-Jones implicitly distinguishes three ways in which a public service can be provided: direct provision, contract, or privatisation with a public authority as market regulator.[958] Just as in France, public authorities in principle have free choice in how to provide public services. EU law also guarantees this free choice. In the following, this principle will be nuanced a bit for local authorities. Harden describes the three categories on the basis of which a public authority may intervene as follows: (a) services provided by a public body directly, (b) services purchased by a public body through contract and (c) services which a private body has a public law duty to provide.[959] The provision of public services is done 'through a hybrid combination of mechanisms of public and private ordering'.[960] The influence of the government will from direct to indirect influence vary depending on which of these ways is chosen. The different ways in which public services are managed today in England do not differ much if at all from the way this occurs in France.

From the perspective of certain case law it may be stated that in England a public authority is free to choose between a direct or 'in house' provision and the conclusion of a contract with a third party. In *Montpellier Estates v. Leeds City Council*[961] Superstone J. considered a public authority 'acted lawfully in deciding to abandon the tender exercise, having discovered that the award of the contract on the basis of the advertised award criteria would not achieve value for money'. The public authority abandoned the tendering procedure and chose for an 'in house'-provision.[962]

The thesis now explores the ways in which public services are provided, albeit with attention primarily focussing on the conclusion of contracts with third parties. The ways of intervening are to be found on both the national level and the local level (local governments). These ways of intervening are also used in Scotland.

956 S. Arrowsmith, *The law of public and utilities procurement*, Vol. I (London, Sweet & Maxwell, 2014), p. 17.

957 Arrowsmith gave a description of value for money in public procurement: 'VMF is commonly assessed by balancing assessment of the quality of tenderers against the price to be charged by the provider under the proposed contract, which equates to the cost of the service for the procuring entity' (S. Arrowsmith, *The law of public and utilities procurement*, Vol. I (London, Sweet & Maxwell, 2014), p. 18).

958 P. Vincent-Jones, 'Responsive Law and Governance in Public Services Provision: A Future for the Local Contracting Authority' (*Modern Law,* 1998), p. 362; see also J. Bell and T.P. Kennedy, 'La notion de service public au Royaume-Unie et en Irlande', in F. Moderne and G.Marcou (eds), *L'idée de service public dans le droit des états de l'Union Européenne* (Paris: l'Harmattan, 2001), pp. 248–254.

959 I. Harden, *The Contracting State* (Buckingham: Open University Press, 1992), p. 9.

960 P. Vincent-Jones, 'The New Public Contracting' (*Indiana Journal of Global Legal Studies,* 2007), p. 259.

961 [2013] EWHC 166.

962 R. Ashmore, 'United Kingdom – reminder that contracting authorities can switch to an inhouse "Plan B" solution if it represents value for money and is done in good faith: Montpellier Estates Ltd v. Leeds City Council' (*PPLR,* 2013), pp. NA68-NA72.

2.2.1. Direct provision

At present, only in a few situations a public authority assumes the direct provision of a public service.[963] This way of intervening was especially common at the beginning of the last century with the advent of the Social Welfare State.[964] Tasks were performed by government departments, which were branches of the central administration staffed by civil servants.[965]

However, the Thatcher government introduced a more modern system of management (New Public Management).[966] It was thought that the organisation of public administration should mirror the way private companies are structured. The idea was to reduce the role of government. The way in which government and citizen faced off against one another would have to be fundamentally altered as a consequence of these reforms. The goals of reform were: efficiency, effectiveness and accountability. Market principles were introduced in the management of public authorities.

One of the reforms was the Next Step-initiative,[967] in which the management of certain powers was transferred from the central administration to executive agencies. These agencies enjoy a certain financial autonomy, but have no legal personality. The relationship between the administration and the agency is governed by a Framework Document. The Framework Document defines the goals and functions of the agency. Some authors consider this relationship to be contractual in nature.[968] The agencies perform mainly the executive functions of government. The presence of these agencies is still required. The present government sees these agencies as the 'default delivery option in cases where there is a need to deliver public functions within central government but with a degree of operational independence'.[969]

The relations between a central administration and these executive agencies can, with a basis in EU case law, be considered as in-house situations. Sometimes the executive agencies are not independent legal persons. The relationship between the central administration and the agency is not a contractual relation. Such situations do not fall under the scope of EU law.[970]

963 D. Guinard, *Réflexions sur la construction d'une notion juridique: l'exemple de la notion de services d'intérêt général* (Paris: l'Harmattan, 2012), p. 95, nr. 91.

964 M. Donnelly, *Delegation of Governmental Power to Private Parties* (Oxford: OUP, 2009), p. 61.

965 A.W. Bradley and K.D. Ewing, *Constitutional and Administrative Law* (London: Pearson, 2005), p. 268; P. Vincent-Jones, *The New Public Contracting* (Oxford: OUP, 2006), p.169.

966 See also M. Donnelly, *Delegation of Governmental Power to Private Parties* (Oxford: OUP, 2009), pp. 62–63.

967 *Improving management in Government: the Next Steps* (1988).

968 M. Freedland, 'Government by Contract and Public Law' (*PL*, 1994), p. 88.

969 Minister for the Cabinet Office (2011), pp. 41–42.

970 Case C-26/03, *Stadt Halle and RPL Recyclingpark Lochau GmbH. v. Arbeitsgemeinschaft Thermische Restabfall- und Energieverwertungsanlage TREA Leuna* [2005] *ECR* I-00001.

In *Portsmouth City Council*[971] the Court of Appeal confirmed the public procurement Directives do not apply to in house provision. In 1991 Portsmouth City Council decided to reorganise its housing repair and maintenance work and to that end it proposed to conclude three contracts with the private sector: a maintenance contract, an improvement contract and a BISF contract (external renovation of a specific group of houses). The conclusion of the first contract was announced in the Official Journal of the European Union, in which it was stated that the contracting partner would be chosen on the basis of best value for money.

Prior to the 1991 decision, Portsmouth City Council had the work done in part by an in-house department, Portsmouth Contract Services (PCS). In taking the decision to do this work Portsmouth City Council was obliged not to act anti-competitively.[972] Portsmouth City Council had to explore what the financial consequences would be of whatever choice it made, i.e. full or partial in-house completion of the work or completion wholly by a third party. In that period, a local government in England could not have any works completed wholly in-house. Under certain circumstances, a public authority was obliged to let an in-house service compete with third parties for the purpose of performing a public service. (see *infra*) This option seemed to present itself in the commented case and an awarding procedure was therefore organised.

Although Portsmouth City Council had earlier chosen to issue a public procurement contract for a maintenance job, it opted during the awarding procedure, to have a cost-benefit analysis done and on the basis of that result decided to have the job partially done in-house. Consequently the PCC reverted in part to its earlier decision to allow the market to come into play for the entire contract. However, this decision to go for in-house execution of the work was not taken on the basis of best value for money. Some tenderers protested against this course of affairs. But the Council of PCC replied that the Regulations on Public Procurement do not apply to the choice for PCS.

The case was ultimately taken to court.[973] According to the judge, when the public authority published the tendering procedure for the conclusion of the three contracts, it should have notified that in awarding the contracts it took into account the influence of the choice on its own financial situation. The judge viewed this as an awarding criterion, which, however, had not initially been made public. The judge argued that this was a violation of the public procurement directives.

But Portsmouth City Council did not agree with this judgment and therefore brought the case before the Court of Appeal where they presented a new defence. They argued that public procurement Directives were not applicable to its relationship with PCS. Indeed, this relationship was not a contract in the sense of the public procurement Directives.

971 *R.v. Portsmouth City Council ex parte Peter Coles and Colwick Builders Limited and George Austin Limited* (C.L.C., 1997), p. 407.

972 Section 9(4) (a a q a) of the Local Government, Planning and Land Act 1980.

973 Mr. Justice Keene, Queen's Bench Division of the High Court.

Legatt PJ reasoned as follows: 'I regard it as inescapable that, when awarding work to PCS the Council were not entering into a public service contract within the meaning of the works directive, which could therefore have no application to the transaction'. He based this opinion on an earlier ruling of the Queen's Bench Division in *R. v. Cumbria* cc Ex p. Cumbria Professional Care Ltd[974]: 'Since, as a matter of law, the respondents cannot contract with themselves, the Directive cannot, in my judgment, be called into play … A contract as recognised by domestic law, is not made when, as the result of an administrative decision a service provider, who happens to/be in-house with the purchasing authority is selected to perform a function which the purchaser can lawfully award to itself'. Holehouse LJ confirmed this: 'Where a local authority, as did this County Council, decides to use its own direct labour department, it is not deciding to award a contract: it is deciding not to award a contract. Such a decision is something which falls outside the purview of the directives'.

The upshot of this judgment from the Court of Appeal was the determination that when a public authority makes use of its own department there is no contract and that consequently public procurement Directives are not applicable. This was later explicitly reconfirmed by the CJEU in *Stadt Halle.*[975] However, the Court of Appeal did not take, nor was it obliged to take, any decision concerning situations that are similar to an in-house situation. In this case at issue was not a cooperative agreement between two independent public authorities, and hence the *Teckal* case law was not applicable.

2.2.2. Contracting

The idea of New Public Management (hereinafter NPM) was applied in England in the 1980's and introduced market principles in the management of administration. One of the objectives of NPM was the increased use of the contract. Before that time, contracts were generally used by public authorities to purchase goods and services (public procurement).

The contract is becoming steadily more important in governance. One aspect of this increased use was the introduction of Compulsory Competitive Tendering in 1980 at the level of local government. Via a contract local authorities request a third party (public or private) to accomplish some tasks for them. The third party accomplishes a task that indirectly benefits the management of the administration or the third party receives directly the responsibility to manage the public service itself. Compulsory Competitive Tendering set down that local public authorities are obliged to open services that they in principle would prefer to perform internally, to competition. On this point the English system went further than even EU law ever required. From the perspective of EU law a public authority retains the option of either having its own departments perform a service or selecting a third party to do this.

974 (C.C.L. Rep 3, 2000), p. 79.

975 Case C-26/03, *Stadt Halle and RPL Recyclingpark Lochau GmbH. v. Arbeitsgemeinschaft Thermische Restabfall- und Energieverwertungsanlage TREA Leuna* [2005] *ECR* I-00001.

The contractual procedure is used in various ways in the provision of public services. Davies recognises six categories: 1) procurement, 2) providing services by contracting with private bodies (e.g. contracting out), 3) the private finance initiative and other public-private partnerships (PPPs), 4) agreement between the government and a self-regulatory organisation, 5) various types of agreement internal to government and 6) contract of employment with staff.[976] The present thesis will only be concerned with the 2nd, 3rd and 5th categories. The first category comes under EU law insofar as a public contract is involved. In this regard English law does not differ from French law. The national laws have transposed the European Directives. The 4th and 6th categories are too far removed from the types of contracts with which the thesis is concerned.

Since the 1980s the English government has, as mentioned earlier on, been looking for other approaches to the organisation of the activities of its various departments. Contracting out was one of the possible alternatives. In the case of contracting out, an in-house service is delivered by a third party, but the public authority remains responsible for the functioning of this service.[977] In fact, public contracting out is comparable to a service concession. In both cases a public function or activity is transferred to a third party and the third party accomplishes the task for the public authority. In such a situation an administration is required to compete with a private partner for a particular service. Competition, it is assumed, should ensure a better, more efficient, more imaginative and cheaper provision of services. In the evolution of contracting out-systems a distinction should be made between central and local government.

Contracting out for central government came into being under Thatcher; Central Government was required to conduct a review to determine if public services should be managed in house or should be contracted out. The 1977 Labour government continued the policy of contracting out, whereby the choice for the method of service provision was determined case by case. The Conservative/Liberal Coalition Government maintained the same policies for central government.[978] According to the government, public services can be provided by a wide range of providers including public providers.[979]

On the other hand, local authorities were required to tender in-house services under the Local Government Act 1980, the Local Government Act 1988 and the Local Government Act 1992. As such 'contracting out' was in principle obligatory. This was called

[976] A. Davies, *Accountability: A public law analysis of government by contract* (Oxford: OUP, 2001), p. 1: see also C. Harlow and R. Rawlings, *Law and administration* (Cambridge: CUP, 2009), p. 339.

[977] M. Freedland, 'Government by Contract and Public Law' (*PL*, 1994), p. 87.

[978] S. Arrowsmith, *The law of public and utilities procurement*, Vol. I (London, Sweet & Maxwell, 2014), p. 33. However, Craig recognises a different approach by the Coalition government: P. Craig, *Administration Law* (London: Sweet and Maxwell, 2012), p. 115.

[979] White paper, *Open public services* (2011), para. 6.1., https://www.gov.uk/government/uploads/system/uploads/attachment_data/file/255288/OpenPublicServices-WhitePaper.pdf.

'Compulsory Competitive Tendering' (hereinafter CCT).[980] Services and activities subject to CCT were explicitly listed in the Local Government Act. After the 1997 elections, 'Best Value' replaced CCT for local authorities.[981] The objective of 'Best Value' is ongoing improvement in the quality of the services provided by local authorities and to secure the efficient and effective provision of local services. The Coalition Government continued this policy.

Use of the Private Finance Initiative in its present form in England goes back to 1992.[982] The original purpose of PFI was to finance public infrastructures with private funds. Public authorities[983] were encouraged to provide public services via private capital funding. The use of PFI was situated within a broader framework of reform of the way the general interest is managed.

A quite recent definition of PFI is as follows: *'PFI is an arrangement whereby the public sector contracts to purchase services, usually derived from an investment in assets, from the private sector on a long-term basis, often between 15 to 30 years'*.[984] They are contracts for the provision of capital and assets.[985] Public-Private partnership (PPP) is a more general notion in which PFI constitutes one element.[986] PPP covers a broad range of business structures and partnership arrangements. The aim of every PPP is to deliver high quality services (better government).

Three types of PPP may be distinguished[987]: 1) the private sector finances the infrastructure and a public authority pays for right of use, 2) the private sector builds the infrastructure and may collect a toll on it and 3) an infrastructure is built by the private sector and is paid for in part from rent and in part from toll. However, it may also act through the private sector whereby the latter takes shares in government companies.

In both PFI and PPP a contract is concluded between two different legal persons.[988] This type of cooperation may be either horizontal or vertical. These are always long-term contracts. The conclusion of these kinds of contracts is generally governed by the public

980 M. Trybus, 'From the indivisible crown to *Teckal*: the In-House provision of works and services in the United Kingdom', in M. Comba and S. Treumer (eds), *The In-House providing in European Law* (Copenhagen: Djöf Publishing, 2010), p. 189.

981 Local Government Act 1999. Departement of the Environment, Transport and the Regions, *Modernising Local Government: Improving Local Services through Best Value* (1997).

982 See N. Lamont, *Chancellor of the exchequer*, Autumn Statement, vol.128, col. 996 (12 November 1992).

983 For local authorities see: P. Craig, *Administration Law* (London: Sweet and Maxwell, 2012), pp. 126–128; *Local Government and the Private Finance Initiative* (1998).

984 H.M. Treasury, *Managing Public Money* (2008), p.18.

985 A. Davies, *The Public Law of Government Contracts* (Oxford: OUP, 2008), p.10.

986 A. Davies, *o.c.*, p.10.

987 M. Freedland, 'Public Law and Private Finance-Placing the Private Finance Initiative in a Public Law' (*PL*, 1998), pp. 290–291; P. Craig, *Administrative Law* (London: Sweet and Maxwell, 2012), p.120.

988 Y. Marique, 'An English Legal perspective on Public-private partnerships', in F. Lichère (eds), *Public-Private Partnership Reports of the XVIII Congress of the Internatinal Academy of Comparative Law* (Brussels: Bruylant, 2011), pp. 111–112.

procurement Directives or the European principle of equality if a contract clearly shows a cross-border interest.

2.3. *Cooperative agreements between public authorities*

In the foregoing the thesis examined some of the ways in which public authorities manage or administer their public services. In England, when legal theory addresses the issue of the ways in which pubic authorities administer a public service there is usually no mention of the situation where a public authority cooperates with another public authority to improve service to the public. This kind of cooperation should, according to the present thesis, also be mentioned among the ways public services are provided.

The thesis is exclusively concerned with the cooperative agreements between public authorities insofar as it may be deemed contractual and, in particular, where said contract is a public procurement or a service concession. The thesis will now look into the use of the contract by public authorities in England (2.3.1.) and the possibilities for the Courts to review the conclusion of these contracts (2.3.2.), after which the thesis will explore the phenomenon of cooperative agreements between public authorities in England and Scotland (2.3.3.) and analyse existing case law in England (2.3.4.).

2.3.1. The use of the capacity to contract by public authorities

In England no legal distinction is made in principle between a situation in which a public authority is a partner in a contract and a situation where solely private persons are involved. Normally the same law is applicable to both forms of contract[989] and accordingly the concept 'contract' is given the same definition. The doctrine of the '*contrat administratif*' is unknown to English or Scottish administrative law. According to some legal theories more recent case law appears to suggest that government contracts do not always come under the same applicable law as private contracts.[990]

The present thesis calls all contracts concluded by a public authority 'government contracts'.[991] The notion 'public contract' has usually a more specific meaning within the scope of the public procurement Directives. This section of the thesis will, however, deal with all contracts concluded by a public authority.

In common law the custom of deducing juridical consequences from the definition of a term is less widespread as in continental law. For this reason most books on contract law provide no clear definition of the notion 'contract'. Nonetheless note should be taken of

989 P. Craig and M. Trybus, 'England and Wales', in R. Nogouellou and U. Stelkens (eds), *Comparative Law on public contracts* (Brussels: Bruylant, 2010), p. 339.

990 P. Birkinshaw, 'Contrats publics et contractualisation' (*RFDA*, 2006), pp. 1028–1029; S. Arrowsmith, *The law of public and utilities procurement*, Vol. I (London: Sweet & Maxwell, 2014), p. 11.

991 Anne Davies uses this concept to determine the contracts used by a public authority. See A. Davies, *The Public Law of Government Contracts* (Oxford: OUP, 2008), pp. 2 et seq.

the following definition of a 'contract': 'A contract consists of an actionable promise or promises. Every such promise involves at least two parties, a promisor and a promise, and an outward expression of common intention and of expectation as to the declaration or assurance contained in the promise'.[992] Common contract law is concerned with the kind of promises that are enforceable, which may trigger binding legal consequences. In the present thesis the term 'contract' is used in the sense given by public procurement Directives.

There is no special law applicable to contracts in which a public authority is one of the contracting parties: 'The legal framework for government contracts in England is a complex blend of internal government guidance, domestic law and EU law requirements'.[993] The requirements in EU law are the subject of this thesis. Public authorities have guidelines that are of help in the conclusion and completion of government contracts.[994] But these guidelines do not purport to be laws in the strict sense of the term. They do not have their origin in legal texts that have been approved by Parliament. They are rather referred to as soft law.[995] This also explains why the provisions that are applicable to a government contract can be quite diverse.

By virtue of these guidelines public authorities are able to diverge widely from the rules that normally apply to a contract. The applicable rules depend largely on the public authority that is the contracting partner in the contract. Although such contracts are concluded under common law the influence of the latter is quite limited in practice.[996] Usually the mutual rights and obligations of the parties to such contracts are determined by standard government contract terms.[997]

The capacity to contract is not equally obvious for all public authorities. The Crown has the power to enter into a contract because it has all the powers of a natural person.[998] Legal scholars associate this capacity with what they call 'the third source of authority for government action': 'the freedom which government has to do anything that is not prohibited by law'.[999] The approval of Parliament is not needed. Crown agents (Ministers and Crown corporations) can conclude contracts on behalf of the Crown in connection with their activities.[1000] Other public bodies need the power to be conferred to them by legislation. These public bodies can only conclude a contract

992 J. Beatson, A. Burrows and J. Cartwright, *Anson's Law of contract* (Oxford: OUP, 2010), p. 29.

993 A. Davies, *The Public Law of Government Contracts* (Oxford: OUP, 2008), p. 33.

994 The Department for Communities and Local Government can provide informal publications to assist local authorities.

995 A. Davies, *op. cit.*, pp. 34–35.

996 A. Davies, *op. cit.*, p. 42.

997 P. Craig, *Administrative law* (London: Sweet and Maxwell, 2012), p. 112.

998 *The Bankers'* Case (1700) 90 E.R. p. 270;C. Harlow and R. Rawlings, *Law and administration* (Cambridge: CUP, 2009), p. 341; M. Freedland, 'Government by Contract and Public Law' (*PL*, 1994), pp. 91–92.

999 B.V. Harris, 'The "Third Source" of Authority' (*LQR*, 1992), pp. 626–627.

1000 S. Arrowsmith, *The law of public and utilities procurement*, Vol. I (London: Sweet & Maxwell, 2014), p. 70.

if they are authorised by statute.[1001] However, a public body can enter into a contract in connection with an activity or project, when it was expressly authorised to carry out this specific activity or project.[1002] For local authorities, the Localism Act 2011 has broadly widened their capacity to enter into a contract. S.1(1) of the Localism Act confers a general power of competence on most local authorities in England. Most local authorities are considered to have the same power as private individuals to enter into a contract.[1003] Some limitations to the general power are provided in S.2 of the Localism Act.

All public authorities are normally free to opt for other than the contractual route. To that extent, the English legal system does not differ from the French system. As already mentioned, EU law does not restrict this choice. Just as in the continental legal system, freedom of contract for an English public authority is not so broadly construed as for a private person.[1004] There are various rules and principles of public law that restrict this freedom to some measure.

The use of a contract to procure public services can, according to Harden, in two ways: 'services performed directly for citizens... or indirectly to support government operations'.[1005] The organisation of the first category of public services via contract has only recently entered into practice.

2.3.2. Judicial review

Citizens only enjoy effective rights, when national judicial system offers them protection (remedies), especially in relation to the activities of a public authority.[1006] This also applies when an operator participates in a public tendering procedure or when an operator is not given the chance to participate. Judicial review is a system that guarantees protection to the citizen against the exercise of public authorities powers.

Remedies against actions of public authorities can be divided in two categories: ordinary remedies and prerogative remedies.[1007] These are the means of obtaining judicial review (challenging the legality of public authority's action). Specific remedies are provided for public contracts above the thresholds in Part 9 of the United Kingdom Public contract Regulations and Utilities Contract Regulations.

[1001] *Hazell v. Hammersmith and Fulham London Burrough Council* (*A.C.* 2, 1992), p. 1. For a discussion on the capacity for Crown agents to contract see P. Craig, *Administration Law* (London: Sweet and Maxwell, 2012), pp. 135–136.

[1002] *Attorney General v. Great Eastern Railway* (*App.Cas.* 5, 1879/1880), p. 473.

[1003] S. Arrowsmith, *The law of public and utilities procurement*, Vol. I (London: Sweet & Maxwell, 2014), p. 87.

[1004] A. Davies, *The Public Law of Government Contracts* (Oxford: OUP, 2008), pp. 121–124.

[1005] I. Harden, *The Contracting State* (Buckingham: Open University Press, 1992), pp. x-xi.

[1006] The notion 'public authorities' is used in this section in a more narrow sense than in Chapter 3.

[1007] W. Wade and C. Forsyth, *Administrative Law* (Oxford: Oxford University Press, 2014).

In general a citizen in England disposes of a significant range of remedies to challenge a decision of a public authority. In general courts recognise that a public authority has to guarantee certain rights to citizens. Public authorities' decisions and actions can be challenged on the basis of illegality, irrationality and procedural unfairness.[1008] The Courts created certain principles to control the exercise of administrative powers: the rule against bias and the right of a fair hearing.[1009] The thesis does not intend to discuss these principles and the system of judicial review. There is no doubt that judicial review has been success in the exercise of control.[1010] There has also been a significant increase of litigation in public procurement.[1011] However, a question arises as to how far aggrieved citizens can invoke principles of judicial review and to what extent they can do this in respect of contractual and procurement powers of public authorities.

In 1990, Arrowsmith acknowledged that there has been a notable increase in the number of reported cases in which the exercise of contractual powers has been challenged on public law grounds, and in several cases the courts have accepted that judicial review is possible.[1012] However, she also saw an ambivalence in the attitude of courts to the availability of judicial review to contractual decisions. Some court decisions demanded the presence of a specific 'public law' element to review pure contractual powers. This condition seems to be predominant now in most contract and procurement cases involving public bodies.[1013]

A public element is present when there is a statutory underpinning to the public authority's decision.[1014] It seems the Courts' approach is that the public element may exist if a specific statute imposes the use of tendering procedures when a public authority wants to conclude a contract.[1015] This is the case for public procurement. In some decisions it is considered that a public element is present if a contract concerns a function of public importance.[1016] Public service concessions are contracts where a public authority transfers a service of general interest to another legal person. It could be considered as a contract that concerns of function of public importance.

1008 *R (Wheeler) v. Office of the Prime Minister* (*EWHC*, 2008), p. 1409 admin.

1009 This is a distinction made by Wade & Forsyth which encompasses all principles of judicial review.

1010 Www.parliament.uk/documents/commons/lib/research/rp2006/rp06-044.pdf; www.gov.uk/government/uploads/system/uploads/attachment_data/file/264091/8703.pdf: in 1998, 4500 applicants were registered whereas in 2012 12.400 applicants.

1011 M. Trybus, 'An Overview of the United Kingdom Public Procurement Review and Remedies System with an Emphasis on England and Wales', in S. Treumer and F. Lichère (eds.), *Enforcement of the EU public procurement rules* (Copenhagen: Djøf Publishing, 2011), p. 201.

1012 S. Arrowsmith, 'Judicial review and the contractual powers of public authorities' (*LQR*, 1990), p. 277.

1013 S. H. Bailey, 'Judicial review of contracting decisions' (*PL*, 2007), pp. 444–463; S. Arrowsmith, *Law of Public and Utilities Procurement Volume 1* (London: Sweet and Maxwell, 2014), pp. 118–119.

1014 *R v. Hibbit and Sanders Ex p. the Lord Chancellor's Department* (C.O.D., 1993), p. 326, DC.

1015 S. Arrowsmith, *Law of Public and Utilities Procurement Volume 1* (London: Sweet and Maxwell, 2014), p. 120.

1016 S. Arrowsmith, *o.c.*, p. 121.

The application of judicial review principles to be considered in procurement cases are: the right to a hearing, breach of natural justice, principles of fairness, fiduciary duty, principle of legitimate expectations.[1017] Consequently, public authorities' decision to cooperate are not only subject to EU (public procurement) law, but also to principles of judicial review.

2.3.3. Cooperation

The preceding pages made it clear that in England public authorities continue to seek original ways to provide public services to citizens. One of these is the cooperation between public authorities. Public authorities set up an independent entity or organise shared services. These 'shared services' have gained currency in recent years. Shared services or joint arrangements are of course no new phenomenon in the business of providing public services in England. Thus, the Local Government Act 1972 already features provisions for Joint Committees, for delegation and for secondment of staff.

Before describing the use of cooperative agreements or shared services, this section will examine how far public authorities in England may conclude cooperative agreements. The thesis has already pointed out that the Crown has a general capacity to conclude contracts and thus also to enter into a cooperative agreement. Since the entry into force of the Localism Act most local authorities have now also the general power to enter into a cooperative agreement. For local authorities and especially for other public bodies a distinction should be made between the acting as a contracting authority, as an operator or to constitute joint companies or other complex shared services agreements. Most local authorities have the power to act as a contracting authority. Other public bodies, than the Crown, must find this power in statutory provisions. Local authorities can also act as providers according to S.1 of the Local Authorities Act 1970. For other public bodies this is less clear. The creation of joint companies by public authorities is covered normally by the general power under the Localism Act. Other public bodies have to look into their applicable legislation.

Shared services are a way whereby public services are mutually created by public authorities in England and Scotland. Public authorities bundle their powers in several different areas to come up with more productive and more efficient public services. This means is of relevance for the present thesis only insofar as this form of cooperation between public authorities displays characteristics of a public contract or a service concession and hence the CJEU case law on cooperative agreements is indeed relevant.

The endeavour to create more efficient public services in England and Scotland dates to around 2004. In England this was the result of 'the Gershon Review'.[1018] According to the original recommendations of this report, savings could be sought through the

1017 S. Arrowsmith, *o.c.*, pp. 122–124.

1018 Www.theworkfoundation.com/assets/docs/publications/119_efficiency,%20efficiency,%20efficiency.%20%20the%20gershon%20review.pdf.

development of shared services.[1019] The need for a new Shared Services approach was also emphasised in the 'Transformational Government' report,[1020] which was an outcrop of the Gershon Review. Customer needs were its focal point. This document also states the purpose of shared services: 'Shared services provide public service organizations with the opportunity to reduce waste and inefficiency by re-using assets and sharing investments with others' (p. 12).

The report 'Building a Better Scotland'[1021] appeared in 2004 in Scotland. The aim of this rapport was to bring efficiency, innovation and productivity to public services. In regard to cooperation between pubic authorities the objective is stated explicitly: 'to examine the public sector as a whole, and realise efficiencies through joining up in purchasing, in accommodation, and in support services'.[1022] One of the points of action is Shared Support Services: 'It should generate substantial efficiency savings'.[1023] Shared Services is one of the five ways suggested by this report to arrive at efficient public services.

The two reports in England and Scotland marked the start of the rise of Shared Services as a way to improve the efficiency of public services. In Scotland in 2006 an advisory document from key players laid out 'A shared approach to building a better Scotland'.[1024] It contained a number of concrete proposals on how Shared Services could be used throughout Scotland. During the consultations that produced this document the key players set out a number of different opinions. In 2007 the Scottish Government produced the following document based on these consultations: 'Shared Services-Guidance Framework December 2007',[1025] which, *inter alia* provides tips for considering where they are on the Shared Services Journey. It aims to provide information, education, guidance and case study examples to those considering Shared Services and to those already on a Shared Services journey (p. 6). This report was updated in 2011.[1026]

In England the present government underscored the importance of Shared Services once again in 2011.[1027] Throughout 2006 and 2007 awareness increased steadily in England and Scotland on the potential influence of European Union Law on Shared Services. Two reports appeared that explored the influence of the EU Public Procurement Rules: 'Shared Services in Government – EU Public Procurement Rules Considerations'[1028] and

1019 Gershon Review, p. 8.
1020 Www.parsdigitalorg/ documentos/docs innovacion/2005/Transformational government.pdf.
1021 Www. scotland.gov.uk/Recource/Doc/26800/0025698.pdf.
1022 Building a Better Scotland, p. 1.
1023 Building a Better Scotland, p. 17.
1024 Www.scotland.gov.uk/recource/Doc/115423/0028606.pdf.
1025 Www.scotland.gov.uk/Resource/Doc/82980/0055049.pdf.
1026 Shared Services Guidance 2011, www.scotland.gov.uk/Topics Government/Public Service Reform/ efficient government/Shared Serices/Guidanceframework 2010.
1027 *Government Shared Services: a strategic vision* (July 2012), www.cabinetoffice.gov.uk/sites/default/files/ recources/government-shared-services-july 2011.pdf.
1028 Cabinet Office, 2006, London.

'Shared Services in the Scottish public sector: Impact of the EU Public Procurement Rules'.[1029]

My training during two weeks at a law office in Edinburgh in the summer of 2012 showed clearly that public authorities in Scotland are aware of the influence of EU law should they want to make use of shared services. This experience in a law office was, however, not sufficient to ascertain that Scottish public authorities check before every form of cooperation with another public authority on conformity with EU law. However, law offices are regularly contacted for advice on the matter.

Although public authorities are using Shared Services increasingly, and the influence of EU law is pervasive, the interplay between them has given little reason for conflicts demanding a resolution at the courts. In the next section the few existing relevant cases will be examined.

2.3.4. Case law

There are two known cases where an English Court had to rule on a cooperative agreement between public authorities regarding the application of EU law, and more specifically the public procurement Directives. At the beginning of 2011 the UK Supreme Court had the occasion to issue a decision on the impact of the *Teckal* case law on the ability of public authorities to cooperate with a third party, of which it is a part, to perform services for it without giving other companies the chance to state their interest in the matter.[1030] At the end of 2013 the Court of Appeal – Queen's Bench Division issued a second decision on the application of the *Teckal* case law.[1031]

In *Brent London Borough Council and others v. Risk Management Partners Ltd*[1032] the Supreme Court issued a judgment on the applicability of Public Contract Regulations 2006[1033] to an insurance contract concluded between various local authorities and London Authorities Mutual Ltd (LAML). In 2006 and 2007 these local authorities concluded mutual insurance arrangements with LAML against various classes of risk. LAML is a company limited by guarantee and is made up exclusively of local authorities. The purpose of participation in LAML was to keep costs down and to raise the standard of risk management for the local authorities.

Brent LBC had, during the period when Brent LBC was considering becoming a shareholder in LAML, announced the awarding of a public contract for which RPM, an

[1029] Www.scotland.gov.uk/Resource/Doc/1265/0051647.pdf.

[1030] See also M. Trybus, 'From the indivisible crown to *Teckal*: the In-House provision of works and services in the United Kingdom', in M. Comba and S. Treumer (eds), *The In-House providing in European Law* (Copenhagen: Djöf Publishing, 2010), pp. 193–211.

[1031] *Tachie v. Welwyn Hatfield BC* [2013] EWHC 3972 (QB); [2014] B.L.G.R. 100 (QBD).

[1032] (2011), UKSC 7 (2011), 2 W.L.R.166.

[1033] 2006 SI/5.

insurance company under private law, had made a tender. The purpose of this public procurement was to conclude an insurance agreement with a third party. However, the moment the participation of Brent LBC in LAML became effective, Brent LBC had stopped the awarding procedure. But RPM found this unacceptable and initiated a judicial procedure. It argued that the contract made between Brent LBC and LAML is a public procurement contract and hence fell under the purview of Regulations 2006. Therefore it should be open to competition. A number of local authorities, shareholders in LAML, one of which was Harrow London Borough Council, intervened in the procedure.

Within the Court of Appeal Stanley Burton LJ argued that Brent had acted in breach of the 2006 Regulations when it abandoned the tender process and awarded (concluded) the insurance contract to LAML.[1034] According to him the control criterion had not been met. Pill LC argued as follows: 'The intention to achieve the aim of operational independence is illustrated by the powers of the board and the arrangements made with the management company and the terms of policies issued. I find it difficult to see how LAML can operate effectively unless its board has considerable freedom to manage its insurance business. The nature of the business and the possibly differing interests of different authorities and affiliates are antithetic to the necessary local authority control'.[1035] Criticism of this judgment was not long in coming. The view was that the Court of Appeal had taken a too one-sided view of the powers of the Board of LAML.[1036]

Brent LBC and Harrow LBC appealed to the Supreme Court. Brent LBC reached a settlement before the Supreme Court handed down its judgment. The Supreme Court was solely required to rule on the dispute between Harrow LBC and RPM on the applicability of Regulations 2006 to the conclusion of the insurance contract between Harrow and LAML.

Hope LJ affirmed in the first place that the *Teckal* exemption is applicable to the 2006 Regulations. The basis for this assertion is to be found in the underlying purposes of the public procurement regulations. They have to give effect to the public procurement Directives.[1037] These Directives and their interpretation have to be applied in a similar way in all Member States. This is an application of the principle of loyal cooperation (see chapter 1). The *Teckal* case law contains such an interpretation of the public procurement Directives. Consequently, this case law is also applicable in England. Therefore Hope LJ judged that the nature of the contract (an insurance contract) was of no relevance in determining whether the *Teckal* case law is applicable. It was necessary to examine whether

1034 (2008), EWHC 1094 (Admin); (2008) LGR429.
1035 (2009), EWCA Civ p. 490, at [131].
1036 See M. Trybus, 'From the indivisible crown to *Teckal*: the In-House provision of works and services in the United Kingdom', in M. Comba and S. Treumer (eds), *The In-House providing in European Law* (Copenhagen: Djöf Publishing, 2010), pp. 207–210.
1037 (2009) EWCA Civ p. 490, at [22].

the *Teckal* criteria had been met.[1038] For this Hope LJ referred to the relevant case law of the Court of Justice. On the basis of the case law of the CJEU Hope LJ judged as follows[1039]:

- an individual control of one local authority is not necessary
- no private interests can be involved in the collective cooperation
- public authorities must act exclusively in the public interest

Hope LJ concluded the members of LAML (local authorities) controlled a subsidiary, which was designed exclusively for the performance of their public functions.[1040] There is a collective control over strategic objectives and significant decisions. Regarding the activity test was observed that LAML only provides insurance to participating members and affiliates. The participating members were all public authorities and the affiliates are associated with the participating members.

Roger LJ also examines in depth the case. He explains in a clear way the purpose of the public procurement Directives and the rationale behind the *Teckal* case law: 'The directive is not intended to protect the commercial sector by forcing public authorities to obtain the services which they need on the commercial market. For instance, a local authority can have its own architect's department and does not need to look outside to obtain the services of an architect or architects to design municipal buildings or housing. It is free to obtain these services in-house. The purpose of the Directive is simply to ensure that, if public authorities do decide to obtain the services which they need from outside bodies, proper procedures are followed to ensure that potential providers of the services have an opportunity'.[1041] Thus Roger LJ reconfirms that in-house provision is beyond the scope of EU law.

According to Roger LJ public authorities may cooperate with other local authorities to ensure that, collectively, they have the necessary resources to do so.[1042] If the cooperation takes the form of establishing a body, the public procurement Directives will not apply if the cooperating public authorities obtain their services or products from the body. They obtain the products or services in-house, in cooperation with other public authorities.[1043] Private investment is excluded and the body cannot be market oriented. Consequently, Roger LJ determined that control can be exercised by all the public authorities combined. A 75% majority of participating members present and voting at the meeting may issue any direction to the board by special resolution. For this reason, according to Roger LJ, the public authorities that contract with LAML have a power of decisive influence over both the strategic objectives and significant decisions of LAML. LAML is a vehicle that the participating London boroughs control, and through which they can arrange for the provision of insurance to each other and to their affiliates. The boroughs achieve this by

1038 At [30].
1039 At [53].
1040 At [57].
1041 At [68].
1042 At [73].
1043 At [74].

utilizing resources in the form of capital contribution and premiums. No capital is contributed by any private body – nor is any such contribution envisaged in the future. The whole purpose of the scheme is to keep it within the ambit of the public authorities and not to transfer it to an outside body.[1044]

The Supreme Court bases its judgment mainly on the objectives of the public procurement Directives and not on the literal wording of the definition of a public contract:

'The 2006 Regulations give effect to the Directive in English law. In other words, they are the way in which English law secures the free movement of services and the opening-up to undistorted competition in relation to contracts, which are to be placed by English local authorities. That being the purpose of the Regulations, they, too, cannot be meant to apply in circumstances where that purpose is not relevant because a contracting authority intends to contract with a body which is not properly to be regarded as an outside body. Although the *Teckal* criteria were formulated with particular reference to the predecessors of the Directive, they are simply a way of identifying situations where the authority can be regarded as obtaining the products or services which it requires in-house and, so, where there is no need to secure the free movement of services and the opening-up to undistorted competition. In my view, the criteria are an equally good indication of situations where, for that reason, the 2006 Regulations have no application. The insight of Advocate General Trstenjak in para 83 of her opinion in *Coditel Brabant* [2008] ECR I-8457, 8482, is instructive. To hold that the Regulations did apply in these circumstances would involve saying that the legislature intended to attach weight to competition law objectives in an area where they have no legitimate application. This would, in turn, involve inappropriate interference with local authorities' right to co-operate in discharging their public functions'.[1045]

The Supreme Court showed the clear link between the TFEU provisions on free movement and public procurement Directives. Both have the same objectives. Only when a cooperative arrangement can distort competition or hinder free movement is the decision to cooperate (state measure) subject to EU law. There can be no such distortion when a public authority applies a measure that affects solely its own organisational structure. The purpose of the measure has no effect on market events.

In *Tachie v. Welwyn Hatfield BC* the Queen's Bench Division of the High Court (before mr. Justice Jay) had to deal with three appeals brought under s.204 of the Housing Act 1996 challenging a decision by Welwyn Hatfield Borough Council to contract out its homelessness functions under Pt VII of the Housing Act 1996 to an arms length management organisation ('ALMO').[1046] ALMOs have a significant degree of independence from their parent local authorities, they are 100% controlled by the latter and are usually

1044 At [90].

1045 At [92].

1046 See also K. Gough, 'Tachie and Ors v. Welwyn Hatfield Borough Council: application of the *Teckal* exemption to arms length management organisations' (*PPLR*, 2014), pp. NA89-NA91.

constituted as companies limited by guarantee. One of the issues that arose was if the *Teckal* 'exemption' was applicable to the process of contracting out to ALMOs.

Mr. Justice Jay confirmed that public authority decisions to engage a contractor are normally subject to the public procurement regulations. However, he also recalled the two *Teckal* criteria as an exception to this general rule. The judgment only concerned the control criterion. Mr. Justice Jay considered: 'I cannot agree … that it is relevant to consider the degree of control in fact exercised … at all material times; the focus must be on the nature of the arrangements between the two entities as constituted by the contractual and other documentation, and these have not changed… It is the presence, or absence, of salient features in these arrangements which will determine whether or not a procurement exercise should have been implemented'.[1047]

In the present case the local authority exercises a complete control on the Trust. No private interests are involved, the Respondent is acting solely in the public interest in the carrying out of its public service task, and there is no contriving to circumvent the rules on public procurement.[1048]

2.4. *Conclusion*

The way the provision of public services in England is organised has undergone a significant evolution. More and more public services have been contracted out or even privatised. This evolution took place without any influence from EU law. Privatisation also reduces the scope of the public procurement Directives. However, if a public authority chooses to cooperate with another public authority to provide public services, EU law may have an influence as to the extent to which the public authority can freely choose its contract partner.

In the first place, the discussed case law confirms that a purely in-house situation lies beyond the reach of EU law and that a public authority can freely choose for such a provision. This case law indicates that the system of Compulsory Competitive Tendering went further than was necessary on the strength of EU law. Second, the English Courts faithfully applies *Teckal* case law. This is somewhat different from the French *Conseil d'État,* which gives a broader interpretation to CJEU case law and seems to go too far. In the event the English courts explicitly devote attention to the objectives of public procurement Directives and on the basis of the latter they have then formulated a specific reply to the question of the applicability of these Directives. It demonstrates that the *Teckal* criteria may be considered a formalised rendition of these objectives.

In *Brent* the Supreme Court emphasises several times the link between case law on vertical and case law on horizontal cooperation.[1049] The question of the applicability of

1047 At [46].
1048 At [47].
1049 At [50], [73] and [75].

EU law to both kinds of cooperation would have to be answered similarly. Indeed, the same objectives determine the applicability of EU law. Although the CJEU has used other criteria to exclude one or the other form of cooperation from the scope of EU law, application of the criteria would have to be driven by the objectives that free trade remains guaranteed and that competition is not distorted.

3. General conclusions

Chapter 6 of the thesis purported to explore how public service tasks in France and England are organised and especially how this organisation is or is not influenced by EU law and more specifically by CJEU case law on cooperative arrangements between public authorities.

First, the idea of 'public service' seems to play totally disparate roles in France and England. In France the concept is of constitutional value, what is more, determines the autonomy of administrative law. Public service is an important juridical concept in France with its own content. This concept is unknown in England and consequently also has no juridical purport. Of course public authorities perform public service tasks as well, but in England such tasks do not mean that public authorities have a special law that is applicable to them. From the research it appears that, in regard to determining whether an activity is a public service task, the French and English systems are converging. More and more a functional interpretation tends to be favoured in these two systems. And in this regard they are coming to conform more and more to the EU understanding of the concept. It is thus first and foremost the purpose of the activity that determines whether it is a public service.

The organisation and management of public service tasks by public authorities is comparable in France and England. The form of organisation to be chosen was not always determined in the same way in France and England. In France it was assumed for a long time that a public authority was always free to organise a public service as it wished. In England the same was the case until the end of the seventies. However, in the eighties legislation was passed that obliged public authorities to allow their in-house departments to participate in tendering procedures when they wished to allow a public task to be carried out. In these circumstances, therefore, there was no free choice in the organisation of a public service task. Since the 1990s this system was abandoned. But with the advent of the *Teckal* case law, the highest courts in both countries determined that when a public authority uses its own services, it need not organise a tendering procedure. The choice of one or another form of organisation is free; it is not determined by EU law.

Clearly, France has had a much longer tradition in matters of cooperative agreements between public authorities than England. Also, the application of public procurement Directives to that kind of arrangement has been a topic of consideration much longer in France. Until 1998 the response to this issue in France was negative. However, under the pressure of EU law the *Conseil d'État* modified its attitudes in this regard. Cooperative arrangements between public authorities can be construed as subject to the application of public procurement Directives. In this regard, the *Conseil d'État* anticipated *Teckal*. In England the High Court was given the chance to confirm this only in 2011.

In both France and England the respective Supreme Courts have assimilated the *Teckal* case law. In both countries the Supreme Courts seem to apply CJEU case law with due consideration given to the EU objectives and the public procurement Directives. This national case law confirms that the criteria developed by the CJEU are simply a concretisation of the aforementioned objectives. They must then also be interpreted and applied in conformity with these objectives. However, in France the *Conseil d'État* goes further and has developed its own criterion to exempt vertical and horizontal cooperative agreements from the requirement to organise a competitive tendering procedure. The interpretation given by the *Conseil d'État* seems to be in conflict with CJEU law. It demonstrates that France still clings to the national competence to organise public tasks. The most recent Directives seem to tend in this direction. Indeed, the Directives contain quite a number of ways for a public authority to cooperate without being subject to EU law (see chapter 5).

In France the legislature also seized the initiative as a consequence of *Teckal* case law. It created new legal forms for local authorities whereby the choice of these new forms would automatically lead to an exception to the application of EU law. Case law shows, however, that this is not the case.

This chapter has shown that CJEU case law has a direct influence on how cooperative agreements between public authorities must be conceived in France and England. In France such agreements fall normally under the scope of administrative law, a branch of law that is outside the ambit of EU competence. However, a teleological interpretation of the CJEU puts this element of national administrative law within the ambit of EU law. It is a good example of how Article 345 TFEU has to be understood. Most of the public authorities decisions fall within the scope of EU law if they hinder or could hinder market access or if they distort or could distort free competition. To that extent the freedom of Member States to regulate the organization and management of public service tasks and the freedom of public authorities to organise or manage their public service tasks is limited. In England, as a consequence of CJEU case law, new soft law inspired by public law, was created for application to cooperative arrangements between public authorities (shared services).

Chapter 7

GENERAL CONCLUSIONS

The main objective of this thesis was to examine if EU (public procurement) law has had some impact and influence on how national public authorities make decisions on how to organise the manner in which they discharge some of their public service tasks. In order to test this the thesis

(i) narrowed the research to cooperative agreements between national public authorities within the EU law on public contracts and service concessions;
(ii) limited the EU Member States to France and the UK.

The two main research questions of this thesis that comply with this objective are:

A) Do agreements between national public authorities whereby they cooperate in discharging their public tasks come within EU law and, in particular, within the scope of the EU public procurement Directives?

In order to answer this question the following sub-research questions have been identified:

(a) What kind of situations regarding the organisation of public tasks are influenced by EU law? (Chapter 3)
(b) How is it possible that these situations been influenced by EU law? (Chapter 4)
(c) To what extent are these situations influenced by EU law? (Chapter 5)

B) Has there been influence of EU law in shaping or changing the national administrative law in France and the UK?

In order to answer this question the thesis has identified the following sub-research questions:

(a) How do public authorities in France discharge their public service tasks? (Chapter 6)
(b) How do public authorities in the UK discharge their public service tasks? Do they cooperate with each other? (Chapter 6)
(c) What, if any, has been the influence of EU law (both legislative and case law) on how France and the UK organise the manner in which their national public authorities discharge their tasks? (Chapter 6)

The central focus of the thesis was the cooperation between public authorities, but not every kind of cooperation was of interest for this study. The study was in the first place limited by the very concept of 'public authority'. Accordingly, of relevance for the thesis was solely the form of cooperation that may be defined in EU law as a public contract or a service concession. For this reason this thesis uses the general term 'cooperative agreements'. Finally, cooperative agreements are only relevant when their object is governed by considerations and requirements in the pursuit of objectives in the general interest. Hence this thesis is constrained by three terms: 1) public authority, 2) public contract or service concession and 3) public service task.

As discussed and demonstrated in Chapter 3, a public authority is an entity capable of making decisions irrespective of any financial or commercial motive. Its actions and decisions are based on general non-commercial considerations, but such actions and decisions may, nevertheless, hinder access to markets and/or distort free competition (Chapter 4). In Chapter 3 the thesis made a distinction between two categories: namely, contracting authorities and public authorities, although both are indifferently referred to as a 'public authorities'. A contracting authority is defined as such in the EU public procurement Directives. The CJEU has itself defined the essence of the term 'public authority'; namely, public authorities are in general entities that do not perform their activities, which are not of a commercial nature, on the market.

Cooperation amongst public authorities, as discussed in Chapter 3, must be a contract and more specifically a service concession or a public contract. According to the CJEU a contract is an agreement concluded between two independent legal persons who have a certain freedom to negotiate the content of the contract. The independent character of the relationship between the two parties defines it as a contract. The major difference between a public contract and a service concession is the nature of the quid pro quo. In a public contract the contracting public authority pays a price. In a service concession the public authority transfers an exploitation right. Additionally, all or a significant share of the risk must also be transferred along with the transfer of this right. In both contracts the public authority charges a third party to execute an economic activity.

The term 'public service task' is defined neither by EU law nor by the CJEU. A premise of the thesis in Chapter 3 is that this term should have the same meaning in regard to the application of EU law as does the term 'service of general interest'. In any definition of this term, there is one element that must be present; namely, the element 'general interest'. Such service exists if a public authority takes measures to entrust an activity that has a universal and compulsory nature.

This thesis thus concerns itself with cooperative agreements between public authorities when these agreements are about the organization or management of public service tasks. The next key question is to establish the applicable law in the case of such a decision to cooperate. As indicated in the chapter 1 of this thesis, a central question is to determine the extent to which EU law has a bearing on national administrative law governing cooperative agreements between public authorities.

In most European countries public authorities discharge services of general interest. A separate body of law gradually came into being in the Member States, applied exclusively to the actions and decisions of public authorities. The functioning and the organisation of these public authorities are also governed by the same body of law that became known as 'national administrative law'. (see chapter 6)

The way public authorities are organised is freely chosen in many of the EU Member States. This means that they are able to discharge the tasks of general interest themselves or they may call upon a third party, a private undertaking, another public authority or choose to privatise public service tasks. In any case each Member State decides by itself which rules shall be applicable to the organisation and management of their public service tasks. This thesis selected in chapter 6 the French and English legal systems as examples to demonstrate how each legal system addresses the situation.

In France, administrative law occupies a separate place in the legal system. This special place is defined by the term *'service public'*. The discharge of tasks in the general interest requires the application of special divergent legal rules to the bulk of the actions of a public authority. To take on tasks of general interest French public authorities provide them in-house or in cooperation with other parties. The choice between these two kinds of management is free. Even the choice to cooperate with another public authority, to this end, is free. There is complete freedom to organise the *'service public'*, as was demonstrated in chapter 6.

The concept of 'public service' is unknown in England according to chapter 6. To develop a separate administrative law was also unimportant. It was not until the second half of the 20th century that administrative law was recognised as a separate branch of law. The actions and decisions of any public authority, for the most part, fell under English common law, even when public authorities wished to conclude a contract. In each and every situation a public authority was free to decide how it wished to organise its public service tasks and moreover, to choose a third party as a contracting partner.

The central question this thesis poses is whether EU law is relevant to cooperative agreements between public authorities and, more precisely to the decision of a public authority to enter into such an agreement. In order to answer this question the thesis examined in chapter 4 how EU law might have impacted on the activities of public authorities and what element of EU internal market law could be relevant to explain the CJEU case law on cooperative agreements between public authorities. Furthermore, the public procurement Directives and the CJEU case law interpreting these Directives were analysed in chapter 5 to verify i) to what extent EU law has a bearing and ii) under what conditions these cooperative agreements fall under the scope of EU law. Finally this thesis examined in chapter 6 to what extent EU law has influenced existing national (administrative) law.

Regarding the first aspect of the research this thesis makes clear in chapter 4 that the influence of EU law on cooperative agreements between public authorities could be explained on the basis of internal market law. EU competition law can not explain this case law. This thesis proposes in Chapter 4 that the decision to cooperate with a third party actually should be deemed equivalent to a 'State measure'. This decision can influence events on the market. This thesis postulates that the third party helps the public authority in the organisation or the management of its public service tasks. Thus the third party provides a service and this service is provided for remuneration. Consequently, the provisions concerning free movement of services is especially relevant. Another premise is that for EU law to be applicable to the cooperative agreements of public authorities, the agreements must not concern a purely internal situation, but a cross-border interest has to be present. Thus EU law is relevant to cooperative agreements between public authorities.

The research and argumentation in chapter 4 demonstrates that the criterion of a 'restriction' is the crucial aspect that may explain why cooperative agreements can be excluded from the scope of EU law. The decisions of a public authority to cooperate are subject to EU internal market rules if they can restrict or hinder market access, if they can distort or likely to distort free competition. If a decision (State measure) of a public authority has such an effect the public authority must meet two obligations: First, it must guarantee that all undertakings that may be interested in the conclusion of an agreement have an equal chance to do so. Second, the public authority must guarantee transparency, which means that it must give notice in an appropriate form that it intends to conclude a cooperation agreement and indicate which factors will be under consideration in the agreement.

This thesis claimed in chapter 4 that a distortion of free competition is absent if the object of the decision to cooperate (State measure) is alien to the regulation of an economic activity. This kind of regulation is absent if a public authority takes a decision that is proper or inherent to its own organisation. If a decision is based solely on considerations of general interest and it does not give any advantage to a private undertaking then EU (public procurement) law is not applicable.

The second aspect of this research (Chapter 5) concerned the conditions that determine the applicability of EU law to cooperative agreements between public authorities. This question first came up in regard to public procurement Directives. The central point was the CJEU's interpretation of the concept of 'public contract' and more specifically the element 'contract'. A (public) contract exists, according to the CJEU, even when the two independent legal persons are public authorities. Consequently, in this situation the public authorities are obliged to organise a tendering procedure. Their freedom is restricted. The CJEU also has made clear that no contract exists if an agreement is made internal to the public authority. If a public authority uses its own administration and its own technical resources to perform public service tasks (in-house provision) the public procurement Directives do not apply. Thus, the CJEU has made a first constitutional choice. EU law is not applicable to public authority decisions that concern its internal organisation according to chapter 5.

The CJEU equated this last situation with a situation where the public authority exercises a control similar to that which it exercises over its own departments and the entity carries out the essential part of its activities with the public authority that owns it (quasi-in-house or vertical cooperative agreements). Later the CJEU ruled that the form of cooperation is not important for determining whether public procurement Directives are applicable and hence horizontal cooperative agreements could also be beyond their scope. CJEU case law also makes clear that the same argument applies to service concessions. The CJEU has developed separate criteria for placing vertical or horizontal cooperative agreements beyond the scope of EU law. This thesis then examined in chapter 5 the criteria more thoroughly to determine the objectives they serve. With this case law the CJEU made a second constitutional choice. Under certain conditions EU (public procurement) law is not applicable to cooperative agreements between public authorities.

As stated earlier a vertical cooperative agreement falls outside the scope of EU law if the public authority exercises a control similar to that which it exercises over its own departments and the entity concerned performs the essential part of its activities with the public authority that owns it. Two criteria should be kept separate: i) the control criterion and ii) the activities criterion. Both criteria reflect the idea of the dependence that must subsist between public authorities that work together cooperatively. In regard to the control criterion the CJEU decided that if the service provider has one private party as shareholder, EU law applies to the decision to cooperate. The choice for such a private undertaking without the presence of any tendering procedure could distort free competition. Even if all shareholders are public authorities, EU law may be applicable. In that situation one has to take into account all the legislative provisions and relevant factual circumstances. If, taking into account all these elements the public authority has a decisive influence over both strategic objectives and significant decisions the control criterion is fulfilled. Three factors may determine whether sufficient control is present: (i) capital, (ii) a market orientation character or (iii) the control mechanisms. Secondly, the operator's activities must sub-serve principally the public authority. According to the CJEU the control and activities criterion can be present even if several public authorities are shareholders of the operator. The control of each shareholder can be minor, but it must be effective.

Horizontal cooperative agreements fall outside the scope of EU law insofar as public authorities establish cooperation with one another with the aim of ensuring that the public task they are required to perform is in fact accomplished. This kind of agreement should be governed solely by considerations and requirements relating to the pursuit of objectives in the general interest. As with vertical cooperative agreements the agreement cannot place a private undertaking in a position of advantage *vis-à-vis* its competitors.

According to chapter 5 of this thesis, the criteria that the CJEU has developed to enable vertical and horizontal cooperation to fall beyond the scope of EU law, is an expression of the same idea. A State measure, i.e. a decision to cooperate in the accomplishment of a public task objective, is of no relevance to EU law if it is guided solely by considerations related to the public interest and the measure does not advantage a private undertaking. EU law is developed on the basis of economic objectives and is solely applicable in an economic context. Only State measures that put these objectives at risk give rise to the application of EU law. The measure has to be alien to the regulation of an economic activity. To avoid the risk of distortion the CJEU has 'invented' criteria that express the need for a strong dependent relation between cooperating public authorities. The criteria are, in the vision of the thesis, the reflection of the objectives of the fundamental freedoms and the public procurement Directives. Taking into account the functional interpretation method of the CJEU it interprets these criteria on the basis of these objectives. The criteria also include the vision of the CJEU on the division of powers between the EU and the Member States related to cooperative agreements.

The new Directives on public procurement and service concessions were published in March 2014, and contain provisions that seek to implement CJEU case law on cooperative agreements. However, this thesis makes it clear in chapter 5 that these Directives go further and apply also to situations other than the ones accepted by the CJEU, and place cooperative agreements outside the scope of EU law. Briefly put, the new Directives grant more powers to the Member States than the CJEU. It remains to be seen how the CJEU will interpret these new provisions. In the light of the Treaty objectives, an 'economic' interpretation is required, taking into account the objectives regarding the realisation of an internal market.

Chapter 6 of this thesis then asked if and how the CJEU case law has influenced the national legal systems of France and England. In France, the *Conseil d'Etat* anticipated the CJEU rulings and already in 1998 affirmed the applicability of public procurement Directives on cooperative agreements between public authorities. Secondly, the French legislature integrated the *Teckal* criteria (control and activities) into the *Code des Marchés Publics* in 2001. However, the *Conseil d'Etat* put forth its own criterion for placing cooperative agreements beyond the scope of EU law. If the entity that concluded an agreement with a public authority is not an operator on a competitive market, the public authority does not have to organise a tendering procedure. It can choose to seek its contractor. The *Conseil d'Etat* uses one criterion to exclude both vertical and horizontal cooperative agreements beyond the scope of EU law. Furthermore, even agreements where one pubic authority performs a service for another public authority for remuneration can be excluded from the scope of EU law according to the *Conseil d'Etat*. This goes far beyond the CJEU case law. The French legislator also took action. It created a new kind of legal person (*société publique locale*), whereby a contract newly concluded between a public authority with such a legal person will necessarily fall beyond the scope of EU law. But the case law of the *Conseil d'Etat* indicates that this is not always the case. (see chapter 6)

In England the influence of EU law is less obvious. Government documents, examined in chapter 6, show that CJEU case law on cooperative agreements is indeed taken into account. The influence is more difficult to show as there is much less case law concerning the application of public procurement Directives or the principle of equality. This consequently is also the situation with cooperative agreements. Existing case law does indeed show that the difference between in-house provision and provision of services by a third party is taken into account. The English courts clearly specify that for the first category no tendering procedure needs be organised. As for cooperative agreements, the Supreme Court reverted to the objective of the public procurement Directives to establish that under certain circumstances EU law was not applicable to cooperative agreements. The Supreme Court applies the CJEU criteria more consistently than the *Conseil d'Etat*. The Supreme Court also seems to draw a link between CJEU case law on vertical and horizontal cooperative agreements. In England there was no legislative initiative to adapt legislation to CJEU case law on cooperative agreements. But this will presumably now be necessary with the new Directives. (see chapter 5)

The research questions that can be found at the beginning of this chapter could be answered in the following way:

A) Cooperative agreements concluded between national public authorities come within the scope of EU (public procurement) law

   (a) The CJEU and the 2014 Directives on public contracts and service concession confirm that the decision to tender or conclude a public contract and service concession comes under the scope of EU law even if the object of these contracts is the organisation of management of a public task.
   (b) The public authority's decision to cooperate is a State measure. As such it can be influenced by EU internal market law. If these decisions have a cross-border interest and they distort competition or hinder market access (restriction), EU internal market law applies. The obstacle to market access or the distortion of competition explains when a decision to cooperate enters into the scope of EU law. According to the thesis this also explains the CJEU case law on cooperative agreements.
   (c) Vertical cooperative agreements fall outside the scope of EU law if the public authority exercises a control similar to that which it exercises over its own departments and the entity concerned performs the essential part of its activities with the public authority that owns it. Horizontal cooperative agreements fall outside the scope of EU law insofar as public authorities establish cooperation with one another with the aim of ensuring that the public task they are required to perform is in fact accomplished. This kind of agreement should be governed

solely by considerations and requirements relating to the pursuit of objectives in the general interest. The agreement cannot place a private undertaking in a position of advantage *vis-à-vis* its competitors.

B) The CJEU case law on cooperative agreements has had an influence on national law in France and England.

(a) In France and England public authorities discharge their public service tasks in house or in cooperation with third parties.
(b) Public authorities also cooperate with one another to discharge public service tasks.
(c) Especially the case law of the Supreme Courts in both countries takes account of the CJEU case law. Moreover, in France the legislator has intervened to provide a framework for vertical cooperation between local public authorities.

This thesis makes clear that the influence of EU law on national law is also significant in areas that in principle are within the exclusive competence of the Member States. In particular, this influence is felt in administrative law. This is an area of the law inextricably associated with the uniquely autonomous nature of each Member State and is applicable to the way Member States and their public authorities organise and manage their public administration. National administrative law is increasingly acquiring an EU coloration so that the notion of 'European administrative law' is becoming more and more apposite.

EU law sees this national administrative law through economic spectacles. This branch of the law governs the decisions of public authorities. However, when decisions (State measures) have consequences for the market, some of the other provisions of the EU treaties may be relevant. These decisions must not imperil the realisation of the internal market.

The driving force behind this influence is the CJEU via its functional interpretation of EU law. But this interpretation is also reaffirmed by the regulatory capacity of EU institutions in this area. Provisions on cooperative agreements between public authorities may now be found in the new Directives adopted in March 2014. Compared to the CJEU's broad interpretation, the new Directives bring within their scope more situations in which cooperative agreements between public authorities fall outside the scope of EU law. Thus the Member States are able to bring their influence to bear and restrict the impact of EU law on its national administrative law.

This also shows that the division of competences between the EU and Member States, and the relationship between Market and State is still evolving. The European economic constitution is continually in evolution. However, the new Directives display a tendency for the Member States to turn inwards toward themselves and also show a certain mistrust of the EU.

BIBLIOGRAPHY

1. Books

Arrowsmith, S., *Civil liability and public authorities,* (Winteringham, Earlsgate Press, 1992)

Arrowsmith, S., *The law of public and utilities procurement* (London: Sweet & Maxwell, 2005).

Arrowsmith, S. and Kunzlik, P. (eds.), *Social and environmental policies in EC procurement law,* (Cambridge, Cambridge University Press, 2009).

Arrowsmith, S., *EU Public Procurement Law: an introduction,* www.nottingham.ac.uk.pprg.

Arrowsmith, S., *The law of public and utilities procurement,* Vol. I, (London, Sweet & Maxwell, 2014).

Auby, J.-B. (dir.), *L'influence du droit européen sur les catégories du droit public* (Paris: Dalloz, 2010).

Auby, J.-B. and Dutheil de la Rochère, J. (dir.), *Droit administratif européen* (Bruxelles: Bruylant, 2007).

Auby, J.-B. and Dutheil de la Rochère, J. (dir.), *Traité de droit administratif européen* (Bruxelles: Bruylant, 2014).

Bamforth, N. and Leyland, P. (eds.), *Public law in a Multi-Layered constitution* (Oxford: Hart Publishing, 2003).

Baquero-Cruz, J., *Between Competition and Free Movement the Economic Constitutional Law of the European Community* (London: Hart Publishing, 2002).

Barnard, C. and Scott, J. (eds.), *The Law of the Single European Market: Unpacking the Premises* (Oxford/Portland: Hart Publishing, 2002).

Barnard, C., *The Substantive Law of the EU,* 4th edn (Oxford: OUP, 2013).

Beatson, J., Burrows, A. and Cartwright, J., *Anson's Law of contract* (Oxford: OUP, 2010).

Bertrand, B., *Le juge de l'Union européenne, juge administratif* (Brussels: Bruylant, 2012).

Bovis, C., *EC Public Procurement: case law and regulation* (Oxford: OUP, 2006).

Bovis, C., *EU public procurement law* (Cheltenham: Edgar European Law, 2012).

Braconnier, S., *Droit des services Publics* (Paris: PUF, 2007).

Bradley, A.W. and Ewing, K.D., *Constitutional and Administrative Law* (London: Pearson, 2005).

Brameret, S., *Les relations des collectivités territoriales avec les sociétés d'économie mixte locales* (Paris: LGDJ, 2012).
Casalini, D., *L'organismo di diritto pubblico e l'organizzazione in house* (Napoli: Jovene Editori, 2003).
Chalmers, D., Davies, G. and Monti, G., *European Union Law* (Cambridge: Cambridge University Press, 2010).
Chapus, R., *Droit administratif Général*, T.1 (Paris: Montchréstien, 2001).
Clamour, G., *Intérêt général et concurrence* (Paris: Dalloz, 2006).
Comba, M. and Treumer, S. (eds.), *The In-house Providing in European Law* (Copenhagen: Djøf Publishing, 2010).
Craig, P. and De Burca, G., *EU Law* (Oxford: OUP, 2011).
Craig, P., *Administration Law* (London: Sweet and Maxwell, 2012).
Craig, P., *The Lisbon Treaty* (Oxford: OUP, 2010).
Dashwood, A., Dougan, M., Rodger, B., Spaventa, E. and Wyatt, D., *Wyatt and Dashwood's European Union Law* (London: Hart Publishing, 2011).
Davies, A., Accountability: *A public law analysis of government by contract* (Oxford: OUP, 2001).
Davies, A., *The Public Law of Government Contracts* (Oxford: OUP, 2008).
De Koninck, C. and Flamey, P., *Overheidsopdrachten* (Antwerpen: Maklu, 2006).
de Laubadère, A., *Traité élémentaire de droit administrative* (Paris: 1953).
de Laubadère, A., Moderne, F. and Delvolvé, P., *Traité des contrats administratifs*, T. 1 (Paris: LGDJ, 1981).
Dicey, A.V., *The Law of the Constitution* (1885).
Donelly, C.M., *Delegation of governmental power to private parties* (Oxford: OUP, 2007).
Dreyfus, J.D., *Contribution a une théorie générale des contrats entre personnes publiques* (Paris: L'Harmattan, 1997).
Duguit, L., *Les transformations du droit public* (1913).
Durviaux, A.L., *Logique de marché et marché public en droit communautaire* (Bruxelles: Larcier, 2006).
Eckert, G., Gautier, Y., Kovar, R. and Ritleng, D. (dir.), *Incidences du droit communautaire sur le droit public français* (Strasbourg: Presses Universitaires de Strasbourg, 2007).
Fallon, M., *Droit matériel général de Union européenne* (Bruxelles: Bruylant, 2002).
Favoreu, L. and Philip, L., *Les grandes décisions du Conseil Constitutionnel* (Paris: Dalloz).
Fernandez Martin, J.M., *The EC Public procurement rules: a critical analysis* (Oxford: Clarendon Press, 1996).
Flamme, M.A., Matheï, Ph., Flamme, Ph., Delvaux, A. and Dardenne, Cl., *Praktische commentaar bij de reglementering van de overheidsopdrachten*, 1A (Brussel: NCB, 1996–1997).
Frier, P.-L. and Petit, J., *Précis de droit administratif* (Paris: Montchrestien, 2010).
Frier, P.-L. and Petit, J., *Droit administratif* (Paris: Montchrestien, 2012).
Gadhouin, P.-Y., *La liberté contractuelle dans la jurisprudence du Conseil constitutionnel* (Paris: Dalloz, 2008).
Gaudemet, Y., *Traité de droit administratif*, T.1 (Paris: LGDJ, 2001).

Gonod, P., Melleray, F. and Yolka, Ph. (dir.), *Traité de droit administratif*, T.2 (Paris: Dalloz, 2011).
Gosselin, F., Molitor, C., Nihoul, P. and Quertainemont, Ph. (eds.), *Les modes de cooperation des services publics locaux au regard du droit européen* (Waterloo: Kluwer, 2008).
Graells, A.S., *Public procurement and the EU Competition Rules* (Oxford: Hart Publishing, 2011).
Guettier, Ph., *Droit des contrats administratifs* (Paris: Thémis, 2008).
Gugliemi, G.J. and Koubi, G. with Dumont, G., *Droit du service public* (Paris: Montchrestien, 2007).
Guinard, D., *Réflexions sur la construction d'une notion juridique: l'exemple de la notion de services d'intérêt général* (Paris: l'Harmattan, 2012).
Hansen, C.R., *Contracts not covered or not fully covered by the Public Sector Directive* (Copenhagen: Djøf Publishing, 2012).
Harden, I., *The Contracting State* (Buckingham: Open University Press, 1992).
Hardraht, K., *In-House-Geschäfte und Europäisches Vergaberecht* (Berlin: Dunckler & Humblot, 2006).
Harlow, C. and Rawlings, R., *Law and administration* (Cambridge: CUP, 2009).
Hatzopoulos, V., *Regulating Services in the European Union* (Oxford: OUP, 2012).
Hauriou, M., *La gestion administrative, étude historique du droit administratif* (Paris: 1899).
Hjelmborg, S.E., Jacobsen, P.S. and Poulsen, S.T., *Public procurement law* (Copenhagen: Djøf Publishing, 2006).
Hughes, O.E., *Public management and Administration: an Introduction* (Basingstoke: Palgrave Macmillan, 2003).
Jans, J.H., De Lange, R., Prechal, S. en Widdershoven, R.J.G.M., *Inleiding tot het Europees bestuursrecht* (Nijmegem: Ars Aequi Libri, 2002).
Jans, J.H., Delange, R., Prechal, S. and Widdershoven, R.J.G.M. (dir.), *Europeanisation of Public law* (Groningen: Europa Law Publishing, 2007).
Kapteyn, P.J.G., McDonnell, A.M., Mortelmans, K.J.M. and Timmermans, C.W.A., *The Law of the European Union and the European Communities* (Alphen aan den Rijn: Kluwer Law International, 2008).
Lamont, N., *Chancellor of the exchequer, Autumn Statement*, vol. 128, col. 996 (12 November 1992).
Leger, P. (éd.), *Commentaire article par article des traités UE et CE* (Paris: Dalloz, 2000).
Lenaerts, K. and Van Nuffel, P., *Constitutional law of the European Union* (Oxford: OUP, 2005).
Lenaerts, K. and Van Nuffel, P., *European Union Law* (London: Sweet & Maxwell, 2011).
Lenaerts, K., *Le juge et la Constitution aux Etats Unis d'Amérique et dans l'ordre juridique européen* (Bruxelles: Bruylant,1988).
Lichère, F., *Droit des contrats publics* (Paris: Dalloz, 2005).
Long, M., Weil, P., Braibant, G., Delvolvé, P. and Genvois, B., *Les grands arrêts de la jurisprudence administrative* (Paris: Dalloz, 2009).

Lott, K., *Die Rechtsprechung des EuGH und die In-House-Vergabe in Deutschland* (Saarbrücken: VDM Verlag Dr. Muller, 2008).Marique, Y., *Public-private partnerships and the law*, (Cheltenham, Edward Elgar, 2014).
Müller-Graff, P.-C., *Gemeinsames Privatrecht in der Europäischen Gemeinschaft* (Baden-Baden: Nomos, 1993).
Neill, P., *The European CJEU: A Case Study in Judicial Activism* (London: European Policy Forum, 1995).
Oliver, D. and Drewry, G., *Public Service Reforms: Issues of Accountability and Public Law* (London: Pinter, 1996).
Oliver, D., *Common Values and the Public-Private Divide* (London: Butterworths, 1999).
Péquignot, G., *Théorie générale du contrat administratif* (Paris: Pédone, 1945).
Pernas Garcia, J.J., *Los operaciones in house y el Derecho comunitario de contratos publicos* (Madrid: Iustel, 2008).
Peters, A., *Theorie der Elemente der Verfassung Europas* (Berlin: Duncker & Humblot, 2001).
Poiares Maduro, M., *We the Court, The European Court of Justice and the European Economic Constitution. A Critical Reading of Article 30 of the EC Treaty* (Oxford: Hart, 1998).
Prechal, S., *Directives in EC law* (Oxford: OUP, 2004).
Pynacker Hordijk, E.H., Van Der Bend, G.W. and Van Nouhuys, J.F., *Aanbestedingsrecht* (Den Haag: Sdu Uitgevers, 2009).
Rasmussen, H., *On Law and Policy in the European Court of justice. A Comparative Study in Judicial Policy-Making* (Dordrecht: Martinus Nijhoff Publishers, 1986).
Reich, N., *Understanding EU law: Objectives, Principles and Methods of Community Law* (Antwerp/Oxford: Intersentia, 2005).
Richer, L., *Droit des contrats administratifs* (Paris: LGDJ, 2008).
Richer, L., *L'Europe des marchés publics* (Paris: LGDJ, 2009).
Richer, L., *La qualité du cocontractant de l'administration; contrats entre collectivités publiques* (Paris: Ed. Le Moniteur, 1996).
Sauter, W., and Schepel, H., *State and Market in European Union Law* (Cambridge: Cambridge University Press, 2009).
Schwarze, J., *European administrative law* (London: Sweet and Maxwell, 1992).
Shiubhne, N.N. (ed.), *Regulating the Internal Market* (Cheltenham/Northampton: Edward Elgar Publishing, 2006).
Sirinelli, J., *Les transformations du droit administratif par le droit de l'Union européenne* (Paris: LGDJ, 2011).
Snell, J., *Goods and Services in EC Law* (Oxford: OUP, 2002).
Symchowisz, N., *Droit public des montages contractuels complexes* (Paris: Imprimerie Nationale Éditions, 2003).
Szyszczak, E., *The Regulation of the State in Competitive Markets in the EU* (Oxford: Hart Publishing, 2007).
Trepte, P., *Regulating procurement. Understanding the ends and means of public procurement regulation* (Oxford: OUP, 2004).
Trepte, P., *Public procurement in the EU* (Oxford: OUP, 2007).
Vedel, G. and Delvolvé, P., *Droit administratif* (Paris: PUF, 1988).
Vincent-Jones, P., *The New Public Contracting* (Oxford: OUP, 2006).

Wade, H.W.R. and Forsyth, C.F., *Administrative law* (Oxford: OUP, 2009).
Waline, M., *Droit administratif* (Paris: Dalloz, 2010).
Waline, M., *Droit administratif* (Paris: Dalloz, 2012).
Wauters, K., *Rechtsbescherming en overheidsovereenkomsten* (Antwerpen: Intersentia, 2009).
Weiss, F., *Public procurement in European Community Law* (London: Athlone, 1993).
Woods, L., *Free Movement of Goods and Services within the European Community* (Ashgate: Aldershot, 2004).

2. Chapters in books

Auby, J.-B., 'La distinction du droit public et du droit privé', in J.-B. Auby (dir.), *L'influence du droit européen sur les catégories du droit public* (Paris: Dalloz, 2010).
Armin, H., 'The Economic Constitution within the Internal Market', in von Bogdandy, A. and Bast, J. (eds.), *Principles of European Constitutional Law* (Munich: C.H. Beck/ Oxford: Hart Publishing, 2011), pp. 589–629.
Arrowsmith, S. and Kunzlik, P., 'EC regulation of public procurement', in Arrowsmith, S. and Kunzlik, P., *Social and environmental Policies in EC Procurement Law* (Cambridge: Cambridge University Press, 2009), pp. 55–107.
Auby, J.-B. and Dutheil de la Rochère, J., 'Introduction générale', in Auby, J.-B. and Dutheil de la Rochère, J. (dir.), *Droit administratif européen* (Bruxelles: Bruylant, 2007), pp. 3–4.
Barnard, C., 'Derogations, Justifications and the Four Freedoms: Is State Interest Really Protected?', in Barnard, C. and Odudu, O. (eds.), *The Outer Limits of European Union Law* (Oregon: Hart Publishing, 2009), pp. 273–315.
Barrière, L.-A., 'Une approche historique de la summa divisio droit public-droit privé', in B. Bonnet et P. Deumier, De *l'interet de la summa divisio droit public-droit prive?*, (Paris: Dalloz, 2010).
Beaud, C., 'La distinction entre droit public et droit privé: un dualisme qui résiste aux critiques', in J.-B. Auby and M. Freedland (eds.), *The Public/Private Divide: une entente assez cordiale?*, (Paris: Editions Panthéon-Arras, 2004).
Bell, J. and Kennedy, T.P., 'La notion de service public au Royaume-Unie et en Irlande', in Moderne, F. and Marcou, G. (eds), *L'idée de service public dans le droit des Etats de l'Union Européenne* (Paris: l'Harmattan, 2001), pp. 259–313.
Bleeker, R.G.T. and Manunza, E.R., 'De invloed van het Europees recht op het Nederlandse aanbestedingsrecht', in Hartkamp, A.S., Sieburgh, C.H. and Keus, L.A.D. (eds.), *De invloed van het Europese recht op het Nederlandse privaatrecht* (Deventer: Kluwer, 2007), pp. 543–598.
Burgi, M., '"In-House" Providing in Germany', in Comba, M. and Treumer, S. (eds.), *The In-House Providing in European Law* (Copenhagen: Djøf Publishing, 2010), pp. 71–93.
Caranta, R., 'The In-House Providing: The Law as it Stands in the EU', in Comba, M. and Treumer, S. (eds.), *The In-House Providing in European Law* (Copenhagen: Djøf Publishing, 2010), pp. 13–52.

Casalini, D., 'Beyond EU Law: the New "Public House"', in Olykke, G.S., Hansen, C.R. and Tvarno, C.D., *EU Public Procurement – Modernisation, Growth and Innovation* (Copenhagen: Djøf Publishing, 2011), pp. 151–178.

Comba, M., 'In-House Providing in Italy: the circulation of a model', in Comba, M. and Treumer, S. (Eds.), *The In-house providing in European law* (Copenhagen: Djøf Publishing, 2010), pp. 95–117.

Cotte, O., 'La répartition des compétences entre l'Union et ses Etats membres dans le domaine des services d'intérêt économique général', in G. Eckert, Y. Gautier, R. Kovar and D. Ritleng, *Incidences du droit communautaire sur le droit public français*, (Strasbourg: Presses universitaires de Strasbourg, 2007).

Craig, P. and Trybus, M., 'England and Wales', in Nogouellou, R. and Stelkens, U. (eds), *Comparative Law on public contracts* (Brussels: Bruylant, 2010), pp. 339–366.

D'Hooghe, D., Vos, I. and De Keyser, Ph., 'Recente evoluties in het aanbestedingsrecht', in De Ketelaere, K. and Verbeke, A. (eds.), *Jaarboek Bouwrecht 2004-2005* (Brugge: Die Keure, 2005), pp. 4–20.

de Broux, P.-O., 'Historique et transformation de la notion de service public à la lumière du droit européen', in Dumont, H., Jadoul, P., Lombaert, B., Tulkens, F. and Van Drooghenbroeck, S. (eds.), *Le service public*, T. 1 (Brussels: La Charte, 2009), pp. 1–56.

De Witte, B., 'Interpreting the EC Treaty like a constitution: the role of the European Court of Justice in comparative perspective', in Bakker, R., Heringa, A.W. en Stroink, F. (eds.), *Judicial Control* (Antwerpen: Maklu, 1995), pp.133–152.

Delvolvé, P., 'Constitution et contrats publics', in *Mouvement du droit public. Mélanges Franck Moderne* (Paris: Dalloz, 2004), pp. 469–499.

Drexl, J., 'Competition Law as Part of the European Constitution', in von Bogdandy, A. and Bast, J. (eds.), *Principles of European Constitutional Law* (Munich: C.H. Beck/ Oxford: Hart Publishing, 2011), pp. 659–698.

Dubouis, L., 'Service public et droit de l'Union européenne un perpétuel débat', in *Juger l'administration, administrer la justice: Mélanges en l'honneur du Daniel Labetoulle* (Paris: Dalloz, 2007), pp. 293–306.

Durviaux, A.L., 'La "logique de marché" dans les relations contractuelles entre le secteur public et le secteur privé: développements récents', in Thirion, N. (ed.), *Le marché et l'Etat à l'heure de la mondialisation* (Bruxelles: Larcier, 2007), pp. 41–102.

Eckert, G., 'La cooperation public-public, entre espoirs et inquiétudes', in *Mélanges en l'honneur du professeur Richer* (Paris: LGDJ, 2013), pp. 617–632.

Eckert, G., 'La distinction entre les services d'intérêt économique général et les services d'intérêt général non-économiques', in Potvin-Solis, L. (dir.), Huitièmes Journées d'Etudes du Pôle Européen Jean Monnet, *La libération des services d'intérêt économique général en réseau en Europe* (Bruxelles: Bruylant, 2010), pp. 3–21.

Flauss, J.-F., 'Rapport français', in Schwarze, J. (ed.), *Das Verwaltungsrecht unter europaïschem Einfluß* (Baden-Baden: Nomos, 1996), pp. 31–121.

Fort, F.-X., 'Les aspects administratifs de la liberté contractuelle', in X., *Contrats publics. Mélanges en l'honneur du Professeur Michel Guibal*, I (Montpellier: CREAM, 2006), pp. 27–43.

Hansen, C.R., 'Defining a Service Concession Contract will the proposed new definition of service concession contracts increase legal legality in the field of concessions', in

Olykke, G.S., Hansen, C.R. and Tvarno, C.D. (eds.), *EU Public procrurement – Modernisation*, Growth and Innovation (Copenhagen: Djøf publishing, 2012), pp. 239–250.

Hatje, A., 'The Economic Constitution within the Internal Market', in Bogdandy, A. v. and Bast, J. (eds), *Principles of European Constitutional Law*, 2nd edn (Oxford: Hart/Beck, 2010), pp. 589–622.

Hulst, R. and Van Montfort, A., 'Inter-municipal cooperation: a widespread phenomenon', in R. Hulst and A. van Montfort (eds.), *Inter-Municipal cooperation in Europe*, (Dordrecht: Springer, 2007).

Jarass, H.D., 'A Unified Approach to the Fundamental Freedoms', in Andenas, M. and Roth, W.-H. (eds.), *Services and Free Movement in EU Law* (Oxford: OUP, 2002), pp. 141–162.

Jegouzo, Y., 'L'administration contractuelle en question', in X., *Mouvement du droit public. Mélanges en l'honneur de Franck Moderne* (Paris: Dalloz, 2004), pp. 543–546.

Joerges, C., 'Unity in Diversity as Europe's Vocation and Conflicts Law as Europe's Constitutional Form', in Nickel, R. and Greppi, A. (eds.), *The Changing Role of Law in the Age of Supra- and Transnational Governance* (Baden-Baden: Nomos, 2012), pp. 99–133.

Joerges, C. and Rödl, F., 'The "Social Market Economy" as Europe's Social Model?', in Magnusson, L. and Stråth, B. (eds.), *A European Social Citizenship? Preconditions for Future Policies in Historical Light* (Brussels: Lang, 2005), pp. 125–158.

Lang, J.T., 'Article 10 EC – The most important "General Principle" of Community Law', in Bernitz, U., Nergelius, J. en Cardner, C. (eds.), *General Principles of EC Law in a Process of Development* (Alphen aan den Rijn: Kluwer Law International, 2007), pp. 76–113.

Lenaerts, K. and Vanvoorden, K., 'The right to property in the case law of the Court of Justice of the European Communities', in Vandenberghe, H. (ed.), *Property and human rights* (Brugge: Die Keure, 2006), pp. 195–240.

Lenaerts, K., 'Les services d'intérêt général et le droit communautaire', in *Rapport public du Conseil d'Etat* (2002), pp. 425–437.

Lichère, F., 'New Award Procedures', in Trybus, M., Caranta, R. and Edelstam, G. (eds.), *European Union Law of Public Contracts* (Brussel: Bruylant, 2013), pp. 83–95.

Maduro, M., 'Contrapunctual [sic] Law: Europe's Consitutional Pluralism in Action', in Walker, N. (ed), *Sovereignty in Transition* (Oxford: Hart, 2003), pp. 501–537.

Picard, E., 'The Public-Private Divide in French law through the History and Destiny of French Administrative Law', in M. Rüffert (ed.), *The Public-Private Law Divide: Potential for transformation*, (London: British Institute of International and Comparative Law, 2009).

Malaret Garcia, E., 'Public service, Public services, Public functions, and Guarantees of the Rights of Citizens: Unchanging needs in a changed context', in M. Freeland and S. Sciarra (eds.), *Public services and citizenship in European law*, (Oxford: Clarendon Press, 1998).

Malvasio, F., 'Les catégories du droit administratif économique et du service public', in Auby, J.-B. (dir.), *L'influence du droit européen sur les catégories du droit public* (Paris: Dalloz, 2010), pp. 739–776.

Marique, Y., 'An English Legal perspective on Public-private partnerships', in Lichère, F. (eds), *Public-Private Partnership Reports of the XVIII Congress of the Internatinal Academy of Comparative Law* (Brussels: Bruylant, 2011), pp. 95–165.

Moderne, F., 'Les transcriptions doctrinales de l'idée de service public', in Moderne, F. and Marcou, G. (dir.), *L'idée de service public dans le droit des états de l'Union européenne* (Paris: L'Harmattan, 2001), pp. 9–82.

Nabli, B., 'L'autorité publique et la puissance publique', in Auby, J.-B. (dir.), *L'influence du droit européen sur les categories du droit public* (Paris: Dalloz, 2010), pp. 331–353.

Neergaard, U., 'Services of general economic interest under EU law constraints', in Schiek, D., Liebert, U. and Schneider, H. (eds.), *European Economic and Social Constitutionalism after the Treaty of Lisbon* (Cambridge: Cambridge University Press, 2011), pp. 174–196.

Neergaard, U., 'Services of General Economic Interest', in Krajewski, M., Neergaard, U. and Van Den Gronden, J. (eds), *The Changing Legal Framework for Services of General Interest in Europe* (TMC Asser Press, 2009), pp. 17–50.

Nicinski, S., 'Le dogme de l'autonomie de la volonté dans les contrats administratifs', in Clamour, G. en Ubaud-Bergeron, M. (eds), *Contrats publics, Mélanges en l'honneur du Professeur Michel Guibal*, T.I (Montpeller: CREAM, 2006), pp. 47–50.

Nielsen, R., 'Framework Agreements', in Nielsen, R. and Treumer, S. (eds), *The new EU Public Procurement Directives* (Copenhagen: Djøf Publishing, 2005), pp. 81–96.

Odudu, O., 'Economic activity as a limit to community law', in Barnard, C. and Odudu, O., *The Outer Limits of European Union Law* (Oregon: Hart Publishing, 2009), pp. 225–243.

Pelikánová, I., 'The Role of Competition Law in the Evolution of Community Law', in H. Kanninen et al. (eds.), *EU Competition Law in Context: Essays in Honour of Virpi Tiili*, (Oxford: Hart Publishing, 2009).Pilone, C., 'Reflexions autour de la notion de contrat "in house"', in Clamour, G. and Ubaud-Bergeron, M. (eds.), *Contrats publics. Mélanges en honneur du Professeur Michel Guibal*, Vol. I (Montpellier: CREAM, 2006), pp. 702–717.

Pini, J., 'Autorité et contrat dans l'administration moderne en France', in X., *Annuaire Européen d'administration publique* (P.U.A., 1997), pp. 73–88.

Poiares Maduro, M., 'The scope of European remedies. The case of purely internal situations and reverse discrimination', in Kilpatrick, C., Novitz, T. and Skidmore, P. (eds), *The Future of European Remedies* (Oxford: Hart publishing, 2000), pp. 117–140.

Poiares Maduro, M., 'The Chameleon State: EU Law and the Blurring of the Private/Public Distinction in the Market', in R. Nickel (ed.), *Conflict of Laws and Laws of Conflict in Europe and Beyond - Patterns of Supranational and Transnational Juridification*, (Antwerp - Oxford - Portland: Intersentia, 2010).

Richer, L., 'L'introduction de la notion d'activité économique dans le droit des contrats publics', in Conseil d'Etat, *Rapport public 2008. Le contrat, mode d'action publique et de production de normes* (Paris: EDCE, 2008), pp. 355–367.

Ritling, D., 'L'incidence du droit de l'Union Européenne sur les catégories organiques du droit administratifs', in J.-B. Auby and J. Duteuil de la Rochère (eds.), *Traité de droit administratif européen*, (Bruxelles: Bruylant, 2014).

Rubach-Larsen, A., 'Competitive Dialogue', in R. Nielsen and S. Treumer (eds.), *The New EU Public Procurement Directives* (Copenhagen: Djøf Publishing, 2005), pp. 71–80.

Rüffert, M., 'The Transformation of Administrative Law as a Transnational Methodological System', in Rüffert, M. (ed.), *The Transformation of Administrative Law* (Sellier: European Law Publishers, 2007), pp. 3–52.

Ruiz-Jarabo Colomer, D., 'L'engagement contractuel dans la jurisprudence de la Cour de justice des Communautés européennes', in *Conseil d'Etat. Rapport public 2008. Le contrat, mode d'action publique et de production de normes* (Paris: La documentation française, 2008), pp. 369–381.

Schweitzer, H., 'Services of general interest: European Law's Impact on the Role of Markets and of Member States', in Cremona, M. (ed.), *Market Integration and Public Services in the European Union* (Oxford: Oxford University Press, 2011), pp. 11–62.

Smit, H. and Herzog, P.E., 'Preliminary observations on article 222', in Smit, H. and Herzog, P.E., *The Law of the European Community – A commentary on the EEC Treaty*, Vol. 5 (New York: Mattew Bunder, 1998).

Taggart, M., 'Reinventing Administrative Law', in Bamforth, N. and Leyland (eds), *Public Law in a multi layered constitution* (Oxford: Hart Publishing, 2003), pp. 311–334.

Triantafyllou, D., 'Les mutations de la notion de service public en droit comparé', in *Service public et Communauté Européenne entre intérêt général et le marché* (Paris: La documentation française, 1998), pp. 33–66.

Truchet, D., 'Le contrat administratif, qualification juridique d'un accord de volontés', in Cadier, L. (ed.), *Le droit contemporain des contrats. Bilan et perspectives* (Paris: Economica, 1987), pp. 185 et s.

Trybus, M. and Caranta, R., 'European Union Law of Public Contracts: Public Procurement and Beyond', in Trybus, M., Caranta, R. and Edelstam, G. (eds.), *European Union Law of Public Contracts* (Brussel: Bruylant, 2013), pp. 1–12.

Trybus, M., 'From the indivisible crown to *Teckal*: the In-House provision of works and services in the United Kingdom', in Comba, M. and Treumer, S. (eds), *The In-House providing in European Law* (Copenhagen: Djöf Publishing, 2010), pp. 187–211.

Trybus, M., 'Public contracts in European Union Internal Market Law: Foundations and Requirements', in Noguellou, R. and Stelkens, U. (eds.), *Comparative law on Public Contracts* (Brussel: Bruylant, 2010), pp. 81–121.

Trybus, M., 'An Overview of the United Kingdom Public Procurement Review and Remedies System with an Emphasis on England and Wales', in S. Treumer and F. Lichère (eds.), *Enforcement of the EU public procurement rules*, (Copenhagen: Djøf Publishing, 2011).

Wang, P., Cavallo Perin, R. and Casalini, D., 'Addressing purchasing agreements between public sector entities: what can the WTO learn from the EU's experience?', in Arrowsmith, S. and Anderson, R.D. (Eds.), *The WTO regime on government procurement: challenge and reform* (Cambridge: Cambridge University Press, 2011), pp. 252–282.

Widdershoven, R., 'The principle of loyal cooperation. Lawmaking by the European Court of Justice and the Dutch Courts', in Stroink, F. and van der Linden, E., *Judicial Law-making and Administrative Law* (Antwerpen: Intersentia, 2005), pp. 3–36.

X, 'Un recours accru au contrat pour conduire l'action publique ou édicter des normes', in *Rapport public 2008. Le contrat, mode d'action publique et de production de normes* (Paris: La Documentation Française, 2008), pp. 17–90.
X, 'Contrat, loi et décision administrative unilatérale: des imbrications croissants', in *Rapport public 2008. Le contrat, mode d'action publique et de production de normes* (Paris: La documentation Française, 2008), pp. 91–167.
Zijlstra, S.E., 'De grenzen van de overheid', in X., *Privaat bestuur?* (Den Haag: Boom Juridische Uitgevers, 2008), pp. 9–93.
Ziller, J., 'Les droits administratifs nationaux: caractéristiques générales', in Auby, J.-B. and Dutheil de la Rochère, J. (dir.), *Traité de droit administratif européen* (Bruxelles: Bruylant, 2014), pp. 539–559.

3. Articles

Akkermans, B. and Ramaekers, E., 'Article 345 TFEU (ex Article 295 EC), Its Meaning and Interpretation' (*ELJ*, 2010), pp. 292–314.
Andrews, J., 'European Charter on Local Self-Government' (*ELRev*, 1986), pp. 180–181.
Arrowsmith, S., 'An Assessment of the New Legislative Package on Public Procurement' (*CMLR* 41, 2004), pp. 1–49.
Arrowsmith, S., 'Public Private Partnerships and the European Procurement Rules: EU Policies in conflict?' (*CMLR*, 2000), pp. 709–737.
Arrowsmith, S., 'The past and future evolution of EC procurement law: from framework to common code?' (*PCLJ*, 2006), pp. 337–384.
Arrowsmith, S., 'The purpose of the EU Procurement Directives: ends, means and the implications for national regulatory space for commercial and horizontal procurement policies' (*CYELS*, 2011–2012), pp. 1–47.
Ashmore, R., 'United Kingdom – reminder that contracting authorities can switch to an inhouse "Plan B" solution if it represents value for money and is done in good faith: *Montpellier Estates Ltd v. Leeds City Council*' (*PPLR*, 2013), pp. NA68-NA72.
Auby, J.-B., 'Comparative approaches to the Rise of Contract in the Public Sphere', (*PL*, 2007).
Auby, J.-B., 'Les sociétés publiques sociales. Un outil aux contours incertains' (*RFDA*, 2012), pp. 99–108.
Auby, J.-M., 'La notion de concession et les rapports des collectivités locales et des établissements publics, de l'électricité et du gaz dans la loi du 8 avril 1946' (*CJEG*, 1949), pp. 1 et s.
Avarkioti, F., 'The application of EU Public Procurement Rules to "In-house" arrangements' (*PPLR*, 2007), pp. 22–35.
Bailey, S. H., 'Judicial review of contracting decisions', (*PL* 2007), pp. 444–463.
Bangui, T., 'L'effectivité du contrôle analogue des Sociétés publiques locales' (*CMP* 5, 2012), pp. 6–9.
Bartels, S., 'Europees privaatrecht: over de bevoegdheidsverdeling tussen Unie en lidstaat met betrekking tot het eigendomsrecht' (*AA*, 1999), pp. 244–251.
Bel, G. and Warner, M.E., 'Factors Explaining Inter-municipal Cooperation in Service Delivery: A Meta-Regression Analysis', www.union.wisc.edu/pmra2013/Paper%20

Submissions/Renamed/Factors%20Explaining%20Intermunicipal%20 Contracting%20A%20Meta%20Analysis.pdf.

Bel, G., Fageda, W. and Mur, M., 'Why do municipalities cooperate to provide local public services? An empirical analysis', (*Local Government Studies*, 2013), http://dx.doi.org/10.1080/03003930.2013.781024.

Berthelot, O., 'Liberté du commerce et de l'industrie et transferts de compétences; socialisation de l'économie ou privatisation du service public' (*AJDA*, 2003), pp. 707–710.

Bertrand, V., 'La réforme européenne des marchés publics dans les secteurs classiques' (*JTE*, 2005), pp. 1–11.

Beuter, R., 'European public procurement reform: main innovations in the Public Sector Directive - a preliminary assessment' (*Eipascope* 3, 2005), pp. 5–11.

Birkinshaw, P., 'Contrats publics et contractualisation' (*RFDA*, 2006), pp. 1015 et s.

Bossard, B., 'Le traitement communautaire des services d'intérêt général non economiques' (*RDP*, 2006), p. 1301–1324.

Boussard, S., 'L'éclatement des catégories de service public et la résurgence du "service public par nature"' (*RFDA*, 2008), pp. 43–49.

Boutayeb, C., 'Une recherche générale sur la place et les fonctions de l'intérêt général en droit communautaire' (*RTDE*, 2003), pp. 587–614.

Bovis, Ch., 'Public procurement in the EU: jurisprudence and conceptual directions' (*PPLR*, 2012), pp. 247–289.

Brechon-Moulènes, C., 'La liberté contractuelle des personnes publiques' (*AJDA*, 1998), pp.643–655.

Brown, A., 'Changing a sub-contractor under a public services concession: Wall AG v. Stadt Frankfut am Main C-91/98' (*PPLR*, 2010), pp. 160–166.

Brown, A., 'Whether German public broadcasters are financed for the most part by the state so as to fall within the EU procurement directives: Bayerischers Rundfunk (C-337/06)' (*PPLR*, 2008), pp. NA 124–127.

Cabral, P., 'The internal market and the right to cross border medical care' (*ELR*, 2004), pp. 673–685.

Cane, P., 'Accountability and the public-private Distinction', in N. Bamforth and P. Leyland (eds.), *Public law in a Multi-Layered constitution,* (Oxford: Hart Publishing, 2003), pp. 247–276.

Caro de Sousa, P., 'Catch me if you can? The Market Freedoms Ever-expanding Outer Limits' (*EJLS*, 2011), pp. 162–191.

Caruso, D., 'Private law and public stakes in European integration: the case of property' (*ELJ*, 2004), pp. 751–765.

Chiti, M.P., 'The EC concept of Public administration: the case of the bodies governed by public law' (*EPL*, 2002), pp. 473–495.

Clamour, G., 'Marchés et concessions "entre entités dans le secteur public"', (*CMP* 6, 2014).

de Corail, J.-L., 'L'approche fonctionnelle du service public: sa réalité et ses limites' (*AJDA*, 1997), pp. 20–29.

de Mars, S., 'The limits of general principles: a procurement case study' (*ELR*, 2013), pp. 316–334.

De Staercke, J., 'De toepassing van de algemene reglementering overheidsopdrachten op privaatrechtelijke (onderwijs)instellingen na het Cambridge-arrest van het Hof van Justitie' (*RW*, 2002–2003), pp. 161–174.
Delvolvé, P., 'Marchés publics: les critères des "contrats-maison"' (*RDUE*, 2002), pp. 53–61.
Delvolvé, P., 'Service public et libertés publiques' (*RFDA*, 1985), pp. 1–11.
Déom, D., 'Quel avenir pour le service public local à l'heure européenne' (*Mouv.comm.*, 2004), pp. 462–471.
Devroe, W., 'Privatizations and community law: neutrality versus policy' (*CMLR*, 1997), pp. 267–306.
di Porto, E., 'Cooperation among local governments to deliver public services: Evidence from France', www.ieb.ub.edu/files/Di%20Porto.pdf.
Dossier: L'administration contractuelle (2003) AJDA, pp. 970–991.
Douence, J.-CL., 'La dévolution contractuelle du service public local' (*Rép. Dalloz Collectivités locales*, 1995), pp. 6150–1 et s.
Dreyfus, J.-D., 'Actualité des contrats entre personnes publiques' (*AJDA*, 2000), pp. 575 et s.
Dreyfus, J.-D., 'Externalisation et liberté d'organisation du service' (*AJDA*, 2009), pp. 1529–1534.
Driguez, L. and Rodrigues, S., 'Services sociaux d'intérêt social et droit communautaire' (*AJDA*, 2008), pp. 191–197.
Drijber, B.J. and Stergiou, H., 'Public procurement law and Internal market law' (*CMLR*, 2008), pp. 805–846.
Dubois, C., 'To be or not to be "In house"? Observations relatives à l'exception "In house" après l'arrêt Carbotermo' (*CDPK*, 2007), pp. 213–240.
Duffy, A., 'La constitutionnalisation de la liberté contractuelle' (*RDP*, 2006), pp. 1569–1600.
Durviaux, A.L. and Thirion, N., 'Les modes de gestion des services publics locaux, la réglementation relative aux marchés publics et le droit communautaire' (*JT*, 2004), pp. 17–27.
Durviaux, A.L., 'Les relations in-house: un pas de plus dans une direction délicate' (*BJCP*, 2007), pp. 22–33.
Eckert, G., 'Contrats entre personnes publiques et droit de la concurrence' (*AJDA*, 2013), pp. 849–852.
Eckert, G., 'Les contrats échappant aux règles de publicité et de mise en concurrence' (*AJDA*, 2013, pp. 849–852), pp. 849.
Estevan de Quesada, C., 'Competition and transparency in public procurement markets', (*PPLR*, 2014), pp. 229–244.
Fatôme, E. and Menemis, A., 'Concurrence et liberté d'organisation des personnes publiques: éléments d'analyse' (*AJDA*, 2006), pp. 67–73.
Fatome, E. and Menemis, A., 'Intérêt général, concurrence et service public' (*AJDA*, 2006), pp. 67 et s.
Fatome, E. and Richer, L., 'Les procédures de passation des contrats et pouvoir d'organisation du service public' (*ACCP* 12, 2002), pp. 60–64.
Fennelly, N., 'Legal Interpretation at the European Court of Justice' (*Fordham International Law Journal*, 1996), pp. 656–679.

Fiedziuk, N., 'Putting services of general economic interest up for tender: reflections on applicable EU rules' (*CMLR*, 2013), pp. 87-114.
Fiedziuk, N., Services of General Economic Interest and the Treaty of Lisbon: Opening Doors to a whole new approach or, maintaing the 'status quo' (*ELR*, 2011), pp. 226-242.
Flamme, M.A., 'La libération de la concurrence dans les marchés publics au sein de la C.E.E.' (*RMC*, 1965), pp. 277–290.
Flamme, Ph. and Flamme, M.-A., 'Les marchés publics de services et la coordination de leurs procédures de passation' (*RMCUE*, 1993), pp. 150–170.
Freedland, M., 'Government by Contract and Public Law' (*PL*, 1994), pp. 86–104.
Freedland, M., 'Public Law and Private Finance-Placing the Private Finance Initiative in a Public Law' (*PL*, 1998), pp. 288–307.
Freedland, M., 'From the Contract of Employment to the Personal Work Nexus', (*Industrial Law Journal*, 2006).
Gerber, J., 'Constitutionalising Economy: German neo-liberalism, Competition Law and the "New" Europe' (*The American Journal of Comparative Law*, Vol. 42, No.1), pp. 25–84.
Gerner-Beuerle, C., 'Shareholders between the market and the state; The VW law and other interventions in the market' (*CMLRev.*, 2012), pp. 97–144.
Guillou, Y.-R., 'L'exonération des relations "in house" du régime des marches publics' (*ACCP* 32, 2004), pp. 72 et seq.
Harlow, C., '"Public" and "Private" Law: Definition without Distinction', (*CMLR*, 1980).
Harris, B.V., 'The "Third Source" of Authority' (*LQR*, 1992), pp. 626–629.
Hausmann, F.L. and Queisner, G., 'In-House Contracts and Inter-Municipal Cooperation – Exceptions from the European Union Procurement Law should be applied with caution' (*EPPPL*, 2013), pp. 231–237.
Hoepffner, H., 'La nouvelle directive Concessions', (*Europe*, 2014, June), pp. 9–16.
Janicot, L., 'L'identification du service public géré par une personne privée' (*RFDA*, 2008), pp. 67–79.
Joerges, C., 'What is left of the European Economic Constitution? A Melancholic Eulogy' (*ELR*, 2005), pp. 461–489.
Kaarreselo, T., 'Procuring in-house: the impact of the EC procurement regime' (*PPLR*, 2008), pp. 242–254.
Kalflèche, G., 'Le contrôle des collectivités sur les sociétés publiques locales faut-il rénover le in house' (*RFDA*, 2012), pp. 1120–1127.
Karayigit, M.T., 'The Notion of Services of General Economic Interest Revisited' (*EPL*, 2009), pp. 575–595.
Karayigit, M.T., 'A new type of exemption from the EU rules on public procurement established: "in the neighbour's house" provision of public interest tasks' (*PPLR*, 2010), pp. 183–197.
Kotschy, B., 'Arrêts Stadt Halle, Coname et Parking Brixen' (*RDUE*, 2005), pp. 845–853.
Kumm, M., 'The Jurisprudence of Constitutional Conflict: Constitutional Supremacy in Europe before and after the Constitutional Treaty' (*ELJ*, 2005), pp. 262–307.
Laurent, D. and Rousset, O., 'Convention de délégation de service public local et loi Sapin: la transparence dans le brouillard' (*LPA* 1994), pp. 1 et s.

Lenaerts, K., 'L'égalité de traitement et droit communautaire' (*Cah.dr.eur.*, 1991), pp. 1–41.
Lenaerts, K., 'Federation and the Rule of Law. Perspectives from the European Court of Justice', (Fordham Int.L.J., 2011).
Llorens, F., 'Le recours des personnes publiques à la vente d'immeuble en l'état futur d'achèvement: une condamnation partielle' (*CJEG*, 1991), pp. 251 et s.
M.T. Karayigit, 'The notion of services of general economic interest' (*EPL*, 2009), pp. 575–595.
Marchegiani, G., 'Les relations in-house et le syndrome du cheval à bascule' (*RMCUE*, 2006), pp. 47–57.
Mattera, A., 'Vers un Code européen des marchés publics. Simplification, modernisation et clarification de la reglementation existante' (*RDUE*, 2000), pp. 528–570.
Mensi, M., L'ouverture à la concurrence des marchés publics de services (*RMCUE*, 1993), pp. 59–86.
Moderne, F., 'L'evolution récente du droit des contrats administratifs: les conventions entre personnes publiques' (*RFDA*, 1984), pp. 1 et s.
Moderne, F., 'La concurrence des services techniques de l'Etat et des techniciens privés auprès des collectivités locales' (*RD.imm.*, 1982), p. 467 et s.
Moderne, F., 'Les Conventions des prestations de services entre l'Etat et les collectivités' (EFE, 1996, no. 29), cited by Dreyfus, J.-D., 'Actualité des contrats entre personnes publiques' (*AJDA*, 2000), pp. 575–580.
Munro, C., 'Competition law and public procurement: two sides of the same coin?' (*PPLR*, 2006), pp. 352–361.
Neergaard, U., 'Public service concessions and related concepts – the increased pressure from Community law on Member States' use of concessions' (*PPLR*, 2007), pp. 387–409.
Nettesheim, M., 'Les services d'intérêt general en droit communautaire entre libre concurrence et état social' (*RIDC*, 2008), pp. 608–615.
Neveu, Ph., 'Contractualisation et mutualisation, outils de l'intercommunalité', in (*La Semaine juridique Administrations et Collectivités territoriales*, 2010, n° 30), p. 2242 et s.
Nicinski, S., 'La loi du 28 mai 2010 pour le développement des sociétés publiques locales' (*AJDA*, 2010), pp. 1759–1765.
Nihoul, P., 'Les marches publics dans l'Union européenne (2003–2005)' (*JDE*, 2006), pp. 264–270.
Odudu, O., 'The public/private distinction in EU Internal Market Law', (*RTDE*, 2010), 826 et seq.
Olykke, G.S., 'How does the Court of Justice of the European Union pursue competition concerns in a public procurement context?' (*PPLR*, 2011), pp. 179–192.
Pescatore, P., 'Le recours, dans la jurisprudence de la Cour de Justice des Communautés Européennes, à des normes déduites de la comparaison des droits des Etats membres' (*RIDC*, 1980) pp. 337–359.
Peyrical, J.-M., Que reste-t-il du in house? (*RFDA*, 2005), pp. 955–958.
Peyrical, J.M., Les contrats de prestation entre collectivités publiques (*AJDA*, 2000), pp. 581–591.

Picard, E., La liberté contractuelle des personnes publiques constitue-t-elle un droit fondamental? (*AJDA*, 1996), pp. 651–666.
Pontier, J.-M., 'Cooperation contractuelle et cooperation institutionnelle' (*Rev.Adm.*, 1994), pp. 162–167.
Poulet-Gebot Leclercq, N., 'La contractualisation des relations entre les personnes publiques' (*RFDA*, 1999), pp. 551–565.
Pouyaud, D., 'Contrats entre personne publiques' (*Juris classeur Administratif*), fasc. 675.
R.S., 'Un organisme public de radioduffusion percevant une redevanve est-il un pouvoir adjudicateur?', under Case C-337/06, Bayerischer Rundfunk a.o. v. GEWA (*BJCP* 4, 2008), p. 98 et s.
Ramsey, I., 'The New Public Procurement Directives: a partial solution to the problems of procurement compliance' (*EPL*, 2006), pp. 275–294.
Raynaud, F. en Fombeur, P., 'Chronique générale de jurisprudence administrative française' (*AJDA*, 1998), pp. 553–575.
Reitz, J.C., 'Political Economy as a Major Architectural Principle of Public Law' (*Tulane L. Rev.*, 2001), pp. 1121–1157.
Richer, L., 'La contractualisation comme technique de gestion des affaires publiques' (*AJDA*, 2003), pp. 973 et s.
Richer, L., Un contrat d'entente intercommunale n'est pas une délégation de service public (*AJDA*, 2012), pp. 555–558.
Richer, L., 'Les contrats entre entités du secteur public', (*ACCP*, 2014, n° 143), pp. 31–35.
Rodrigues, S., Les qualifications concurrentes des activités d'intérêt général en droit communautaire (*AJDA*, 2006), pp. 84–90.
Samson-Dye, A., 'Irrégularité du recours à un contrat in house entre une SPLA et une collectivité très minoritaire' (*CMP*, 2013), pp. 36–38.
Sauter, W., 'The Economic Constitution of the European Union' (*Col. J. Eur. L.*, 2 1998), pp. 27–68.
Sauter, W., 'Services of General Economic Interest and Universal Service in EU Law' (*ELR*, 2008), pp. 167–192.
Schutyser, B., 'Het toepassingsgebied van de wetgeving overheidsopdrachten: een aantal evoluties in de rechtspraak van het Hof van Justitie (1998–2003)' (*TBP*, 2004), pp. 259–279.
Semmelmann, C., 'The European Union's economic constitution under the Lisbon Treaty soul-searching among lawyers shifts the focus to procedure' (*ELR*, 2010), pp. 516–542.
Semmelmann, C., 'Theoretical reflections on the public-private distinction and their traces in European Union law', (*Social legal series*, 2), http://opo.iisj.net/index.php/osls/article/viewFile/102/71, pp. 29–30.
Semmelmann, C., 'The Public-Private Divide in European Union Law or an Overkill of Functionalism', http://papers.ssrn.com/sol3/papers.cfm?abstract_id=2056311, p. 13.
Simon, D. en Lagondet, F., La communication de la Commission sur les services d'intérêt général en Europe continuité ou rupture? (*Europe 1*, 1997), pp. 4–6.
Simon, D., 'L'intérêt général national vu par les droits européens' (*Cah. const.*, 2006), pp. 1–18.

Smith, J., 'The European Charter on Local Self-Government: does the UK Government comply' (*Journal of Local Government Law*, 2002), pp. 90–96.
Snell, J., 'The notion of Market access: a concept or a Slogan?' (*CMLR*, 2010), pp. 437–472.
Spaventa, E., 'Leaving Keck behind? The Free Movement of Good after the rulings in commission v. Italy and Michelsson and Roos' (*ELR*, 2009), pp. 914–932.
Stewart, J. and Walsh, K., 'Change in The Managemenet of Public Services' (*Public Administration*, 1992), pp. 499–518.
Stirn, B., 'La liberté contractuelle, droit fondamental en droit administratif' (*AJDA*, 1998), pp. 673–675.
Szydlo, M., 'Contracts beyond the scope of the EC procurement directives – who is bound by the requirement for transparency?' (*ELR*, 2009), pp. 724–730.
T.C. Hartley, 'The European Court, Judicial Objectivity and the Constitution of the European Union' (*The Law Quarterly Review*, 1996), pp. 95–109.
Terneyre, Ph., 'A propos de la liberté contractuelle' (*AJDA*, 2007), pp. 1906–1911.
Trepte, P.-A., 'Public procurement and the Community competition rules' (*PPLR*, 1993), pp. 93–114.
Tridimas, T., 'The Court of Justice and judicial activism' (*ELRev*, 1996), pp. 199–210.
Truchet, D., 'Label de service public et statut du service public' (*AJDA*, 1982), pp. 427–439.
Tryfonidou, A., 'Further steps on the road to convergence among the market freedoms' (*ELR*, 2010), pp. 36–56.
Tryfonidou, A., 'Reverse discrimination in purely internal situations: An incongruity in a Citizens' Europe' (*LIEI*, 2008), pp. 43–67.
Van Garsse, S., 'Nieuwe richtlijn overheidsopdrachten. Codificatie van het Europees aanbestedingsrecht in de klassieke sectoren' (*NjW*, 2004), pp. 944–949.
Verhoeven, A., 'Privatisation and EC Law: Is the European Commission 'neutral' with respect to public versus private ownership of companies?' (*ICLQ*, 1996), pp. 861–887.
Vincent-Jones, P., 'The New Public Contracting' (*Indiana Journal of Global Legal Studies*, 2007), pp. 259–278.
Vincent-Jones, P., 'Responsive Law and Governance in Public Services Provision: A Future for the Local Contracting Authority' (*Modern Law*, 1998), pp. 362–381.
Weiler, Joseph H.H., 'Does Europe Need a Constitution? Reflections on Demos, Telos and the German Maastricht Decision' (*ELR*, 1995), pp. 219–258.
Weltzien, K., 'Avoiding the procurement rules by awarding contracts to an in-house entity – scope of the the procurement directives in the classical sector' (*PPLR*, 2005), pp. 237–255.
Wiggen, J., 'Public procurement rules and cooperation between public sector entities: the limits of the in-house doctrine under EU procurement law' (*PPLR*, 2011), pp. 157–172.
Wiggen, J., 'Directive 2014/24/EU: the new provision on co-operation in the public sector', (*PPLR*, 2014), pp. 83–93.
Williams, R., 'Public-public cooperation – *Teckal* in practise' (*PPLR*, 2012), pp. NA1–10.
Williams, R., 'The New Procurment Directives of the European Union' (*PPLR*, 2004), pp. 153–159.

Withofs, V., Artikel 345 VWEU: een rem op de Europese harmonisatie van het goederenrecht? (*TBBR*, 2013), pp. 67–87.
Wolfswinkel, J., 'The allocation of a Limited Number of Authorisations' (*Review of European Administrative Law*, 2010), pp. 61–104.
Young, K., 'Local public service agreements and performance incentives for local government', (*Local Government Studies*, 2005, 1), pp. 3–20.
X., 'Les Nouvelles directives européennes' (*ACCP* 33, 2004), pp. 45–68.
Zimmer, W., 'Convention conclue par deux collectivités territoriales en vue d'exercer en coopération un service public' (*CMP* 3, 2012), pp. 19–20.
'Dossier: Les nouvelles directives "marchés"', (*ACCP*, 2014, n° 143) and (*ACCP*, 2014, n° 144).
'Special issue – the new EU procurement directives', (*PPLR*, 2014, Issue 3) and (*PPLR*, 2014, Issue 4).

4. Table of Cases

4.1. CJEU

C-26/62, *NV Algemene Transport- en Expeditie Onderneming van Gend & Loos v. Netherlands Inland Revenue Administration* [1963] *ECR* 00001.
C-13/63, *Italian Republic v. Commission of the European Economic Community* [1963] *ECR* 00165.
C-2/74, *Reyners v. Belgium* [1974] ECR 631.
C-8/74, *Procureur du Roi v. Dassonville* [1974] *ECR* 837.
C-33/74, *Johannes Henricus Maria van Binsbergen v. Bestuur van de Bedrijfsvereniging voor de Metaalnijverheid* [1974] *ECR* 1299.
C-41/74, *Yvonne van Duyn v. Home Office* [1974] *ECR* 1337.
C-36/74, *B.N.O. Walrave and L.J.N. Koch v. Association Union cycliste internationale* [1974] *ECR* 1405.
C-36/75, *Roland Rutili v. Ministre de l'intérieur* [1975] *ECR* 01219.
C-13/76, *Gaetano Donà v. Mario Mantero* [1976] *ECR* 1333.
C-71/76, *Jean Thieffry v. Conseil de l'ordre des avocats à la Cour de Paris* [1977] *ECR* 765.
C-22/67, *Fonds national de retraite des ouvriers mineurs v. Giovanni Mura* [1977] *ECR* 1699.
C-30/77, *Régina v. Pierre Bouchereau* [1977] *ECR* 1999.
C-82/77, *Public Prosecutor of the Kingdom of the Netherlands v. Jacobus Philippus van Tiggele* [1978] *ECR* 837.
C-120/78, *Rewe v. Bundesmonopolverwaltung für Bramtwein* [1978] *ECR* 649.
C-175/78, *R. v. Saunders* [1979] *ECR* 1129.
C-249/81, *Commission v. Ireland* [1982] *ECR* 4005.
C-182/83, *Robert Fearon & Company Limited v. Irish Land Commission* [1984] *ECR* 3677.
C-98/86, *Ministère public v. Arthur Mathot* [1987] ECR 809.
C-20/87, *Ministère public v. André Gauchard* [1987] *ECR* 4879.
C-31/87, *Gebroeders Beentjes BV v. State of the Netherlands* [1988] *ECR* 4635.

C-45/87, *Commission v. Ireland ("Dundalk")* [1988] *ECR* 4929.
C-186/87, *Ian Willam Cowan v. Trésor public* [1989] *ECR* 195.
C-3/88, *Commission v. Italy* ("*Re Data Processing*") [1989] ECR 4035.
C-103/88, *Fratelli Costanzo SpA v. Comune di Milano* [1989] *ECR* 1839.
C-41/90, *Klaus Höfner and Fritz Elser v. Macrotron GmbH* [1991] *ECR* I-1979.
C-1/90, *Aragonesa de Publicidad v. Departmento de Sanidad* [1991] ECR I-4151.
C-76/90, *Manfred Säger v. Dennemeyer & Co. Ltd* [1991] *ECR* I-4221.
C-78/90, *Compagnie Commerciale de l'Ouest and others v. Receveur Principal des Douanes de La Pallice Port* [1992] *ECR* I-1847.
C-46/93 and C-48/93, *Brasserie du Pêcheur v. Bundesrepublik Deutschland and The Queen v. Secretary of State for Transport, ex parte: Factortame Ltd and others* [1993] *ECR* I-1839.
C-17/92, *Federación de Distribuidores Cinematográficos v. Estado Español en Unión de Productores de Cine y Televisión* [1993] *ECR* I-02239.
C-55/94, *Reinhard Gebhard v. Consiglio dell'Ordine degli Avvocati a Procuration de Milano* [1995] *ECR* I-4165.
C-83/94, *Leifer and Others* [1995] *ECR* I-3231.
C-87/94, *Commission of the European Communities v. Kingdom of Belgium* [1996] *ECR* I-2043.
C-84/95, *Bosphorus Hava Yollari Turizm ve Ticaret AS v. Minister for Transport, Energy and Communications and Others* [1996] *ECR* I-03953.
C-64/96 and C-65/96, *Land Nordrhein-Westfalen v. Uecker and Jacquet v. Land Nordrhein-Westfalen* [1997] *ECR* I-3177.
C-44/96, *Mannesmann Anlagenbau Austria AG and Others v. Strohal Rotationsdruck GesmbH* [1998] *ECR* I-73.
C-158/96, *Raymond Kohll v. Union des caisses de maladie* [1998] *ECR* I-1931.
C-107/98, *Teckal Srl v. Comune di Viano* [1999] *ECR* I-8121.
C-51/96 and C-191/97, *Christelle Deliège v. Ligue francophone de judo et disciplines associées ASBL, Ligue belge de judo ASBL, Union européenne de judo and François Pacquée* [2000] *ECR* I-2549.
C-108/98, *RI.SAN. Srl v. Comune di Ischia, Italia Lavoro SpA and Ischia Ambiente SpA* [2000] *ECR* I-05219.
C-9/99, *Echirolles Distribution SA v. Association du Dauphiné and Others* [2000] *ECR* I-8207.
C-94/99, *Arge Gewässerschutz v. Bundesministerium für Land- und Forstwirtschaft* [2000] *ECR* I-11037.
C-162/99, *Commission of the European Communities v. Italian Republic* [2001] *ECR* I-00541.
C-19/00, *SIAC Construction Ltd v. County Council of the County of Mayo* [2001] ECR I-7725.
C-59/00, *Bent Mousten Vestergaard v. Spotrup Boligselkab* [2001] *ECR* I-9505.
C-92/00, *Hospital Ingenieure Krankenhaustechnik Planungs-Gesellschaft mbH v. Stadt Wien* [2002] *ECR* I-5553.
C-6/01, *Associação Nacional de Operadores de Máquinas Recreativas (Anomar) and Others v. Estado português* [2003] *ECR* I-8261.

C-18/01, Arkkitehtuuritoimisto Riitta Korhonen Oy and Others v. Varkauden Taitotalo Oy [2003] ECR I-5321.
C-98/01, *Commission v. United Kingdom* [2003] *ECR* I-4641.
C-126/03, *Commission v. Germany* [2004] *ECR* I-11197.
C-26/03, *Stadt Halle and RPL Recyclingpark Lochau GmbH v. Arbeitsgemeinschaft Thermische Restabfall- und Energieverwertungsanlage TREA Leuna* [2005] *ECR* I-00001.
C-31/03 and C-34/03, *Fabricom SA v. Belgian State* [2005] *ECR* I-1559.
C-84/03, *Commission v. Spain* [2005] *ECR* I-00139.
C-29/04, *Commission of the European Communities v. Republic of Austria* [2005] *ECR* I-9705.
Joined Cases C-180/98 to C-184/98, *Pavel Pavlov and Othus v. Stichting Pensioenfonds Medische specialisten* [2006] *ECR* I-6451.
Joined Cases C-158/04 and C-159/04, *Alfa Vita Vassilopoulos AE and Carrefour Marinopoulos AE v. Elliniko Dimosio and Nomarchiaki Aftodioikisi Ioanninon* [2006] *ECR* I-08135.
C-112/05, *Commission v. Germany* [2007] *ECR* I-8995.
Joined Cases C-147/06 and C-148/06, *SECAP SpA and Santorso Soc. coop. arl v. Comune di Torino* [2008] *ECR* I-03565.
C-49/07, *Motosykletistiki Omospondia Ellados NPID (MOTOE) v. Elliniko Dimosio* [2008] *ECR* I-4863.
C-110/05, *Commission of the European Communities v. Italian Republic* [2009] *ECR* I-519.
C-142/05, *Mickelsson and Roos* [2009] *ECR* I-4273.
C-305/08, *Consorzio Nazionale Interuniversitario per le Scienze del Mare (CoNISMa) v. Regione Marche* [2009] ECR I-12129.
C-91/08, *Wall AG v. La ville de Francfort-sur-le-Main and Frankfurter Entsorgungs- und Service* (FES) GmbH [2010] *ECR* I-2815.
C-64/08, *Engelmann* [2010] *ECR* I-8219.
C-171/08, *Commission v. Portugal* [2010] *ECR* I-06817.
C-95/10, *Strong Segurança SA v. Município de Sintra and Securitas-Serviços e Tecnologia de Segurança* [2011] *ECR* I-01865.
C-72/10 and C-77/10, *Costa and Cifone* [2012] *ECR* I-0000.
C-159/11, *Azienda Sanitaria Locale di Lecce, Università del Salento v. Ordine degli Ingegneri della Provincia di Lecce and Others* [2012] *ECR* I-00000.
Joined Cases C-182/11 and C-183/11, *Econord SpA v. Comuni di Cagno, Comune di Varese, Comune di Solbiate* [2012] *ECR* I-00000.
Joined Cases C-186/11 and C-209/11, *Stanleybet International Ltd, William Hill Organization Ltd, William Hill Plc, Sportingbet plc v. Ypourgos Oikonomias kai Oikonomikon, Ypourgos Politismou* [2013] *ECR* I-0000.
C-94/12, *Swm Costruzioni 2 SpA, Mannocchi Luigino DI v. Provincia di Fermo* [2013] *ECR* I-00000.
Case C-574/12, *Centro Hospitalar de Setúbal EPE, Serviço de Utilização Comum dos Hospitais (SUCH) v. Eurest (Portugal) – Sociedade Europeia de Restaurantes Lda* [2014] *ECR* I-00000.

C-15/13, *Technische Universität Hamburg-Harburg, Hochschul-Informations-System GmbH v. Datenlotsen Informationssysteme GmbH* [2014] *ECR* I-00000.
C-196/08, *Acoset SpA v. Conferenza Sindaci e Presidenza Prov. Reg. ATO Idrico Ragusa and Others* [2009] *ECR* I-09913.
C-196/96, *Steymann v. Staatssecretaris van Justitie* [1988] *ECR* 2085.
Joined Cases C-197/11 and C-203/11, *Eric Libert and Others v. Gouvernement flamand and All Projects & Developments NV and Others v. Vlaamse Regering* [2013] *ECR* I-00000.
C-198/89, *Commission of the European Communities v. Hellenic Republic* [1991] *ECR* I-00727.
C-203/08, *Sporting Exchange Ltd v. Minister van Justitie* [2010] *ECR* I-04695.
C-205/03P, *Federación Española de Empresas de Tecnología Sanitaria (FENIN) v. Commission of the European Communities* [2006] *ECR* I-6295.
C-205/07, *Lodewijk Gysbrechts and Santurel Inter BVBA* [2008] *ECR* I-09947.
C-206/08, *Wasser- und Abwasserzweckverband Gotha und Landkreisgemeinden (WAZV Gotha) v. Eurawasser Aufbereitungs- und Entsorgungsgesellschaft mbH* [2009] *ECR* I-0000.
C-212/06, *Government of the French Community and Walloon Government v. Flamish Government* [2008] *ECR* I-1683.
C-214/00, *Commission v. Spain* [2003] *ECR* I-4667.
C-220/05, *Jean Auroux and Others v. Commune de Roanne* [2007] *ECR* I-389.
C-220/06, *Asociación Profesional de Empresas de Reparto y Manipulado de Correspondencia v. Administración General del Estado* [2007] *ECR* I-12175.
C-221/12, *Belgacom NV v. Interkommunale voor Teledistributie van het Gewest Antwerpen (INTEGAN) and Others* [2013] *ECR* I-00000.
Joined Cases C-223/99 and C-260/99, *Agorà Srl and Excelsior Snc di Pedrotti Bruna & C. v. Ente Autonomo Fiera Internazionale di Milano and Ciftat Soc. coop. arl.* [2001] *ECR* I-3605.
C-226/09, *European Commission v. Ireland* [2010] *ECR* I-11807.
C-231/03, *Consorzio Aziende Metano (Coname) v. Comune di Cingia de' Botti* [2005] *ECR* I-7287.
C-237/99, *Commission v. France* [2001] *ECR* I-939;
C-240/06, *Commission v. Italy* [2007] *ECR* I-09413.
C-243/89, *Commission v. Denmark (Storebaelt)* [1993] *ECR* I-2253.
C-244/94, *Fédération Française des Sociétés d'Assurance, Société Paternelle-Vie, Union des Assurances de Paris-Vie and Caisse d'Assurance et de Prévoyance Mutuelle des Agriculteurs v. Ministère de l'Agriculture et de la Pêche* [1995] *ECR* I-4013.
C-244/97, *Erich Ciola v. Land Vorarlberg* [1999] *ECR* I-02517.
C-250/03, *Giorgio Emanuele Mauri v. Ministero della Giustizia and Commissione per gli esami di avvocato presso la Corte d'appello di Milano* [2005] *ECR* I-1267.
C-260/89, *Elliniki Radiophonia Tiléorassi AE and Panellinia Omospondia Syllogon Prossopikou v. Dimotiki Etairia Pliroforissis and Sotirios Kouvelas and Nicolaos Avdellas and others* [1991] *ECR* I-02925.
C-263/86, *Belgian State v. René Humbel* [1988] *ECR* 5365.

Joined Cases C-267/91 and C-268/91, *Criminal proceedings v. Bernard Keck and Daniel Mithouard* [1993] *ECR* I-6097.
C-268/99, *Aldona Malgorzata Jony and Others v. Staatssecretaris van Justitie* [2001] *ECR* I-8615.
C-274/09, *Privater Rettungsdienst und Krankentransport Stadler v. Zweckverband für Rettungsdienst und Feuerwehralarmierung Passau* [2011] *ECR* I-1335.
C-275/98, *Unitron Scandinavia A/S and 3-S A/S, Danske Svineproducenters Serviceselskab v. Ministeriet for Fødevarer, Landbrug og Fiskeri* [1999] *ECR* I-08291.
C-281/06, *Jundt v. Finanzamt Offenburg* [2007] *ECR* I-12231.
Joined Cases C-282 and C-283/04, *Commission v. Netherlands* [2006] *ECR* I-9141.
C-283/00, *Commission v. Spain* [2003] *ECR* I-11697.
Joint Cases C-285/99 and C-286/99, *Impresa Lombardini SpA – Impresa Generale di Costruzioni v. ANAS – Ente nazionale per le strade and Società Italiana per Condotte d'Acqua SpA and Impresa Ing. Mantovani SpA v. ANAS – Ente nazionale per le strade and Ditta Paolo Bregoli* [2001] *ECR* I-09233.
C-292/12, *Ragn Sells v. Sillamäe Linnavalitsus* [2013] *ECR* I-00000.
C-295/05, *Asociación Nacional de Empresas Forestales (Asemfo) v. Transformación Agraria SA (Tragsa)* [2007] *ECR* I-02999.
C-300/01, *Doris Salzmann* [2003] *ECR* I-4899.
C-300/07, *Hans & Christophorus Oymanns GbR, Orthopädie Schuhtechnik v. AOK Rheinland/Hamburg* [2009] *ECR* I-04779.
C-300/89, *Commission of the European Communities v. Council of the European Communities* [1991] *ECR* I-2901.
C-302/97, *Klaus Konle v. Republik Österreich* [1999] *ECR* I-3099.
C-305/08, *Consorzio Nazionale Interuniversitario per le Scienze del Mare (CoNISMA) v. Regione Marche* [2009] *ECR* I-12129.
C-306/97, *Connemara Machine Turf Co. Ltd v. Coillte Teoranta* [1998] *ECR* I-8761.
C-309/99, *J.C.J. Wouters, J. W. Savelbergh and Price Waterhouse Belastingadviseurs BV v. Algemene Raad van de Nederlandse Orde van Advocaten* [2002] *ECR* I-1577.
Joined Cases C-321/94 to C-324/94, *Christian Poucet v. Assurances Générales de France and Caisse Mutuelle Régionale du Languedoc-Roussillon and Daniel Pistre v. Caisse Autonome Nationale de Compensation de l' Assurance Vieillesse des Artisans (Cancava)* [1997] *ECR* I-2343.
C-323/96, *Commission v. Belgium* [1998] *ECR* I-5063.
C-324/07, *Coditel Brabant SA v. Commune d'Uccle and Région de Bruxelles-Capitale* [2008] *ECR* I-8457.
C-324/98, *Telaustria Verlags GmbH and Telefonadress GmbH v. Telekom Austria AG* [2000] *ECR* I-10745.
C-336/12, *Ministeriet for Forskning, Innovation og Videregående Uddannelser v. Manova A/S* [2013] *ECR* I-00000.
C-337/05, *Commission v. Italy* [2008] *ECR* I-02173.
C-337/06, *Bayerischer Rundfunk e.a. v. GEWA*, [2007] *ECR* I-11173.
C-337/82, *St. Nikolaus Brennerei v. Hauptzollamt Krefeld* [1984] *ECR* 1051.
C-339/89, *Alsthom Atlantique SA v. Compagnie de construction mécanique Sulzer SA* [1991] *ECR* I-00107.

C-340/04, *Carbotermo SpA and Consorzio Alisei v. Comune di Busto Arsizio and AGESP SpA* [2006] *ECR* I-04137.
C-347/06, *ASM Brescia SpA v. Comune di Rodengo Saiano* [2008] *ECR* I-05641.
C-348/10, *Norma-A SIA and Dehon-ASIA v. Latgales planasanas regions* [2011] *ECR* I-0000.
C-352/12, *Consiglio Nazionale degli Ingegneri v. Comune di Castelvecchio Subequo et Comune di Barisciano* [2013] *ECR* I-00000.
C-353/96, *Commission v. Ireland* [1998] *ECR* I-8565.
C-355/85, *Driancourt v. Cognet* [1986] *ECR* 3231.
Joined Cases C-357/10 and C-358/10, *Duomo Gpa Srl, Gestione Servizi Pubblici Srl and Irtel Srl v. Comune di Baranzate and Comune di Venegono Inferiore* [2012] *ECR* I-00000.
C-359/93, *Commission v. The Netherlands (UNIX)* [1995] *ECR* I-157.
C-360/96, *Gemeente Arnhem and Gemeente Rheden v. BFI Holding BV* [1998] *ECR* I-6821.
C-367/98, *Commission of the European Communities v. Portuguese Republic* [2002] *ECR* I-04731.
C-368/10, *Commission v. Netherlands* [2012] *ECR* I-00000.
C-371/05, *Commission of the European Communities v. Italian Republic* [2008] *ECR* I-00110.
C-373/00, *Adolf Truley GmbH v. Bestattung Wien GmbH* [2003] *ECR* I-1931.
C-379/98, *Preussen Elektra AG v. Schleswag AG* [2001] *ECR* I-2099.
C-380/98, *The Queen v. H.M. Treasury, ex parte The University of Cambridge* [2000] *ECR* I-8035.
C-381/93, *Alpine Investments v. Minister van Financiën* [1995] *ECR* I-1141.
C-382/05, *Commission of the European Communities v. Italian Republic* [2007] *ECR* I-6657.
C-382/85, *Bond van Adverteerders and others v. The Netherlands* [1988] *ECR* 2085.
C-384/93, *Alpine Investments v. Minister van Financiën* [1995] *ECR* I-1141.
C-386/11, *Piepenbrock Dienstleistungen & Co. KG v. Kreis Düren* [2013] *ECR* I-00000.
C-388/01, *Commission v. Italy* [2003] *ECR* I-00721.
C-388/12, *Comune di Ancona v. Regione Marche* [2013] *ECR* I-00000.
C-393/06, *Ing. Aigner, Wasser-Wärme-Umwelt, GmbH v. Fernwärme Wien GmbH* [2008] *ECR* I-2339.
C-399/98, *Ordine degli Architetti delle province di Milano e Lodi, Piero De Amicis, Consiglio Nazionale degli Architetti and Leopoldo Freyrie v. Comune di Milano, and Pirelli SpA, Milano Centrale Servizi SpA and Fondazione Teatro alla Scala* [2001] *ECR* I-05409.
C-410/04, *Associazione Nazionale Autotrasporto Viaggiatori (ANAV) v. Comune di Bari and AMTAB Servizio SpA* [2006] *ECR* I-03303.
C-412/04, *Commission of the European Communities v. Italian Republic* [2008] *ECR* I-00619.
C-412/93, *Société d'Importation Edouard Leclerc-Siplec v. TF1 Publicité SA and M6 Publicité SA* [1995] *ECR* I-179.
C-415/93, *Union Royale des Sociétés de Football Association v. Bosman* [1995] *ECR* I-4921.

C-419/92, *Ingetraut Scholz v. Opera Universitaria di Cagliari and Cinzia Porcedda* [1994] *ECR* I-505.
C-421/01, *Traunfellner GmbH v. Österreichische Autobahnen- und Schnellstraßen-Finanzierungs-AG* [2003] *ECR* I-11941.
C-425/12, *Portgás - Sociedade de Produção e Distribuição de Gás SA v. Ministério da Agricultura, do Mar, do Ambiente e do Ordenamento do Territó* [2013] *ECR* I-00000.
C-434/09, *McCarthy v. Secretary of State for the Home Department* [2011] *ECR* I-3375.
C-441/02, *Commission v. Germany* [2006] *ECR* I-3449.
C-448/98, *Criminal proceedings against Jean-Pierre Guimont* [2000] *ECR* I-10663.
C-451/08, *Helmut Müller GmbH v. Bundesanstalt für Immobilienaufgaben* [2010] *ECR* I-02673.
C-452/01, *Margarethe Ospelt and Schlössle Weissenberg Familienstiftung* [2003] *ECR* I-9743.
C-454/06, *Pressetext Nachrichtenagentur GmbH v. Republik Österreich (Bund), APA-OTS Originaltext-Service GmbH and APA Austria Presse Agentur registrierte Genossenschaft mit beschränkter Haftung* [2008] *ECR* I-04401.
C-458/03, *Parking Brixen GmbH v. Gemeinde Brixen and Stadtwerke Brixen AG* [2005] *ECR* I-08585.
Joined Cases C-463 and C-464/04, *Federconsumatori and Others and Associazione Azionariato Diffuso dell'AEM SpA and Others v. Comune di Milano* [2007] *ECR* I-10419.
C-470/99, *Universale-Bau AG, Bietergemeinschaft: 1) Hinteregger & Söhne Bauges.m.b.H. Salzburg, 2) ÖSTÜ-STETTIN Hoch- und Tiefbau GmbH v. Entsorgungsbetriebe Simmering GmbH* [2002] *ECR* I-11617.
C-480/06, *Commission of the European Communities v. Federal Republic of Germany* [2009] *ECR* I-04747.
C-483/99, *Commission v. France* [2002] *ECR* I-4781.
C-503/04, *Commission v. Germany* [2007] *ECR* I-6153.
C-503/99, *Commission v. Belgium* [2002] *ECR* I-4809.
C-507/03, *Commission of the European Communities v. Ireland* [2007] *ECR* I-09777.
C-513/03, *Heirs of M. E. A. van Hilten-van der Heijden v. Inspecteur van de Belastingdienst/Particulieren/Ondernemingen outsideland te Heerlen* [2006] *ECR* I-10653.
Joined Cases C-515/99, C-519/99, C-524/99 and C-526/99 till C-540/99, *Hans Reisch and Others v. Bürgermeister der Landeshauptstadt Salzburg and Grundverkehrsbeauftragter des Landes Salzburg and Anton Lassacher and Others v. Grundverkehrsbeauftragter des Landes Salzburg and Grundverkehrslandeskommission des Landes Salzburg* [2002] *ECR* I-2147.
C-518/06, *Commission v. Italy* [2009] *ECR* I-3491.
C-526/11, *IVD GmbH & Co. KG v. Ärztekammer Westfalen-Lippe* [2013] *ECR* I-00000.
C-532/03, *Commission v. Ireland* [2007] *ECR* I-11353.
C-532/06, *Emm. G. Lianakis AE, Sima Anonymi Techniki Etaireia Meleton kai Epivlepseon and Nikolaos Vlachopoulos v. Dimos Alexandroupolis and Others* [2008] *ECR* I-251.
C-543/08, *Commission v. Portugal* [2010] *ECR* I-11241.
C-564/11, *Consulta Regionale Ordine Ingegneri della Lombardia e.a. v. Comune di Pavia* [2013] *ECR* I-00000.

C-573/07, *Sea Srl v. Comune de Ponte Nossa* [2010] *ECR* I-08127.
C-599/10, *SAG ELV Slovensko a.s., FELA Management AG, ASCOM (Schweiz) AG, Asseco Central Europe a.s., TESLA Stropkov a.s., Autostrade per l'Italia SpA, EFKON AG, Stalexport Autostrady SA v. Úrad pre verejné obstarávanie* [2012] *ECR* I-00000.
C-810/79, *Peter Uberschär v. Bundesversicherungsanstalt für Angestellte* [1980] *ECR* 2747.

4.2. General Court (EU)

Joined Cases T-228/99 and T-233/99, *Westdeutsche Landesbank Girozentrale and Land Nordrhein-Westfalen v. Commission of the European Communities* [2003] *ECR* II-435.
T-313/02, *Meca-Medina and Majcen v. Commission* [2004] *ECR* II-3291.
T-17/02, *Fred Olsen v. Commission* [2005] *ECR* II-2031.
T-155/04, *SELEX Sistemi Integrati SpA v. Commission* [2006] *ECR* II-4797.
T-289/03, *British United Provident Association Ltd (BUPA), BUPA Insurance Ltd and BUPA Ireland Ltd v. Commission of the European Communities* [2008] *ECR* II-00081.
T-50/05, *Evropaïki Dynamiki - Proigmena Systimata Tilepikoinonion Pliroforikis kai Tilematikis AE v. European Commission* [2010] *ECR* II-01071.
T-289/09, *Evropaïki Dynamiki - Proigmena Systimata Tilepikoinonion Pliroforikis kai Tilematikis AE v. Europese Commissie* [2011] *ECR* II-0000.

4.3. Conseil d'Etat (France)

CE fr. 26 June 1930, *Bourrageas, Lebon* 659.
CE fr. 20 December 1935, *Etablissements Vézia* (*RDP*, 1936) p. 119.
CE fr. 13 May 1938, *Caisse primaire d'aide et de protection, Rec.* 41.
CE fr. 31 July 1942, *Monpeurt, Lebon* 239.
CE fr. 2 April 1943, *Bouguen, Lebon* 86;
CE fr. 3 November 1950, *Com.*, p. 534.
CE fr. 20 April 1956, *Epoux Bertin, Rec.* 167.
CE fr. 13 January 1961, *Magnier*, no. 43548, *Lebon* 32.
CE fr. 18 June 1963, *Narcy, Lebon* 401.
CE fr. 28 June 1963, *Narcy, Rec.* 401.
CE fr. 29 April 1970, *Soc. Unipain* (*AJDA*, 1970), p. 430.
CE fr. 30 October 1980, *Fédération française des professionnels immobiliers et commerciaux, Lebon* 348.
CE fr. 20 January 1989, *SA GBA Berry-Loire, Lebon* 26.
CE fr. 17 March 1989, *Synd. psychiatre français* (*RFDA*, 1991), p. 267.
CE fr. 20 July 1990, *Ville de Melun et Association "Melun-culture-loisirs", Lebon* 220.
CE fr. 28 January 1998, *Société Borg Warner* (*AJDA*, 1998) p. 287.
CE fr. 20 May 1998, *Communauté de communes du Piémont de Barr*, nr. 188.239 (*AJDA*, 1998) p. 553.
CE fr. 8 February 1999, *Service départemental incendie et Secours.*

CE fr. 9 July 2003, *Féd. Française des entreprises gestionnaires des services, aux équipements, à l'énergie et à l'environnement et autres*, Req. N° 239879 (*CMP comm.*, 2003) p. 169.
CE fr. 22 February 2007, *Association du personnel relevant des établissements pour inadaptés, Rec.* 92.
CE fr. 6 April 2007, *Commune d'Aix en Provence* (*RFDA*, 2007), p. 812.
CE fr. 4 March 2009, *Syndicat national des industries d'information de gaz* (*AJDA*, 2009), p. 891.
CE fr. 3 February 2012 (*AJDA*, 2012) p. 555.
CE fr. 23 December 2012, no. 337396, *Conseil national de l'ordre des médecins.*
CE fr. 6 November 2013, *Commune de Marsannay-la-Côte*, n° 365079.

4.4. Cour constitutionnelle (France)

C.c. no. 2000–437, 19 December 2000.
C.c. no. 2006–543, 30 November 2006.

4.5. English Courts

The Bankers' Case, (1700) 90 E.R. p. 270.
Attorney General v. Great Eastern Railway, (*App.Cas.* 5, 1879/1880), p. 473.
Bulmer Ltd v. J. Bollinger SA (1974) 2:401,418–19.
Foster v. British Gas (1991) 2 AC, pp. 206–317.
Hazell v. Hammersmith and Fulham London Burrough Council, (*A.C.* 2, 1992), p. 1.
R v. Hibbit and Sanders Ex p. the Lord Chancellor's Department, (*C.O.D.*, 1993), p. 326, DC.*R. v. Portsmouth City Council ex parte Peter Coles and Colwick Builders Limited and George Austin Limited*, C.L.C. (1997), p. 407.
R (Wheeler) v. Office of the Prime Minister (*EWHC*, 2008), p. 1409 admin.
Brent London Borough Council and others v. Risk Management Partners Ltd (UKSC 7, 2011), 2 W.L.R.166.
Tachie v. Welwyn Hatfield BC (2013) EWHC 3972 (QB); (2014) B.L.G.R. 100 (QBD).

IUS COMMUNE EUROPAEUM

A peer-reviewed book series in which the common foundations of the legal systems of the Member States of the European Union are the central focus.

The *Ius Commune Europaeum* series includes horizontal comparative legal studies as well as studies on the effect of treaties within the national legal systems. All the classic fields of law are covered. The books are published in various European languages under the auspices of METRO, the Institute for Transnational Legal Research at Maastricht University.

Recently published:

Volume 123: *The Treaty on European Union 1993-2013. Reflections from Maastricht*, M. de Visser and A.P. van der Mei (eds.)

Volume 124: *Inside Policy Custody. Training Framework on the Provisions of Suspects' Rights*, T. Spronken, J. Blackstock, E. Lloyd-Cape, J. Hodgson, A. Ogorodova and M. Vanderhallen

Volume 125: *Coordinating Ombudsmen and the Judiciary. A Comparative View on the Relations between Ombudsmen and the Judiciary in the Netherlands, England and the European Union*, M. Remac

Volume 126: *Legal Evolution and Hybridisation. The Law of Shares Transfer in England*, M. Solinas

Volume 127: *The Role of EU State Aid Law in Promoting a Pro-Innovation Policy. A Review from the Perspective of University-Industry R&D Cooperation*, M. Cisneros

Volume 128: *Tradition, Codification and Unification. Comparative – Historical Essays on Developments in Civil Law*, J.M. Milo, J.H.A. Lokin and J.M. Smits

Volume 129: *Nobody's Perfect. Comparative Essays on Appeals and Other Means of Recourse Against Judicial Decisions in Civil matters*, A. Uzelac and C.H. van Rhee (eds.)

Volume 130: *Legal Aid in the Low Countries*, B. Hubeau and A. Terlouw (eds.)

Volume 131: *State Aid and Public Procurement in the European Union*, S. Schoenmaekers, W. Devroe and N. Philipsen (eds.)

Volume 132: *Property Law Perspectives III*, A. Apers, S. Bouly et al. (eds.)

Volume 133: *Multi-Party Redress Mechanisms in Europe: Squeaking Mice?*, V. Harsági and C.H. van Rhee (eds.)

www.ingramcontent.com/pod-product-compliance
Ingram Content Group UK Ltd.
Pitfield, Milton Keynes, MK11 3LW, UK
UKHW051927100926
8556IPUK00022B/1407

9 781780 683126